THE MODERN LIBRARY
OF THE WORLD'S BEST BOOKS

THE PLAYS OF
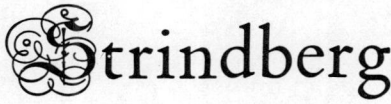

VOLUME I

*The publisher will be pleased to send, upon request,
an illustrated folder listing each volume in*
THE MODERN LIBRARY

THE PLAYS OF
Strindberg

VOLUME I

*Introduced, and translated
from the Swedish, by*

MICHAEL MEYER

THE MODERN LIBRARY · NEW YORK

FIRST MODERN LIBRARY EDITION, *September, 1966*

© Copyright, 1964, by Michael Meyer

All rights reserved under International and Pan-American Copyright Conventions. Published in New York by Random House, Inc.

CAUTION: Professionals and amateurs are hereby warned that these translations of the PLAYS OF STRINDBERG, being fully protected under the Copyright Laws of the United States of America, the British Empire, including the Dominion of Canada, and all other countries of the Berne and Universal Copyright Conventions, are subject to royalty. All rights, including professional, amateur, motion picture, recitation, lecturing, public reading, and radio and television broadcasting, are strictly reserved. Particular emphasis is laid on the question of readings, permission for which must be secured from the author's agent in writing. All inquiries regarding performances, etc., in the United States and Canada should be addressed to: *Harold Freedman, Brandt & Brandt, 101 Park Avenue, New York 17, N. Y.* Inquiries for all other parts of the world should be addressed to: *Margaret Ramsay, Ltd., 14 Goodwin's Court, London, W.C. 2.*

MANUFACTURED IN THE UNITED STATES OF AMERICA

THE MODERN LIBRARY

is published by

RANDOM HOUSE, INC.

BENNETT CERF   DONALD S. KLOPFER

CONTENTS

Foreword	7
Acknowledgements	13
Introduction to THE FATHER	15
THE FATHER	27
Introduction to MISS JULIE	89
Author's Preface to MISS JULIE	99
MISS JULIE	113
Introduction to CREDITORS	163
CREDITORS	169
Introduction to THE STRONGER	221
THE STRONGER	225
Introduction to PLAYING WITH FIRE	235
PLAYING WITH FIRE	239
Introduction to ERIK THE FOURTEENTH	281
ERIK THE FOURTEENTH	287

Introduction to STORM	371
STORM	375
Introduction to THE GHOST SONATA	419
THE GHOST SONATA	425
Chronological List of Strindberg's Plays	468
Appendix	469

FOREWORD

JOHAN AUGUST STRINDBERG was born in Stockholm on 22 January 1849, the fourth child of a shipping merchant and his former maidservant. His father went bankrupt four years after Strindberg's birth, and his mother died when he was thirteen; the next year, his father married his housekeeper. At the age of eighteen he went to Upsala University where he began to read medicine, but after failing an intermediate examination he left and went on the stage at the Royal Dramatic Theatre in Stockholm. He was a failure as an actor, turned to writing and went back to Upsala to study modern languages and political science. In 1870 his fourth play, a one-act drama entitled IN ROME, was performed at the Royal Theatre. In 1872 he left Upsala for good and, after another abortive attempt to go on the stage, he worked for two years as a journalist and then for eight years as a librarian at the Royal Library in Stockholm.

Shortly after he had taken this post he met, in 1875, Baron Carl Gustaf Wrangel and his wife, a Finnish actress named Siri von Essen. Strindberg and Siri fell in love, and in 1877 they married. In 1879 Strindberg published his novel THE RED ROOM, about life among the young writers and artists of Stockholm, and this made his name as an author. His playwriting was less successful; most of his plays were rejected, and the first half-success he had in the theatre was in 1883 with his ninth play, LUCKY PETER'S JOURNEY, a slight work halfway between PEER GYNT and the ARABIAN NIGHTS. It was tepidly received by the critics, but ran for seventy-six performances. By that time, however, Strindberg had left Sweden with his family, and they spent the next six years (1883-1889) abroad, moving between France, Switzerland, Germany and Denmark.

He had turned his back on the theatre, as he was to do at intervals throughout his life, and poured out a miscellany of volumes in both verse and prose. In 1884 he published a volume of short stories entitled MARRIAGE, for which he was quickly prosecuted for blasphemy; he returned to Sweden to face his trial, and was acquitted. He returned to his family in Switzerland, and wrote a series of autobiographical volumes under the general title THE SON OF A MAIDSERVANT. By this time he and Siri had three children, but they were very poor and their marriage had become unhappy, largely on account of Strindberg's pathological jealousy. In 1886 he turned again to the theatre and wrote his first play for four years, THE ROBBERS (which he shortly rewrote as THE COMRADES). The remainder of Strindberg's story is told in the introductions to the various plays in this volume.

He wrote sixty-two plays, of very uneven quality, in violent and spasmodic bursts of activity punctuated by years of, as far as the theatre was concerned, silence. Thus, after his first major play THE FATHER (1887), he wrote six plays in 1888-1889; none in 1890-1891; seven in 1892; none from 1892 to 1898; twenty-six in 1898-1903; none in 1904-1906; ten and a fragment in 1907-1909; and no more before his death in 1912. In addition, he composed innumerable novels, volumes of essays and short stories, memoirs, poems and theses on science, philosophy and philology; his collected works fill over fifty volumes.

Strindberg has never received his due as a dramatist in England or America. To begin with, he excelled in depicting people driven by love, hatred, jealousy or a mixture of all three to that nightmare border county where hysteria abuts on madness. All of his finest plays, from THE FATHER to THE GHOST SONATA and THE GREAT HIGHWAY, are set in this appalling landscape, which all of us, at some time in our lives, enter, though few of us, mercifully, are imprisoned in it as he was.

Now we in England and America are prepared to read about this no-man's-land in an armchair, but we do not, or did not until a few years ago, want to be confronted with it in the theatre. A Strindberg play well acted is an almost unbearable experience, both for the audience and for those taking part. Moreover, it requires a kind of acting which has, regrettably, become suspect with us—the kind that is not afraid to approach the precipice. In Sweden, as in Germany, the unforgivable sin is to underact; in England and America, it is to overact; how often have we not seen our best actors, when faced by the peaks of King Lear or Othello, take refuge in gentlemanly underplaying? There are some parts—Lear and Othello, Cleopatra, Clytemnestra, Oedipus, Prometheus, Wozzeck, Brand, Peer Gynt, Borkman—which have got to be done big or they had better not be done at all; and Strindberg's greatest creations—the Captain in THE FATHER, Miss Julie, the two protagonists in THE DANCE OF DEATH, Hummel in THE GHOST SONATA—belong to this category. It is no coincidence that the only two actors who have entirely succeeded in Strindberg in England, Robert Loraine and Wilfrid Lawson, have been actors of a most un-English, one might almost say continental vehemence, and consequently, like that other great actor Frederick Valk, difficult to cast in roles of ordinary human dimensions. For a parallel reason, there has never yet been a fully adequate Miss Julie in England or America, though there are perhaps one or two young actresses who might achieve it today.

Strindberg, too, has been unlucky in that none of the great Swedish producers, such as Olof Molander, Alf Sjöberg and Ingmar Bergman, have ever come to show foreigners how his plays should be staged. Tchehov remained similarly unappreciated in London until Theodore Komisarjevsky showed the way with his productions at Barnes in the nineteen-twenties. One has to know Sweden and the Swedes to be able to stage Strindberg. Although they appear on the surface to treat sex lightly, it is to them a game played on very thin ice, and Strindberg's characters have heard it crack under their feet, if they are not already struggling in the dark and greedy waters. We have a deep distrust of those waters; we are not drawn towards them, as Strindberg's characters are; and to play these dramas amiably, even mate-ily, as they usually have been played in England and America, is to render them ridiculous.

I am thinking here of Strindberg's realistic dramas, which form the bulk of his work. His symbolical or expressionistic plays, which he wrote towards the end of his life after his INFERNO crisis,* such as TO DAMASCUS, A DREAM PLAY and THE GHOST SONATA, are difficult for a different reason. They are to drama what ULYSSES was to be to the novel and THE WASTE LAND to poetry. In them Strindberg was, to quote his own words, trying "to imitate the inconsequent yet transparently logical shape of a dream. Everything can happen.... Time and place do not exist; on an insignificant basis of reality the imagination spins, weaving new patterns...." Thirty years earlier, Ibsen had attempted something of the kind in PEER GYNT, but not, as Strindberg did, consciously; Ibsen never deliberately implies that in the fifth act he is showing us the inside of a dead or a dying man's mind, though we can infer this if we wish to. But Strindberg, twenty-one years the younger man, was writing TO DAMASCUS and A DREAM PLAY at the same time that Freud was formulating his theories in Vienna, and although Strindberg did not, as far as we know, read Freud, he had studied Freud's predecessors, such as Max Nordau, Hippolyte Bernheim and the Nancy school, and was moving on a parallel road.

Much that is commonplace in modern drama stems from Strindberg; Toller and Kaiser, O'Neill and O'Casey, Pinter and Ionesco have all acknowledged him as their ancestor. Apart from his expressionistic experiments, he perfected, in such plays as MISS JULIE and CREDITORS, a terse, nervous dialogue, less deliberate and more fragmentary than Ibsen's, the shorthand of speech. Ibsen had reduced dialogue from

* See page 282. Strindberg's own terrible account of this period in his life, INFERNO, has recently been well translated into English by Mary Sandbach (Hutchinson, 1962).

poetic verbosity to a taut and spare colloquial prose, but Strindberg reduced it even further. Structurally, too, he achieved an economy beyond Ibsen's; he proudly pointed out that the plots of MISS JULIE and CREDITORS would each have sufficed for a five-act play but that he had reduced each of them to a single act of less than ninety minutes. Take a lamb cutlet, he said; it looks large, but three-quarters of it is bone and fat, containing a kernel of meat. I strip off the bone and fat and give you the kernel.

Psychologically, too, he was a pioneer; he explored, as D. H. Lawrence did, those dark corners of the human soul which most of us seal off like poisoned wells. He was unbalanced, but so were most explorers of that country: Swift, Melville, Dostoevsky, Kafka. One can say of him what one has said of his disciple, Stig Dagerman: reality and fantasy, the world of the countryman and the world of the city—he was never fully able to reconcile them. Although he wanted to be the conscience of the world, his world was in fact a small private one. Yet he photographed his small, split world with a vivid and faithful clarity, and sometimes one is haunted by a secret and uneasy suspicion that his private vision may in some respects be nearer the truth of things than those visions of the great humanists, such as Tolstoy and Balzac, which people call universal.

MICHAEL MEYER

ACKNOWLEDGEMENTS

I GLADLY ACKNOWLEDGE my debt to four pioneers in the field of Strindberg research: the late Professor Martin Lamm, for his books STRINDBERGS DRAMER and AUGUST STRINDBERG; Docent Torsten Eklund, for his monumental edition of Strindberg's letters, of which the first seven volumes (to December 1889) have to date appeared; Docent Carl Reinhold Smedmark, of whose definitive edition of Strindberg's plays two volumes have so far been published; and Docent Gunnar Ollén, for his admirable survey, STRINDBERGS DRAMATIK (revised edition, 1962). Docent Eklund and Docent Smedmark have also given me much valuable information personally. I also wish to thank Mr. Casper Wrede for innumerable suggestions concerning the translation of CREDITORS; the 59 Theatre Company for commissioning that translation; the Royal Shakespeare Company for commissioning the translation of PLAYING WITH FIRE; the British Broadcasting Corporation for commissioning the translation of THE GHOST SONATA; and, not least, the Royal Dramatic Theatre of Stockholm for the memorable Strindberg productions they have enabled me to see over the past sixteen years.

Strindberg's plays present a formidable textual problem. Once anything had been published, he lost interest in the manuscript, so that many of these have disappeared. He was, moreover, the most indolent of proof-readers; and sometimes his various publishers made surreptitious amendments on the ground of supposed libel or obscenity. But even where the manuscript exists and shows corrections in a hand other than the author's, we cannot ignore them, since some at least may well have been made at Strindberg's own oral or written request. For example, the manuscript of MISS JULIE contains some corrections in Strindberg's hand, some in the hand of his publisher Joseph Seligmann, and some (e.g., deletions) that might have been made by either. Strindberg's own word counts for nothing in this matter, for one line that he swore was a miserable invention of Seligmann appears clearly on the manuscript in his (Strindberg's) own handwriting. Many of Seligmann's amendments seem to me to be obvious dramatic improvements, tightening the dialogue; they are of the kind much more likely to have been made by a playwright than a publisher, and it is difficult to see why Seligmann should have made them except at Strindberg's request. Where this play is concerned, I have followed my own judgment, based on a close study of Strindberg's manuscript. For an analysis of the respective merits of the three different endings to PLAYING WITH FIRE, see p. 280.

This Vintage paperback edition contains a few amendments to the texts of THE FATHER AND MISS JULIE as originally published in hardback in 1964.

M.M.

Introduction to
THE FATHER

STRINDBERG wrote THE FATHER at Issigatsbühel in Bavaria in January and February of 1887, shortly after his thirty-eighth birthday.

The previous autumn he had completed a play—his first for four years—entitled THE ROBBERS (MARODÖRER), which he described to his publisher, Albert Bonnier, as "a comedy in five acts—the last four written during the past eight days, which doesn't mean they're not good, for I can't write slowly". This play, which he was later to rewrite under the title of THE COMRADES, was set in Paris and dealt with the marital troubles of a young female painter named Bertha, who smoked cigarettes, wore her hair short and dressed like a man. Bonnier did not much like it, and on 12 January 1887 he wrote to Strindberg that Ludwig Josephson, the director of the New Theatre in Stockholm, had rejected it. "His refusal does not surprise me", commented Bonnier, "for, as you know, I have already expressed a similar opinion, *which I still hold*. I fear that these last months you have been living too isolated a life to be able to keep acquainted with public opinion and really understand it, and if you are not willing even to read a country's newspapers I think it must be difficult to go on writing for that country and to partake in its literary polemics."

Strindberg replied on 6 February: "One does not *choose* what one writes about.... Just now I am preoccupied with this question of women's rights, and shall not drop it until I have investigated and experimented in this field. I have just completed Act One of THE FATHER, the first play in the trilogy of which THE ROBBERS is the second. I beg you therefore not to reject THE ROBBERS, but to make the amendments I have suggested, and in the fulness of time you will see a remarkable work which the wise will still think mad, but which just because of that contains the future. If you reject it, I shall have to go to another publisher, for I won't let myself be silenced in so big and important a matter as this, which has been befogged and made a farce of by such *sometime* men as Ibsen and Björnson. In a fortnight, I shall have completed my tragedy, THE FATHER. Wait till then."

The feminist campaign, which Ibsen had championed in such plays as THE PILLARS OF SOCIETY (1877) and A DOLL'S HOUSE (1881) was something to which Strindberg was violently antipathetic. His own marriage, with the actress Siri von Essen, was, after ten feverish years, dreadfully on the rocks. He suspected her of being unfaithful to him, both with other men and with a young Danish girl, short-haired and cigarette-smoking like Bertha in THE ROBBERS, named Marie David. On 4 January he had explained to Gustaf av Geijerstam: "I am writing for the theatre now because otherwise the bluestockings will take it over; and the theatre is a weapon", and on 22 January he had complained to Edvard Brandes of Ibsen's "scandalous attacks on the male sex. I am about to rewrite Act 5 [of THE ROBBERS]. Then Part 1 [of the trilogy], THE FATHER, and in ten years, when we shall have these women-devils over us with their right to vote and everything, down-trodden men will dig up my trilogy, but will not dare to stage it. . . .* I shall fight as long as I have a nerve left in my body, and if they peck me to death you can write a play about 'the

---

* In 1886, just before he wrote THE FATHER, Strindberg had been much impressed by an article which he read in a magazine by Paul Lafargue. Lafargue postulated the theory that the family was originally a matriarchy and only became a patriarchy as the result of a long and violent war between the sexes. A return to the matriarchal pattern would involve an equally long and bloody war. At about the time when he was working on THE FATHER Strindberg wrote an essay in which he expresses his fear that this battle will mean the defeat of man, and that if this takes place it will herald an age of barbarism. Lafargue refers a great deal in his essay to the ORESTEIA of Aeschylus, and this may have influenced Strindberg into composing THE FATHER more closely according to the classical principles than any of his previous plays.

last man'. Actually, my misogyny is entirely theoretical, and I can't live a day without supposing that I warm my soul at the flame of their unconscious, vegetable way of life."

He finished THE FATHER on 15 February, having apparently completed it in two to three weeks (we do not know the exact date on which he started it). Like so many of Strindberg's plays, it is largely autobiographical, or at any rate an imagined picture of his past and present situation.* As long ago as 1872, he had, like the Captain, written to the director of a private asylum asking to be admitted for treatment. "I have been reading a lot about insanity," he had told Verner von Heidenstam on 5 October 1886. "It would seem that all human beings are mad except doctors." Like the Captain, he had quarrelled with his wife about the future of his two daughters; he wanted them to become nurses, Siri wanted them to train for the stage. (In fact, one became an actress and the other, with dreadful irony when one thinks of Bertha in THE ROBBERS, a painter.)

The subject of hypnotism and "suggestion" was one that deeply interested Strindberg—as, at this same time, it did Ibsen, who had explored it in ROSMERSHOLM and was to do so again the next year (1888) in THE LADY FROM THE SEA and, four years later, in THE MASTER BUILDER. Dr. Gunnar Ollén has noted that Strindberg "knew of the experiments of Bernheim and the so-called Nancy School in influencing people by suggestion when they are awake, and in the autumn of 1886 he had eagerly devoured Max Nordau's *Paradoxes*, with their demonstrations of the effect of alien suggestion upon ordinarily healthy minds. He knew his Darwin. Man, in his plays, was to be shown as the more refined sex, but also the more debilitated by civilisation, and thus doomed to be crushed by the more primitive and stronger female sex. Her weapon of victory was to be not, as in the days of Aeschylus and Shakespeare, poison or dagger,

---

* Almost all the situations in THE FATHER reappear in Strindberg's autobiographical novel THE APOLOGY OF A FOOL, and some of the lines from the play are repeated word for word.

but the much subtler weapon of spiritual murder through suggestion."

Unlike Ibsen, Strindberg was a revealing correspondent, and although he made few references to THE FATHER while actually at work on it his letters over the next twelve months contain many passages that throw light upon the state of mind that caused him to write it. On 25 February he remarked to his brother Axel: "You will know that, as a poet, I blend fiction with reality, and all my misogyny is theoretical, for I couldn't live without the company of women. . . . So you mustn't get depressed when you read THE FATHER, for it is a work of fiction. Like THE ROBBERS." A week later he wrote to Georg Lundström: "I am a misogynist only in theory, and live quite idyllically here in the country alone in a house with six women. My wife and I sing student songs, play backgammon, drink beer and live like newlyweds. We aren't petty, and so never nag each other; I am the most humane of men in everyday matters, and my wife's great virtue is that she isn't smallminded. So we are very happy; and she cooks splendidly and thinks life is wonderful. I keep my play to myself."

He harps continually on the disservice that Ibsen has done to their sex. "What would have happened to A DOLL'S HOUSE", he asked Edvard Brandes (6 April 1887) "if Helmer had received a little justice? Or to GHOSTS if Mr. Alving had been allowed to live and tell the audience that his wife was lying about him? No—just blame everything on them, blacken their names, tread them in the mud so that they haven't a square inch left clean—that makes for good theatre!" And on 3 June he warned the actor August Lindberg, who was negotiating with a Copenhagen theatre to do a season of Ibsen plays: "You can't go on with Ibsen for long; he probably won't write much more; his *genre* is his speciality and is on the way out. You ought to read what the Germans have to say about ROSMERSHOLM!" In this, as in so many other matters, Strindberg proved a bad prophet, for Ibsen was about to embark on his great final sextet of THE LADY FROM THE SEA, HEDDA

GABLER, THE MASTER BUILDER, LITTLE EYOLF, JOHN GABRIEL BORKMAN and WHEN WE DEAD AWAKEN.

That summer Strindberg broke with Siri and applied for a divorce (though they did not finally part until four years later). On 3 September 1887 he wrote a long and hysterical letter to Pehr Staaff: "Her witchcraft was unbelievable! Notwithstanding her crimes and all her debts she succeeded in making the first man she met believe that I was the guilty one! She got me to imagine for three years that I was ill, got me to imagine I was mad—and everyone pitied and believed her! ... Remember that Siri tricked me into writing to Forssberg [the family doctor, and an old friend of Strindberg's from their Upsala days] that I believed I was mad. ... It'll be interesting to see how this drama ends; probably in tragedy. But I won't let her go too soon, or she'll raise an army against me, and female cunning is stronger than male intelligence. Divorce? Yes—then I'll have to sit celibate, masturbating and paying for other men to fornicate with her! That prospect doesn't much amuse me. And her talent for squeezing money out of me is monstrous!"

That autumn Hans Riber Hunderup, the director of the Casino Theatre in Copenhagen, decided to stage THE FATHER (which had been rejected by all the Swedish theatres to which it had been offered), and commissioned a young Swedish writer, Axel Lundegård, to translate it and to negotiate with Strindberg for the rights; also, if possible, to persuade him to attend the première. On 17 October Strindberg wrote Lundegård a lengthy and detailed letter in which the precision and clear-sightedness of his observations about the play stand in astonishing contrast to the wildness and woolliness of his remarks on other subjects. After a characteristic opening ("I rejoice to hear from one of the younger generation, who understand what I write and realise that I represent the spirit of our age ..."), he continued: "But who is to be the Captain, and what woman is prepared to act Laura? The play can easily be destroyed and become ridiculous! I suggest, though I don't usually interfere in these matters, that the Captain be given to an actor of normally healthy temper who, conscious of his superiority, goes loftily and cynically, almost joyfully, to meet his fate, wrapping himself in death as in a spider's web which he is impotent to tear asunder. A deceived husband is a comic figure in the eyes of the world, and especially to a theatre audience. He must show that he is aware of this, and that he too would laugh if only the man in question were someone other than himself. This is what is *modern* in my tragedy, and alas for me and the clown who acts it if he goes to town and plays an 1887 version of the Pirate King! No screams, no preachings! Subtle, calm, resigned!—the way a normally healthy spirit accepts his fate today, as though it were an erotic passion. Remember that a cavalry officer is always a rich man's son who has had an education,* is exacting in his demands upon himself as a social animal, and behaves like a civilised human being even when addressing a common soldier. He mustn't be caricatured into a hidebound military reactionary. He stands above his profession—has seen through it, and turned to science. In particular, he symbolises for me a masculinity which people have tried to pound or wheedle out of us and transfer to the third sex! It is only when he is with the woman that he is unmanly, because that is how she wants him, and the law of adaptation forces us to play the role that our sexual partner demands. Yes, we sometimes have to act chaste, naïve or ignorant, simply to get our marital rights! . . . As regards appearing personally, I don't believe in that. I've tried it and it hasn't worked. My presence has usually injured my cause, and I am content to stay at my desk. I am gauche, stupid and tactless in company, and too cynical to play the blushing author."

Despite these and further protestations, however, Strindberg eventually agreed to attend the première, and on 6 November he arrived in Denmark, where he was to spend a harassing and

* In Bavaria he had met army officers who knew Latin and Greek, and they seem to have corresponded to his idea of a male hero.

miserable six months. On 12 November, two days before the première, he wrote to Lundegård, to whom he appears to have taken a fancy, warning him that he might "in a fit of romanticism", absent himself (i.e. commit suicide), and asking the unfortunate young man to act as his executor, listing a series of extraordinary requests. "Rehabilitate my wife by throwing a cloak of obscurity over everything that has happened, for the children's sake. . . . Force Albert Bonnier to publish Part Four of my autobiography. . . . See that my collected writings are published, when the time is ripe, in Flensburg, Leipzig, Copenhagen or Chicago; *everything* that I have written, every word, from newspapers, almanacs, abroad and at home, including my letters. . . . Arrange pensions for my children who, whether they are mine or not, were adopted by me (we don't need to mention my wife). . . . Urge Zola to get a publisher for THE FATHER, or have it printed in Copenhagen in French . . . try to get it acted in Paris. Get in touch with my brother Axel at the Royal Theatre in Stockholm, but don't obey him, for he doesn't understand me and has been talked over by Albert Bonnier and the Younger Generation. . . ."

He goes on to the impossibility, if one is a romantic, of living without an ideal. "Mine was incarnated in a woman, because I was a woman-worshipper. When it fell, I fell! In my letters you will see . . . a trusting and credulous fool, who allowed himself to believe anything, even that he was trash, which he wasn't at all—believe anything, so that the crimes of others might be concealed. . . . It seems to me as though I walk in my sleep—as though reality and imagination are one. I don't know if THE FATHER is a work of the imagination, or if my life has been; but I feel that at a given moment, possibly soon, it will cease, and then I will shrivel up, either in madness and agony, or in suicide. Through much writing my life has become a shadow-play; it is as though I no longer walk the earth, but hover weightless in a space that is filled not with air but with darkness. If light enters this darkness, I shall fall, broken. What is curious is that in a dream which often recurs to me at night I feel that

I am flying weightless, and I find this quite natural, as though all conception of right and wrong, true and false, had ceased to exist for me, so that everything that happens, however strange, seems inevitable. Well, I suppose this is the logical consequence of the new philosophy of indeterminism, and perhaps it is because I am unaccustomed to this new intellectual climate that I am amazed and fearful."

Two days later, on 14 November 1887, the première of THE FATHER took place at the Casino Theatre and was, against all expectation, quite a success—partly, no doubt, because the great Georg Brandes had condescended to advise on the production. Hunderup himself played the Captain, with his future wife, Johanne Krum, as Laura. The Danish newspapers praised the play warmly, and Strindberg found himself referred to as a genius. The normal fare offered to the Casino's audience consisted of light comedy and burlesque, and to sugar this particular pill, which must have perplexed such regular patrons as had not studied their newspapers, the evening was concluded with a farce. Even in this promising situation, however, Strindberg's ill fortune pursued him, for after eleven performances, through no fault of the play, the theatre went bankrupt. He did not receive a penny from the production, and had to pawn some of his belongings to see himself and his family through the worst of the winter.

Largely as a result of the Danish reviews, Ludwig Josephson, who had previously rejected the play, decided to stage it at his New Theatre in Stockholm, and on 23 December Strindberg wrote a long and perceptive letter of advice to the actor who was to direct and play the lead, August Falck.* "Act the play as Lindberg acted Ibsen, i.e. not tragedy, not comedy, but somewhere midway between. Don't take it too quickly, as we did here at the Casino. Rather let it creep forward, quietly, evenly, until it gathers momentum of its own accord towards

* The father of the more famous actor of the same name, who twenty years later was to be one of the leading spirits of Strindberg's own Intimate Theatre in Stockholm.

the last act. Exception: the Captain's lines when his obsession has manifested itself. They should be spoken quickly, abruptly, repeatedly breaking the atmosphere. Remember: the Captain is not a coarse soldier, but a scholar who has risen above his profession. (Think, without copying him, of the late Capt. P. v. Möller, member of the Academy of History and Literature; v. Holst the painter, v. Kock the philanthropist, etc.); gentle in Act 1, a good child; hardens, becomes angry, and at last mad. Detail: when he enters in Act 3 he is in shirt-sleeves (woollen shirt), has books under one arm and the saw under the other. If Laura is played by a young and beautiful woman, she should be hard, for her appearance will have a softening effect, from which her influence on her husband gains strength. If she is played by someone older, she must accentuate the maternal and somewhat underplay the hardness. The priest is an ordinary priest, serious, absorbed in the role he finds himself playing, not comic. The doctor is an ordinary doctor, torn between the influence of the woman and his natural sympathy for his fellow man. The daughter must be healthy and captivating, vital, alert, a breath of fresh air in the midst of all this gloom.... You will have received a copy showing the cuts. Cut more if you wish! You'll hear at rehearsal what doesn't work. The throwing of the lamp must be devised somehow; here the lamp was of wicker; the glass and shade should be fixed with putty, so that the lamp can be lifted without the glass falling off; it must be thrown past Laura's head out through the door *after* she has retreated through it, so that the audience is left uncertain whether or not it has hit her. Laura screams, and the stage is plunged into darkness.... Laura has a good moment in Act 3, Scene 1, when she sits at the secretaire where the Captain had previously sat. If she then repeats or imitates some gesture of the Captain's (e.g., sucking the pen and speaking a line with it between her lips, provided of course that he has done the same), the contrast will prove effective. That's about all I have to say. My greetings to the cast, and every good wish."

On 12 January 1888 THE FATHER received its Swedish première at the New Theatre in Stockholm, and was a disastrous failure. "It can suitably be summed up", wrote one critic, "in Hamlet's exclamation: 'O horrible, O horrible, most horrible!' Any other comment seems superfluous." The audience began to express its disapproval before the end of the evening, and the play was removed after only nine performances. From this production, Strindberg received approximately £2.

The following year, however, some consolation came with a production at the Freie Buhne in Berlin, the experimental theatre which Otto Brahm had just founded on the model of Antoine's Théâtre Libre in Paris. It was the first time a play by Strindberg had been performed outside Scandinavia, and established him in the country in which his influence and reputation were to remain most constant.

Hunderup, the original producer of THE FATHER, having improved his financial position, revived the play on frequent occasions in Denmark, but in the absence of any binding copyright law Strindberg earned practically nothing from these performances. In 1891, Hunderup took his production to Christiania, where it was seen by at least one notable spectator. Vilhelm Petersen has described in his memoirs how, one hot summer evening, the theatre was almost empty. But in the front row, in lonely majesty, sat Henrik Ibsen, who had been invited to attend and who had just returned to live in Norway after twenty-seven years abroad.* After the interval, when there was to have been a farce, Ibsen had gone, and the theatre was left completely empty.

In 1894, Lugné-Poe, Ibsen's champion, staged THE FATHER

---

* More accurately, he had returned to Norway for a holiday, but in fact stayed for the remaining fifteen years of his life. Unfortunately his opinion of THE FATHER is not on record. Later he kept a painting of Strindberg on his study wall, not, he explained, because of any sympathy or friendship with either the painter or Strindberg, but because "I am now not able to write a word without having that madman staring down at me!"

Introduction to THE FATHER

in Paris at his Théâtre de l'Œuvre, the première being attended by Zola, Rodin, Prévost, Sardou, Gauguin and Becque, but (apart from a single performance in 1893), it was to be twenty years before the play was to receive another production in Strindberg's native country, and then only at his own recently-founded Intimate Theatre in Stockholm. There in 1908, it was staged by August Falck, junior, the son of the actor who had been responsible for the ill-fated New Theatre production. This time the play was acclaimed, and ran for seventy-seven performances. Three years later, the Intimate Theatre production was filmed, out of doors in Stockholm "on an autumn day so cold that the breath of the actors was visible". Dr. Gunnar Ollén, who saw the film, comments that the style of acting is, for the period, surprisingly restrained, partly, perhaps, because the company was used to playing in so tiny an auditorium.

The same year, 1911, THE FATHER was performed in London, first in Yiddish at the Pavilion Theatre in Whitechapel and subsequently in English at the little Rehearsal Theatre in Maiden Lane.* *The Times* remarked that Strindberg seemed "extraordinarily naïve in some of his dramatic processes", and *The Academy* asked: "Why use the theatre for unrelieved depression and brutal aspects of human nature and relationships exploited in the name of art?" It might with luck have been seen twenty years earlier in London; J. T. Grein, the founder of the Independent Theatre which introduced Ibsen to English audiences, subsequently put on record (*The Sketch*, 31 July 1929) that he "tried in vain to cast it for our Independent Theatre, because all the women I approached to play the Captain's wife rebuffed me with the same answer: "You do not expect me to play that awful part?"

In 1912 THE FATHER was produced in New York, with Warner Oland in the title role, but the only two countries in which the play really succeeded before the First World War

* For the cast of this and subsequent London productions, see Appendix (page 469).

were Germany and Russia. By 1914 it had been produced in Berlin, Hamburg, Leipzig, Munich, Nuremburg, Stuttgart, Graz and Brunn, as well as twice in Vienna. In 1904 it was staged in St. Petersburg, and in 1905 in Moscow; the latter production was so successful that it toured many of the Russian cities, and in Nijni Novgorod the police had to remove four women who had been overcome with hysterics during the last act.

After the First World War, the climate of theatrical taste had changed, and THE FATHER came into its own in many countries. In London, in 1927, Robert Loraine achieved a great success at the Everyman Theatre, which he repeated when the play was transferred to the Savoy.* In 1929 Malcolm Morley played it in modern dress, again at the Everyman; and three weeks later, by what seems to have been a generous arrangement, Morley produced the play at the Apollo Theatre in period costume, with Loraine back in his old part. Since the Second World War, THE FATHER has twice been finely acted in London, in 1948 by Michael Redgrave and in 1953 by Wilfrid Lawson.** The latter, in particular, gave an unforgettable performance. Among the many notable interpretations of the role on the Continent may be named those of Paul Wegener in Berlin in 1915 (at Max Reinhardt's Kammerspiele), Fritz Kortner in Munich in 1949, and Lars Hanson in Stockholm in 1953. The play has also been produced as far abroad as Turkey and India.

* When Loraine first read the play to his wife, she fell on her knees halfway through to assure him that his children were his own and that he was not to believe a word of the play. Loraine commented: "If it upsets you like that, there must be something in it."

** And, since this introduction was written, in 1964 by Trevor Howard.

THE FATHER

A Tragedy in Three Acts
(1887)

CHARACTERS

THE CAPTAIN
LAURA, his wife
BERTHA, their daughter
DR. ÖSTERMARK
THE PASTOR
THE NURSE
NÖJD, a servant
THE CAPTAIN'S BATMAN

This translation of THE FATHER was first performed on 14 January 1964 at the Piccadilly Theatre, London. The cast was:

THE CAPTAIN	Trevor Howard
LAURA	Joyce Redman
BERTHA	Jo Maxwell-Muller
DR. ÖSTERMARK	Nigel Stock
THE PASTOR	Alfred Burke
THE NURSE	Gwen Nelson
NÖJD	Trevor Peacock
THE CAPTAIN'S BATMAN	Malcolm Tierney

Designed by Malcolm Pride
Directed by Casper Wrede

ACT ONE

A room in the CAPTAIN's house. Upstage right, a door. In the centre of the room is a large round table, with newspapers and magazines. On the right, a leather sofa and a table. In the right-hand corner, a concealed door. On the left, a secretaire, with an ornamental clock on it, and a door which leads to the rest of the house. There are weapons on the wall; rifles and game-bags. By the door, clothes-hangers with military tunics on them. On the large table a lamp is burning.

Scene 1

The CAPTAIN and the PASTOR on the leather sofa. The CAPTAIN is in undress uniform, with riding-boots and spurs. The PASTOR is in black, with a white stock, but without his clerical bands. He is smoking a pipe.

The CAPTAIN rings. The BATMAN enters.

BATMAN: Sir?

CAPTAIN: Is Nöjd out there?

BATMAN: He's waiting for orders in the kitchen, sir.

CAPTAIN: In the kitchen again! Send him here at once!

BATMAN: Sir! [*Goes.*]

PASTOR: What's the matter now?

CAPTAIN: Oh, the blackguard's been mucking about with one of the girls again. Damned nuisance, that fellow!

PASTOR: Nöjd? Why, you had trouble with him last year too!

CAPTAIN: You remember? Perhaps you'd give him a friendly

talking-to—that might have some effect. I've sworn at him, and given him a tanning, but it doesn't do any good.

PASTOR: So you want me to read him a sermon! Do you think the Word of God will have any effect on a cavalryman?

CAPTAIN: Well, brother-in-law, it doesn't have much effect on me, as you know——

PASTOR: Yes, I know!

CAPTAIN: But on him——? Try, anyway.

Scene 2

The CAPTAIN. *The* PASTOR. NÖJD.

CAPTAIN: Well, Nöjd, what have you been up to now?

NÖJD: God bless you, Captain, I couldn't tell you before his Reverence.

PASTOR: Come, come, don't be bashful, my lad!

CAPTAIN: Own up, or you know what'll happen!

NÖJD: Well, sir, it was like this, you see. We was dancing up at Gabriel's, and then, yes, well, Louis said——

CAPTAIN: What's Louis got to do with it? Stick to the facts!

NÖJD: Well, Emma suggested we should go to the barn.

CAPTAIN: I see! So it was Emma who seduced you!

NÖJD: Not far off. And I'll say this—if a girl ain't willing, she don't run no danger.

CAPTAIN: Out with it! Are you the child's father or not?

NÖJD: How should I know?

CAPTAIN: What! You don't know!

NÖJD: Well, you can never be sure.

CAPTAIN: Weren't you the only one, then?

NÖJD: I was that time, but that don't mean to say I was the only one.

CAPTAIN: Are you saying Louis's to blame? Is that it?

NÖJD: It ain't easy to say who's to blame.

CAPTAIN: But you've told Emma you want to marry her.

NÖJD: Yes, well, you have to tell them that.

CAPTAIN [*to* PASTOR]: This is monstrous!

PASTOR: It's the old story. Now, look here, Nöjd, surely you're man enough to know whether you're the father!

NÖJD: Well, I did go with her, but, as your Reverence knows, that don't necessarily mean anything need happen.

PASTOR: Come, come, my lad, don't start trying to evade the issue! You surely don't want to leave the girl alone with the child! Of course we can't force you to marry her, but you must accept responsibility for the child. You must!

NÖJD: All right, but Louis must pay his share.

CAPTAIN: Oh, very well, it'll have to go to court. I can't unravel the rights and wrongs of this, and I don't feel inclined to try. Right, get out!

PASTOR: Nöjd! One moment. Hm! Don't you regard it as dishonourable to leave a girl high and dry like that with a child? Eh? Well? Don't you feel such behaviour would be—hm——?

NÖJD: Oh, yes, if I knew I was the child's father. But that's something a man can never be sure of, your Reverence. And it's no joke spending your whole life sweating for other men's children. I'm sure you and the Captain'll both appreciate that.

CAPTAIN: Get out!

NÖJD: Sir! [*Goes.*]

CAPTAIN: And keep out of the kitchen, damn you!

Scene 3

CAPTAIN: Well, why didn't you lay into him?

PASTOR: What? I thought I spoke very strictly.

CAPTAIN: Oh, you just sat there mumbling to yourself.

PASTOR: To be honest, I don't know what one ought to say. It's bad luck on the girl, yes. But it's bad luck on the boy, too. Suppose he isn't the father? The girl can suckle the child four months at the orphanage, and then she'll be shot of him, but the boy can't dodge his responsibility like that. She'll get a good job afterwards in some decent home, but if he gets thrown out of his regiment, he's finished.

CAPTAIN: Yes, I wouldn't like to be the magistrate who has to judge this case. I don't suppose the lad's completely innocent —one can't be sure. But one thing you can be sure of. The girl's guilty—if you can say anyone's guilty.

PASTOR: Yes, yes! I'm not condemning anyone! But what were we speaking about when this blessed business intervened? Bertha's confirmation, wasn't it?

CAPTAIN: It's not just her confirmation. It's the whole question of her upbringing. This house is stuffed with women every one of whom wants to bring up my child. My mother-in-law wants to make her a spiritualist, Laura wants her to be a painter, her governess wants her to be a Methodist, old Margaret wants her to be a Baptist, and the maids are trying to get her into the Salvation Army. Well, you can't patch a soul together like a damned quilt. I have the chief right to decide her future, and I'm obstructed whichever way I turn. I've got to get her out of this house.

PASTOR: You've too many women running your home.

CAPTAIN: You needn't tell me that. It's like a cage full of tigers—if I didn't keep a red-hot iron in front of their noses, they'd claw me to the ground the first chance they got. Yes, you can laugh, you old fox! It wasn't enough that I married your sister, you had to palm your old stepmother off on me too!

PASTOR: Well, good heavens, one can't have one's stepmother living under one's roof.

CAPTAIN: But one's mother-in-law is all right! Yes, under someone else's roof.

PASTOR: Well, well. We all have our cross to bear.

CAPTAIN: Yes, but I've a damned sight too many. I've got my old nurse too, and she treats me as though I was still in a bib! Oh, she's a dear old soul, heaven knows, but she doesn't belong here!

PASTOR: You should keep your women in their place, Adolf. You let them rule you.

CAPTAIN: My dear brother-in-law, will you kindly tell me how one keeps women in their place?

PASTOR: To speak frankly, Laura—I know she's my sister, but—well, she was always a little difficult.

CAPTAIN: Oh, Laura has her moods, but she's not too bad.

PASTOR: Ah, come on! I know her!

CAPTAIN: Well, she's had a romantic upbringing, and has a little difficulty in accepting life, but, after all, she is my wife——

PASTOR: And is therefore the best of women. No, Adolf, she's the biggest stone round your neck.

CAPTAIN: Yes, well, anyway, now the whole house has become impossible. Laura doesn't want to let Bertha out of her sight. But I can't let her stay in this asylum.

PASTOR: So? Laura won't—? Hm, then I'm afraid things aren't going to be easy. When she was a child, she used to lie absolutely still like a corpse until she'd got what she wanted. And when she'd got it, she'd give it back, explaining that it wasn't the *thing* she wanted, simply the fact of having her will.

CAPTAIN: I see, she was like that already, was she? Hm! She gets so emotional sometimes that I become frightened, and wonder if she isn't—well—sick.

PASTOR: But what is it you want for Bertha that she finds so unacceptable? Can't you meet each other halfway?

CAPTAIN: You mustn't imagine I want to build the child into a prodigy, or a copy of myself. But I don't want to play the pimp and educate her just simply for marriage—if I do that and she stays single, she'll become one of these embittered spinsters. On the other hand, I don't want to train her for some masculine vocation that'll need years of study and be completely wasted if she does get married.

PASTOR: What do you want, then?

CAPTAIN: I'd like her to become a teacher. Then, if she stays single she'll be able to look after herself, and won't be worse off than these wretched schoolmasters who have to support a family. And if she does marry, she can use the knowledge she's gained in bringing up her own children. That's logical, isn't it?

PASTOR: Perfectly. But hasn't she shown a great talent for painting? Wouldn't it be bad for her to repress that?

CAPTAIN: No, no. I've shown her efforts to a prominent artist, and he says it's only the kind of thing people learn to do at schools. But then some young ass came here last summer who knew more about such matters, and said she was a genius—and as far as Laura was concerned, that settled it.

PASTOR: Was he in love with the girl?

CAPTAIN: I presume so.

PASTOR: Then God help you, my dear fellow, for there'll be nothing you can do about that! But this is a sad business, and of course Laura has allies—in there.

CAPTAIN: Oh, yes, never you fear! The whole household is up in arms—and, between you and me, they're not fighting strictly according to the rules of chivalry.

PASTOR [*gets up*]: Do you think I haven't been through all this?

CAPTAIN: You too?

PASTOR: Are you surprised?

CAPTAIN: But the worst is, it seems to me Bertha's future is being decided in there from motives of hatred. They keep dropping hints that men will see that women can do this and do that. Man versus woman, that's their theme, all day long. Must you go now? No, stay for supper. I can't offer you much, but, did I tell you, I'm expecting the new doctor to pay a call? Have you seen him?

PASTOR: I caught a glimpse of him on my way here. He looks a pleasant, straightforward chap.

CAPTAIN: Does he? Good! Think he might be on my side?

PASTOR: Who knows? It depends how much he's had to do with women.

CAPTAIN: Oh, come on, do stay!

PASTOR: No thanks, my dear fellow. I've promised to be home for supper, and my old lady gets so worried if I'm late.

CAPTAIN: Worried? Angry, you mean! Well, as you wish. Let me give you a hand with your coat.

PASTOR: It's certainly very cold tonight. Thank you. You want to look after yourself, Adolf. You look nervy.

CAPTAIN: Do I?

PASTOR: You're not quite yourself, are you?

CAPTAIN: Has Laura given you that idea? She's been treating me like a budding corpse for twenty years.

PASTOR: Laura? No, no, I just wondered—— Take care of yourself! That's my advice. Well, goodbye, old chap. But didn't you want to talk to me about confirmation?

CAPTAIN: No, that'll have to take its course. Chalk that one up to society's conscience. I don't intend to be a martyr for the sake of truth. I'm past all that. Goodbye! Give my regards to your wife!

PASTOR: Goodbye, brother! Give mine to Laura!

Scene 4

The CAPTAIN. *Then* LAURA.

CAPTAIN [*opens the secretaire, sits down at it and starts counting*]: Thirty-four—nine—forty-three—seven, eight—fifty-six.

LAURA [*enters from the main part of the house*]: Would you mind——

CAPTAIN: In a moment. Sixty-six, seventy-one, eighty-four, eighty-nine, ninety-two, one hundred. What is it?

LAURA: Perhaps I'm disturbing you.

CAPTAIN: Not at all. The housekeeping money, I suppose?

LAURA: Yes. The housekeeping money.

CAPTAIN. Leave the bills there, and I'll go through them.

LAURA: Bills?

CAPTAIN: Yes.

LAURA: Oh, you want bills now?

CAPTAIN: Of course I want bills. We are financially embarrassed, and if things come to a head I've got to be able to produce accounts. Otherwise I can be punished as a negligent debtor.

LAURA: It isn't my fault if we're financially embarrassed.

CAPTAIN: That's just what the bills will establish.

LAURA: I'm not to blame if our tenant won't pay the lease of his farm.

CAPTAIN: Who recommended him? You. Why did you recommend such a—what shall we call him? Drone?

LAURA: If he's such a drone, why did you take him?

CAPTAIN: Because you wouldn't let me eat in peace, sleep in peace or work in peace until you'd got him here. You wanted to have him because your brother wanted to be rid of him, your mother wanted to have him because I didn't want to have him, the governess wanted to have him because he was a Methodist, and old Margaret wanted to have him because she'd known his grandmother since they were children. So we took him, and if I hadn't I should now be either sitting in an asylum or lying in the family vault. However, here is your household allowance, and some pin money. You can give me the bills later.

LAURA [*curtseys*]: Thank you, sir. Do you keep bills for your private expenses?

CAPTAIN: That's none of your business.

LAURA: True; no more than my child's upbringing. Have you gentlemen reached a decision now, after your evening session?

CAPTAIN: I had already made my decision. I merely wished to impart it to the only friend whom I and my family have in common. Bertha is to live in town. She will leave in a fortnight.

LAURA: And where is she to live, if I may be allowed to ask?

CAPTAIN: I have arranged for her to lodge with my lawyer, Mr. Saevberg.

LAURA: That freethinker!

CAPTAIN: The law states that a child is to be brought up in her father's faith.

LAURA: And the mother has no say in the matter?

CAPTAIN: None. She has sold her birthright by legal contract, and has surrendered all her claims. In return, the husband supports her and her children.

LAURA: So she has no rights over her own child?

CAPTAIN: None whatever. Once you have sold something, you can't get it back and keep the money.

LAURA: But if the father and mother should agree on a compromise——?

CAPTAIN: How is that possible? I want her to live in town, you want her to stay at home. The arithmetical mean would be that she should live at the railway station, halfway between. This is a situation which cannot be resolved by compromise.

LAURA: Then it must be resolved by force. What did Nöjd want here?

CAPTAIN: That is my professional secret.

LAURA: The whole kitchen knows.

CAPTAIN: Then you should.

LAURA: I do.

CAPTAIN: And have passed judgment?

LAURA: The law is quite explicit on the matter.

CAPTAIN: The law is not explicit as to who is the child's father.

LAURA: No. But one usually knows.

CAPTAIN: Wise men say one can never be sure about such things.

LAURA: Not be sure who is a child's father?

CAPTAIN: They say not.

LAURA: How extraordinary! Then how can the father have all these rights over her child?

CAPTAIN: He only has them if he accepts responsibility for the child—or has the responsibility forced upon him. And in marriage, of course, the question of paternity does not arise.

LAURA: Never?

CAPTAIN: I should hope not.

LAURA: But if the wife has been unfaithful?

CAPTAIN: That is not relevant to our discussion. Are there any other questions you want to ask me?

LAURA: None whatever.

CAPTAIN: Then I shall go to my room. Please be so good as to inform me when the Doctor comes. [*Shuts the secretaire and rises.*]

LAURA: Very well.

CAPTAIN [*going through concealed door right*]: The moment he arrives! I don't wish to insult him. You understand? [*Goes.*]

LAURA: I understand.

Scene 5

LAURA *alone. She looks at the banknotes she is holding in her hand.*

GRANDMOTHER [*offstage*]: Laura!

LAURA: Yes?

GRANDMOTHER: Is my tea ready?

LAURA [*in the doorway left*]: I'll bring it in a moment.

Goes towards the door upstage. Just before she reaches it, the BATMAN *opens it.*

BATMAN: Dr. Östermark!

DOCTOR [*enters*]: Mrs. Lassen?

LAURA [*goes to greet him, and stretches out her hand*]: How do you do, Doctor! Welcome to our home. The Captain is out, but he will be back shortly.

DOCTOR: Please forgive me for coming so late. I've already had to visit some patients.

LAURA: Won't you sit down?

DOCTOR: Thank you, Mrs. Lassen, thank you.

LAURA: Yes, there's a lot of illness around here just now. However, I do hope you'll be happy here. We lead such a lonely life out here in the country, so it's important for us to have a doctor who takes an interest in his patients. And

I've heard many flattering reports of you, so I hope we shall see a good deal of each other.

DOCTOR: You are too kind, Mrs. Lassen. But I trust, for your sake, that my visits will not always have to be professional! Your family enjoys good health——?

LAURA: We've never had any serious illnesses, I am glad to say. But things aren't quite as they should be——

DOCTOR: Indeed?

LAURA: I'm afraid they are not at all as we could wish.

DOCTOR: Really? You alarm me!

LAURA: There are certain domestic matters which a woman's honour and conscience require her to conceal from the world——

DOCTOR: But not from her doctor.

LAURA: Precisely. So I feel it is my painful duty to be quite open with you from the start.

DOCTOR: Could we not postpone this conversation until I have had the pleasure of making the Captain's acquaintance?

LAURA: No. You must hear what I have to say before you see him.

DOCTOR: It concerns him, then?

LAURA: Yes—my poor, beloved husband!

DOCTOR: You alarm me, Mrs. Lassen. Believe me, I am deeply touched by your distress.

LAURA [*takes out her handkerchief*]: My husband is mentally unbalanced. Now you know. You will be able to judge for yourself later.

DOCTOR: What! But I have read with admiration the Captain's excellent dissertations on mineralogy, and have always received the impression of a powerful and lucid intelligence.

LAURA: Indeed? I should be most happy if it could be proved that we have all been mistaken.

THE FATHER

DOCTOR: It is of course possible that his mind may be unhinged where other matters are concerned. Pray proceed.

LAURA: That is what we fear. You see, sometimes he has the most extraordinary ideas, which we would gladly indulge if they didn't threaten the existence of his whole family. For example, he has a mania for buying things.

DOCTOR. That is unfortunate. But what does he buy?

LAURA: Whole crates of books, which he never reads.

DOCTOR: Well, it isn't so unusual for a scholar to buy books.

LAURA: You don't believe me?

DOCTOR: Yes, Mrs. Lassen, I am sure that what you say is true.

LAURA: But is it reasonable for a man to claim that he can see in a microscope what is happening on another planet?

DOCTOR: Does he say that?

LAURA: Yes.

DOCTOR: In a microscope?

LAURA: Yes, in a microscope.

DOCTOR: If that is so, it is serious——

LAURA: *If* it is so! You don't believe me, Doctor. And I sit here telling you all our family secrets——

DOCTOR: Now listen, Mrs. Lassen. I am honoured that you should confide in me. But as a doctor, I must investigate the matter thoroughly before I can make a diagnosis. Has the Captain shown any symptoms of capriciousness or vacillation?

LAURA: Any symptoms! We've been married for twenty years, and he has never yet taken a decision without reversing it.

DOCTOR: Is he stubborn?

LAURA: He always insists on having his own way, but once he has got it he loses interest and begs me to decide.

DOCTOR: This is serious. I must observe him closely. You see, my dear Mrs. Lassen, will is the backbone of the mind. If the will is impaired, the mind crumples.

LAURA: God knows I've done my best to meet his wishes during all these long years of trial. Oh, if you knew the things I have had to put up with! If you knew!

DOCTOR: Mrs. Lassen, your distress moves me deeply, and I promise you I will see what can be done. But after what you have told me, I must ask you one thing. Avoid touching on any subject that might excite your husband. In a sick brain, fancies grow like weeds, and can easily develop into obsessions or even monomania. You understand?

LAURA: You mean I must take care not to make him suspicious?

DOCTOR: Exactly. A sick man is receptive to the slightest impression, and can therefore be made to imagine anything.

LAURA: Really? I understand. Yes. Yes. [*A bell rings within the house.*] Excuse me, my mother wishes to speak with me. Wait a moment—this must be Adolf!

Scene 6

The DOCTOR. *The* CAPTAIN *enters through the concealed door.*

CAPTAIN: Ah, you here already, Doctor? Delighted to meet you!

DOCTOR: Good evening, Captain. It is a great honour for me to make the acquaintance of so distinguished a scientist.

CAPTAIN: Oh, nonsense. My military duties don't allow me much time for research. All the same, I think I'm on to a new discovery.

DOCTOR: Indeed?

CAPTAIN: You see, I've been submitting meteorites to spectral analysis, and I've discovered carbon! Evidence of organic life! What do you say to that?

DOCTOR: You can see that in the microscope?

CAPTAIN: Microscope? Good God, no—spectroscope!

DOCTOR: Spectroscope? Ah—yes, of course, I mean spectroscope. Well, then, you'll soon be able to tell us what is happening on Jupiter.

CAPTAIN: Not what *is* happening, but what *has* happened. If only that damned shop in Paris would send those books! I really believe all the booksellers in the world have entered into a conspiracy against me. Would you believe it, for two months I haven't had a reply to a single order, letter or even telegram! It's driving me mad. I just don't understand it.

DOCTOR: Oh, that's just common laziness. You mustn't take it too seriously.

CAPTAIN: Yes, but, damn it, I won't be able to get my thesis ready in time—I know there's a fellow in Berlin working on the same lines. Still, we haven't met to talk about that, but about you. If you'd care to live here, we have a small apartment in the wing—or would you rather take over your predecessor's lodgings?

DOCTOR: Just as you please.

CAPTAIN: No, as *you* please. Say, now.

DOCTOR: You must decide, Captain.

CAPTAIN: No, no, I can't decide. You must say what you want. I've no feelings in the matter, no feelings at all.

DOCTOR: Yes, but I can't decide——

CAPTAIN: For God's sake, man, say what you want! I've no inclinations in the matter, I couldn't care less what you do! Are you such a nitwit that you don't know what you want? Answer, or I'll get angry!

DOCTOR: If I must decide, then I'll live here!

CAPTAIN: Good! Thank you. Oh—! Forgive me, Doctor, but nothing annoys me so much as to hear people say it's all the same to them!

He rings. The NURSE *enters.*

CAPTAIN: Oh, is it you, Margaret? Tell me, old dear, do you know if the wing is ready for the doctor?

NURSE: Yes, sir, it's all ready.

CAPTAIN: Good. Then I won't keep you, Doctor—I expect you're tired. Good night. I'll look forward to seeing you again tomorrow.

DOCTOR: Good night, Captain.

CAPTAIN: I suppose my wife told you a few things about conditions here, to put you in the picture?

DOCTOR: She did mention one or two details she thought it might be useful for a stranger to know. Good night, Captain.

Scene 7

The CAPTAIN. *The* NURSE.

CAPTAIN: What do you want, old darling? Is something the matter?

NURSE: Now, listen, Mr. Adolf, pet.

CAPTAIN: What is it, Margaret? Speak out, my dear. You're the only one I can listen to without getting spasms.

NURSE: Now, listen, Mr. Adolf. Why don't you go halfway to meet madam about the child? Remember, she's a mother.

CAPTAIN: Remember I'm a father, Margaret.

NURSE: Now, now, now! A father has other things beside his child, but a mother has nothing. She's only got her child.

CAPTAIN: Exactly. She has only one burden, but I have three, including hers. Do you think I'd have stayed a soldier all my life if I hadn't been saddled with her and her child?

NURSE: Oh, I didn't mean that.

CAPTAIN: No, I'm sure you didn't. You're trying to put me in the wrong.

NURSE: Surely you think I want what's best for you, Mr. Adolf?

CAPTAIN: Yes, yes, my dear, I'm sure you do. But you don't know what's best for me. You see, it isn't enough for me to have given the child life. I want to give it my soul too.

NURSE: Well, I don't understand that. But I still think you ought to be able to come to some agreement.

CAPTAIN: You are not my friend, Margaret.

NURSE: I? Why, Mr. Adolf, how can you say such a thing? Do you think I can forget you were my baby when you were little?

CAPTAIN: Have *I* ever forgotten it, my dear? You've been like a mother to me—you've supported me, up to now, when everyone's been against me—but now, when I need you most, now you betray me and go over to the enemy.

NURSE: Enemy!

CAPTAIN: Yes, enemy! You know how things are in this house. You've seen it all, from beginning to end.

NURSE: Yes, I've seen enough. Blessed Jesus, why must two human beings torment the life out of each other? You're both so good and kind—madam's never like that to me or anyone else.

CAPTAIN: Only to me. Yes, I know. But I'm telling you, Margaret—if you betray me now, you are committing a sin. A web is being spun around me here, and that doctor is not my friend.

NURSE: Oh, Mr. Adolf, you think bad of everyone. But that's because you don't follow the true faith. That's the cause of it.

CAPTAIN. And you've found the only true faith, you and your Baptists. Aren't you lucky!

NURSE: Well, I'm luckier than you, Mr. Adolf. And happier. Humble your heart, and you'll see. God will make you happy, and you'll love your neighbour.

CAPTAIN: It's extraordinary—as soon as you start talking about God and love, your voice becomes hard and your eyes fill with hatred. No, Margaret, you haven't found the true faith.

NURSE: Ah, you're proud. All your learning won't get you far at the Day of Judgment.

CAPTAIN: How arrogantly thou speakest, O humble heart! Yes, I know learning means nothing to animals like you.

NURSE: Shame on you! Never mind. Old Margaret loves her big, big boy best of all, and when the storm comes he'll creep back to her like the good little child he is.

CAPTAIN: Margaret! Forgive me, but—believe me, there's no one here who loves me except you. Help me. I feel something is going to happen here—I don't know what, but there's something evil threatening—— [*There is a scream from within the house.*] What's that? Who's screaming?

Scene 8

The CAPTAIN. *The* NURSE. BERTHA *enters.*

BERTHA: Father, father! Help me! Save me!

CAPTAIN: What is it, my beloved child? Tell me.

BERTHA: Help me! I think she wants to hurt me!

CAPTAIN: Who wants to hurt you? Tell me. Tell me.

BERTHA: Grandmamma. But it was my fault. I played a trick on her.

CAPTAIN: Tell me about it.

BERTHA: But you mustn't say anything! Promise you won't!

CAPTAIN: Very well. But tell me what it is.

The NURSE *goes.*

BERTHA: Well—in the evenings, she turns down the lamp and sits me down at the table with a pen and paper. And then she says that the spirits are going to write.

CAPTAIN: What! Why haven't you told me about this before?

BERTHA: Forgive me—I didn't dare. Grandmamma says the spirits take their revenge if anyone talks about them. And then the pen writes, but I don't know if it's me. And sometimes it goes all right, but sometimes it won't move at all. And when I'm tired, nothing comes—but it's *got* to come! And tonight I thought I was writing well, but then grandmamma said I was copying from some old poem and playing a trick on her—and then she became so horribly angry!

CAPTAIN: Do you believe that spirits exist?

BERTHA: I don't know.

CAPTAIN: But I know they do not!

BERTHA: But grandmamma says you don't understand, and that you have much worse things, that can see what's happening on other planets.

CAPTAIN: She says that, does she? What else does she say?

BERTHA: She says you can't work magic.

CAPTAIN: I haven't said I can. You know what meteors are? Yes, stones that fall from other heavenly bodies. I can study them and say whether they contain the same elements as our earth. That's all I can see.

BERTHA: But grandmamma says there are things that she can see but you can't.

CAPTAIN: Well, she's lying.

BERTHA: Grandmamma doesn't tell lies.

CAPTAIN: How do you know?

BERTHA. Then mother would be lying too.

CAPTAIN: Hm!

BERTHA: If you say mother's lying, I'll never believe you again!

CAPTAIN: I haven't said that, and you must believe me when I tell you that your happiness and your whole future depend on your leaving this house. Would you like that? Would you like to go and live in town, and learn something new?

BERTHA: Oh, I'd so love to live in town and get away from here! As long as I can see you sometimes—often! In there everything's so gloomy, so horrible, like a winter night—but when you come, father, it's like throwing open the window on a spring morning!

CAPTAIN: My child! My child!

BERTHA: But, father, you must be nice to mother, do you hear? She cries so often.

CAPTAIN: Hm! So you want to go and live in town?

BERTHA: Yes! Yes!

CAPTAIN: But if your mother doesn't want you to?

BERTHA: But she must!

CAPTAIN: But if she doesn't?

BERTHA: Well, then—I don't know. But she must! She must!

CAPTAIN: Will you ask her?

BERTHA: You must ask her, nicely. She doesn't pay any attention to me.

CAPTAIN: Hm! Well, if you want it and I want it, and she doesn't want it, what shall we do then?

BERTHA: Oh, then everything'll be difficult again. Why can't you both——?

Scene 9

The CAPTAIN. BERTHA. LAURA.

LAURA: Oh, she's here. Now perhaps we can hear her opinion. Since her fate is about to be decided.

CAPTAIN: The child can hardly be expected to hold an informed opinion on what a young girl ought to do with her life. We are at least partly qualified to judge, since we have seen a good many young girls grow up.

LAURA: But since we differ, let Bertha decide.

CAPTAIN: No! I permit no one to usurp my rights—neither woman nor child. Bertha, leave us.

BERTHA *goes*.

LAURA: You were afraid to let her speak, because you knew she'd agree with me.

CAPTAIN: I happen to know she wants to leave home. But I also know that you have the power to alter her will at your pleasure.

LAURA: Oh, am I so powerful?

CAPTAIN: Yes. You have a satanic genius for getting what you want. But that's always the way with people who aren't scrupulous about what means they use. How, for example, did you get rid of Dr. Norling, and find this new man?

LAURA: Well, how did I?

CAPTAIN: You insulted Norling, so that he went, and got your brother to fix this fellow's appointment.

LAURA: Well, that was very simple, wasn't it? And quite legal. Is Bertha to leave at once?

CAPTAIN: In a fortnight.

LAURA: Is that final?

CAPTAIN: Yes.

LAURA: Have you spoken to Bertha?

CAPTAIN: Yes.

LAURA: Then I shall have to stop it.

CAPTAIN: You can't.

LAURA: Can't? You think I'm prepared to let my daughter live with people who'll tell her that everything I taught her is nonsense, so that she'll despise her mother for the rest of her life?

CAPTAIN: Do you think I am prepared to allow ignorant and conceited women to teach my daughter that her father is a charlatan?

LAURA: That should matter less to you.

CAPTAIN: Why?

LAURA: Because a mother is closer to her child. It has recently been proved that no one can be sure who is a child's father.

CAPTAIN. What has that to do with us?

LAURA: You can't be sure that you are Bertha's father.

CAPTAIN: I—can't be sure——!

LAURA: No. No one can be sure, so you can't.

CAPTAIN: Are you trying to be funny?

LAURA: I'm only repeating what you've said to me. Anyway, how do you know I haven't been unfaithful to you?

CAPTAIN: I could believe almost anything of you, but not that. Besides, if it were true you wouldn't talk about it.

LAURA: Suppose I were prepared for anything—to be driven out, despised, anything—rather than lose my child? Suppose I am telling you the truth now, when I say to you: "Bertha is my child, but not yours!" Suppose——!

CAPTAIN: Stop!

LAURA: Just suppose. Your power over her would be ended.

CAPTAIN: If you could prove I was not the father.

LAURA: That wouldn't be difficult. Would you like me to?

CAPTAIN: Stop it! At once!

LAURA: I'd only need to name the true father, and tell you the time and place. When was Bertha born? Three years after our marriage——

CAPTAIN: Stop it, or——!

LAURA: Or what? All right, I'll stop. But think carefully before you take any decision. And, above all, don't make yourself ridiculous.

CAPTAIN: God—I could almost weep——!

LAURA: Then you *will* be ridiculous.

CAPTAIN: But not you!

LAURA: No. Our relationship to our children is not in question.

CAPTAIN: That is why one cannot fight with you.

LAURA: Why try to fight with an enemy who is so much stronger?

CAPTAIN: Stronger?

LAURA: Yes. It's strange, but I've never been able to look at a man without feeling that I am stronger than him.

CAPTAIN: Well, for once you're going to meet your match. And I'll see you never forget it.

LAURA: That'll be interesting.

NURSE [*enters*]: Dinner's ready. Will you come and eat?

LAURA: Thank you.

The CAPTAIN *hesitates, then sits in a chair by the table, next to the sofa.*

LAURA: Aren't you going to eat?

CAPTAIN: No, thank you. I don't want anything.

LAURA: Are you sulking?

CAPTAIN: No. I'm not hungry.

LAURA: Come along, or there'll be questions asked. Be sensible, now. Oh, very well. If you won't, you'd better go on sitting there. [*Goes.*]

NURSE: Mr. Adolf! What is all this?

CAPTAIN: I don't know. Can you explain to me how it is that you women can treat an old man as though he was a child?

NURSE: Don't ask me. I suppose it's because, whether you're little boys or grown men, you're all born of woman.

CAPTAIN: But no woman is born of man. Yes, but I *am* Bertha's father! Tell me, Margaret! You do believe that? Don't you?

NURSE: Lord, what a child you are! Of course you're your own daughter's father. Come and eat now, and don't sit there sulking. There! There now, come along!

CAPTAIN [*gets up*]: Get out, woman! Back to hell, you witches! [*Goes to the door leading to the hall.*] Svaerd! Svaerd!

BATMAN [*enters*]: Sir?

CAPTAIN: Harness the sleigh! At once!

NURSE: Captain! Now, listen——!

CAPTAIN: Out, woman! At once!

NURSE: Lord help us, what's going to happen now?

CAPTAIN [*puts on his hat and makes ready to go out*]: Don't expect me home before midnight! [*Goes.*]

NURSE: Blessed Jesus preserve us, how's all this going to end?

ACT TWO

As in Act One. The lamp is burning on the table. It is night.

Scene 1

The DOCTOR. LAURA.

DOCTOR: After my conversation with your husband, I am by no means convinced that your fears are justified. You made a mistake when you told me he had reached these surprising conclusions about other heavenly bodies by the use of a microscope. Now that I hear it was a spectroscope, he must not only be acquitted of any suspicion of derangement, but appears to have made a genuine contribution to science.

LAURA: But I never said that.

DOCTOR: Madam, I took notes of our conversation, and I remember I questioned you on this very point, because I thought I must have misheard you. One must be most meticulous in such accusations, for they could result in a man being certified as incapable of managing his affairs.

LAURA: Certified as incapable——?

DOCTOR: Yes. Surely you know that a person who is *non compos* loses all his civic and family rights?

LAURA: No, I didn't know that.

DOCTOR: There is one further point on which I feel uneasy. He told me that his letters to booksellers had remained unanswered. Permit me to ask whether you, no doubt from the best of motives, perhaps intercepted them?

LAURA: Yes, I did. I had to protect my family. I couldn't let him ruin us all without doing something.

DOCTOR: Forgive me, but I don't think you can have realised the consequences of such an action. If he finds that you have been secretly interfering in his affairs, his suspicions will be confirmed, and they will grow like an avalanche. Besides, by doing this you have fettered his will and further inflamed his impatience. You must have felt yourself how agonising it is when one's most fervent wishes are obstructed, and one's wings are clipped.

LAURA: Yes, I have felt it.

DOCTOR: Well, then, judge how he must feel.

LAURA [*rises*]: It's midnight, and he hasn't come home. We must be ready for the worst.

DOCTOR: But, tell me, Mrs. Lassen, what happened this evening after I left? I must know everything.

LAURA: Oh, he raved and said the most extraordinary things. Can you imagine—he asked if he really was the father of his child!

DOCTOR: How very strange! Where did he get that idea?

LAURA: I can't imagine. Unless—well, he'd been questioning one of the servants about who was the father to some baby, and when I took the girl's side he became furious and said no one could know for sure who was any child's father. God knows I tried my best to calm him, but now I don't see that there's anything more we can do. [*Weeps.*]

DOCTOR: This mustn't be allowed to continue. Something must be done. But we mustn't arouse his suspicions. Tell me, has the Captain had such hallucinations before?

LAURA: It was the same six years ago. Then he actually admitted in a letter to the doctor that he feared for his own sanity.

DOCTOR: Dear me! This obviously springs from something very deep-rooted. I mustn't enquire into the sacred secrets of family life, etcetera; I must confine myself to visible symptoms. What is done cannot, alas, be undone; but some steps should have been taken earlier. Where do you suppose he is now?

LAURA: I can't imagine. He gets such crazy ideas nowadays.

DOCTOR: Would you like me to wait till he comes back? I could say that your mother has been feeling poorly, and that I have been attending her. That would lull his suspicions.

LAURA: Yes, do that. Oh, please don't leave us! If you knew how worried I am! But wouldn't it be better to tell him straight out what you think about his condition?

DOCTOR: No, one must never do that with people who are mentally sick. Certainly not until they raise the subject themselves, and then only under certain circumstances. It all depends how things develop. But we mustn't sit in here. Perhaps I should go next door? Then he won't suspect anything.

LAURA: Yes, that's a good idea. Margaret can sit in here. She always stays up when he goes out, and she's the only one who can do anything with him. [*Goes to the door, left.*] Margaret! Margaret!

NURSE: What is it, madam? Is the master home?

LAURA: No, but I want you to sit here and wait for him. When he comes, tell him that my mother is ill and the doctor has come to visit her.

NURSE: Very well. You leave it to me.

LAURA [*opens the door, left*]: Will you come in here, Doctor?

DOCTOR: Thank you.

Scene 2

NURSE [*at the table; picks up a prayerbook and her spectacles*]:
Yes, yes! Yes, yes!

[*Reads half to herself.*]

> A wretched and a grievous thing
> Is life, this vale of suffering.
> Death's angel hovers ever near,
> And whispers into each man's ear:
> "All's vanity! All's vanity!"
> Yes, yes! Yes, yes!
>
> All things that live upon the earth
> Fall to the ground before his wrath;
> And only sorrow's ghost survives
> To carve above the green-dug grave:
> "All's vanity! All's vanity!"
> Yes, yes! Yes, yes!

BERTHA [*enters with a tray of coffee and a piece of embroidery. She whispers*]: Margaret, can I sit with you? It's so horrid up there.

NURSE: Heaven preserve us! Are you still up?

BERTHA: I've got to finish father's Christmas present, you see. And, look! I've something for you!

NURSE: But, my dear Miss Bertha, you can't do this. You've got to get up in the morning, and it's past midnight.

BERTHA: Well, what of it? I daren't sit up there alone. I'm sure there are ghosts about.

NURSE: You see! What did I say? Yes, mark my word, there's no good spirit guarding this house. What kind of thing did you hear?

BERTHA: Oh, do you know—I heard someone singing in the attic!

THE FATHER

NURSE: In the attic! At this time of night!

BERTHA: Yes. It was a sad song—so sad—I've never heard anything like it before. And it sounded as if it came from the cupboard where the cradle is—you know, on the left——

NURSE: Oi, oi, oi! And with such a storm blowing tonight! I'm frightened it'll bring the chimney-pots down. "What is this life but toil and care? A moment's hope, then long despair!" Well, my dear child, may God grant us a happy Christmas!

BERTHA: Margaret, is it true father is ill?

NURSE: I'm afraid so.

BERTHA: Then we won't be able to *have* Christmas. But how can he be up, if he's ill?

NURSE: Well, my child, with his kind of illness you can stay up. Ssh! There's someone on the steps. Go to bed, now, and hide this [*indicates the coffee tray*], or the master'll be angry.

BERTHA [*goes out with the tray*]: Good night, Margaret.

NURSE: Good night, my child. God bless you.

Scene 3

The NURSE. *The* CAPTAIN.

CAPTAIN [*takes off his greatcoat*]: Are you still up? Go to bed!

NURSE: I only wanted to wait till you——

The CAPTAIN *lights a candle, opens the secretaire, sits down at it immediately and takes from his pocket letters and newspapers.*

NURSE: Mr. Adolf!

CAPTAIN: What do you want?

NURSE: The old lady's sick. And the doctor's here.

CAPTAIN: Is it dangerous?

NURSE: No, I don't think so. Just a chill.

CAPTAIN [*gets up*]: Who was the father of your child, Margaret?

NURSE: Oh, I've told you so many times. That good-for-nothing Johansson.

CAPTAIN: Are you sure it was he?

NURSE: Don't be silly. Of course I'm sure. He was the only one.

CAPTAIN: Yes, but was *he* sure he was the only one? No, he couldn't be. But you could be. There's a difference, you see.

NURSE: I can't see the difference.

CAPTAIN: No, you can't see it, but the difference is there. [*Turns the pages of a photograph album on the table.*] Do you think Bertha is like me? [*Looks at a portrait in the album.*]

NURSE: You're as alike as two berries on a bough.

CAPTAIN: Did Johansson admit he was the father?

NURSE: He had to.

CAPTAIN: It's horrible—! There's the doctor.

Scene 4

The CAPTAIN. *The* NURSE. *The* DOCTOR.

CAPTAIN: Good evening, Doctor. How is my mother-in-law?

DOCTOR: Oh, it's nothing serious. She's just sprained her left foot slightly.

CAPTAIN: I thought Margaret said she had a chill. There seem to be two rival diagnoses. Go to bed, Margaret.

[*The* NURSE *goes. Pause.*]

CAPTAIN: Please sit down, Doctor.

DOCTOR [*sits*]: Thank you.

CAPTAIN: Is it true that if you cross a zebra with a horse, you get striped foals?

DOCTOR [*surprised*]: That is perfectly correct.

CAPTAIN: Is it also true that if you cross the same mare with an ordinary stallion, the foals may continue to be striped?

DOCTOR: Yes, that is also true.

CAPTAIN: Then, in certain circumstances a brown stallion can sire a striped foal, and vice versa?

DOCTOR: Apparently.

CAPTAIN: *Ergo*, the resemblance that a child bears to its father means nothing?

DOCTOR: Oh——

CAPTAIN: *Ergo*, it can never be proved who is a child's father?

DOCTOR: Er—hm——!

CAPTAIN: You are a widower and have had children?

DOCTOR: Er—yes——

CAPTAIN: Didn't you sometimes feel that your position was ridiculous? I know nothing so ludicrous as to see a father walking with his child on the street, or hear a father talking about his children. "My wife's children", he should say. Did you never feel the falseness of your position, had you never any pinpricks of doubt? I don't use the word suspicion, for as a gentleman I assume that your wife was above suspicion.

DOCTOR: Indeed I did not! Has not Goethe written: "A man must take his children on trust"?

CAPTAIN: Trust, where a woman's concerned? That's risky!

DOCTOR: But there are so many kinds of women.

CAPTAIN: Recent research has proved that there is only one kind. When I was young, I was strong and, I flatter myself, handsome. Let me quote you just two incidents which subsequently caused me to ponder. Once I was travelling on a steamer. I was sitting with some friends in the lounge. The young waitress came and sat herself opposite me in tears, and told me that her fiancé had been drowned. We pitied her, and I ordered some champagne. After the second glass, I touched her foot; after the fourth, her knee; and before morning, I had consoled her.

DOCTOR: That was just a fly in winter.

CAPTAIN: Now to my second; and this was a fly in summer. I was at Lysekil. There was a young wife there, with her children—but her husband was in town. She was religious, had very strict principles, read me moral lectures, preached sermons at me—was completely honourable, I still believe. I lent her a book, two books. When the time came for her to leave, strange to relate, she returned them. Three months later, I found in one of these books a visiting card bearing a pretty explicit declaration of love. It was innocent, as innocent as a declaration of love can be from a married woman to a stranger who has never made an advance to her. The moral? Never trust anyone too much!

DOCTOR: Or too little!

CAPTAIN: Exactly; just so far and no further. But, you see, Doctor, that woman was so unconsciously mischievous that she told her husband she had developed a passion for me. That's just the danger, they don't realise their instinctive capacity for creating mischief. It's an extenuating circumstance, but it doesn't nullify their guilt, it merely lessens it.

DOCTOR: Captain, these are unhealthy thoughts. You should keep a watch on yourself——

CAPTAIN: You mustn't use that word, unhealthy. You see, all boilers explode when the manometer reaches breaking-point; but they don't all have the same breaking-point—you understand? Still, you're here to keep an eye on me. If I were not a man I would have the right to accuse—or, as the polite phrase is, to lay a complaint. Then I might perhaps be able to give you a complete diagnosis of my illness, and, what is more, its history. But unfortunately, I am a man, and so I can only, like a Roman, fold my arms across my breast and hold my breath until I die. Good night.

DOCTOR: Captain! If you are ill, it cannot be any reflection on your honour as a man to tell me the truth. I must hear both sides.

CAPTAIN: I should have thought you'd had enough listening to one.

DOCTOR: No, Captain. Do you know, when I sat in the theatre the other evening and heard Mrs. Alving orating over her dead husband, I thought to myself: "What a damned shame the fellow's dead and can't defend himself!"

CAPTAIN: If he'd been alive, do you think he'd have dared to open his mouth? If any dead man rose from his grave, do you think he'd be believed? Good night, Doctor. As you can hear, I am perfectly calm, so you can sleep in peace.

DOCTOR: Good night, then, Captain. I cannot take any further part in this matter.

CAPTAIN: Are we enemies?

DOCTOR: By no means. The pity is that we cannot be friends. Good night. [*Goes.*]

CAPTAIN [*accompanies the* DOCTOR *to the door upstage. Then he goes to the door left, and opens it slightly*]: Come in, and let's talk. I heard you listening.

Scene 5

LAURA *enters embarrassed. The* CAPTAIN *sits down at the secretaire.*

CAPTAIN: It's late, but we must talk this matter out. Sit down! [*Pause.*] This evening I went to the post office and collected my letters. It is evident from them that you have been intercepting both my outgoing and my incoming correspondence. The resultant waste of time has virtually destroyed the value of my researches.

LAURA: I was acting from kindness. You were neglecting your duties for this work.

CAPTAIN: You were not acting from kindness. You feared that some day I might win more honour through these researches than through my military career, and you were determined that I should not win any honour, because that would throw into relief your insignificance. Now I have confiscated some letters addressed to you.

LAURA: How noble of you.

CAPTAIN: I'm glad you appreciate my qualities. It is clear from these letters that for some time you have been turning all my former friends against me by spreading a rumour concerning my sanity. And you've succeeded, for now hardly one of them, from my commanding officer to my cook, regards me as sane. The situation regarding my mental condition is as follows. My brain is, as you know, unaffected, since I can perform both my professional duties and my duties as a father. I still have my emotions more or less under control, and my will is, to date, fairly unimpaired, but you have been chipping and chafing at it so that soon the cogs will disengage and the wheels will start whirling backwards. I shall not appeal to your feelings, for you have none—that is your strength. But I appeal to your self-interest.

LAURA: Go on.

CAPTAIN: By your behaviour you have succeeded in filling my mind with doubt, so that soon my judgment will be clouded and my thoughts begin to wander. This is the approaching dementia for which you have been waiting, and which may come at any time. Now you must ask yourself the question: is it not more to your interest that I should be well rather than ill? Think carefully? If I break down, I shall lose my job, and you will be without support. If I die, you will receive the insurance on my life; but if I kill myself, you will get nothing. So it is to your own interest that I should go on living.

LAURA: Is this a trap?

CAPTAIN: Yes. It is up to you whether you go round it or stick your neck in it.

LAURA: You say you'll kill yourself. You won't!

CAPTAIN: Are you sure? Do you think a man can live when he has nothing and no one to live for?

LAURA: Then you capitulate?

CAPTAIN: No. I propose an armistice.

LAURA: And your conditions?

CAPTAIN: That I retain my sanity. Free me from my doubts, and I will abandon the battle.

LAURA: What doubts?

CAPTAIN: About Bertha's parentage.

LAURA: Are there any doubts about that?

CAPTAIN: In my mind there are. You have awoken them.

LAURA: I?.

CAPTAIN: Yes. You have dripped them into my ear like poison, and events have fostered their growth. Free me from my uncertainty, tell me straight out: "It is so!" and already I forgive you.

LAURA: How can I confess to a crime I have not committed?

CAPTAIN: What does it matter? You know I shan't reveal it. Do you think a man goes around trumpeting his shame?

LAURA: If I say it isn't true, you won't be sure; but if I say it is, you will be. So you would rather it was true.

CAPTAIN: Yes. It's strange, but I suppose it's because the one cannot be proved, whereas the other can.

LAURA: Have you any grounds for your suspicions?

CAPTAIN: Yes and no.

LAURA: I suppose you'd like me to be guilty so that you could throw me out and keep the child to yourself. But you won't catch me with a trick like that.

CAPTAIN: Do you think I'd want to keep some other man's child if I knew you were guilty?

LAURA: I'm sure you wouldn't. And that's why I realise you were lying just now when you said you already forgave me.

CAPTAIN [*gets up*]: Laura, save me and my sanity. You don't understand what I'm saying. If the child is not mine, I have no rights over her, and want none—and that is all that *you* want. Isn't it? Or do you want something else too? Do you want to retain your power over the child, but to keep me here as the breadwinner?

LAURA: Power? Yes. What has this life-and-death struggle been for if not for power?

CAPTAIN: I do not believe in resurrection, and to me this child was my life hereafter. She was my idea of immortality—perhaps the only one that has any roots in reality. If you take her away, you cut short my life.

LAURA: Why didn't we part while there was still time?

CAPTAIN: Because the child bound us together. But the bond became a chain. How did it become that? How? I've never thought about it, but now memories return, accusing, condemning. We had been married for two years, and had no children, you best know why. I fell ill, and lay near to death. In a lucid moment I heard voices from the drawing-room. It was you and the lawyer, talking about my money—I still had some then. He is explaining that you cannot inherit anything because we have no children, and he asks if you are pregnant. I didn't hear your reply. I got better, and we had a child. Who is the father?

LAURA: You!

CAPTAIN: No, it is not I! A crime lies buried here, and it's beginning to come to light. And what a fiendish crime! You women were soft-hearted enough to free your black slaves, but you keep your white ones! I have worked and slaved for you, for your child, your mother, your servants. I have sacrificed my life and my career, I have undergone torture, scourging, sleeplessness, every kind of torment for you, my hair has turned grey, all so that you might live free from care and, when you grow old, enjoy new life through your child. All this I have borne without complaint, because I believed I was the father to this child. This is the most arrant form of theft, the most brutal slavery. I have served seventeen years of hard labour for a crime I did not commit. What can you give me in return?

LAURA: Now you really *are* mad.

CAPTAIN [*sits*]: So you hope. And I have seen how you worked to hide your crime. I pitied you, because I didn't understand why you were sad. I often calmed your evil conscience, supposing that I was driving away some sick thought. I heard you cry aloud in your sleep, though I didn't want to listen. Now I remember—the night before last! It was Bertha's birthday. It was between two and three o'clock in the morning, and I was sitting up, reading. You screamed as though someone was trying to strangle you: "Don't come, don't come!" I banged on the wall because—because I didn't want to hear any more. I have had my suspicions for a long time, but I didn't dare to hear them confirmed. I have suffered all this for you. What will you do for me?

LAURA: What can I do? I will swear by God and all that is sacred that you are Bertha's father.

CAPTAIN: What good will that do, when you have already said that a mother can and should commit any crime for the sake of her child? I entreat you, by the memory of the past—I beg you, as a wounded man begs for mercy—tell me everything! Don't you see that I am as helpless as a child, can't you hear me crying for pity like a child crying to its mother, can't you forget that I am a man, a soldier who with a word can tame men and beasts? I ask only for the pity you would extend to a sick man, I lay down the insignia of my power and cry for mercy—for my life.

LAURA [*has approached him and lays her hand on his forehead*]: What! Man, you're crying!

CAPTAIN: Yes, I am crying, although I am a man. But has not a man eyes? Has not a man hands, limbs, heart, thoughts, passions? Does he not live by the same food, is he not wounded by the same weapons, warmed and cooled by the same summer and winter as a woman? If you prick us, do we not bleed? If you tickle us, do we not laugh? If you poison us, do we not die? Why should a man be forbidden to complain, or a soldier to weep? Because it is unmanly? Why is it unmanly?

LAURA: Weep, my child. Your mother is here to comfort you. Do you remember, it was as your second mother that I first entered into your life? Your big, strong body was afraid. You were a great child who had come too late into the world, or had come unwanted.

CAPTAIN: Yes, I suppose it was that. Father and mother had me against their will, and so I was born without a will. When you and I became one, I thought I was making myself whole; so I let you rule; and I who, in the barracks, among the soldiers, issued commands, was, with you, the one who obeyed. I grew up at your side, looked up to you as though to a superior being, listened to you as though I was your innocent child.

LAURA: Yes. That's how it was, and I loved you as my child. But, do you know—I suppose you noticed it—every time your feelings towards me changed, and you approached me as my lover, I felt bashful, and your embrace was an ecstasy followed by pangs of conscience, as though my blood was ashamed. The mother became the mistress—ugh!

CAPTAIN: Yes. I saw it, but I didn't understand. I thought you despised my lack of masculinity, and I wanted to win you as a woman by being a man.

LAURA: That was where you made your mistake. The mother was your friend, you see, but the woman was your enemy. Love between man and woman is war. And don't think I gave myself. I didn't give, I took—what I wanted to have. But you had the upper hand. I felt it, and I wanted to make you feel it.

CAPTAIN: No, you were always the one who had the upper hand. You could hypnotise me so that I neither saw nor heard, but only obeyed. You could give me a raw potato and make me think it was a peach, you could force me to admire your stupid ideas as strokes of genius, you could have driven me to crime, yes, even to vice. For you lacked intelligence, and instead of following my advice you did as *you* wanted. But when, later, I awoke and looked about me and saw that my honour had been sullied, I wanted to wipe out the stain through a noble action, a brave deed, a discovery, or an honourable suicide. I wanted to go to war, but I couldn't. It was then that I turned to science. Now, when I should stretch out my hand to receive the fruits of my labour, you chop off my arm. Now I am without honour, and I cannot go on living, for a man cannot live without honour.

LAURA: But a woman——

CAPTAIN: She has her children, but he has none. Yet you and I and all the other men and women in the world have gone on living, as innocently as children, living on fancies, ideals and illusions. And then we awoke. Yes, we awoke, but with our feet on the pillow, and He Who woke us was Himself a sleepwalker. When women grow old and cease to be women, they get beards on their chins. I wonder what men get when they grow old and cease to be men? We who greeted the dawn were no longer cocks but capons, and the hens answered our false call, so that when the sun should have risen we found ourselves sitting in moonlight among ruins, just like in the good old days. It had only been a fretful slumber, a wild dream. It was no awakening.

LAURA: You know, you ought to have been a poet.

CAPTAIN: Perhaps I ought.

LAURA: Well, I'm sleepy. If you've any more fantasies, keep them until morning.

CAPTAIN: One word more—and this isn't a fantasy. Do you hate me?

LAURA: Sometimes. When you are a man.

CAPTAIN: This is like racial hatred. If it is true that we are descended from the ape, it must have been from two different species. We aren't of the same blood, are we?

LAURA: What do you mean by all that?

CAPTAIN: I feel that, in this war, one of us must go under.

LAURA: Which one?

CAPTAIN: The weaker, of course.

LAURA: And the stronger is in the right?

CAPTAIN: Always. Because he is the one with power.

LAURA: Then I am in the right.

CAPTAIN: You think you have the power?

LAURA: Yes. And tomorrow I shall have it legally, when I have you certified.

CAPTAIN: Certified——?

LAURA: Yes. And then I shall bring up the child myself, without having to listen to your visions.

CAPTAIN: And who will pay for the child's upbringing, when I am gone?

LAURA: Your pension.

CAPTAIN [*goes towards her threateningly*]: How can you have me certified?

LAURA [*takes out a letter*]: By this letter, an attested copy of which I have deposited with the authorities.

CAPTAIN: What letter?

THE FATHER

LAURA [*moves backwards towards the door*]: Yours! The one you wrote to the doctor telling him you were mad. [*The* CAPTAIN *looks at her dumbly.*] You have done your job as a father and a breadwinner. Now you are no longer needed, and you can go. You realise that my intelligence is equal to my will, and since you are not prepared to stay and admit it, you can go!

The CAPTAIN *goes to the table, takes the burning lamp and throws it at* LAURA, *who has retreated through the door.*

ACT THREE

As in Act Two. But another lamp. The concealed door is barricaded with a chair.

Scene 1

LAURA. *The* NURSE.

LAURA: Did he give you the keys?

NURSE: Give them to me? No, God forgive me, I took them out of his pocket. He'd left them in the coat he'd given Nöjd to brush.

LAURA: So Nöjd's on duty today, is he?

NURSE: Yes.

LAURA: Give them to me.

NURSE: But that's like stealing! Very well. Oh, listen to him up there, madam! To and fro, to and fro.

LAURA: Is the door safely locked?

NURSE: Yes. It's locked all right.

LAURA [*opens the secretaire and sits down to it*]: You must try to control your feelings, Margaret. Our only hope is to remain calm. [*There is a knock on the door.*] Who's that?

NURSE [*opens the door to the hall*]: It's Nöjd.

LAURA: Tell him to come in.

NÖJD [*enters*]: A despatch from the Colonel!

LAURA: Give it to me. [*Reads.*] Nöjd, have you removed all the cartridges from the rifles and pouches?

NÖJD: As you ordered, ma'am.

LAURA: Then wait outside, while I answer the Colonel's letter.

NÖJD goes. LAURA writes.

NURSE: Madam, listen! Whatever can he be doing up there?

LAURA: Be quiet while I'm writing.

The sound of sawing is heard.

NURSE [*half to herself*]: Merciful Jesus preserve us all! Where's this going to end?

LAURA: There. Give this to Nöjd. My mother must know nothing of this. You hear!

The NURSE goes to the door. LAURA opens the drawers of the secretaire and takes out some papers.

Scene 2

LAURA. *The PASTOR takes a chair and sits beside LAURA at the secretaire.*

PASTOR: Good evening, sister. I've been away all day, as you know, so I couldn't come before. Well, this is a sad story.

LAURA: Yes, brother. It's the worst twenty-four hours I have ever experienced.

PASTOR: At all events I see no harm has come to you.

LAURA: No, thank God. But think what could have happened.

PASTOR: But tell me one thing. How did it begin? I've heard so many different versions.

LAURA: Well, it started with him talking some nonsense about not being Bertha's father, and ended with him throwing the burning lamp in my face.

PASTOR: But this is terrible! This is real madness. What are we to do?

LAURA: Try to prevent any further violence. The doctor has sent to the asylum for a straitjacket. I've written to the Colonel, and am trying to get these accounts into some kind of order. It's really disgraceful the way he's neglected them.

PASTOR: What a tragedy! Mind you, I've always feared something like this might happen! Fire and water, you know—they're bound to end in an explosion. What have you got in that drawer?

LAURA [*has pulled a drawer out of the desk*]: Look. This is where he's been hiding everything.

PASTOR [*looks in the drawer*]: Great heavens! Why, there's your doll! And your christening-cap—and Bertha's rattle—and your letters—and that locket——! [*Touches his eyes with his handkerchief.*] He must have loved you very much, Laura, in spite of everything. I haven't kept things like that.

LAURA: I think he used to love me once. But time—time changes so many things.

PASTOR: What's that big paper? Why, it's a receipt for—for a grave! Well, better a grave than the asylum. Laura! Tell me—have you no share of the blame for all this?

LAURA: I? How could I be to blame for a man going mad?

PASTOR: Well, well. I shan't say anything. After all, blood is thicker than water.

LAURA: What do you mean by that?

PASTOR [*looks at her*]: Now, listen, Laura.

LAURA: Yes?

PASTOR: Listen to me. You cannot deny that this fits in very nicely with your wish that you should bring up the child yourself.

LAURA: I don't understand.

PASTOR: I can't help but admire you!

LAURA: Me! Hm!

PASTOR: And I am to become the guardian of that freethinker! Do you know, I have always regarded him as a tare among our wheat.

LAURA [*gives a short, stifled laugh. Then, suddenly serious*]: And you dare say that to me—his wife?

PASTOR: You are too strong for me, Laura. Incredibly strong! Like a fox in a trap; you'd rather bite off your own leg than let yourself be caught. Like a master-thief; you scorn any accomplice, even your own conscience. Look at yourself in the mirror! You daren't!

LAURA: I never use mirrors.

PASTOR: No, you daren't. May I look at your hand? Not one spot of blood to betray you, no trace of the poison that lies hidden there! One small, innocent murder, that the law cannot touch; an unconscious crime—unconscious? Brilliant, my dear, brilliant! But do you hear how he's working away up there? Take care? If that man gets free, he'll cut you to pieces!

LAURA: You talk too much. Have you a bad conscience? Accuse me; if you can.

PASTOR: I cannot.

LAURA: You see! You can't; I am innocent. You do your duty, and I'll do mine. Here comes the Doctor.

Scene 3

LAURA. *The* PASTOR. *The* DOCTOR.

LAURA [*rises*]: Good evening, Doctor. At least you'll help me, won't you? Though I'm afraid there's not much anyone can do. You hear how he's carrying on up there? Are you convinced now?

DOCTOR: I am convinced that an act of violence has been committed. The question is whether it was an outbreak of anger or of madness.

PASTOR: Even if one ignores the actual assault, you must surely admit that he suffers from fixed ideas.

DOCTOR: I think your ideas are even more fixed, Pastor.

PASTOR: If you are referring to my spiritual convictions——

DOCTOR: I wasn't. Madam, it is up to you whether you choose to condemn your husband to imprisonment and a fine, or the asylum. How would you describe the Captain's conduct?

LAURA: I can't answer that now.

DOCTOR: You mean you are not certain which course would best serve the interests of your family? Well, Pastor, what do you say?

PASTOR: There'll be a terrible scandal either way. I really don't know——

LAURA: If he only has to pay a fine, he may commit violence again.

DOCTOR: And if he goes to prison he will soon be released. Then I suppose we must regard it as best for all concerned that he be treated as insane. Where is the nurse?

LAURA: Why do you ask?

DOCTOR: She must put the straitjacket on him, after I have talked with him and given her the signal. But not before! I have the thing outside. [*Goes into the hall and returns with a large package.*] Please ask the nurse to come in.

LAURA *rings.*

PASTOR: Dreadful, dreadful!

The NURSE *enters.*

DOCTOR [*unpacks the straitjacket*]: You see this? When I decide that the moment has come, you must approach the Captain from behind and put this coat on him, to prevent

THE FATHER

any further outbreaks. As you see, it has unusually long sleeves, to limit his movements. You must fasten these behind his back. These two straps go through these buckles here, and you can then tie them to the back of the chair, or the sofa, whichever is more convenient. Will you do this?

NURSE: No, Doctor, I can't. I can't!

LAURA: Why don't you do it yourself, Doctor?

DOCTOR: Because the patient mistrusts me. You, madam, would be the most proper person to do it; but perhaps he mistrusts you too? [LAURA *does not reply.*] Perhaps you, Pastor——?

PASTOR: No, no! I couldn't possibly!

Scene 4

LAURA. *The* PASTOR. *The* DOCTOR. *The* NURSE. NÖJD.

LAURA: Have you delivered the letter already?

NÖJD: Yes, madam.

DOCTOR: Ah, it's you, Nöjd. Now you know what's happened, don't you? The Captain is—ill. You must help us to take care of him.

NÖJD: If there's anything I can do for the Captain, he knows I'll do it.

DOCTOR: Good. Now you must put this coat on him——

NURSE: No, he mustn't touch him! He'd hurt him. No, I'll do it myself—so gently, gently. Let him wait outside, to help me if need be. He can do that.

There is a banging on the concealed door.

DOCTOR: There he is! Hide this under the shawl—yes, on that chair—and go outside, all of you. The Pastor and I will wait in here. That door won't hold for long. Get outside, now, all of you!

NURSE [*goes out left*]: Blessed Jesus, help us!

LAURA *closes the secretaire and goes out.* NÖJD *exits upstage.*

Scene 5

The lock snaps, the chair crashes to the floor and the concealed door is flung open. The CAPTAIN *enters with a pile of books under his arm. The* DOCTOR. *The* PASTOR.

CAPTAIN [*puts the books on the table*]: It's all here. I wasn't mad, you see. For example—*The Odyssey*, Book 1, line 215, page 6 in the Upsala translation. Telemachus speaking to Athene. "Truly my mother asserts that he whom men call Odysseus is my father. But of this I cannot be sure, for no man knows for sure from whom he springs." And he says this of Penelope, the chastest of women! Pretty, eh? And here we have the prophet Ezekiel. "The fool saith: 'See, here is my father!' But who can tell whose loins have begotten him?" That's clear enough. Now, what have we here? Merslåkow's *History of Russian Literature*. "Alexander Pushkin, Russia's greatest poet, died more of grief at the widespread rumours of his wife's infidelity than of the bullet he received in the breast in a duel. On his deathbed, he swore that she was innocent." Idiot! Idiot! How could he swear to *that*? You see! I read my books! Hullo, Jonas, you here? And the Doctor—yes, of course! Have they told you what I once said to an Englishwoman who complained that the Irish throw burning lamps in their wives' faces? "God, what women!" I said. "Women?" she lisped. "Yes!" I replied. "When things have reached the pitch that a man who has loved and worshipped a woman takes a burning lamp and throws it in her face, then you know——!"

PASTOR: Then you know what?

CAPTAIN: Nothing! One never knows—one only believes—eh, Jonas? One believes, and is saved. Yes, saved! But I know that belief can damn a man! I know that.

DOCTOR: Captain!

CAPTAIN: Oh, shut up. I don't want to talk to you. I don't want to hear you echoing everything they say in there like one of these damned telephones! Yes, you know what I mean! Tell me, Jonas, do you believe that you are your children's father? I remember you used to have a tutor living with you whom people talked about. Such beautiful eyes, they said he had

PASTOR: Adolf! Take care, now——!

CAPTAIN: Put your hand under your hair and see if you can't feel a couple of bumps there! I'm blessed if he hasn't gone pale! Yes, yes, it was only talk—but, my God, how they talked! But we're all objects of ridicule, we husbands. Isn't that true, Doctor? How about your marriage couch? Didn't you have a lieutenant billeted on you? Wait, now, let me guess—wasn't he called——? [*Whispers in the* DOCTOR's *ear.*] You see, he's gone pale too! Don't cry, now. She's dead and buried, and what's done can't be done again! I knew him, though—now he's a—look at me, Doctor!—no, in the eyes! —a major in the Dragoons. By God, I believe he's grown horns too!

DOCTOR: Captain, can we please discuss something else?

CAPTAIN: You see! As soon as I mention the word horns, he wants to talk about something else!

PASTOR: My poor brother, don't you realise you are mad?

CAPTAIN: Yes, I know. But if I had the care of your antlered heads for a week or two, I'd have you all behind bars too! I am mad, but how did I become mad? You don't care. Nobody cares. Let's talk about something else. [*Takes the photograph album from the table.*] Dear God—there is my child! Mine? How can we tell? Do you know what we have to do to be sure? First, marry to become socially respectable; then, soon afterwards, get divorced; and become lovers; and adopt the child. Then at least you can be sure it's your own adopted child. That's right, isn't it? But what good is all this to me? What good is anything to me now that you have taken away my hope of immortality, what good is my science and my philosophy now that I have nothing to live for, what use is my life to me now that I have no honour left? I grafted my right arm, half my brain, half my spinal cord on to another stem, because I believed they would unite into a single, more perfect tree, and then someone comes with a knife and cuts beneath the graft, so that now I am only half a tree—but the other tree goes on growing with my arm and half my brain, while I wither and die, for I gave the best parts of myself. Now I want to die! Do what you will with me! I no longer exist!

The DOCTOR whispers to the PASTOR. They go into the room on the left. A few moments later, BERTHA enters.

Scene 6

The CAPTAIN. BERTHA.

The CAPTAIN *sits huddled at the table.* BERTHA *goes over to him.*

BERTHA: Are you ill, father?

CAPTAIN [*looks up dully*]: I?

BERTHA: Do you know what you've done? Do you know you threw a burning lamp at mother?

CAPTAIN: Did I?

BERTHA: Yes, you did! Think if you'd hurt her!

CAPTAIN: What would that have mattered?

BERTHA: You aren't my father if you can talk like that!

CAPTAIN: What's that you say? I'm not your father? How do you know? Who has told you that? Who is your father, then? Who?

BERTHA: Well, not you, anyway.

CAPTAIN: Still not me! Who, then? Who? You seem well informed. Who's been priming you? Must I endure this, that my child comes and tells me to my face that I am not her father? But do you realise you're insulting your mother by saying that? Don't you understand that, if this is true, she is the one who has sinned?

BERTHA: Don't say anything against Mother, do you hear?

CAPTAIN: No, you stick together, you're all against me! And you've done so all the time!

BERTHA: Father!

CAPTAIN: Don't use that word again!

BERTHA: Father, father!

CAPTAIN [*draws her to him*]: Bertha, my darling, my beloved child, of course you are my child! Yes, yes—it must be so—it *is* so. Those were just sick thoughts that came with the wind like pestilence and fever. Look at me, let me see my soul in your eyes! But I see her soul too! You have two souls, and you love me with one and hate me with the other! You must only love me! You must only have one soul, or you will never find peace, nor shall I. You must have only one thought, the child of my thought, and you shall have only one will, mine.

BERTHA: I don't want that! I want to be myself!

CAPTAIN: You mustn't do that! You see, I'm a cannibal, and I want to eat you. Your mother wanted to eat me, but she couldn't. I am Saturn, who ate his children because it had been prophesied that otherwise they would eat him. To eat or be eaten! That is the question. If I don't eat you, you will eat me, and you have already shown me your teeth. But don't be afraid, my beloved child. I won't hurt you. [*Goes to where the guns are on the wall and takes a revolver.*]

BERTHA [*tries to escape*]: Help, mother, help! He wants to murder me!

NURSE [*enters*]: Mr. Adolf, what is it?

CAPTAIN [*looks at the revolver*]: Have you taken the cartridges?

NURSE: Yes, I've hidden them away. But sit down and calm yourself, and I'll bring them back to you.

She takes the CAPTAIN *by the arm and coaxes him down into the chair, where he remains sitting dully. Then she takes the straitjacket and goes behind his chair.* BERTHA *tiptoes out left.*

NURSE: Do you remember, Mr. Adolf, when you were my dear little baby, how I used to tuck you up at night and say your prayers with you? And do you remember how I used to get up in the night to fetch you a drink? Do you remember how I lit the candle and told you pretty stories when you had bad dreams and couldn't sleep? Do you remember?

CAPTAIN: Go on talking, Margaret. It soothes my head so. Go on talking.

NURSE: All right, but you must listen, then. Do you remember how once you took the carving knife and wanted to make boats, and how I came in and had to get the knife away from you by telling you a story? You were such a silly baby, so we had to tell you stories, because you thought we all wanted to hurt you. Give me that snake, I said, otherwise he'll bite you. And you let go of the knife. [*Takes the gun from the* CAPTAIN's *hand.*] And then, when you had to get dressed and you didn't want to. Then I had to coax you and say I'd give you a gold coat and dress you like a prince. And I took your little body-garment, which was only of green wool, and held it in front of you and said: "Put your arms in", and then I said: "Sit still, now, and be a good boy while I button up the back!" [*She has got the straitjacket on him.*] And then I said: "Stand up now, and walk nicely, so I can see how you look." [*She leads him to the sofa.*] And then I said: "Now it's time to go to bed."

CAPTAIN: What's that, Nanny? Must I go to bed when I'm dressed? Damnation! What have you done to me? [*Tries to free himself.*] Oh, you damned cunning woman! Who would have believed you were so crafty? [*Lies down on the sofa.*] Caught, cropped, and cozened! And not to be allowed to die!

NURSE: Forgive me, Mr. Adolf, forgive me! But I wanted to stop you from killing the child!

CAPTAIN: Why didn't you let me kill the child? Life is a hell, and death a heaven, and the child belongs to heaven.

NURSE: What do you know about what comes after death?

CAPTAIN: That is all one does know. About life, one knows nothing. Oh, if one had only known from the beginning!

NURSE: Mr. Adolf! Humble your proud heart and pray to God to forgive you. It still isn't too late. It wasn't too late for the robber on the cross, when our Saviour said to him: "Today shalt thou be with me in Paradise."

CAPTAIN: Are you croaking for carrion already, you old crow? [*The NURSE takes a prayer-book from her pocket. The CAPTAIN roars.*] Nöjd! Is Nöjd there?

Nöjd *enters.*

CAPTAIN: Throw this woman out! She wants to choke me to death with her prayer-book! Throw her out through the window, or up the chimney! Anywhere!

NÖJD [*looks at the* NURSE.] God bless you, Captain, I can't do that! I just can't! If there were six men, yes, but a woman——

CAPTAIN: Aren't you stronger than a woman?

NÖJD: Of course I'm stronger, but there's something special about a woman that stops a man raising his hand against her.

CAPTAIN: What's special about them? Haven't they raised their hands against me?

NÖJD: Yes, but I can't, Captain! It's just as though you was to ask me to strike the Pastor. It's something that's in a man's blood, like religion. I can't!

Scene 7

As before. LAURA *gestures to* NÖJD *to go.*

CAPTAIN: Omphale! Omphale! Now you play with the club while Hercules winds your wool!

LAURA [*comes over to the sofa*]: Adolf! Look at me! Do you think I am your enemy?

CAPTAIN: Yes, I do. I think you are all my enemies. My mother was my enemy. She didn't want to bring me into the world because my birth would cause her pain. She robbed my first embryo of its nourishment, so that I was born half-crippled. My sister was my enemy, when she taught me that I was her inferior. The first woman I kissed was my enemy—she gave me ten years of sickness in return for the love I gave her. My daughter became my enemy, when you forced her to choose between you and me. And you, my wife, you were my mortal enemy, for you didn't let go of me until you had throttled the life out of me.

LAURA: I don't know that I ever planned, or intended, what you think I have done. I may have felt a vague desire to be rid of you, because you were an obstacle in my path; but if you see a plan in the way I have acted, then perhaps there was one, though I wasn't aware of it. I didn't plot any of this—it just glided forward on rails which you laid yourself—

and before God and my conscience, I feel that I am innocent, even if I am not. Your presence has been like a stone on my heart, pressing and pressing until my heart rebelled against its suffocating weight. This is the truth, and if I have unintentionally hurt you, I ask your forgiveness.

CAPTAIN: That all sounds plausible. But how does it help me? And who is to blame? Perhaps the idea of marriage is to blame. In the old days, one married a wife; now one forms a company with a woman who goes out to work, or moves in to live with a friend. And then one seduces the partner, or defiles the friend. What became of love—healthy, sensuous love? It died, starved. And what is the offspring of this broker's-love, a blank cheque drawn on a bankrupt account? Who will honour it when the crash comes? Who is the bodily father to the spiritual child?

LAURA: Those suspicions of yours about the child are completely unfounded.

CAPTAIN: That's just what's so horrible. If they were real, at least one would have something to grip on, something to cling to. Now there are only shadows, hiding in the bushes and poking out their heads to laugh—it's like fighting with air, a mock battle with blank cartridges. A real betrayal would have acted as a challenge, roused my soul to action. But now my thoughts dissolve in twilight, my brain grinds emptiness until it catches fire! Give me a pillow under my head! And put something over me, I'm cold. I'm so terribly cold!

LAURA takes her shawl and spreads it over him. The NURSE goes out to fetch a pillow.

LAURA: Give me your hand, friend.

CAPTAIN: My hand! Which you have tied behind my back? Omphale! Omphale! But I feel your soft shawl against my mouth. It's warm and smooth like your arm, and it smells of vanilla, as your hair did when you were young. Laura—

when you were young—and we walked in the birch woods among the primroses—and thrushes sang! Beautiful, beautiful! How beautiful life was! And now it has become like this. You didn't want it to be like this, I didn't want it, and yet it happened. Who rules our lives?

LAURA: God alone rules——

CAPTAIN: The God of battle, then! Or the goddess, nowadays! Take away this cat that's lying on me! Take it away! [*The* NURSE *enters with the pillow and removes the shawl.*] Give me my tunic. Put it over me! [*The* NURSE *takes his military tunic from the clothes-hanger and drapes it over him.*] Ah, my brave lion's skin, that you would take from me! Omphale! Omphale! O cunning woman, who so loved peace that you discovered the art of disarming men! Awake, Hercules, before they take your club from you! You would rob us of our armour and have us believe that it is only tinsel. No, it was iron before it became tinsel. In the old days it was the smith who forged the soldier's tunic; now it is the seamstress. Omphale! Omphale! Strength has been vanquished by craft and weakness! Curse you, damned woman, and all your sex! [*Rises himself to spit, but falls back on the couch.*] What kind of a pillow have you given me, Margaret? It's so hard, and so cold, so cold! Come and sit beside me here, on the chair. That's right. May I rest my head in your lap? So. That's warm! Bend over so that I can feel your breast. Oh, it is sweet to sleep at a woman's breast, whether a mother's or a mistress's, but sweetest at a mother's!

LAURA: Do you want to see your child, Adolf? Speak!

CAPTAIN: My child? A man has no children. Only women have children, and so the future belongs to them, while we die childless. Gentle Jesus, meek and mild, look upon this little child—!

NURSE: Listen! He's praying to God!

CAPTAIN: No, to you, to send me to sleep. I'm so tired, so

tired. Good night, Margaret. Blessed be thou amongst women——

He raises himself, but falls with a cry in the NURSE's *lap.*

Scene 8

LAURA *goes left, and calls the* DOCTOR, *who enters with the* PASTOR.

LAURA: Help us, Doctor, if it isn't too late. Look, he's stopped breathing!

DOCTOR [*takes the* CAPTAIN's *pulse*]: He has had a stroke.

PASTOR: Is he dead?

DOCTOR: No. He may still awake, and live. But to what he will awake, we do not know.

PASTOR: "Once to die, but after this the judgment——"

DOCTOR: We must not judge or accuse him. You, who believe that there is a God who rules men's destinies, must plead this man's cause before the bar of Heaven.

NURSE: Oh, Pastor, he prayed to God in his last moment!

PASTOR [*to* LAURA]: Is this true?

LAURA. It is true.

DOCTOR: Then my art is useless. Now you must try yours, Pastor.

LAURA: Is that all you have to say at this death-bed, Doctor?

DOCTOR: That is all. My knowledge ends here. He who knows more, let him speak.

BERTHA [*enters left and runs to her mother*]: Mother, mother!

LAURA: My child! *My* child!

PASTOR: Amen!

Introduction to
MISS JULIE

STRINDBERG wrote MISS JULIE in July-August 1888 at the age of thirty-nine. He completed it, as he had THE FATHER, in about a fortnight.

After coming to Denmark the previous November for the première of THE FATHER, he had settled with his wife and three children in the village of Lyngby not far from Copenhagen. There they had leased rooms in an old castle belonging to an eccentric lady, aged around forty, who called herself the Countess Frankenau, though she was not in fact of noble birth. Her estate was managed by her bailiff Ludwig Jansen, a fellow of gipsy-like appearance with whom the Countess appeared to be having an affair. Hansen at first got on well with Strindberg; he shared the latter's interest in hypnotism, and gave him a demonstration of the art. Years later it transpired that Hansen was in fact not the Countess's lover but her half-brother, being the illegitimate son of her late father, and that they had kept this matter secret out of respect to the dead man's memory. But Strindberg did not know this at the time, and their supposed relationship formed one of the starting-points of MISS JULIE.

Another starting-point for the play lay in Strindberg's old feeling of social inferiority towards his wife. Siri, when he first met her, had been a baroness. He, as he could never forget, was the son of a servant-girl, and all his life he retained a sense of resentment against people with an upper-class background. He was to use the valet, Jean, as a mouthpiece for this resentment.

Shortly after Strindberg had completed THE FATHER the previous year, André Antoine, an employee in a Paris gas company, had started an experimental theatre in the Place Pigalle of exactly the kind of which Strindberg had long been dreaming. "In view of the hoped-for generation of new playwrights", Antoine had declared, "there will be needed a new generation of actors.... The actor will no longer 'speak his lines' in the classic manner; he will say them naturally, which is just as difficult to learn.... Purely mechanical movements, vocal effects, irrational and superfluous gestures will be banished. Dramatic action will be simplified by a return to reality and natural gestures. The old stagy attitudes will be replaced by effects produced only by the voice. Feelings will be expressed by familiar and real accessories; a pencil turned round, a cup overturned, will be as significant and have an effect as intense on the mind of the spectator as the grandiloquent exaggerations of the romantic drama. Is it necessary to note that this apparent revolution is nothing but a return to the great traditions, and that the most famous actors of the French stage got their finest effects from simple means? Has not Salvini moved us deeply by his sobriety of gesture?... Did not Molière himself, in two or three instances, take care to affirm the necessity of 'acting as one speaks'?"

Strindberg had sent Antoine a French translation of THE FATHER, and Antoine was astute enough to perceive its merits. He wrote enthusiastically to Strindberg telling him that he would have produced it immediately but for the fact that he had committed himself to a production of Ibsen's GHOSTS, and promising that he would try to present it in the near future. This encouragement acted as a considerable stimulus to Strindberg to continue with the kind of half-length, one-set play of which THE FATHER had been an example. Moreover, he had himself for some time been interested in the possibility of starting just such an experimental theatre in Scandinavia, and Antoine's success caused him to renew his efforts. On 3 June 1887 he sent a lengthy prospectus to the Swedish actor August Lindberg, who had played a leading role in the championing of Ibsen's works and had, in 1883, been the first European to dare to produce GHOSTS. Strindberg's theatre was to be a travelling one. "Only plays by August Sg. are to be acted", he wrote, with characteristic arrogance, "and none of his old ones. I

Introduction to MISS JULIE

will write plays which will obviate the need for carrying round costumes, sets and properties. . . . There need never be any shortage of material, for I can write a one-act play in two days."

Antoine's ideas and the success of his theatre exercised an important influence on Strindberg at this period; not because they were new to him, but because they confirmed what he already believed. Strindberg's own preface to MISS JULIE* echoes many of Antoine's sentiments. His hope that he might some time "see the full back of an actor throughout an important scene" is a reference to Antoine's already famous habit of turning his back on the audience for long periods; the Théâtre Libre had, indeed, acquired the nickname of "Antoine's Back". (It was facetiously suggested that a rich uncle had threatened to cut him off if he ever showed his face on the stage.)

Another, though perhaps more indirect influence upon Strindberg at the time he was writing MISS JULIE was Friedrich Nietzsche, to whose writings Georg Brandes had introduced him that summer. "Buy a modern German philosopher called *Nietzsche*, about whom G.B. has been lecturing," he wrote to Verner von Heidenstam on 17 May 1888, "You will find everything worth reading there! Don't deny yourself this pleasure! N. is a poet too." On 4 September he told Edvard Brandes: "My spiritual uterus has found a tremendous fertiliser in Friedrich Nietzsche, so that I feel like a dog about to litter! He is the man for me!" He was much attracted by Nietzsche's theory of the Superman, which seemed to him to offer some consolation against the impending domination of the world by women; here at last was a fellow spirit to support him against Ibsen, whose championship of the female sex Strindberg abominated. Later that year he wrote four letters to Nietzsche, three in French and one in an eccentric mixture of Greek and Latin. "Je termine toutes mes lettres à mes amis: lisez Nietzsche!" he assured him in December. "C'est mon *Carthago est delenda*!"

* See page 99.

On 10 August 1888 he posted MISS JULIE triumphantly to his Stockholm publisher, Karl Otto Bonnier. "I take the liberty", he wrote, "of hereby offering you the first naturalistic tragedy of the Swedish drama, and I beg you not to reject it without serious thought, or you will later regret it, for, as the German says 'Ceci datera!' = this play will be remembered in history.... P.S. MISS JULIE is the first of a forthcoming series of naturalistic tragedies." Eleven days later, having received no reply, he wrote again to Bonnier, telling him that Antoine was planning to stage THE FATHER, and adding that "in a week I shall be sending you a new naturalistic tragedy, even better than MISS JULIE, with three characters, a table and two chairs, and no sunrise!" This was a reference to CREDITORS, which he had already begun.

But Bonnier had already written to Strindberg the previous day rejecting MISS JULIE, and their letters crossed. "It is much too 'risky'", Bonnier explained, "much too 'naturalistic' for us. We therefore dare not publish the play, as likewise I fear you will find difficulty in getting it produced." A descendant of Bonnier has described this decision as the most unfortunate ever perpetrated by that distinguished house; but Karl-Otto Bonnier was right in his final prognostication, for it was to be sixteen years before MISS JULIE was performed in Sweden.

Strindberg accordingly offered the play to another publisher, Joseph Seligmann, who a decade earlier had published THE RED ROOM, Strindberg's autobiographical account of life among the young artists and writers of Stockholm. "It is nearly ten years", Strindberg wrote to him on 22 August 1888, "since the first Swedish naturalistic novel appeared under your imprint, with the consequences that we know. Today I send for your perusal the first Swedish naturalistic drama, written as I think it should be, for the reasons I have given in the foreword."

Seligmann accepted MISS JULIE, on condition that he was allowed to make certain amendments. Strindberg had by now been thrown out of the castle at Lyngby after a row with his gipsy friend, and must have been feeling somewhat desperate. He therefore agreed to Seligmann's conditions, and for many years, until Alf Sjöberg's Stockholm production in 1949 based on the original manuscript, this slightly bowdlerised version was the only one used even, apparently, for the première in Denmark. (See above, pp. 13-14.)

Despite this precaution, MISS JULIE was widely attacked on publication for its immorality, its assailants including, rather surprisingly, Bjoernsterne Bjoernson. However, that winter, with the help of Hans Riber Hunderup (who had produced and played THE FATHER) and others, Strindberg at last succeeded in fulfilling his old ideal of founding a Scandinavian experimental theatre.* On 17 November 1888 he inserted an advertisement in the Danish newspaper *Politiken*:

"Since I intend at the earliest opportunity to open a Scandinavian Experimental Theatre on the pattern of the Théâtre Libre in Paris, I hereby announce that I invite plays of whatever kind to be sent to me for reading. Preferably they should have a contemporary setting, be of not too great a length, and not require elaborate machinery or a large cast."

They acquired the little Dagmar Theatre in Copenhagen, and planned to open it in the beginning of January. Although the advertisement elicited no very exciting contributions, they had enough plays to make a start, for by the end of the year, in the five months since he had completed MISS JULIE, Strindberg had written four more short plays, CREDITORS, THE STRONGER, PARIAH and SIMOOM. After several postponements for this reason and that, it was eventually decided to inaugurate the season on 2 March with a double bill consisting of MISS JULIE and CREDITORS. But the day before the première was due to take place, police arrived at the theatre with the news that the Danish censor had, somewhat belatedly, decided to ban MISS JULIE. Siri tried to get the censor to relent, but without success, and the theatre was forced to open a week later, on

* On 14 November 1888—the anniversary, as Strindberg noted with gratification, of the first performance of THE FATHER.

9 March, with a triple bill of CREDITORS, PARIAH and THE STRONGER.

Since the rehearsals of MISS JULIE had reached so advanced a stage, Strindberg and his associates sought around desperately for some way of overcoming the censor's ban, and eventually hit on the idea of giving a private performance at the Copenhagen University Students' Union. On 14 March 1889 MISS JULIE thus received its première before an audience of a hundred and fifty students, their friends, and a handful of critics. Siri played the title role, and the part of Jean was taken by a young Danish actor named Viggo Schiwe, whom Strindberg immediately suspected of having an affair with his wife. The scene at this first performance was described by the correspondent of the Swedish newspaper *Dagens Nyheter*:

> We find ourselves in a depressing little room on the first floor of a building in Bath-house Street in Copenhagen. The window-shutters are screwed shut, and only a single lamp illuminates the stage in front of us. The room is packed, and when our eyes have accustomed themselves to the relative darkness, we are able to study the people sitting or standing under the low ceiling. Most of them are students, only six or seven are women, but not so few of the *coryphées* of Copenhagen are seated in the front rows. But we search in vain for August Strindberg, though it has been announced that he is to attend the performance....
>
> In front of the chairs a long, blue, half-transparent curtain hangs from ceiling to floor. The bottom of it is concealed by a broad board, behind which are the footlights. A gas-light shines through at one side (later in the evening it was to serve as the setting sun).
>
> "Nine o'clock" it said on the tickets, for which the students have been fighting for two days. The academic quarter* has already passed, the hall—if one can so describe

---

* In Scandinavia, academic events, such as lectures, normally begin fifteen minutes after the advertised time.

this large room—is more than full, and people are beginning to grow a little impatient. Feet are stamped, and a cry of "Ring it up!" is heard.

"Shut up those galleryites!" shouts a witty citizen to those sitting behind him.

"Galleryite yourself!" is the retort, and the stamping of feet continues until at length a few faint sounds of a teaspoon being tapped against a toddy glass make themselves heard. There is a deal of hushing, and then, after another teaspoon-tap, the blue curtain is drawn aside. A deathly silence reigns in the "auditorium", where the heat begins to be oppressive. The ceiling is not so high but that a man standing on his chair might not touch it with his hand, and there is no ventilation.

The play, as is known, takes place in a kitchen, and completely new decor has had to be bought for the evening's performance. To our surprise, it resembles a real kitchen. A plate-rack, a kitchen table, a speaking tube to the floor above, a big stove with rows of copper pots above it—in short, everything is there, presenting the living image of a real kitchen.

From the little programme sheets which have been handed out we see that the title role is to be played by Fru Essen-Strindberg, Christine by Fru Pio and the servant Jean by Hr. Schiwe. As regards the first-named, her performance appears to be precisely opposed to what the author intended. She is too cold, much too cold, and one gets no impression at all of the kind of woman who would seduce a man like Jean. Hr. Schiwe hardly suggested a servant; his manner was much more that of a gentleman and a *viveur*. Fru Pio, however, spoke her lines excellently.

Although the play was performed before an audience almost exclusively male, the author had been compelled to accept several deletions. The promised midsummer romp by farm-hands and serving girls did not materialise; we merely heard a violin playing a dance.

And so, after rather a tame final scene, the curtain fell, or, more correctly, the sacking was pulled across the stage. There is resounding applause and the actors are called to take their bow.

Then we gather round the tables, and our theatrical evening ends like any student party.

The author himself, we are told, "stood half-hidden behind a door, his face pale and twisted with jealousy." He was convinced that Siri and Schiwe were having an affair.

The performance—not surprisingly, considering the inadequacy of the presentation—aroused no great enthusiasm, and it was three more years before MISS JULIE was publicly staged, on 3 April 1892 in Berlin, at Otto Brahm's Freie Bühne. But there were such vehement public protests that even Brahm dared not continue with the play, which had to be removed from the repertory after a single performance. The following year, however, on 16 January 1893, André Antoine fulfilled Strindberg's hopes by presenting it at his Théâtre Libre—the first time a Swedish dramatist had been performed in Paris since a play by King Gustav III had been staged at the Comedie Francaise in 1803. MISS JULIE received a mixed reception from the audience and most of the critics were hostile; but Antoine was well satisfied with the result of the evening. "MISS JULIE has created a tremendous sensation," he noted. "Everything gripped the audience—the subject, the *milieu*, this concentration into a single ninety-minute act of a plot that would suffice for a full-length play. Of course there were laughter and protests, but one found oneself in the presence of something quite new."

After the turn of the century, the climate of taste had sufficiently mellowed for MISS JULIE to be publicly presented in other countries. In 1902 it was performed in Stuttgart, in 1903 in Hamburg, and in 1904 the young Max Reinhardt produced it in Berlin. The same year, sixteen years after it had been written, MISS JULIE was at last staged in Sweden, for a single, somewhat surreptitious performance at Upsala. In 1905 it was performed in New York in Russian, with Alla Nazimova; and in 1906 in St. Petersburg. The same year August Falck junior toured a production round the Swedish provinces, bringing it in December to Stockholm, where it was a great success. In 1907 the play was presented at Strindberg's own Intimate Theatre in Stockholm, where it was performed, on and off, no less than 134 times. In 1908 Strindberg arranged a special performance for Bernard Shaw, who was on a visit to Stockholm, and watched it with him.*

MISS JULIE first reached London in 1912, when Octavia Kenmore presented it at the Little Theatre. It was received with complete bewilderment, and although it has since been revived seven times in London it has yet, at the time of writing, to be worthily performed here. Among the many interpretations of the role on the Continent one of the most notable was that of the young Elizabeth Bergner in Vienna in 1924.

MISS JULIE has been filmed no less than four times: in 1912 in Sweden, in 1922 in Germany (with Asta Nielsen and William Dieterle), in 1947 in Argentina, and in 1951 again in Sweden. The last-named was a memorable production by Alf Sjöberg, containing magnificent performances by Anita Björk and Ulf Palme, and deservedly won the Grand Prix at the Cannes Film Festival of that year. It is one of the best translations of a classic ever made for the screen.

* This performance was witnessed only by Strindberg, Shaw and Mrs. Shaw. August Falck and Manda Björling, who played the leading roles, had to be summoned especially from the archipelago where they were holidaying; since it was some little time since they had last performed the play, they studied their parts on the boat in. This was, astonishingly, the first time Strindberg ever saw MISS JULIE performed (although present on the occasion of the 1889 première in Copenhagen, he had refused to watch the play). He hated visiting the theatre and, though he sometimes came to rehearsals, he seldom witnessed an actual performance, even of his own works.

Author's Preface to
MISS JULIE

THE THEATRE, and indeed art in general, has long seemed to me a *Biblia pauperum*, a Bible in pictures for the benefit of the illiterate; with the dramatist as a lay preacher hawking contemporary ideas in a popular form, popular enough for the middle classes, who comprise the bulk of playgoers, to be able to grasp without too much effort what the minority is arguing about. The theatre has always been a primary school for the young, the semi-educated, and women, all of whom retain the humble faculty of being able to deceive themselves and let themselves be deceived—in other words, accept the illusion, and react to the suggestion, of the author. Nowadays the primitive process of intuition is giving way to reflection, investigation and analysis, and I feel that the theatre, like religion, is on the way to being discarded as a dying form which we lack the necessary conditions to enjoy. This hypothesis is evidenced by the theatrical crisis now dominating the whole of Europe; and, not least, by the fact that in those cultural strongholds which have nurtured the greatest thinkers of our age, namely England and Germany, the art of writing plays is, like most of the other fine arts, dead.

In other countries, men have tried to create a new drama by pouring new ideas into the old forms. But this has failed, partly because the new thinkers have not yet had time to become popularised and thus educate the public to understand the issues involved; partly because polemical differences have so inflamed emotions that dispassionate appreciation has become impossible —the cheers and whistles of the majority exercise a pressure that upsets one's instinctive reaction—and partly also because we have not succeeded in adapting the old form to the new content, so that the new wine has burst the old bottles.

In my previous plays, I have not tried to do anything new—

for that one can never do—but merely to modernise the form so as to meet the demands which I supposed that the new men and women of today would make of this art. To this end I chose, or let myself be caught up by, a theme which may be said to lie outside current party conflicts. For the problem of social ascent and decline, of higher or lower, better or worse, man or woman, is, has been and will be of permanent interest. When I took this theme from an actual incident which I heard about some years ago, and which at the time made a deep impression on me, it seemed to me suitable matter for tragedy; for it is still tragic to see one on whom fortune has smiled go under, much more to see a line die out. But the time may come when we shall have become so developed and enlightened that we shall be able to observe with indifference the harsh, cynical and heartless drama that life presents—when we shall have discarded those inferior and unreliable thought-mechanisms called feelings, which will become superfluous and harmful once our powers of judgment reach maturity. The fact that the heroine arouses our sympathy is merely due to our weakness is not being able to resist a feeling of fear lest the same fate should befall us. Even so, the hyper-sensitive spectator may possibly even feel that sympathy is not enough, while the politically-minded will doubtless demand positive measures to remedy the evil—some kind of "programme". But there is no such thing as absolute evil, since the death of a family is good luck for some other family that will be able to take its place, and social change constitutes one of the main pleasures of life, happiness being dependent on comparison. As for the political planner, who wishes to remedy the regrettable fact that the bird of prey eats the dove, and the louse eats the bird of prey, I would ask him: "Why should this state of affairs be remedied?" Life is not so foolishly and mathematically arranged that the great always devour the small. It happens equally often that a bee kills a lion, or at any rate drives it mad.

If my tragedy makes a tragic impression on people, they have only themselves to blame. When we become as strong as the first French revolutionaries, we shall feel uninhibited pleasure and relief at seeing our national forests thinned out by the removal of decayed and superannuated trees which have too long obstructed the growth of others with an equal right to live and fertilise their age—a relief such as one feels when one sees an incurable invalid at last allowed to die.

Recently, people complained of my tragedy THE FATHER that it was too tragic—as though tragedies ought to be jolly. One hears pretentious talk about "the joy of life",* and theatrical managers feverishly commission farces, as though joy consisted in behaving idiotically and portraying the world as though it were peopled by lunatics with an insatiable passion for dancing. I find "the joy of life" in life's cruel and mighty conflicts; I delight in knowledge and discovery. And that is why I have chosen a case that is unusual but from which one can learn much—an exception, if you like, but an important exception which proves the rule—though I dare say it will offend those people who love only what is commonplace. Another thing that will offend simple souls is the fact that the motivation of my play is not simple, and that life is seen from more than one viewpoint. An incident in real life (and this is quite a new discovery!) is usually the outcome of a whole series of deep-buried motives, but the spectator commonly settles for the one that he finds easiest to understand, or that he finds most flattering to his powers of judgment. Someone commits suicide. "Bad business!", says the business man. "Unrequited love!", say the ladies. "Bodily illness!", says the invalid. "Shattered hopes!", says the man who is a failure. But it may be that the motive lay quite elsewhere, or nowhere, and that the dead man concealed his true motive by suggesting another more likely to do credit to his memory!

I have suggested many possible motivations for Miss Julie's unhappy fate. The passionate character of her mother; the upbringing misguidedly inflicted on her by her father; her

* "The joy of life" (*livsglæde*) is a key-phrase in Ibsen's GHOSTS, published seven years before Strindberg wrote MISS JULIE. (Translator's note.)

own character; and the suggestive effect of her fiancé upon her weak and degenerate brain. Also, more immediately, the festive atmosphere of Midsummer Night; her father's absence; her menstruation; her association with animals; the intoxicating effect of the dance; the midsummer twilight; the powerfully aphrodisiac influence of the flowers; and, finally, the chance that drove these two people together into a private room—plus of course the passion of the sexually inflamed man.

I have therefore not suggested that the motivation was purely physiological, nor that it was exclusively psychological. I have not attributed her fate solely to her heritage, nor thrown the entire blame on to her menstruation, or her lack of morals. I have not set out to preach morality. This, in the absence of a priest, I have left to a cook.

This multiplicity of motives is, I like to think, typical of our times. And if others have done this before me, then I congratulate myself in not being alone in my belief in these "paradoxes" (the word always used to describe new discoveries).

As regards characterisation, I have made my protagonists somewhat lacking in "character", for the following reasons:

The word "character" has, over the years, frequently changed its meaning. Originally it meant the dominant feature in a person's psyche, and was synonymous with temperament. Then it became the middle-class euphemism for an automaton; so that an individual who had stopped developing, or who had moulded himself to a fixed role in life—in other words, stopped growing—came to be called a "character"—whereas the man who goes on developing, the skilful navigator of life's river, who does not sail with a fixed sheet but rides before the wind to luff again, was stigmatised as "characterless" (in, of course, a derogatory sense) because he was so difficult to catch, classify and keep tabs on. This *bourgeois* conception of the immutability of the soul became transferred to the stage, which had always been *bourgeois*-dominated. A character, there, became a man fixed in a mould, who always appeared drunk, or comic, or pathetic, and to establish whom it was only necessary to equip

Author's Preface to MISS JULIE

with some physical defect, such as a club-foot, a wooden leg or a red nose, or else some oft-repeated phrase, such as "Absolutely first-rate!", "Barkis is willin'!", etc. This over-simplified view of people we find even in the great Molière. Harpagon is a miser and nothing else, although he might have been both miserly and a first-class financier, a loving father, a good citizen. And, what is worse, his "defect" is in fact extremely advantageous to both his daughter and his son-in-law, who are his heirs and are thus the last people who ought to blame him if they have to wait a little before gathering the fruits of his parsimony. So I do not believe in "theatrical characters". And these summary judgments that authors pronounce upon people —"He is stupid, he is brutal, he is jealous, he is mean", etc.— ought to be challenged by naturalists, who know how richly complex a human soul is, and who are aware that "vice" has a reverse image not dissimilar to virtue.

Since they are modern characters, living in an age of transition more urgently hysterical at any rate than the age which preceded it, I have drawn my people as split and vacillating, a mixture of the old and the new. And I think it not improbable that modern ideas may, through the media of newspapers and conversation, have seeped down into the social stratum which exists below stairs.

My souls (or characters) are agglomerations of past and present cultures, scraps from books and newspapers, fragments of humanity, torn shreds of once-fine clothing that has become rags, in just the way that a human soul is patched together. I have also provided a little documentation of character development, by making the weaker repeat words stolen from the stronger, and permitting the characters to borrow "ideas", or, as the modern phrase is, accept suggestions from each other.

Miss Julie is a modern character—not that the half-woman, the man-hater, has not existed in every age, but because, now that she has been discovered, she has stepped forward into the limelight and begun to make a noise. The half-woman is a type that pushes herself to the front, nowadays selling herself for power, honours, decorations and diplomas, as formerly she used to for money. They are synonymous with corruption. They are a poor species, for they do not last, but unfortunately they propagate their like by the wretchedness they cause; and degenerate men seem unconsciously to choose their mates from among them, so that their number is increased. They engender an indeterminate sex to whom life is a torture, but fortunately they go under, either because they cannot adapt themselves to reality, or because their repressed instinct breaks out uncontrollably, or because their hopes of attaining equality with men are shattered. It is a tragic type, providing the spectacle of a desperate battle against Nature—and tragic also as a Romantic heritage now being dissipated by Naturalism, which thinks that the only good lies in happiness—and happiness is something that only a strong and hardy species can achieve.

But Miss Julie is also a relic of the old warrior nobility, which is now disappearing in favour of the new neurotic or intellectual nobility; a victim of the discord which a mother's "crime" implanted in a family; a victim of the errors of her age, of circumstances, and of her own flawed constitution, all of which add up to the equivalent of the old concept of Destiny or the Universal Law. The naturalist has abolished guilt with God, but he cannot expunge the consequences of her action—punishment, and prison, or the fear of it—for the simple reason that, whether or not he acquits her, the consequences remain. One's injured fellow-beings are not as indulgent as outsiders who have not suffered can afford to be. Even if her father felt impelled to postpone the moment of Nemesis, vengeance would be taken on his daughter, as it is here, by that innate or acquired sense of honour which the upper classes inherit—from where? From barbarism, from their Aryan forefathers, from mediaeval chivalry. It is very beautiful, but nowadays it is fatal to the continuation of the species. It is the nobleman's *hara-kiri*, the Japanese law of inner conscience which commands a man to slit his stomach when another has insulted him, and which survives in a modified form in that ancient privilege of the nobility, the duel. Thus, the servant, Jean, lives; but Miss Julie cannot live without honour. The slave has this advantage over the knight, that he lacks the latter's fatal preoccupation with honour; but in all of us Aryans there is a little knight or Don Quixote who makes us sympathise with the man who kills himself because he has committed a dishonourable act and thereby lost his honour. We are aristocrats enough to be sad when we see the mighty fallen and stinking corpse-like on the garbage-heap—yes, even if the fallen should arise and make atonement by honourable action. The servant Jean is the type who founds a species; in him, we trace the process of differentiation. He was the son of a poor peasant, and has now educated himself to the point where he is a potential gentleman. He has proved a quick student, possesses finely developed senses (smell, taste, sight), and an eye for beauty. He has already risen in the world, and is strong enough not to worry about using other people's shoulders to climb on. He has already reacted against his fellow servants, whom he despises as representing the world which he has left behind him; he fears them and shrinks from them because they know his secrets, sniff out his intentions, envy his rise and hopefully await his fall. Hence his dual, uncrystallised character, wavering between sympathy for the upper class and hatred of those who constitute it. He is, as he himself says, an aristocrat; he has learned the secrets of good society, is polished, but coarse underneath; he knows how to wear a tail-coat, but can offer us no guarantee that his body is clean beneath it.

He respects Miss Julie, but is afraid of Christine, because she knows his dangerous secrets; and he is sufficiently callous not to allow the events of the night to interfere with his future plans. With the brutality of a slave and the indifference of a tyrant he can look at blood without fainting and shake off misfortune. So he survives the battle unharmed, and will quite possibly end as an *hôtelier;* and even if he does not become a Rumanian count, his son will probably get to university and very likely end up on the bench.

Incidentally, the information he gives us about the lower classes' view of life as seen from below is by no means negligible —when, that is, he speaks the truth, which is not often, for his tendency is to say what is likely to prove to his own advantage rather than what is true. When Miss Julie throws out the suggestion that the lower classes find the pressure from above intolerable, Jean naturally agrees, because he wants to win her sympathy, but he immediately corrects himself when he sees the advantage of differentiating between himself and the mass.

Apart from the fact that Jean's star is rising, he has the whip-hand of Miss Julie simply because he is a man. Sexually he is an aristocrat by virtue of his masculine strength, his more finely developed senses and his ability to seize the initiative. His sense of inferiority arises chiefly from the social *milieu* in which he temporarily finds himself, and he will probably throw it off when he discards his livery.

His slave-mentality expresses itself in his respect for the Count (the boots) and in his religious superstition; but he respects the Count principally as the holder of the social position which he himself covets. And this respect remains even when he has won the daughter of the house and seen the emptiness of that pretty shell.

I do not think that any "love relationship" in the higher sense can exist between two spirits of such unequal quality, and I have therefore made Miss Julie imagine herself to be in love so as to excuse her action and escape her feeling of guilt; and I make Jean fancy that he might be able to fall in love with her, provided he could improve his social standing. I think it is the same with love as with the hyacinth, which has to strike roots in darkness before it can produce a strong flower. With these two, it shoots up, flowers and goes to seed in a moment, and that is why it so quickly dies.

What of Christine? She is a female slave, utterly conventional, bound to her stove and stuffed full of religion and morality, which serve her as both blinkers and scapegoats. She goes to church in order to be able to shift the guilt of her domestic pilferings on to Jesus, and get herself recharged with innocence. She is a supporting character, and I have therefore deliberately portrayed her as I did the priest and the doctor in THE FATHER; I wanted them to appear everyday human beings, as provincial priests and doctors usually are. And if these supporting characters seem somewhat abstract, that is because ordinary people are, to a certain degree, abstract in the performance of their daily work—conventional, and showing only one side of themselves—and as long as the spectator feels no need to see their other sides, my abstract portrayal of them will serve well enough.

Finally, the dialogue. Here I have somewhat broken with tradition by not making my characters catechists who sit asking stupid questions in order to evoke some witty retort. I have avoided the symmetrical, mathematically constructed dialogue of the type favoured in France, and have allowed their minds to work irregularly, as people's do in real life, when, in conversation, no subject is fully exhausted, but one mind discovers in another a cog which it has a chance to engage. Consequently, the dialogue, too, wanders, providing itself in the opening scenes with matter which is later taken up, worked upon, repeated, expanded and added to, like the theme in a musical composition.

The plot is, I fancy, passable enough, and since it really only concerns two persons I have confined myself to them, introducing but one minor character, a cook, and making the unhappy spirit of the father hover over and behind the whole of the action. I have done this because I believe that what most interests people today is the psychological process. Our prying minds are not content merely with seeing something happen— they must know why it happens. We want to see the wires, see the machinery, examine the box with the false bottom, finger the magic ring to find the join, look at the cards to see how they are marked.

In this context I have been mindful of the realistic novels of the Goncourt brothers, which have attracted me more than anything else in contemporary literature.

On the question of technique, I have, by way of experiment, eliminated all intervals. I have done this because I believe that our declining capacity for illusion is possibly affected by intervals, which give the spectator time to reflect and thereby withdraw from the suggestive influence of the author-hypnotist. My play will probably run for about one and a half hours, and if people can listen to a lecture, a sermon or a parliamentary debate for that length of time, I think they should be able to endure a play for ninety minutes. As long ago as 1872, in one of my first dramatic attempts, THE OUTLAW, I aimed at this concentrated form, though with little success. I originally plotted it in five acts, and had already completed it before I noticed how broken and restless was its effect. I burned it, and from the ashes arose a single, long, integrated act of some fifty printed pages, which played for a full hour. This form is by no means new, though it appears at present to be my monopoly, and perhaps, thanks to the changing laws of taste, it may prove appropriate to the spirit of our time. My ultimate hope would be to educate an audience to the point where they will be able to sit through a full evening in the theatre without an interval. But one would have to examine the matter first. Meanwhile, in order to provide short periods of rest for the audience and the actors, without allowing the former to escape from my word of illusion, I have used three art-forms all of which properly belong to the drama—namely, the monologue, mime, and ballet. These were originally a part of ancient tragedy, the monody having developed into the monologue and the Greek chorus into ballet.

The monologue is nowadays abominated by our realists as being contrary to reality, but if I motivate it I make it realistic, and can thus use it to advantage. It is after all realistic that a speaker should walk up and down alone in his room reading his speech aloud, that an actor should rehearse his part aloud, a servant-girl talk to her cat, a mother prattle to her child, an old maid jabber at her parrot, a sleeper talk in his sleep. And, to give the actor the chance for once to create for himself, and get off the author's leash, it is better that monologues should be implied rather than specified. For, since it matters little what one says in one's sleep, or to one's parrot or cat (for it does not influence the action), so a talented actor, attuned to the atmosphere and situation, may be able to improvise better than the author, who cannot calculate in advance how much needs to be said, or for how long the audience will accept the illusion.

As is known, the Italian theatre has, in certain instances, returned to improvisation, and thereby created actors who themselves create, on the author's blueprint. This may well be a step forward, or even a new species of art, of which we shall be able to say that it is an art that engenders art.

Where a monologue would seem unrealistic, I have resorted to mime, which leaves the player even more freedom to create, and so gain independent recognition. But in order not to make too great a demand upon the audience, I have allowed music, well motivated by the midsummer dance, to exercise its illusory power during the dumb play. Here I would ask the musical director to take care when choosing his pieces not to evoke an alien atmosphere by echoes from popular operettas or dance tunes, or folk melodies with specific associations.

The ballet which I have introduced must not be smudged into a so-called "crowd scene", because crowd scenes are always badly acted, and a mob of buffoons would seize the chance to be clever and so destroy the illusion. Since simple people do not improvise when they wish to be spiteful, but use ready-to-hand material, I have not written new words for them but have borrowed a little-known song which I discovered myself in the countryside near Stockholm. The words are circumlocutory rather than direct, but that is as it should be, for the cunning (weakness) of servile people is not of the type that engages in direct assault. So there must be no chattering or clowning in what is, after all, a serious piece of action, no coarse sniggering in a situation which drives the nails into the coffin of a noble house.

As regards the décor, I have borrowed from the impressionist painters asymmetry and suggestion (i.e., the part rather than the whole), believing that I have thereby helped to further my illusion. The fact that one does not see the whole room and all the furniture leaves room for surmise—in other words, the audience's imagination is set in motion and completes its own picture. I have also profited by eliminating those tiresome exits through doors; for stage doors are made of canvas and flap at the slightest touch; they will not even allow an angry father to express his fury by stumping out after a bad dinner and slamming the door "so that the whole house shakes". (In the theatre, the door simply waves.) I have likewise confined myself to a single set, both to enable the characters to accustom themselves to their milieu, and to get away from the tradition of scenic luxury. But when one has only one set, one is entitled to demand that it be realistic—though nothing is more difficult than to make a room which looks like a room, however skilful the artist may be at creating fire-spouting volcanoes and waterfalls. Even if the walls have to be of canvas, it is surely time to stop painting them with shelves and kitchen utensils. We have so many other stage conventions in which we are expected to believe that we may as well avoid overstraining our imagination by asking it to believe in painted saucepans.

I have placed the rear wall and the table at an angle so that the actors shall be able to face each other and be seen in demi-profile when they sit opposite each other at the table. In a performance of the opera AIDA I once saw a backcloth at an angle which led one's eyes off into an unknown perspective; nor did it look as though it had been arranged thus simply out of a spirit of reaction against the boredom of straight lines.

Another perhaps not unnecessary innovation would be the removal of the footlights. This illumination from below is said to serve the purpose of making actors fatter in the face; but I would like to ask: "Why should all actors be fat in the face?"

Does not this under-lighting annihilate all subtle expressions in the lower half of the face, particularly around the mouth? Does it not falsify the shape of the nose, and throw shadows up over the eyes? Even if this were not so, one thing is certain: that pain is caused to the actors' eyes, so that any realistic expression is lost. For the footlights strike the retina on parts of it which are normally protected (except among sailors, who see the sun reflected from the water), so that one seldom sees any attempt at ocular expression other than fierce glares either to the side or up towards the gallery, when the whites of the eyes become visible. Perhaps this is also the cause of that tiresome habit, especially among actresses, of fluttering eyelashes. And when anyone on the stage wishes to speak with his eyes, he has no alternative but to look straight at the audience, thereby entering into direct contact with them outside the framework of the play—a bad habit which, rightly or wrongly, is known as "greeting one's friends".

Would not side-lights of sufficient power (with reflectors, or some such device) endow the actor with this new resource, enabling him to reinforce his mime with his principal weapon of expression, the movement of his eyes?

I have few illusions of being able to persuade the actor to play *to* the audience and not with them, though this would be desirable. I do not dream that I shall ever see the full back of an actor throughout the whole of an important scene, but I do fervently wish that vital scenes should not be played opposite the prompter's box as though they were duets milking applause. I would have them played at whatever spot the situation might demand. So no revolutions, but simply small modifications; for to turn the stage into a room with the fourth wall missing, so that some of the furniture would have its back to the audience, would, I suppose, at this juncture, simply serve as a distraction.

A word about make-up; which I dare not hope will be listened to by the ladies, who prefer beauty to truth. But the actor might well ponder whether it is to his advantage to paint an abstract character upon his face which will remain sitting there like a mask. Imagine a gentleman dipping his finger into soot and drawing a line of bad temper between his eyes, and suppose that, wearing this permanently fierce expression, he were called upon to deliver a line smiling? How dreadful would be the result! And how is this false forehead, smooth as a billiard ball, to wrinkle when the old man gets really angry?

In a modern psychological drama, where the subtler reactions should be mirrored in the face rather than in gesture and sound, it would surely be best to experiment with strong side-lights on a small stage and with the actor wearing no make-up, or at best a minimum.

If we could then dispense with the visible orchestra, with their distracting lampshades and faces turned towards the audience; if we could have the stalls raised so that the spectator's sightline would be above the actors' knees; if we could get rid of the side-boxes (my particular *bête noire*), with their tittering diners and ladies nibbling at cold collations, and have complete darkness in the auditorium during the performance; and, first and foremost, a *small* stage and a *small* auditorium—then perhaps a new drama might emerge, and the theatre might once again become a place for educated people. While we await such a theatre, one must write to create a stock of plays in readiness for the repertoire that will, some day, be needed.

I have made an attempt! If it has failed, there will, I hope, be time enough to make another!

MISS JULIE

A Naturalistic Tragedy
(1888)

CHARACTERS

MISS JULIE, 25
JEAN, her father's valet, 30
CHRISTINE, her father's cook, 35

The action takes place in the Count's kitchen, on midsummer night.

This translation of MISS JULIE was first performed by the National Theatre Company at the Festival Theatre, Chichester, on 27 July 1965. The cast was:

MISS JULIE	Maggie Smith
JEAN	Albert Finney
CHRISTINE	Jeanne Watts
OTHER SERVANTS	Chloe Ashcroft, Elizabeth Burger, Kay Gallie, Jennie Heslewood, Caroline John, Carolyn Jones, Pauline Taylor, Michael Byrne, Alan Collins, Neil Fitzpatrick, John Hallam, Ron Pember, Edward Petherbridge, Ronald Pickup, David Ryall, John Savident.
MUSICIANS	Sydney Bliss, Pierre Tas, Henry Krein

Movement by Litz Pisk

Designed by Richard Negri

Directed by Michael Elliott

THE SCENE

A large kitchen, the roof and side walls of which are concealed by drapes and borders. The rear wall rises at an angle from the left; on it, to the left, are two shelves with utensils of copper, iron and pewter. The shelves are lined with scalloped paper. Over to the right we can see three-quarters of a big, arched exit porch, with twin glass doors, through which can be seen a fountain with a statue of Cupid, lilac bushes in bloom, and tall Lombardy poplars.

On the left of the stage is visible the corner of a big tiled stove, with a section of an overhead hood to draw away fumes. To the right, one end of the kitchen table, of white pine, with some chairs. The stove is decorated with birch-leaves; the floor is strewn with juniper twigs. On the end of the table is a big Japanese spice-jar containing flowering lilacs. An ice-box, a scullery table, a sink. Above the door is a big old-fashioned bell, of the alarm type. To the left of this emerges a speaking-tube.

> CHRISTINE *is standing at the stove, frying in a pan. She is dressed in a light cotton dress, with apron.* JEAN *enters, dressed in livery and carrying a pair of big riding boots, with spurs. He puts them down on the floor where we can see them.*

JEAN: Miss Julie's crazy again tonight. Completely crazy!

CHRISTINE: Oh, you're here at last?

JEAN: I went with his lordship to the station, and as I passed the barn on my way back I went in for a dance, and who do I see but Miss Julie leading the dance with the gamekeeper? But as soon as she sees me, she rushes across and offers her arm for the ladies' waltz. And then she danced like—I've never known the like! She's crazy.

CHRISTINE: She always has been. Especially this last fortnight, since the engagement got broken off.

JEAN: Yes, what about that? He was a gentleman, even if he wasn't rich. Oh, they're so full of caprices. [*Sits down at the table.*] It's odd, though, that a young lady should choose to stay at home with the servants, eh? rather than go off to her relations with her father.

CHRISTINE: Oh, I expect she doesn't feel like seeing anyone after that hullaballoo she had with her young man.

JEAN: Very likely! He knew how to stand up for himself, though. Know how it happened, Christine? I saw it, you know, though I took care not to let on I had.

CHRISTINE: No! You saw it?

JEAN: Indeed I did. They were down at the stable yard one evening, and Miss Julie was putting him through his paces, as she called it—do you know what that meant? She made him leap over her riding whip, the way you teach a dog to jump. He leaped twice, and each time she gave him a cut; but the third time, he snatched the whip out of her hand and broke it across his knee. And that was the last we saw of him.

CHRISTINE: Was that what happened? You can't mean it.

JEAN: Yes, that's the way it was. Now, what have you got to tempt me with this evening, Christine?

CHRISTINE [*serves from the pan and lays a place*]: Oh, just a bit of kidney I cut from the joint.

JEAN [*smells the food*]: Lovely! *Cel-ci est mon grand délice!* [*Feels the plate*]. You might have warmed the plate, though.

CHRISTINE: You're fussier than his lordship himself, once you start. [*Pulls his hair affectionately.*]

JEAN [*angrily*]: Don't pull my hair. You know how sensitive I am.

CHRISTINE: Now, now. It's only love, you know.

JEAN *eats.* CHRISTINE *brings a bottle of beer.*

JEAN: Beer—on midsummer eve? No, thank you. I can do better than that. [*Opens a drawer in the table and takes out a bottle of red wine with yellow sealing-wax on the cork.*] See that? Yellow seal! Give me a glass, now. A wine glass, I'm drinking this *pur*.

CHRISTINE [*goes back to the stove and puts a small saucepan on*]: God have mercy on whoever gets you for a husband. I never met such a fusspot.

JEAN: Oh, rubbish. You'd be jolly pleased to get a gentleman like me. And I don't think you've lost anything through people calling you my fiancée [*Tastes the wine.*] Good! Very good! Just not quite sufficiently *chambré*. [*Warms the glass with his hands.*] We bought this one in Dijon. Four francs a litre it cost—and then there was the bottling—and the duty. What are you cooking now? The smell's infernal.

CHRISTINE: Oh, some filthy mess Miss Julie wants for Diana.

JEAN: Please express yourself more delicately, Christine. But why should you have to cook for that confounded dog on midsummer eve? Is it ill?

CHRISTINE: It's ill all right! It managed to slip out with the gatekeeper's pug, and now it's in trouble—and *that* Miss Julie won't allow.

JEAN: Miss Julie is stuck-up about some things, in others she demeans herself, exactly like her ladyship when she was alive. She was most at home in the kitchen or the stables, but one horse wasn't enough to pull her carriage. She went around with dirty cuffs, but there had to be a crest on every button. Miss Julie, now, to return to her—she doesn't bother about herself and her person. To my mind, she is not what one would call a lady. Just now, when she was dancing in the barn, she grabbed the gamekeeper from Anna and made him dance with her. We'd never do that—but that's how it is when the gentry try to lower themselves—they become really common. But she's a magnificent creature! What a figure! What shoulders! and—etcetera, etcetera!

CHRISTINE: No need to overdo it. I've heard what Clara says, and she dresses her.

JEAN: Oh, Clara! You women are always jealous of each other. I've been out riding with her—and the way she dances——!

CHRISTINE: Well, aren't you going to dance with me, when I'm ready?

JEAN: Yes, of course.

CHRISTINE: Promise?

JEAN: Promise? When I say I'll do a thing, I do it. Thank you for that, it was very nice. [*Corks the bottle.*]

MISS JULIE [*in the doorway, talking to someone outside*]: I'll be back immediately. Don't wait for me.

> JEAN *hides the bottle in the drawer of the table and gets up respectfully.*

MISS JULIE [*enters and goes up to* CHRISTINE *by the stove*]: Well, is it ready?

> CHRISTINE *indicates that* JEAN *is present.*

JEAN [*gallantly*]: Have you ladies secrets to discuss?

MISS JULIE [*flips him in the face with her handkerchief*]: Don't be inquisitive!

JEAN: Ah! Charming, that smell of violets.

MISS JULIE [*coquettishly*]: Saucy fellow! So you know about perfumes, too? You certainly know how to dance—stop looking, now, go away!

JEAN [*boldly, yet respectfully*]: Is this some magic brew you ladies are preparing on midsummer eve, which will reveal the future and show whom fate has in store for you?

MISS JULIE [*sharply*]: You'd need sharp eyes to see him. [*To* CHRISTINE.] Pour it into a bottle, and cork it well. Come now, and dance a schottische with me, Jean.

JEAN [*slowly*]: I don't wish to seem disrespectful, but this dance I had promised to Christine——

MISS JULIE: Well, she can have another dance with you, can't you, Christine? Won't you lend me Jean?

CHRISTINE: That's hardly up to me. If Miss Julie condescends, it's not his place to refuse. Go ahead, Jean, and thank madam for the honour.

JEAN: To be frank, without wishing to offend, I wonder if it would be wise for Miss Julie to dance twice in succession with the same partner. These people soon start talking——

MISS JULIE [*flares up*]: Talking? What kind of talk? What do you mean?

JEAN [*politely*]: If madam doesn't understand, I must speak more plainly. It looks bad if you show a preference for one of your servants while others are waiting to be similarly honoured——

MISS JULIE: Preference! What an idea! I am astounded. I, the lady of the house, honour my servants by attending their dance, and when I take the floor I want to dance with someone who knows how to partner a lady. I don't want to be made ridiculous——

JEAN: As madam commands. I am at your service.

MISS JULIE [*softly*]: Don't regard it as a command. Tonight we are ordinary people trying to be happy, and all rank is laid aside. Come, give me your arm! Don't worry, Christine! I won't steal your lover!

JEAN *offers* MISS JULIE *his arm, and escorts her out.*

PANTOMIME

This should be played as though the actress were actually alone. When the occasion calls for it she should turn her back on the audience. She does not look towards them; and must not hasten her movements as though afraid lest they should grow impatient.

CHRISTINE *alone. A violin can be faintly heard in the distance, playing a schottische.* CHRISTINE *hums in time with the music; clears up after* JEAN, *washes the plate at the sink, dries it and puts it away in a cupboard. Then she removes her apron, takes a small mirror from a drawer, lights a candle and warms a curling-iron, with which she then crisps the hair over her forehead. Goes out into the doorway and listens. Returns to the table. Finds* MISS JULIE'S *handkerchief, which the latter has forgotten; picks it up and smells it; then spreads it out, as though thinking of something else, stretches it, smooths it, folds it into quarters, etc.*

JEAN [*enters alone*]: No, she really *is* crazy! What a way to dance! Everyone was grinning at her from behind the doors. What do you make of it, Christine?

CHRISTINE: Oh, it's that time of the month for her, and then she always acts strange. Well, are you going to dance with me now?

JEAN: You're not angry with me for leaving you like that——?

CHRISTINE: No, a little thing like that doesn't bother me. Besides, I know my place——

JEAN [*puts his arm round her waist*]: You're a sensible girl, Christine. You'd make a good wife——

MISS JULIE [*enters; is disagreeably surprised; speaks with forced lightness*]: Well, you're a fine gentleman, running away from your partner like that!

JEAN: On the contrary, Miss Julie. As you see, I have hastened to return to the partner I forsook!

MISS JULIE [*changes her tone*]: Do you know, you dance magnificently. But why are you wearing uniform on midsummer eve? Take it off at once.

JEAN: Then I must ask madam to go outside for a moment. I have my black coat here—— [*Goes right with a gesture.*]

MISS JULIE: Does my presence embarrass you? Can't you change a coat with me here? You'd better go into your room, then. Or stay, and I'll turn my back.

JEAN: With your permission, Miss Julie.

Goes right. We see his arm as he changes his coat.

MISS JULIE [*to* CHRISTINE]: Christine, Jean is very familiar with you. Are you engaged to him?

CHRISTINE: Engaged? If you like. We call it that.

MISS JULIE: Call——?

CHRISTINE: Well, you've been engaged yourself, madam——

MISS JULIE: We were properly engaged.

CHRISTINE: Didn't come to anything, though, did it?

JEAN *enters in black tails and a black bowler hat.*

MISS JULIE: *Très gentil, monsieur Jean! Très gentil!*

JEAN: *Vous voulez plaisanter, madame!*

MISS JULIE: *Et vous voulez parler francais!* Where did you learn that?

JEAN: In Switzerland. I was wine waiter at the biggest hotel in Lucerne.

MISS JULIE: You look quite the gentleman in those tails. *Charmant!* [*Sits at the table.*]

JEAN: Oh, you're flattering me.

MISS JULIE [*haughtily*]: Flattering *you*?

JEAN: My natural modesty forbids me to suppose that you would pay a truthful compliment to one so humble as myself, so I assumed you were exaggerating, for which I believe the polite word is flattering.

MISS JULIE: Where did you learn to talk like that? You must have spent a lot of your time at the theatre.

JEAN: Yes. And I've been around a bit, too.

MISS JULIE: But you were born here, weren't you?

JEAN: My father worked on the next farm to yours. I used to see you when I was a child, though you wouldn't remember me.

MISS JULIE: No, really?

JEAN: Yes. I remember one time especially—no, I oughtn't to mention that.

MISS JULIE: Oh, yes! Tell me. Come on! Just this once.

JEAN: No, I really couldn't now. Some other time, perhaps.

MISS JULIE: Some other time means never. Is it so dangerous to tell it now?

JEAN: It isn't dangerous, but I'd rather not. Look at her! [*Indicates* CHRISTINE, *who has fallen asleep in a chair by the stove.*]

MISS JULIE: A charming wife she'll make. Does she snore too?

JEAN: She doesn't do that, but she talks in her sleep.

MISS JULIE [*cynically*]: How do you know?

JEAN [*coolly*]: I've heard her.

Pause. They look at each other.

MISS JULIE: Why don't you sit?

JEAN: I wouldn't permit myself to do that in your presence.

MISS JULIE: But if I order you to?

JEAN: Then I shall obey.

MISS JULIE: Sit, then. No, wait. Can you give me something to drink first?

JEAN: I don't know what we have in the ice-box. Only beer, I think.

MISS JULIE: What do you mean, only beer? My taste is very simple. I prefer it to wine.

JEAN *takes a bottle of beer from the ice-box, opens it, gets a glass and plate from the cupboard and serves her.*

MISS JULIE: Thank you. Won't you have something yourself?

JEAN: I'm not much of a drinker, but if madam orders me——

MISS JULIE: Orders? Surely you know that a gentleman should never allow a lady to drink alone.

JEAN: That's perfectly true. [*Opens another bottle and pours a glass.*]

MISS JULIE: Drink my health, now! [JEAN *hesitates.*] Are you shy?

JEAN [*kneels in a parody of a romantic attitude, and raises his glass*]: To my mistress's health!

MISS JULIE: Bravo! Now kiss my shoe, and the ceremony is complete.

> JEAN *hesitates, then boldly takes her foot in his hands and kisses it lightly.*

MISS JULIE: Excellent. You ought to have been an actor.

JEAN [*gets up*]: We mustn't go on like this, Miss Julie. Someone might come in and see us.

MISS JULIE: What then?

JEAN: People would talk, that's all. And if you knew how their tongues were wagging up there just now——

MISS JULIE: What kind of thing were they saying? Tell me. Sit down.

JEAN [*sits*]: I don't want to hurt you, but they were using expressions which—which hinted that—well, you can guess! You aren't a child, and when people see a lady drinking alone with a man—let alone a servant—at night—then——

MISS JULIE: Then what? Anyway, we're not alone. Christine is here.

JEAN: Asleep.

MISS JULIE: Then I shall wake her. [*Gets up.*] Christine! Are you asleep?

> CHRISTINE *mumbles to herself in her sleep.*

MISS JULIE: Christine! My God, she is asleep!

CHRISTINE [*in her sleep*]: Are his lordship's boots brushed? Put on the coffee. Quickly, quickly, quickly! [*Laughs, then grunts.*]

MISS JULIE [*takes her by the nose*]: Will you wake up?

JEAN [*sharply*]: Don't disturb her!

MISS JULIE [*haughtily*]: What!

JEAN: People who stand at a stove all day get tired when night comes. And sleep is something to be respected——

MISS JULIE: A gallant thought, and one that does you honour. [*Holds out her hand to* JEAN.] Come outside now, and pick some lilac for me.

> *During the following dialogue,* CHRISTINE *wakes and wanders drowsily right to go to bed.*

JEAN: With you?

MISS JULIE: With me.

JEAN: Impossible. I couldn't.

MISS JULIE: I don't understand. Surely you don't imagine——?

JEAN: I don't, but other people might.

MISS JULIE: What? That I have fallen in love with a servant?

JEAN: I'm not being conceited, but such things have happened—and to these people, nothing is sacred.

MISS JULIE: Quite the little aristocrat, aren't you?

JEAN: Yes, I am.

MISS JULIE: If I choose to step down——

JEAN: Don't step down, Miss Julie, take my advice. No one will believe you did it freely. People will always say you fell——

MISS JULIE: I have a higher opinion of people than you. Come and see! Come!

She fixes him with her eyes.

JEAN: You know, you're strange.

MISS JULIE: Perhaps. But so are you. Everything is strange. Life, people, everything, is a scum which drifts, drifts on and on across the water until it sinks, sinks. I have a dream which recurs every so often, and I'm reminded of it now. I've climbed to the top of a pillar, and am sitting there, and I can see no way to descend. When I look down, I become dizzy, but I must come down—but I haven't the courage to jump. I can't stay up there, and I long to fall, but I don't fall. And yet I know I shall find no peace till I come down, down to the ground. And if I could get down, I should want to burrow my way deep into the earth. . . . Have you ever felt anything like that?

JEAN: No. I dream that I'm lying under a high tree in a dark wood. I want to climb, up, up to the top, and look round over the bright landscape where the sun is shining—plunder the bird's nest up there where the gold eggs lie. And I climb and climb, but the trunk is so thick and slippery, and it's so far to the first branch. But I know that if I could only get to that first branch, I'd climb my way to the top as though up a ladder. I haven't reached it yet, but I shall reach it, even if it's only in a dream.

MISS JULIE: Why do I stand here prattling with you about dreams? Come, now! Just into the park!

She offers him her arm, and they go.

JEAN: We must sleep with nine midsummer flowers under our pillow tonight, Miss Julie, and our dreams will come true!

They turn in the doorway. JEAN *puts a hand to one of his eyes.*

MISS JULIE: Have you something in your eye?

JEAN: It's nothing. Only a speck of dust. It'll be all right soon.

MISS JULIE: My sleeve must have brushed it. Sit down and I'll take it out. [*Takes him by the arm, makes him sit, takes his head and pushes it backwards, and tries to remove the dust with the corner of her handkerchief.*] Sit still now, quite still! [*Slaps his hands.*] Come, obey me! I believe you're trembling, you great, strong lout! [*Feels his biceps.*] What muscles you have!

JEAN [*warningly*]: Miss Julie!

MISS JULIE: Yes, monsieur Jean?

JEAN: *Attention! Je ne suis qu'un homme!*

MISS JULIE: Sit still, will you! There! Now it's gone. Kiss my hand and thank me.

JEAN [*gets up*]: Miss Julie, listen to me. Christine's gone to bed now—will you listen to me!

MISS JULIE: Kiss my hand first.

JEAN: Listen to me!

MISS JULIE: Kiss my hand first.

JEAN: All right. But you've only yourself to blame.

MISS JULIE: For what?

JEAN: For what? Are you a child? You're twenty-five. Don't you know it's dangerous to play with fire?

MISS JULIE: Not for me. I am insured.

JEAN [*boldly*]: No, you're not. And if you are, there's inflammable material around that isn't.

MISS JULIE: Meaning you?

JEAN: Yes. Not because I'm me, but because I'm a young man——

MISS JULIE: Of handsome appearance! What incredible conceit! A Don Juan, perhaps? Or a Joseph! Yes, upon my word, I do believe you're a Joseph!

JEAN: Do you?

MISS JULIE: I almost fear it.

JEAN *moves boldly forward and tries to take her round the waist to kiss her.*

MISS JULIE [*slaps him*]: Stop it!

JEAN: Are you joking or serious?

MISS JULIE: Serious.

JEAN: Then you were being serious just now too. You play games too seriously, and that's dangerous. Well, now I'm tired of this game and must ask your permission to get back to my work. His lordship's boots must be ready in time, and it's long past midnight.

MISS JULIE: Forget the boots.

JEAN: No. They're part of my job, which doesn't include being your playmate. And never will. I flatter myself I'm above that.

MISS JULIE: Aren't we proud!

JEAN: In some respects. In others, not.

MISS JULIE: Have you ever been in love?

JEAN: We don't use that word. But I've been fond of a lot of girls, and once I was sick because I couldn't get the one I wanted. Yes, sick, do you hear, like those princes in the Arabian Nights, who couldn't eat or drink because of love.

MISS JULIE: Who was she? [JEAN *is silent.*] Who was she?

JEAN: You cannot order me to answer that.

MISS JULIE: If I ask you as an equal? As a friend! Who was she?

JEAN: You.

MISS JULIE [*sits*]: How absurd!

JEAN: Yes, if you like. It was absurd. Look, this was the story I didn't want to tell you just now—but now I will tell you. Do you know how the world looks from down there? No, you don't. Like hawks and eagles, whose backs one seldom sees because most of the time they hover above you! I lived in a hut with seven brothers and sisters and a pig, out in the grey fields where never a tree grew. But from the window I could see the wall of his lordship's park, with apple trees rising above it. It was the Garden of Paradise, and there stood many evil angels with flaming swords to guard it.

But despite them I and other boys found a way in to the tree of life— You despise me now?

MISS JULIE: Oh, I suppose all boys steal apples.

JEAN: You can say that now, but you do despise me. However. One day I entered the garden with my mother, to weed the onion beds. On one side of the garden stood a Turkish pavilion in the shadow of jasmine trees and overgrown with honeysuckle. I didn't know what it could be for, but I'd never seen such a beautiful building. People went in and came out again; and, one day, the door was left open. I crept in and saw the walls hung with pictures of kings and emperors, and there were red curtains on the windows with tassels—ah, now you understand! I—— [*Breaks a flower from the lilac and holds it beneath* MISS JULIE's *nose.*] I'd never been into the palace itself, never seen anything except the church—but this was more beautiful—and however my thoughts might stray, they always returned there. And gradually I began to long just once to experience the full ecstasy of actually—*enfin*, I crept inside, saw and marvelled. But then—someone's coming! There was only one exit—for the lords and ladies. But for me—there was another—and I had no choice but to take it. [MISS JULIE, *who has taken the lilac blossom, lets it fall on the table.*] Then I ran, broke through a raspberry bush, charged across a strawberry patch, and found myself on a terrace with a rose garden. There I saw a pink dress and a pair of white stockings. You. I lay down under a pile of weeds—*under*, can you imagine that?—under thistles that pricked me and wet earth that stank. And I looked at you as you walked among the roses, and I thought: "If it is true that a thief can enter heaven and dwell with the angels, then it's strange that a peasant's child here on earth cannot enter the great park and play with the Count's daughter."

MISS JULIE [*romantically*]: Do you suppose all poor children have had the same ideas as you about this?

JEAN [*at first hesitant, then with conviction*]: Have *all* poor——? Yes! Of course! Of course!

MISS JULIE: It must be a terrible misfortune to be poor.

JEAN [*deeply cut, speaks with strong emotion*]: Oh, Miss Julie! Oh! A dog may lie on the Countess's sofa, a horse may have its nose patted by a young lady's hand, but a servant——! [*Changes his tone*]. Oh, now and then a man has strength enough to hoist himself up in the world, but how often does it happen? But do you know what I did? I ran down into the millstream with my clothes on. They dragged me out and beat me. But the following Sunday, when my father and all the others had gone to visit my grandmother, I managed to fix things so that I stayed at home. And then I scrubbed myself with soap and hot water, put on my best clothes, and went to church, in order that I might see you. I saw you, and returned home, determined to die. But I wanted to die beautifully, and pleasantly, without pain. Then I remembered it was dangerous to sleep under an elder bush. We had a big one, in flower. I plundered it of everything it held, and then I lay down in the oat-bin. Have you ever noticed how beautiful oats are? Soft to the touch like human skin. Well, I shut the lid and closed my eyes. I fell asleep, and woke up feeling really very ill. But I didn't die, as you can see. What did I want? I don't know. I had no hope of winning you, of course—but you were a symbol to me of the hopelessness of my ever climbing out of the class in which I was born.

MISS JULIE: Do you know you're quite a *raconteur*? Did you ever go to school?

JEAN: A bit. But I've read a lot of novels, and gone to theatres. And I've heard gentlefolk talk. That's where I've learned most.

MISS JULIE: Do you listen to what we say?

JEAN: Certainly! And I've heard plenty, too, sitting on the

coachman's box or rowing the boat. One time I heard you and a lady friend——

MISS JULIE: Indeed? What did you hear?

JEAN: Oh, I wouldn't care to repeat it. But it surprised me a little. I couldn't imagine where you'd learned all those words. Maybe at bottom there isn't as big a difference as people suppose between people and—people.

MISS JULIE: Oh, nonsense. We don't act like you do when we're engaged.

JEAN [*looks at her*]: Are you sure? Come, Miss Julie, you don't have to play the innocent with me——

MISS JULIE: The man to whom I offered my love was a bastard.

JEAN: That's what they always say—afterwards.

MISS JULIE: Always?

JEAN: I've heard the expression several times before on similar occasions.

MISS JULIE: What occasions?

JEAN: Like the one in question. The last time——

MISS JULIE [*rises*]: Be quiet! I don't wish to hear any more.

JEAN: *She* didn't want to, either. Strange. Well, have I your permission to go to bed?

MISS JULIE [*softly*]: Go to bed? On midsummer eve?

JEAN: Yes. Dancing with that pack up there doesn't greatly amuse me.

MISS JULIE: Get the key of the boat and row me out on the lake. I want to see the sun rise.

JEAN: Is that wise?

MISS JULIE: You speak as though you were frightened of your reputation.

JEAN: Why not? I don't want to make myself a laughing-stock, and maybe get sacked without a reference, now that I'm beginning to make my way. And I think I have a certain responsibility towards Christine.

MISS JULIE: Oh, I see, it's Christine now——

JEAN: Yes, but you too. Take my advice. Go back to your room and go to bed.

MISS JULIE: Am *I* to obey *you*?

JEAN: For once. For your own sake. I beg you! It's late, drowsiness makes one drunk, one's head grows dizzy. Go to bed. Besides—if my ears don't deceive me—the other servants are coming here to look for me. And if they find us together here, you are lost!

Approaching voices are heard, singing.

VOICES: One young girl in a big dark wood!
    Tridiridi-ralla, tridiridi-ra!
    Met a boy she never should!
    Tridiridi-ralla-ra!

    O lay me down in the grass so soft!
    Tridiridi-ralla, tridiridi-ra!
    And her m-m-m she lost!
    Tridiridi-ralla-ra!

    O thank you sir, but I must go!
    Tridiridi-ralla, tridiridi-ra!
    Another loves me now, so—
    Tridiridi-ralla-la!

MISS JULIE: I know these people, and I love them, as I know they love me. Let them come here, and I'll prove it to you.

JEAN: No, Miss Julie, they don't love you. They take your food, but they spit at you once you've turned your back. Believe me! Listen to them, listen to what they're singing! No, don't listen!

MISS JULIE [*listens*]: What are they singing?

JEAN: It's a filthy song. About you and me.

MISS JULIE: How vile! Oh! The little traitors——!

JEAN: The mob is always cowardly. One can't fight them. One can only run away.

MISS JULIE: Run away? But where? We can't go out—or into Christine's room!

JEAN: No. Into my room, then. We can't bother about conventions now. And you can trust me. I am your true, loyal and respectful—friend.

MISS JULIE: But suppose—suppose they look for you in there?

JEAN: I'll bolt the door. And if anyone tries to break in, I'll shoot. Come! [*Drops to his knees.*] Come!

MISS JULIE [*urgently*]: You promise——

JEAN: I swear.

MISS JULIE *runs out right.* JEAN *hastens after her.*

BALLET

The peasants stream in, wearing their best clothes, with flowers in their hats and a fiddler at their head. A barrel of beer and a keg of schnapps decorated with greenery are set on a table, glasses are produced, and they drink. They form a ring and dance, singing: "Two girls crept out of a big, dark wood!" When this is finished, they go out, singing.

MISS JULIE enters, alone. She sees the chaos in the kitchen, clasps her hands, then takes out a powder puff and powders her face.

JEAN [*enters, agitated*]: There—you see! And you heard them. Do you think you can possibly stay here now?

MISS JULIE: No. I don't. But what can we do?

JEAN: Go away—travel—far away from here——

MISS JULIE: Travel? Yes, but where?

JEAN: To Switzerland, the Italian lakes! Have you never been there?

MISS JULIE: No. Is it beautiful there?

JEAN: Ah! An eternal summer! Oranges, laurel trees—ah!

MISS JULIE: But what shall we do there?

JEAN: I'll start a hotel. *De luxe*—for *de luxe* people.

MISS JULIE: Hotel?

JEAN: Ah, that's a life, believe me! New faces all the time, new languages! Never a minute for worry or nerves, or wondering what to do. There's work to be done every minute, bells ringing night and day, trains whistling, buses coming and going, and all the time the golden sovereigns roll into the till. Yes, that's a life!

MISS JULIE: It sounds exciting. But—I——?

JEAN: Shall be the mistress of the house; the pearl of the establishment. With your looks—and your style—why, we're made! It'll be terrific! You'll sit at your desk like a queen, setting your slaves in motion by pressing an electric bell. The guests will defile before your throne, humbly laying their tribute upon your table—you've no idea how people tremble when they get a bill in their hand. I shall salt the bills, and you shall sugar them with your prettiest smile! Oh, let's get away from here! [*Takes a timetable from his pocket.*] Now, at once, by the next train! We'll be in Malmö by 5.30, Hamburg 8.40 tomorrow morning, Frankfurt to Basel will take a day, through the Gothard Pass—we'll be in Como in, let me see, three days. Three days!

MISS JULIE: It sounds wonderful. But, Jean—you must give me courage. Tell me you love me. Come and kiss me.

JEAN [*hesitates*]: I'd like to—but I daren't. Not in this house—not again. I love you—never doubt that—can you doubt it, Miss Julie?

MISS JULIE [*shy, feminine*]: *Miss!* Call me Julie! There are no barriers between us now. Call me Julie!

JEAN [*tormented*]: I can't! There are still barriers between us—there always will be, as long as we're in this house. There's the past, there's his lordship—I've never met anyone I respected as I do him—I only have to see his gloves on a chair and I feel like a small boy—I only have to hear that bell ring and I jump like a frightened horse—and when I see his boots standing there, so straight and proud, I cringe. [*Kicks the boots.*] Superstition—ideas shoved into our heads when we're children—but we can't escape them. Come to another country, a republic, and others will cringe before my porter's livery—yes, they'll cringe, I tell you, but I shan't! I wasn't born to cringe—I'm a man, I've got character, just let me get my fingers on that first branch and watch me climb! Today I'm a servant, but next year I'll own my own hotel, in ten years I'll be a landed gentleman! Then I'll go to Rumania, get a decoration—why, I might—might, mind you—end up with a title.

MISS JULIE: How wonderful!

JEAN: Oh, in Rumania I could buy myself a title. I'd be a Count, and you'd be a Countess. My Countess!

MISS JULIE: What do I care about all that? That's what I'm giving up now. Tell me you love me, otherwise—yes, otherwise—what am I?

JEAN: I'll tell you a thousand times—later. Only—not here. Above all, no emotional scenes, or it'll be all up with us. We must think this over coolly, like sensible people. [*Takes a cigar, cuts and lights it.*] Sit down there now, and I'll sit here and we'll talk as though nothing had happened.

MISS JULIE [*in despair*]: Oh, my God! Have you no feelings?

JEAN: I? No one has more feelings than I. But I can control them.

MISS JULIE: A moment ago you could kiss my shoe—and now——!

JEAN [*harshly*]: Yes, that was a moment ago. Now we've something else to think about.

MISS JULIE: Don't speak so harshly to me.

JEAN: I'm not speaking harshly. I'm talking sense. One folly has been committed, don't let's commit any more. His lordship may be here any moment, and by then we've got to decide what we're going to do with our lives. What do you think of my plans for our future? Do you approve of them?

MISS JULIE: They seem to me quite sensible, but—just one question. A big project like that needs a lot of capital. Have you that?

JEAN [*chews his cigar*]: I? Certainly. I have my professional expertise, my experience, my knowledge of languages. We've adequate capital, I should say.

MISS JULIE: But all that doesn't add up to the price of a railway ticket.

JEAN: That's perfectly true; which is why I need a backer to advance me the money.

MISS JULIE: Where are you going to find one quickly?

JEAN: You'll find one, if you come with me.

MISS JULIE: I couldn't. And I haven't any money of my own.

Pause.

JEAN: Then our whole plan collapses.

MISS JULIE: And——?

JEAN: Things must stay as they are.

MISS JULIE: Do you suppose I'm going to remain under this roof as your whore? With *them* sniggering at me behind their fingers? Do you think I can look my father in the face after this? No! Take me away from here, from the shame and the dishonour—oh, what have I done, my God, my God! [*Sobs.*]

JEAN: Come, don't start that. What have you done? The same as many others before you.

MISS JULIE [*screams convulsively*]: Oh, now you despise me! I'm falling—I'm falling——!

JEAN: Fall down to me, and I'll lift you up again.

MISS JULIE: What dreadful power drew me to you? The attraction of the weak to the strong? Of the faller to the climber? Or was it love? Was this love? Do you know what love is?

JEAN: I? Yes, of course. Do you think I've never had a woman before?

MISS JULIE: How can you think and talk like that?

JEAN: That's life as I've learned it. And that's me. Now don't get nervous and act the lady. We're both in the same boat now. Come here, my girlie, and I'll give you another glass of wine. [*Opens drawer, takes out the bottle of wine and fills two used glasses.*]

MISS JULIE: Where did you get that wine from?

JEAN: The cellar.

MISS JULIE: My father's burgundy!

JEAN: Is it too good for his son-in-law?

MISS JULIE: And I drink beer! I!

JEAN: That only proves you have an inferior palate to mine.

MISS JULIE: Thief!

JEAN: Going to tell?

MISS JULIE: Oh, oh! Accomplice to a sneakthief! Was I drunk, was I dreaming? Midsummer night! The night of innocent festival——

JEAN: Innocent? Hm!

MISS JULIE [*paces to and fro*]: Is there anyone on this earth as miserable as I?

JEAN: Why should you be miserable after such a conquest? Think of Christine in there. Don't you suppose she has feelings too?

MISS JULIE: I thought so just now, but I don't any longer. Servants are servants——

JEAN: And whores are whores.

MISS JULIE [*kneels and clasps her hands*]: Oh, God in Heaven, end my miserable life! Save me from this mire into which I'm sinking! Save me, save me!

JEAN: I can't deny I feel sorry for you. When I lay in the onion bed and saw you in the rose garden—I might as well tell you now—I had the same dirty thoughts as any small boy.

MISS JULIE: You—who wanted to die for me?

JEAN: The oat-bin? Oh, that was just talk.

MISS JULIE: A lie?

JEAN [*begins to get sleepy*]: More or less. I once read a story in a paper about a sweep who curled up in a wood-chest with some lilacs because he'd had a paternity order brought against him——

MISS JULIE: I see. You're the kind who——

JEAN: Well, I had to think up something. Women always fall for pretty stories.

MISS JULIE: Swine!

JEAN: *Merde!*

MISS JULIE: And now you've managed to see the eagle's back——

JEAN: Back?

MISS JULIE: And I was to be the first branch——

JEAN: But the branch was rotten——

MISS JULIE: I was to be the signboard of the hotel——

JEAN: And I the hotel——

MISS JULIE: I was to sit at the desk, attract your customers, fiddle your bills——

JEAN: No, I'd have done that——

MISS JULIE: Can a human soul become so foul?

JEAN: Wash it, then!

MISS JULIE: Servant, lackey, stand up when I speak!

JEAN: Servant's whore, lackey's bitch, shut your mouth and get out of here. You dare to stand there and call me foul? None of my class ever behaved the way you've done tonight. Do you think any kitchen-maid would accost a man like you did? Have you ever seen any girl of my class offer her body like that? I've only seen it among animals and prostitutes.

MISS JULIE [*crushed*]: You're right. Hit me, trample on me, I've deserved nothing better. I'm worthless—but help me, help me out of this—if there is a way out.

JEAN [*more gently*]: I don't want to disclaim my share in the honour of having seduced you, but do you imagine a man in my position would have dared to so much as glance at you if you hadn't invited him? I'm still dumbfounded——

MISS JULIE: And proud.

JEAN: Why not? Though I must confess I found the conquest a little too easy to be really exciting.

MISS JULIE: Hurt me more.

JEAN [*gets up*]: No. Forgive me for what I've said. I don't hit defenceless people, least of all women. I can't deny it gratifies me to have found that it was only a gilt veneer that dazzled our humble eyes, that the eagle's back was as scabbed as our own, that the whiteness of those cheeks was only powder, that those polished fingernails had black edges, that that handkerchief was dirty though it smelt of perfume——
But on the other hand, it hurts me to have discovered that what I was aspiring towards was not something worthier

and more solid. It hurts me to see you sunk so low, to find that deep down you are a kitchen slut. It hurts me, like seeing the autumn flowers whipped to tatters by the rain and trodden into the mud.

MISS JULIE: You speak as though you were already above me.

JEAN: I am. You see, I could make you into a Countess, but you could never make me into a Count.

MISS JULIE: But I am of noble blood, and you can never be that.

JEAN: That's true. But my children could be noblemen, if——

MISS JULIE: But you're a thief. That's something I am not.

JEAN: There are worse things than being a thief. Besides, when I work in a house I regard myself more or less as a member of the family, a child of the house, and people don't call it stealing when a child takes a berry from a bush heavy with fruit. [*His passion rises again.*] Miss Julie, you're a fine woman, much too good for someone like me. You've been the victim of a drunken folly, and you want to cover it up by pretending to yourself that you love me. You don't, unless perhaps physically—and then your love is no better then mine—but I can never be content with being just your animal, and I can never make you love me.

MISS JULIE: Are you sure of that?

JEAN: You mean it might happen? I could love you, easily—you're beautiful, you're refined—— [*Approaches her and takes her hand.*] Educated, lovable when you want to be, and once you have awoken a man's passion, it could never die. [*Puts his arm round her waist.*] You are like hot wine, strongly spiced, and a kiss from you——! [*Tries to lead her towards his room, but she tears herself free.*]

MISS JULIE: Let me go! You won't win me like that!

JEAN: How, then? Not like that. Not by flattery and fine words. Not by thinking of your future, rescuing you from what you've done to yourself. How, then?

MISS JULIE: How? How? I don't know. There is no way. I detest you as I detest rats, but I cannot run away from you.

JEAN: Run away with me!

MISS JULIE [*straightens herself*]: Run away? Yes, we must run away. But I'm so tired. Give me a glass of wine. [JEAN *pours her some. She looks at her watch.*] But we must talk first. We have a little time. [*Drains the glass and holds it out for more.*]

JEAN: Don't drink so much, you'll get drunk.

MISS JULIE: What does that matter?

JEAN: What does it matter? It's stupid to get drunk. What were you going to say to me just now?

MISS JULIE: We must run away! But first we must talk—that is, I must talk—so far you've been doing all the talking. You've told me about your life, now I want to tell you about mine, so that we know all about each other before we go away together.

JEAN: One moment. Forgive me, but—consider—you may later regret having revealed your private secrets to me.

MISS JULIE: Aren't you my friend?

JEAN: Yes—sometimes. But don't rely on me.

MISS JULIE: You're only saying that. Anyway, everyone else knows. You see, my mother was a commoner, of quite humble birth. She was brought up with ideas about equality, freedom for women and all that. And she had a decided aversion to marriage. So when my father proposed to her, she replied that she would never become his wife, but—well, anyway, she did. I came into the world, against my mother's wish as far as I can gather. She wanted to bring me up as a child of nature, and into the bargain I was to learn everything that a boy has to learn, so that I might stand as an example of how a woman can be as good as a man. I had to wear boy's clothes, and learn to look after horses—though I was never allowed to enter the cowshed. I had to groom and saddle them, and hunt—and even learn to slaughter. That was horrible. Meanwhile, on the estate, all the men were set to perform the women's tasks, and the women the men's—with the result that the estate began to fail, and we became the laughing-stock of the district. In the end my father came to his senses and put his foot down, and everything was changed back to the way he wanted it. My mother fell ill—what illness, I don't know—but she often had convulsions, hid herself in the attic and the garden, and sometimes stayed out all night. Then there was the great fire which you have heard about. The house, the stables and the cowshed were all burned down, under circumstances suggesting arson—for the accident happened the very day our quarterly insurance had expired, and the premium my father sent had been delayed through the inefficiency of the servant carrying it, so that it hadn't arrived in time. [*Fills her glass and drinks.*]

JEAN: Don't drink any more.

MISS JULIE: Oh, what does it matter? So we were left penniless, and had to sleep in the carriages. My father couldn't think where he would be able to find the money to rebuild the house. Then mother advised him to ask for a loan from an old friend of hers, a brick merchant who lived in the neighbourhood. Father got the money free of interest, which rather surprised him. So the house was rebuilt. [*Drinks again.*] Do you know who burned the house down?

JEAN: Your mother!

MISS JULIE: Do you know who the brick merchant was?

JEAN: Your mother's lover!

MISS JULIE: Do you know whose the money was?

JEAN: Wait a moment. No, that I don't know.

MISS JULIE: It was my mother's.

JEAN: His lordship's too, then. Unless he'd made a marriage settlement.

Miss Julie: No, there wasn't any marriage settlement. My mother had had a little money of her own, which she didn't want my father to have the use of. So she entrusted it to her —friend.

Jean: Who kept it!

Miss Julie: Exactly. He kept it. All this came to my father's knowledge—but he couldn't start an action, repay his wife's lover, or prove that the money was his wife's. It was my mother's revenge on him, for taking control of the house out of her hands. He was on the verge of shooting himself—the rumour was that he had done so, but had failed to kill himself. Well, he lived; and he made my mother pay for what she had done. Those five years were dreadful for me, I can tell you. I was sorry for my father, but I took my mother's side, because I didn't know the circumstances. I'd learned from her to distrust and hate men—she hated men, as I've told you. And I promised her that I would never be a slave to any man.

Jean: And then you got engaged to that young lawyer?

Miss Julie: So that he should be my slave.

Jean: And he wasn't willing?

Miss Julie: He was willing enough, but he didn't get the chance. I tired of him.

Jean: I saw it. In the stable.

Miss Julie: Saw what?

Jean: How he broke off the engagement.

Miss Julie: That's a lie! It was I who broke it off! Has he been saying he did it, the little wretch?

Jean: He wasn't a wretch. You hate men, Miss Julie.

Miss Julie: Yes. Most of the time. But sometimes—when the weakness comes—when nature burns—! Oh, God! Will the fire never die?

Jean: You hate me too?

MISS JULIE: Immeasurably! I'd like to shoot you like an animal——

JEAN: "The woman gets two years penal servitude and the animal is shot". That's the law for that, isn't it? But you've nothing to shoot with. So what shall we do?

MISS JULIE: Go away!

JEAN: To torment each other to death?

MISS JULIE: No. To be happy—for two days—a week—as long as one can be happy—and then—die——

JEAN: Die? Don't be stupid. I'd rather start the hotel than do that.

MISS JULIE [*not hearing him*]: —— on the Lake of Como, where the sun always shines, where the laurels are green at Christmas, and the orange-trees flame!

JEAN: The Lake of Como is about as beautiful as a puddle, and I never saw any oranges there except in the grocers' shops. But it's a good spot for tourists, there are a lot of villas to hire out to loving couples, and that's a profitable industry—you know why? Because they lease them for six months, and then leave after three weeks.

MISS JULIE [*naïvely*]: Why after three weeks?

JEAN: They quarrel, of course! But they have to pay the full rent, and then you hire it out again. So it goes on, couple after couple. For love must go on, if not for very long.

MISS JULIE: You don't want to die with me?

JEAN: I don't want to die at all. Partly because I like life, and partly because I regard suicide as a crime against the Providence which gave us life.

MISS JULIE: You believe in God—*you*?

JEAN: Certainly I do. And I go to church every other Sunday. Quite frankly now, I'm tired of all this, and I'm going to bed.

MISS JULIE: I see. And you think I'm going to rest content with that? Don't you know what a man owes to a woman he has shamed?

JEAN [*takes out his purse and throws a silver coin on the table*]: Here. I always pay my debts.

MISS JULIE [*pretends not to notice the insult*]: Do you know what the law says——?

JEAN: Unfortunately the law doesn't demand any penalty from a woman who seduces a man.

MISS JULIE: Can you see any other solution than that we should go away, marry, and part?

JEAN: And if I refuse to enter into this *mésalliance*?

MISS JULIE: *Mésalliance?*

JEAN: Yes—for me! I've got a better heritage than you. None of my ancestors committed arson.

MISS JULIE: How do you know?

JEAN: You couldn't prove it, because we don't have any family records—except with the police. But I've studied your pedigree in a book I found on the table in the drawing-room. Do you know who the first of your ancestors to get a title was? He was a miller who let the King sleep with his wife one night during the Danish war. I haven't any noble ancestors like that—I haven't any noble ancestors at all. But I could become one myself.

MISS JULIE: This is my reward for opening my heart to a servant, for giving my family's honour——!

JEAN: Dishonour! Don't say I didn't tell you. One shouldn't drink, it loosens the tongue. And that's fatal.

MISS JULIE: Oh God, how I regret it, how I regret it! If you at least loved me——!

JEAN: For the last time—what do you want? Shall I burst into tears, shall I jump over your riding crop, shall I kiss you, lie to you for three weeks on Lake Como, and then—what?

What shall I do? What do you want me to do? This is beginning to get tiresome. It's always like this when one gets involved with women. Miss Julie! I see you are unhappy, I know you are suffering, but I do not understand you! We don't fool around like you do—we don't hate—love is a game we play when we have a little time free from work, but we aren't free all day and all night like you! I think you're ill. Yes, undoubtedly, you're ill.

MISS JULIE: You must be kind to me. Now at last you're speaking like a human being.

JEAN: Act like one yourself, then. You spit at me, and won't let me wipe it off—on you.

MISS JULIE: Help me, help me! Just tell me what to do. Where shall I go?

JEAN: For God's sake! If I only knew!

MISS JULIE: I've been out of my mind, I've been mad, but isn't there some way out?

JEAN: Stay here, and keep calm. No one knows.

MISS JULIE: Impossible. The servants know. And Christine.

JEAN: They don't know for sure. They wouldn't really believe it could happen.

MISS JULIE [*hesitantly*]: But—it could happen again.

JEAN: That is true.

MISS JULIE: And—then?

JEAN [*frightened*]: Then? My God, why didn't I think of that? Yes, there's only one answer—you must go away. At once. I can't come with you—then we'd be finished—you must go alone—far away—anywhere.

MISS JULIE: Alone? Where? I can't!

JEAN: You must! And before his lordship returns. If you stay, you know what'll happen. Once one has made a mistake one wants to go on, because the damage has already been done. Then one gets more and more careless and—in the end one gets found out. So go! You can write to his lordship later and tell him everything—except that it was me! He'll never guess that. And I don't suppose he'll be over-keen to find out who it was.

MISS JULIE: I'll go, if you'll come with me.

JEAN: Are you mad, woman? Miss Julie run away with her servant! It'd be in the newspapers in a couple of days, and his lordship'd never live that down.

MISS JULIE: I can't go. I can't stay. Help me! I'm so tired, so dreadfully tired. Order me! Make me do something! I can't think, can't act——

JEAN: Now you see what a comtemptible creature you are! Why do you prink yourselves up and stick your noses in the air as though you were the lords of creation? Very well, I shall order you. Go up to the house, get dressed, get some money for the journey and come back here.

MISS JULIE [*half-whispers*]: Come with me.

JEAN: To your room? Now you're being crazy again. [*Hesitates for a moment.*] No! Go, at once! [*Takes her hand and leads her out.*]

MISS JULIE [*as she goes*]: Speak kindly to me, Jean!

JEAN: An order always sounds unkind. Now you know how it feels!

> JEAN, *left alone, heaves a sigh of relief, sits at the table, takes out a notebook and pencil, and makes some calculations muttering occasionally to himself. Dumb mime, until* CHRISTINE *enters, dressed for church, with a man's dickey and white tie in her hand.*

CHRISTINE: Blessed Jesus, what a mess! What on earth have you been up to?

JEAN: Oh, it was Miss Julie—she brought the servants in. You must have been fast asleep—didn't you hear anything?

CHRISTINE: I slept like a log.

JEAN: Dressed for church already?

CHRISTINE: Yes. You promised to come with me to Communion this morning.

JEAN: So I did. And I see you've brought my uniform. O.K., then.

Sits. CHRISTINE *dresses him in his dickey and white tie. Pause.*

JEAN [*sleepily*]: What's the lesson today?

CHRISTINE: Execution of John the Baptist, I expect. [*Makes a cutting motion across her throat.*]

JEAN: Oh God, that's a long one. Hi, you're strangling me! Oh, I'm so tired, so tired.

CHRISTINE: Yes, what have you been doing, up all night? You're quite green in the face.

JEAN: Sitting here, talking with Miss Julie.

CHRISTINE: She doesn't know what's right and proper, that one.

Pause.

JEAN: I say, Christine.

CHRISTINE: Mm?

JEAN: It's strange, you know, when you think of it. Her.

CHRISTINE: What's strange?

JEAN: Everything.

Pause.

CHRISTINE [*sees the glasses, half empty, on the table*]: Have you been drinking together, too?

JEAN: Yes.

CHRISTINE: For shame! **Look me in the eyes!**

JEAN: Yes?

CHRISTINE: Is it possible? **Is it *possible?***

JEAN [*after a moment*]: Yes.

CHRISTINE: Ugh! *That* I'd never have believed! No! Shame on you, shame!

JEAN: You aren't jealous of her, are you?

CHRISTINE: No, not of her! If it had been Clara or Sophie—then I'd have torn your eyes out. But her—no—I don't know why. Ah, but it's disgusting!

JEAN: Are you angry with her, then?

CHRISTINE: No, with you! It's a wicked thing to have done, wicked! Poor lass! No, I don't care who hears it, I don't want to stay any longer in a house where people can't respect their employers.

JEAN: Why should one respect them?

CHRISTINE: Yes, you're so clever, you tell me! But you don't want to work for people who lower themselves, do you? Eh? You lower yourself by it, that's my opinion.

JEAN: Yes, but it's a comfort for us to know they aren't any better than us.

CHRISTINE: Not to my mind. If they're no better than we are, there's no point our trying to improve ourselves. And think of his lordship! Think of him and all the misery he's had in his time! No, I don't want to stay in this house any longer. And with someone like you! If it'd been that young lawyer fellow—if it'd been a gentleman——

JEAN: What's wrong with me?

CHRISTINE: Oh, you're all right in your way, but there's a difference between people and people. No, I'll never be able to forget this. Miss Julie, who was always so proud, so cool with men—I never thought she'd go and give herself to someone—and to someone like you! She, who all but had poor Diana shot for running after the gatekeeper's pug! Yes, I'm not afraid to say it! I won't stay here any longer. On the 24th of October I go!

JEAN: And then?

CHRISTINE: Yes, since you've raised the subject, it's time you started looking round for something, seeing as we're going to get married.

JEAN: What kind of thing? I can't have a job like this once I'm married.

CHRISTINE: No, of course not. Still, you might get something as a porter, or maybe a caretaker in some factory. A bird in the hand's worth two in the bush; and there'll be a pension for your wife and children.

JEAN [*grimaces*]: Yes, that's all very fine, but I don't intend to die to oblige my wife and children just yet, thank you. I've higher ambitions than that.

CHRISTINE: Ambitions? What about your responsibilities? Think of them.

JEAN: Oh, shut up about responsibilities, I know my duty. [*Listens towards the door.*] But we've plenty of time to think about that. Go inside now and get yourself ready, and we'll go to church.

CHRISTINE: Who's that walking about upstairs?

JEAN: I don't know. Probably Clara.

CHRISTINE [*going*]: It surely can't be his lordship. He couldn't have come back without our hearing him.

JEAN [*frightened*]: His lordship? No, it can't be, he'd have rung.

CHRISTINE [*goes*]: Well, God help us. I've never been mixed up in the likes of this before.

The sun has now risen and is shining on the tops of the trees in the park. Its beams move gradually until they fall at an angle through the windows. JEAN *goes to the door and makes a sign.*

MISS JULIE [*enters in travelling clothes with a small birdcage, covered with a cloth, which she places on a chair*]: I'm ready now.

JEAN: Ssh! Christine is awake!

MISS JULIE [*very nervous throughout this dialogue*]: Does she suspect anything?

JEAN: She knows nothing. But, my God—what a sight you look!

MISS JULIE: What's wrong——?

JEAN: You're as white as a sheet, and—forgive me, but your face is dirty.

MISS JULIE: Let me wash, then. Here. [*Goes to the washbasin and washes her face and hands.*] Give me a towel. Oh—the sun's rising!

JEAN: And then the Devil loses his power.

MISS JULIE: Yes, the Devil's been at work tonight. But Jean, listen. Come with me! I've got some money now.

JEAN [*doubtfully*]: Enough?

MISS JULIE: Enough to start with! Come with me! I can't go alone today. Think—midsummer day, on a stuffy train, squashed among crowds of people staring at me—having to stand still on stations, when one longs to be flying away! No, I can't, I can't! And then—memories—memories of midsummers in childhood, the church garlanded with birch-leaves and lilac, dinner at the long table, the family, friends—the afternoons in the park, dancing, music, flowers, games! Oh, one runs, one runs away, but memories follow in the baggage-wagon—and remorse—and guilt!

JEAN: I'll come with you—but it must be now, at once, before it's too late. Now, this minute!

MISS JULIE: Get dressed, then. [*Picks up the birdcage.*]

JEAN: No luggage, though. That'd give us away.

MISS JULIE: No, nothing. Only what we can have in the compartment with us.

JEAN [*has taken his hat*]: What have you got there? What is it?

MISS JULIE: It's only my greenfinch. I don't want to leave him.

JEAN: For heaven's sake! We can't take a birdcage with us now. You're crazy. Put that cage down.

MISS JULIE: My one memory of home—the only living thing that loves me, since Diana was unfaithful to me. Don't be cruel! Let me take her with me!

JEAN: Put that cage down, I tell you. And don't talk so loud, Christine will hear us.

MISS JULIE: No, I won't leave her for strangers to have. I'd rather you killed her.

JEAN: Bring the little beast here then, and I'll wring its neck.

MISS JULIE: All right—but don't hurt her. Don't—no, I can't!

JEAN: Bring it here. I can.

MISS JULIE [*takes the bird out of its cage and kisses it*]: Ah, poor little Serina, are you going to die now and leave your mistress?

JEAN: Please don't make a scene. Your life and your happiness are at stake. Here, quickly! [*Snatches the bird from her, takes it to the chopping block and picks up the kitchen axe.* MISS JULIE *turns away.*] You ought to have learned how to wring chickens' necks instead of how to fire a pistol. [*Brings down the axe.*] Then you wouldn't have been frightened of a drop of blood.

MISS JULIE [*screams*]: Kill me too! Kill me! You, who can slaughter an innocent bird without a tremor! Oh, I hate and detest you! There is blood between us now! I curse the moment I set eyes on you, I curse the moment I was conceived in my mother's womb!

JEAN: What's the good of cursing? Come!

MISS JULIE [*goes towards the chopping block, as though drawn against her will*]: No, I don't want to go yet. I can't—I must see—ssh! There's a carriage outside! [*Listen, but keeps her eyes fixed all the while on the chopping block and the axe.*] Do you think I can't bear the sight of blood? You think I'm so weak—oh, I should like to see your blood, your brains, on a chopping block—I'd like to see all your sex swimming in a lake of blood—I think I could drink from your skull, I'd like to bathe my feet in your guts, I could eat your heart, roasted! You think I'm weak—you think I loved you, because my womb wanted your seed, you think I want to carry your embryo under my heart and feed it with my blood, bear your child and take your name! By the way, what is your name! I've never heard your surname—you probably haven't any. I'd have to be "Mrs. Kitchen-boy", or "Mrs. Lavator"—you dog, who wear my collar, you lackey who carry my crest on your buttons—am I to share with my own cook, compete with a scullery slut? Oh, oh, oh! You think I'm a coward and want to run away? No, now I shall stay. Let the storm break! My father will come home—find his desk broken open—his money gone! He'll ring—this bell—twice, for his lackey—then he'll send for the police—and I shall tell everything. Everything. Oh, it'll be good to end it all—if only it could be the end. And then he'll have a stroke and die. Then we shall all be finished, and there'll be peace—peace—eternal rest! And the coat of arms will be broken over the coffin—the title extinct—and the lackey's line will be carried on in an orphanage, win laurels in the gutter, and end in a prison!

JEAN: That's the blue blood talking! Bravo, Miss Julie! Just give the miller a rest, now——!

> CHRISTINE *enters, dressed for church, with a prayer-book in her hand.* MISS JULIE *runs towards her and falls into her arms, as though seeking shelter.*

MISS JULIE: Help me, Christine! Help me against this man!

CHRISTINE [*motionless, cold*]: What kind of a spectacle's this on a Sunday morning? [*Looks at the chopping block.*] And what a pigsty you've made here. What does all this mean? I never heard such shouting and bawling.

MISS JULIE: Christine! You're a woman, and my friend. Beware of this vile man!

JEAN [*somewhat timid and embarrassed*]: While you ladies discuss the matter, I'll go inside and shave. [*Slips out right.*]

MISS JULIE: You must understand! You must listen to me!

CHRISTINE: No, this kind of thing I don't understand. Where are you going in those clothes? And what's he doing with his hat on—eh?—eh?

MISS JULIE: Listen to me, Christine. Listen, and I'll tell you everything——

CHRISTINE: I don't want to know anything——

MISS JULIE: You must listen to me——

CHRISTINE: About what? What you've done with Jean? That doesn't bother me—that's between you and him. But if you're thinking of trying to fool him into running away, we'll soon put a stop to that.

MISS JULIE [*very nervous*]: Now try to be calm, Christine, and listen to me. I can't stay here, and Jean can't stay here—so we have to go——

CHRISTINE: Hm, hm!

MISS JULIE [*becoming brighter*]: Listen, I've just had an idea—why don't we all three go away—abroad—to Switzerland—and start a hotel together—I've money, you see—and Jean and I could run it—and you, I thought you might take charge of the kitchen—isn't that a good idea? Say yes, now! And come with us, and then everything'll be settled! Say yes, now!

CHRISTINE [*coldly, thoughtfully*]: Hm, hm!

MISS JULIE [*speaks very rapidly*]: You've never been abroad, Christine—you must get away from here and see the world. You've no idea what fun it is to travel by train—new people all the time—new countries—we'll go through Hamburg and look at the zoo—you'll like that—and then we'll go to the theatre and listen to the opera—and when we get to Munich there'll be all the museums, Christine, and Rubens and Raphael, those great painters, you know—you've heard of Munich—where King Ludwig lived, you know, the King who went mad. And we'll see his palaces—they've still got palaces there, just like in the fairy tales—and from there it isn't far to Switzerland—and the Alps, Christine—fancy, the Alps, with snow on them in the middle of summer—and oranges grow there, and laurel trees that are green all the year round——

> JEAN *can be seen in the wings right, whetting his razor on a strop which he holds between his teeth and his left hand. He listens contentedly to what is being said, every now and then nodding his approval.*

MISS JULIE [*more rapidly still*]: And we'll start a hotel there—I'll sit at the desk while Jean stands in the doorway and receives the guests—I'll go out and do the shopping—and write the letters—oh Christine, what a life it'll be! The trains will whistle, and then the buses'll arrive, and bells will ring on all the floors and in the restaurant—and I'll write out the bills—and salt them, too—you can't imagine how timid tourists are when they have to pay the bill! And you—you'll be in charge of the kitchen—you won't have to do any cooking yourself, of course—and you'll wear fine clothes, for the guests to see you in—and you, with your looks, I'm not flattering you, Christine, you'll get yourself a husband one fine day, a rich Englishman, you'll see—English people are so easy to—[*slowing down*]—catch—and we'll become rich—and build ourselves a villa on Lake Como—it rains there sometimes, of course, but—[*slows right down.*]—the sun must shine there too, sometimes—though it looks dark—and—so—if it doesn't we can come home again—back to—[*Pause.*] Back here—or somewhere——

CHRISTINE: Now listen. Do you believe all this?

MISS JULIE [*crushed*]: Do I believe it?

CHRISTINE: Yes.

MISS JULIE [*wearily*]: I don't know. I don't believe in anything any longer. [*She falls on to the bench and puts her head on the table between her hands.*] Nothing. Nothing at all.

CHRISTINE [*turns right to where* JEAN *is standing*]: So! You were thinking of running away!

JEAN [*crestfallen, puts his razor down on the table*]: Running away? Oh now, that's exaggerating. You heard Miss Julie's plan, and although she's tired now after being up all night I think it's a very practical proposition.

CHRISTINE: Listen to him! Did you expect me to act as cook to that——?

JEAN [*sharply*]: Kindly express yourself respectfully when you refer to your mistress. Understand?

CHRISTINE: Mistress!

JEAN: Yes.

CHRISTINE: Listen to him, listen to him!

JEAN: Yes, listen to me, and talk a little less. Miss Julie is your mistress, and what you despise in her you should despise in yourself too.

CHRISTINE: I've always had sufficient respect for myself——

JEAN: To be able to turn up your nose at others.

CHRISTINE: To stop me from demeaning myself. You tell me when you've seen his lordship's cook mucking around with the groom or the pigman! Just you tell me!

JEAN: Yes, you managed to get hold of a gentleman for yourself. You were lucky.

CHRISTINE: Yes, a gentleman who sells his lordship's oats, which he steals from the stables——

JEAN: You should talk! You get a percentage on all the groceries, and a rake-off from the butcher——

CHRISTINE: What!

JEAN: And you say you can't respect your employers! You, you, you!

CHRISTINE: Are you coming with me to church, now? You need a good sermon after what you've done.

JEAN: No, I'm not going to church today. You can go by yourself, and confess what you've been up to.

CHRISTINE: Yes, I will, and I'll come home with my sins forgiven, and yours too. The blessed Saviour suffered and died on the cross for all our sins, and if we turn to Him with a loyal and humble heart He'll take all our sins upon Him.

JEAN: Including the groceries?

MISS JULIE: Do you believe that, Christine?

CHRISTINE: With all my heart, as surely as I stand here. I learned it as a child, Miss Julie, and I've believed it ever since. And where the sin is exceeding great, His mercy shall overflow.

MISS JULIE: Oh, if only I had your faith! Oh, if——!

CHRISTINE: Ah, but you can't have that except by God's special grace, and that isn't granted to everyone——

MISS JULIE: Who has it, then?

CHRISTINE: That's God's great secret, Miss Julie. And the Lord's no respecter of persons. There shall the last be first——

MISS JULIE: Then He has respect for the last?

CHRISTINE [*continues*]: And it is easier for a camel to pass through the eye of a needle than for a rich man to enter the Kingdom of Heaven. That's how it is, Miss Julie. Well, I'll be going—and as I pass the stable I'll tell the groom not to let any of the horses be taken out before his lordship comes home, just in case. Goodbye. [*Goes.*]

JEAN: Damned bitch! And all this for a greenfinch!

MISS JULIE [*dully*]: Never mind the greenfinch. Can you see any way out of this, any end to it?

JEAN [*thinks*]: No.

MISS JULIE: What would you do in my place?

JEAN: In your place? Wait, now. If I were a lady—of noble birth—who'd fallen——? I don't know. Yes. I know.

MISS JULIE [*picks up the razor and makes a gesture*]: This?

JEAN: Yes. But *I* wouldn't do it, mind. There's a difference between us.

MISS JULIE: Because you're a man and I am a woman? What difference does that make?

JEAN: The difference—between a man and a woman.

MISS JULIE [*holding the razor*]: I want to do it—but I can't. My father couldn't do it, either, the time he should have.

JEAN: No, he was right. He had to be revenged first.

MISS JULIE: And now my mother will be revenged again, through me.

JEAN: Have you never loved your father, Miss Julie?

MISS JULIE: Yes—enormously—but I've hated him too. I must have done so without realising it. But it was he who brought me up to despise my own sex, made me half woman and half man. Who is to blame for what has happened—my father, my mother, myself? Myself? I haven't any self. I haven't a thought I didn't get from my father, not an emotion I didn't get from my mother—and this last idea—that all people are equal—I got that from him, my fiancé whom I called a wretched little fool because of it. How can the blame be mine, then? Put it all on to Jesus, as Christine did— no, I'm too proud to do that, and too clever—thanks to my father's teaching. And that about a rich person not being able to get into heaven, that's a lie, and Christine has money in the savings bank so she won't get there either. Whose fault is it all? What does it matter to us whose fault it is? I shall have to bear the blame, carry the consequences——

JEAN: Yes, but—

There are two sharp rings on the bell. MISS JULIE *jumps up.* JEAN *changes his coat.*

JEAN: His lordship's home! Good God, do you suppose Christine——? [*Goes to the speaking tube, knocks on it, and listens.*]

MISS JULIE: Has he been to his desk?

JEAN: It's Jean, milord. [*Listens. The audience cannot hear what is said to him.*] Yes, milord. [*Listens.*] Yes, milord. At once. [*Listens.*] Yes, milord. In half an hour.

MISS JULIE [*desperately frightened.*] What does he say? For God's sake, what does he say?

JEAN: He wants his boots and his coffee in half an hour.

MISS JULIE: In half an hour, then——! Oh, I'm so tired! I can't feel anything, I can't repent, can't run away, can't stay, can't live—can't die. Help me! Order me, and I'll obey you like a dog. Do me this last service, save my honour, save his name! You know what I ought to will myself to do, but I can't. Will me to, Jean, order me!

JEAN: I don't know—now I can't either—I don't understand—it's just as though this coat made me—I *can't* order you—and now, since his lordship spoke to me—I can't explain it properly, but—oh, it's this damned lackey that sits on my back—I think if his lordship came down now and ordered me to cut my throat, I'd do it on the spot.

MISS JULIE: Then pretend that you are he, and I am you. You acted so well just now, when you went down on your knees—then you were an aristocrat—or—haven't you ever been to the theatre and seen a hypnotist? [JEAN *nods.*] He says to his subject: "Take the broom!", and he takes it. He says: "Sweep!", and he sweeps——

JEAN: But the subject has to be asleep.

MISS JULIE [*in an ecstasy*]: I am already asleep—the whole room is like smoke around me—and you look like an iron stove—

which resembles a man dressed in black, with a tall hat—and your eyes shine like coals, when the fire is dying—and your face is a white smear, like ash—— [*The sun's rays have now reached the floor and are shining on* JEAN.] It's so warm and good——! [*She rubs her hands as though warming them before a fire.*] And so bright—and so peaceful——!

JEAN [*takes the razor and places it in her hand*]: Here's the broom. Go now—while it's bright—out to the barn—and—— [*Whispers in her ear.*]

MISS JULIE [*awake*]: Thank you. Now I am going to rest. But just tell me this—those who are first—they too can receive grace? Say it to me—even if you don't believe it.

JEAN: Those who are first? No, I can't! But, wait—— Miss Julie—now I see it! You are no longer among the first. You are—among the last!

MISS JULIE: That's true. I am among the last of all. I am the last. Oh! But now I can't go! Tell me once more—say I must go!

JEAN: No, now I can't either. I can't!

MISS JULIE: And the first shall be last.

JEAN: Don't think, don't think! You take all my strength from me, you make me a coward. What? I thought the bell moved! No. Shall we stuff paper in it? To be so afraid of a bell! Yes, but it isn't only a bell—there's someone sitting behind it—a hand sets it in motion—and something else sets the hand in motion—you've only got to close your ears, close your ears! Yes, but now he's ringing louder! He'll ring till someone answers—and then it'll be too late. The police will come—and then——!

Two loud rings on the bell.

JEAN [*cringes, then straightens himself up*]: It's horrible. But there can be no other ending. Go!

MISS JULIE *walks firmly out through the door.*

Introduction to
CREDITORS

STRINDBERG wrote CREDITORS at Holte in Denmark almost immediately after MISS JULIE, in August-September 1888. It seems to have taken him about a month.

He began it in the old castle at Lyngby where he had written MISS JULIE, but before he completed it he was forced to leave after an undignified row with the bailiff, his former friend, the gipsy-like Ludwig Hansen. Hansen had a seventeen-year-old sister named Martha Magdalene, and Strindberg, who had for some time been deprived by Siri of his conjugal rights, had a brief affair with the girl. She promptly accused him of raping her, and Strindberg, as he sadly reported to Edvard Brandes on 4 September: "was driven out by revolver shots, unlawful entry, gipsy dances and eight dogs, after I had paid my September rent in advance." The Danish newspapers learned about this and created a scandal. To escape from the publicity, Strindberg departed with his friend Pehr Staaff on a short trip to Berlin, without informing his family and leaving Siri to face the music.

From Berlin, on 19 September, he sent Siri a characteristic explanation of the affair. "You knew about my relationship with the girl Martha. I never had any intentions towards her, but Hansen sent her over on errands in the evenings after I had gone to bed and in the mornings when I was getting up, and so——! I only went with her once, and then with a sheath, so that I am (almost) sure she didn't get pregnant; if she is I shall pay for the child's upkeep, though I think other men are the father [sic]. But not until a doctor has certified that she is pregnant. . . . I regarded our marriage as dissolved, you agreed, and I kept the matter no more secret from you than delicacy demanded."

After a few days, he returned to Denmark and settled in a hotel at Holte. From there, on 29 September, he wrote to Joseph Seligmann, the Swedish publisher who had recently accepted MISS JULIE after its rejection by Bonnier:

"The attached tragedy was written for the Théâtre Libre at the same time as MISS JULIE. I didn't want to publish it in Swedish because my enemies always write commentaries on my work designed to damage me. But now that I have seen from the attached advertisement [of a translation of Ernst Alhgren's *roman à clef* MONEY] how intimately one is allowed to write, I send for your perusal this play, which is finer than MISS JULIE and in which I have more successfully achieved this new form, in the hope that you may be willing to print it with the other play in one volume. The plot is exciting, as spiritual murder must be; the analysis and the motivation are exhaustive, the viewpoint impartial; the author judges no one, he merely explains and forgives; and although he has made even the promiscuous woman sympathetic, this does not mean that he is advocating promiscuity. On the contrary, he says specifically that it is a bad thing, because of the disagreeable consequences which it brings."

Seligmann, however, refused CREDITORS, on the ground not that it was immoral but that it was too intimate and too obviously descriptive of Strindberg's own marriage. Strindberg replied that he had based Tekla on the authoress Victoria Benedictsson, who had committed suicide a few months earlier —an explanation which it is difficult to accept, for CREDITORS paints a very accurate picture of his own marital troubles, or at any rate his view of them. The previous spring he had completed an autobiographical novel in French entitled LE PLAIDOYER D'UN FOU (THE APOLOGY OF A FOOL), which deals in embarrassing detail with Strindberg's relations with his wife and her former husband, Baron Carl Gustav von Wrangel. CREDITORS overlaps to a considerable degree with this novel, in which Strindberg describes how his wife prepares to free herself from "her troublesome creditor", and refers to her former husband as "an idiot". Strindberg still feared that Wrangel (who, like the former husband in the play, was called Gustav) might reappear and regain her affections, or take some kind of revenge. At the same time, Strindberg put much of himself into this character, as well as into Adolf; he was already seeking a divorce from Siri, and this was how he would like to behave towards any future husband whom she might acquire.

Adolf was his present self; Gustav a kind of idealised future self. This ideal of the strong and ruthless man he had taken, at any rate partly, from Nietzsche, with whom he was at this time in correspondence. The power of "suggestion" was something that had interested him for a long time. In 1886–7, just before he began THE FATHER, Strindberg had written a series of essays on what we would nowadays call psychological warfare between individuals; he intended to collect them into a volume which was to be entitled VIVISECTIONS. He had recently read and been much influenced by Hippolyte Bernheim's book DE LA SUGGESTION and Max Nordau's PARADOXES. In one of these essays Strindberg described how he had, by means of his superior brain and stronger nerve-power, been able to "crush into powder" the brain of a man who he believed was trying to do the same to him. This power of suggestion he had of course used as thematic material in both THE FATHER and MISS JULIE. But in the opening scene of CREDITORS he shows it actually taking place on the stage. In an essay on Ibsen's ROSMERSHOLM, which Strindberg wrote after THE FATHER, he refers to Rebecca, whom he regarded as having driven Rosmer's wife to her death by suggestion, as "an unconscious cannibal, who has devoured the dead wife's soul". This image of the "suggester" as a cannibal he was to use in CREDITORS, as indeed he already had in THE FATHER.

On 16 October 1888 he wrote again to Seligmann asking him to reconsider his decision and publish CREDITORS. "It is a great favourite with me, and I read it again and again, continually discovering new subtleties. Everything is intimate nowadays . . . [he lists several examples, including work by

Zola, Daudet and the Goncourts] . . . MISS JULIE is still a compromise with romanticism and *coulisses* . . . but CREDITORS is modern right through, humane, lovable, all three of its characters sympathetic, interesting from start to finish." He did not receive a reply to this letter, and on 4 November he wrote to Seligmann: "Upon mature consideration I have now decided not to publish CREDITORS in Swedish, and beg you to return it." Accordingly, CREDITORS was first published in Danish in February 1889, and did not appear in Swedish until a year later.

That winter (as described above in the Introduction to MISS JULIE) Strindberg formulated his plans for a Scandinavian Experimental Theatre on the model of Antoine's Théâtre Libre. CREDITORS was to form one of the first offerings, and astonishingly, except that no action of Strindberg's is really astonishing, he offered the part of Tekla to Siri. Even more astonishingly, considering that the character was so plainly and spitefully based on her, she accepted it. On 16 November he wrote to his French translator, David Bergström, in a mixture of incredulity and jubilation: "Here's news for you! My wife has read *both* the plays [i.e. MISS JULIE and CREDITORS], is thrilled with the parts, and is willing to play them. So there'll be no difficulties about anything being too "intimate", for who is in a better position to judge than she?" On 21 November he tells Bergström that his theatre is to open around 6 January with the two plays in a double bill. "MISS JULIE entirely in Swedish; CREDITORS in Danish, acted by Danes. Two performances at the Dagmar Theatre, and then out on the road!"

As has been explained, however, various delays postponed the opening, and when it had been finally fixed for 2 March MISS JULIE was banned by the Danish censor. CREDITORS thus had to wait until the following week, 9 March 1889, before receiving its première, at the Dagmar Theatre in Copenhagen, where it shared a triple bill with PARIAH and THE STRONGER, both of which Strindberg had written that January. Tekla was played, not by Siri but by a young and inexperienced Danish actress named Nathalia Larsen; Gustav by Hans Riber Hunderup, who had played the Captain in THE FATHER sixteen months before; and Adolf by Gustav Wied, a young man who was later to make something of a name for himself as a comic writer. The last-named's performance as the weakling husband was apparently most unfortunate. The correspondent of *Vort Land* wrote: "People laughed till the tears sprang to their eyes as the tiny, slender author writhed like a snake in a monster of an armchair up there on the stage. There was no question of hearing his lines; he practically whispered, partly from stage-fright, partly through lack of voice." Nathalia Larsen was obviously too inexperienced for the difficult role of Tekla, and the play, not surprisingly, created only a moderate impression. A week later the company crossed the Sound and repeated their performance in Malmö, where the critic of *Sydsvenska Dagbladet* disliked the play and complained of "the acting style of these dilettantes, which is very different from what we are accustomed to seeing and hearing. (Among other things, we are used to hearing the actor speak louder than the prompter and not, as here, vice versa.)"

The only member of the cast to escape censure was Hunderup, to whom Strindberg, shortly before the première, gave some interesting advice on how to play Gustav. "For God's sake", he wrote on 3 March 1889, "act it throughout with a playful *bonhomie*, like a man who knows he is superior. And above all the scene when Gustav tells how his divorce took place, merely as an experiment in psychological destruction—so that Tekla speaks the truth when she says of Gustav that he doesn't 'preach or moralise'. . . . In a word: Gustav must be like a cat playing with a mouse before he sinks his teeth into it. Never malignant, never moralising, never preaching!"

The following year, CREDITORS was acted in Stockholm for a single matinée by a more experienced cast, and succeeded in creating some interest. "The absence of banal artificialities in the plot", commented one critic, "is as striking as the consistency of the characterisation." But as with so many of

Strindberg's plays it was in Germany and France that CREDITORS first achieved any real success. On 22 January 1893 it was performed at the Residenztheater in Berlin with Rosa Bertens as Tekla, and aroused much admiration; while on 21 June 1894, Aurélien Lugné-Poe produced it, in a somewhat cut version, at his newly-founded Théâtre de L'Oeuvre in Paris, himself taking the part of Adolf, and the public received it with "tumultuous applause". In 1895 it was played at the Freie Bühne of Munich, in the corner of a room in a private apartment before an audience of fifty people; in 1898 it received a full-scale production in the same city at the new Schauspielhaus; and in 1899 it was staged in Vienna. But it was not until after the turn of the century that it was again performed in Sweden, and only after Strindberg's death did his countrymen acclaim it as the masterpiece which it is.

CREDITORS has since come to be regarded, both in Scandinavia and elsewhere, as one of Strindberg's most powerful plays. In 1959 it was presented by the Fifty-Nine Theatre Company at the Lyric Opera House, Hammersmith, with Mai Zetterling, Michael Gough and Lyndon Brook acting under the direction of the Finnish producer Casper Wrede, in one of the few effective performances of a Strindberg play that this country has seen. T. C. Worsley, in the *Financial Times*, wrote of "the richness and compression of this superbly taut, tense and terrible little play"; Milton Shulman in the *Evening Standard* observed: "Strindberg's character delineation and barbed, incisive prose vibrate with a subtle intellectual power that has a fresh contemporary ring to it even after seventy years"; and Sir Gerald Barry, in the B.B.C. Critics programme, remarked upon "the enormous and amazing psycho-analytical insight of a man writing before a word of Freud had ever been read."

CREDITORS

A Tragi-Comedy
(1888)

CHARACTERS

TEKLA
ADOLF, her husband, a painter
GUSTAV, her former husband, a teacher, travelling under an assumed name
TWO LADIES
A PORTER

This translation of CREDITORS was commissioned by the 59 Theatre Company, and was first performed on 3 March 1959 at the Lyric Opera House, Hammersmith. The cast was:

ADOLF	Lyndon Brook
GUSTAV	Michael Gough
TEKLA	Mai Zetterling
TWO LADIES	June Bailey, Helen Montague
A PORTER	Howard Baker

Designed by Malcolm Pride
Produced by Casper Wrede

A drawing room at a seaside resort. In the background, a door leading to a verandah with a view of the landscape. Right, a table with newspapers. A chair stands to the left of the table, and a sofa to the right. In the right-hand wall is a door to another room.

> ADOLF *and* GUSTAV *are at the table, right.* ADOLF *is modelling a wax figure on a miniature stand. His two crutches are beside him.* GUSTAV *is smoking a cigar.*

ADOLF: . . . and for all this, I have to thank you, my dear Gustav.

GUSTAV: Oh, nonsense.

ADOLF: No, I mean it. The first few days my wife was away, I just lay on a sofa absolutely helpless, couldn't do anything, I just lay there longing for her to come back. It was as if she'd gone off with my crutches. I couldn't move. Then, when I had slept for a few days, I began to come alive again and collect my thoughts. My brain, which had been in a fever, gradually cooled, my old ideas came back to me, my passion for work, my urge to create, returned, my eye re-discovered its old sureness, its daring. And then you came.

GUSTAV: You were in a miserable state when I met you, I admit, hobbling around on those crutches. But I don't think you should assume that I'm responsible for your recovery. You just needed rest, and a man to talk to.

ADOLF: Yes, I suppose that's true, like everything you say. I used to have a lot of friends, but when I married I didn't think I needed them any more. I was content with the woman of my choice. Then I began to mix in new circles and made new friends. But my wife grew jealous of them. She wanted to have me to herself, and, what was worse, she wanted to have my friends to herself, too. And I was left alone with my jealousy.

GUSTAV: You are prone to that disease, aren't you?

ADOLF: [I was afraid of losing her—and wanted to make sure I wouldn't. Was that so strange?]* Mind you, I was never afraid of her being unfaithful to me——

GUSTAV: Oh no, husbands never fear that.

ADOLF: Yes, isn't that strange? What I was afraid of was that her friends might gain influence over her, and so come indirectly to have power over me. And I couldn't bear that.

GUSTAV: You and your wife didn't always agree, then?

ADOLF: My wife's a very independent woman—why are you smiling?

GUSTAV: Go on. A very independent woman.

ADOLF: Who doesn't want to take anything from me.

GUSTAV: But will take anything from anyone else?

ADOLF [*pauses*]: Yes. She seems to hate everything I say simply because I say it, not because it's unreasonable. In fact, she often repeats my ideas as though she'd thought of them herself. It's even happened that a friend of mine has repeated something to her which I'd said to him, and she's thought it splendid. Anything's splendid as long as it doesn't come from me.

GUSTAV: In other words, you're not really happy?

ADOLF: No, I'm very happy. I've got the woman I wanted, and I've never wanted anyone else.

GUSTAV: And you've never wanted to be free?

* Square brackets indicate cuts made for the 1959 Hammersmith production.

ADOLF: No, I don't think so. Sometimes I've thought I might find a kind of peace if I was free, but every time she goes away I long for her as I long for the use of my legs. It's funny, but sometimes I feel she doesn't really exist except as a part of me, an intestine which has been taken out and has carried my will and my appetite for life with it. [As though my spirit had passed from me into her.]

GUSTAV: Perhaps you're right. Perhaps she has.

ADOLF: Oh, no, she wouldn't. She's a very independent woman, with lots of ideas of her own. When I first met her, I was nothing. A would-be artist, a child, whom she decided to bring up and educate.

GUSTAV: But later you developed her mind and educated her?

ADOLF: No. She stopped developing. I went on.

GUSTAV: Yes, it's odd the way her writing deteriorated after that first book, or at any rate got no better. But of course she had a rewarding subject. Her first husband, they say? You never met him, did you? He's said to have been an idiot.

ADOLF: No, I never met him. He'd gone abroad for six months. But, judging by the picture she drew of him, he must have been a prize idiot. [*Pause.*] And her picture was a true one, you can be sure of that.

GUSTAV: Mm. Then why do you suppose she married him?

ADOLF: Because she didn't know him. You can't really know a person until you've—er——

GUSTAV: Exactly. Which is why people should not marry until they've—er——! Well, he was a tyrant, of course.

ADOLF: Of course?

GUSTAV: Aren't all husbands? [*Chancing his arm.*] You, for instance?

ADOLF: I? I let my wife come and go exactly as she pleases.

GUSTAV: What else could you do, lock her up? But, tell me, do you like her being away for the night?

ADOLF: No, I do not!

GUSTAV: You see! [*Changes his tone.*] Between us, it might make you look a bit ridiculous.

ADOLF: Ridiculous? Can a man become ridiculous simply because he shows he trusts his wife?

GUSTAV: Certainly he can. And you are. Utterly ridiculous.

ADOLF [*violently*]: Am I? We'll soon change that.

GUSTAV: Now don't get so excited. You'll have a fit.

ADOLF: But why doesn't it make her look ridiculous if I'm away for the night?

GUSTAV: That's the way things are. And while you sit here working out the whys and wherefores, the damage is done.

ADOLF: What damage?

GUSTAV: However, that first husband of hers was a tyrant, and she married him to make herself independent. A girl can only become independent by acquiring a *chaperon*, the so-called husband.

ADOLF: I see what you mean.

GUSTAV: And you're the *chaperon*.

ADOLF: I?

GUSTAV: Well, you're her husband, aren't you? [ADOLF *is speechless.*] Aren't I right?

ADOLF [*uneasily*]: I don't know. You live with a woman for years, without ever really thinking about your relationship with her, then one day you ask yourself a question about it, and then there's no end to it. Gustav, you are my friend! You are the only real friend I have ever had. These last eight days, since you came to this hotel, you have given me courage to face life again. Your magnetism has infected me, you've been like a watchmaker, mending the works inside my head and winding up the mainspring. You can hear for yourself how much more clearly I think, how much more freely I talk. My voice has got back its old resonance—I think, anyway.

GUSTAV: Yes, why is that?

ADOLF: I don't know, perhaps it becomes a habit to lower one's voice when one speaks to a woman. Tekla is always telling me that I shout.

GUSTAV: So you drop your voice to a whisper and creep back under the doormat?

ADOLF: Don't say that! [*Reflects.*] Perhaps it's even worse—but don't let's talk about it now. Where was I? Ah, yes. You came here, and opened my eyes to the secrets of my art. Mind you, I'd been conscious for some time of a waning interest in painting, because it didn't afford me an adequate means of expressing what I wanted to say, and when you rationalised it for me, when you explained why painting is not contemporary enough to be a satisfactory medium for the creative artist today, then it all suddenly became clear, and I realised I could never work in colour again.

GUSTAV: Are you quite sure you'll never be able to paint again? You don't think there's any danger of your having a relapse?

ADOLF: Absolutely none! I've proved it! When I went to bed the evening after our conversation, I went through your line of reasoning point by point, and I was convinced you were right. But when I woke, after a good night's sleep which had cleared my head, it suddenly hit me that you might have been wrong; so I jumped out of bed, picked up my brushes to start painting—but I couldn't! The illusion was gone—the canvas was just a daub of colours—it seemed incredible that anything I'd ever done had ever been more than a square of canvas smudged with paint. The veil had fallen from my eyes, and I could no more have started to paint again than I could have become a child again.

GUSTAV: You realised that the fundamental yearning of our

age for reality, its craving for the concrete and tangible, could only find expression through sculpture—wrestling with the third dimension?

ADOLF [*uncertainly*]: The third dimension—yes.

GUSTAV: So you became a sculptor. Or rather, you were a sculptor already, but had lost your way and needed a guide to put you back on the right road again. [Tell me, do you feel the true creative urge when you work now?

ADOLF: Now I am alive!]

GUSTAV: May I see what you are doing?

ADOLF: A female figure.

GUSTAV: No model! And so full of life!

ADOLF [*dully*]: Yes, but it does resemble someone. It's strange; she's got into my blood, as I have into hers.

GUSTAV: There's nothing strange about that. You know what transfusion is?

ADOLF: Blood transfusion? Yes.

GUSTAV: You have bled yourself too much. Looking at this figure, I understand a thing or two I had only guessed at before. You have loved her tremendously.

ADOLF: Yes. So much so that I couldn't tell whether she is I or I am she. When she smiles, I smile. When she cries, I cry. And, imagine it, when she bore our child, I distinctly felt the labour pains.

GUSTAV: My dear friend, it hurts me to say this, but you are already displaying the first symptoms of epilepsy.

ADOLF [*shaken*]: I? How can you say that?

GUSTAV: I've seen the same symptoms in a younger brother I once had who indulged in carnal excess.

ADOLF: How—what were the symptoms?

> GUSTAV *demonstrates vividly.* ADOLF *listens attentively, unconsciously imitating him.*

GUSTAV: It was a horrible sight, and if you're not feeling well I shan't torture you with a description of it.

ADOLF [*in agony*]: No, no, go on, go on.

GUSTAV: Well, the poor boy had gone and married an innocent young girl—you know, pretty curls, doe eyes, a baby face, and a mind as pure as an angel's. But none the less, she managed to usurp the male prerogative——

ADOLF: What's that?

GUSTAV: The initiative, of course; and the result was that his angel very nearly wafted him up to Heaven. But first he had to hang upon his cross and feel the nails in his flesh. It was horrifying.

ADOLF [*breathlessly*]: How do you mean?

GUSTAV [*slowly*]: We'd be sitting, talking, he and I—and after a while, his face would go as white as chalk. His arms and legs went stiff, and his thumbs twisted round inside his hands, like this. [*Makes a gesture, which* ADOLF *imitates.*] Then his eyes became bloodshot, and he began to chew, like this. [*Chews.* ADOLF *copies him.*] The saliva rattled in his throat, his chest contracted as though it was being crushed in a vice, the pupils of his eyes flickered like gas-jets, his tongue whipped the saliva into a froth, and he sank—slowly—back—and—down—in his chair, as though he was drowning. Then——

ADOLF [*whispers*]: Stop.

GUSTAV: Aren't you feeling well?

ADOLF: No.

GUSTAV [*gets up and fetches a glass of water*]: Drink this, and we'll talk about something else.

ADOLF [*feebly*]: Thank you. But—go on.

GUSTAV: Oh, yes. Well, when he came to he couldn't remember anything that had happened. He'd been quite unconscious. Has that happened to you?

ADOLF: Yes, I've had fainting fits once or twice, but the doctor says it's due to anaemia.

GUSTAV: That's the way it begins, but, believe me, it'll develop into epilepsy if you don't take care of yourself.

ADOLF: What shall I do?

GUSTAV: Well, to begin with you must abstain entirely from intercourse.

ADOLF: How long for?

GUSTAV: Six months, at least.

ADOLF: I can't. It'd upset our marriage.

GUSTAV: Goodbye to you, then.

ADOLF [*drapes a cloth over the wax figure*]: I can't.

GUSTAV: You can't save your life? But, tell me, since you've already taken me so deeply into your confidence, is there nothing else, [no little secret that torments you? It's rare to find only one cause of discord—life is so varied and full of occasions for conflict. Have you] no skeleton you're hiding away? [You said just now that you had a child whom you—gave away. Why didn't you keep it?

ADOLF: My wife wanted it that way.

GUSTAV: Why? You can tell me.

ADOLF: At the age of three it began to look like him. Her former husband.

GUSTAV: Ah!!] Have you seen this former husband?

ADOLF: No, never. [I caught a glimpse of a bad portrait of him once, but I couldn't see any likeness.

GUSTAV: Well, you can never trust portraits. Anyway, he might have become quite a different person since. But, tell me, didn't this arouse your suspicions at all?

ADOLF: Not at all. The child was born a year after our marriage, and anyway her husband was abroad when I met Tekla—here, in this very house, as a matter of fact. That's why we come here every summer.]

GUSTAV: [Well then, you've no possible ground for suspicion. And why should you have any? It often happens when a widow remarries that her new child resembles her dead husband. Tiresome business—that's why they used to burn widows in India, as you know.] But have you never been jealous of him? Of his memory? Wouldn't it sicken you if you met him when you were out for a walk, and with his eyes on your Tekla he said "we" instead of "I"? "We"!

ADOLF: I won't deny that idea has haunted me.

GUSTAV: There you are! And you'll never be rid of it. Don't you realise there are false notes in life which can never be tuned? The only thing to do is to stop your ears with wax and work. Work, grow old, pile as many new impressions as you can into the cupboard to keep the skeleton from rattling.

ADOLF: Sorry to interrupt you, but it's extraordinary how much you resemble Tekla sometimes when you talk. You've a habit of half-closing your left eye as though you were squinting down a rifle. And your eyes—almost seem to hypnotise me, the way hers sometimes do.

GUSTAV: Oh, really?

ADOLF: There! You said: "Oh, really?" in just the same casual way that she does.

GUSTAV: Perhaps we're distantly related—since all human beings are related. Still, it is curious, and it'll be most interesting to meet your wife and see these things for myself.

ADOLF: Mind you, she never borrows any of my expressions. Indeed, she seems to avoid using phrases which I use. And I've never seen her imitate my mannerisms, the way married people usually do.

GUSTAV: This woman has never loved you.

ADOLF: What!

GUSTAV: Forgive me, but—for a woman loving means taking, taking, and if she doesn't take anything from a man it means she doesn't love him. She has never loved you.

ADOLF: Do you think it's impossible for her to love more than once?

GUSTAV: Yes. One only gets fooled once; after that, one goes round with one's eyes open. You've never been deceived—beware of those who have. They're dangerous.

ADOLF: Your words are like knives—I can feel them cutting something to pieces inside me—but I can't prevent it, and it's good, because I know these are boils that are being lanced. She has never loved me! Why did she take me, then?

GUSTAV: Tell me first how she came to take you. [And whether it was you who took her or she who took you.]

ADOLF: God knows if I can do that. [Or how it came about. It didn't happen in a day.]

GUSTAV: Shall I try to guess how it happened?

ADOLF: You can't!

GUSTAV: Oh, from what you've told me about yourself and your wife, I think I can work it out. [Listen, and I'll tell you.] [*Nonchalantly, almost jokingly.*] Her husband is away on a study trip, and she is alone. First, she is aware of the pleasure of being free; then of a feeling of emptiness—she must have felt a bit empty after living alone for a fortnight. Then he turns up, and gradually the emptiness is filled. She begins to compare the two men, and the memory of her husband begins to pale—well, he's a long way away—the square of the distance, etcetera. But when they find their passions awakening, they become uneasy, their consciences prick them, they remember him. They look for some kind of protection, cover their shame with fig-leaves, and play at being brother and sister—and the more their bodies want each other, the more desperately they try to persuade themselves that their relationship is spiritual.

ADOLF: Brother and sister? How do you know that?

GUSTAV: I guessed. Children play mummy and daddy, but when they're grown up they play brother and sister. To hide what must be hidden. They take a vow of chastity, and begin a little game of hide-and-seek, until, one day, their hands touch in a dark corner where they are sure no one can see them. [*With assumed severity*.] But in their hearts they know that there is someone who can see them through the darkness, and they become frightened, and then, once they are frightened, the absent one begins to haunt them—he looms larger, is transformed, and becomes a nightmare which disturbs their blissful slumbers, a creditor knocking on the door. They see his black hand between theirs as they eat at table, they hear his harsh breathing in the stillness of the night, which no sound should disturb but the thumping of their pulses. He cannot stop them from having each other, but he can disturb their happiness. And then they sense his invisible power, they try, vainly, to flee from the memory which dogs them, from the debt they have left unpaid, [from the reproach of public opinion] and because they lack the strength to carry the burden of their guilt, a scapegoat must be found and sacrificed. They were freethinkers, but dared not go to him and tell him to his face: "We love each other!" Well, they were cowards, and so they had to lay his ghost. Am I right?

ADOLF: Yes. But you forget that she educated me and gave me new ideas——

GUSTAV: No, I hadn't forgotten. But, tell me, why didn't she succeed in educating the other fellow too, and turn him into a freethinker?

ADOLF: Oh, he was an idiot.

GUSTAV: True, he was an idiot. But that's a very vague word, and in her novel the main proof of his idiocy seems to have been that he didn't understand her. Forgive me, but is your wife such a profound person? I have found no evidence of it in her writing.

ADOLF: Neither have I. But I confess that I, too, have some difficulty in understanding her. Our minds don't work the same way. Every time I try to understand her, something seems to break inside my head.

GUSTAV: Perhaps you're an idiot, too.

ADOLF: No, I don't think so. I almost invariably think she's wrong. For example, read this letter that I received from her today. [*Takes a letter from his pocket-book.*]

GUSTAV [*glances through it*]: Hm. This handwriting seems familiar.

ADOLF: Almost like a man's, isn't it?

GUSTAV: Yes, I know at least one man whose handwriting it resembles. She calls you "brother". Do you still act that little comedy? The fig-leaf stays in position, if somewhat withered.

ADOLF: I like to show respect for her.

GUSTAV: I see, it's to make you respect her that she calls herself "sister"?

ADOLF: I want to respect her more than myself. [I want her to be my better self.

GUSTAV: Be that yourself! It's more uncomfortable, but do you want to be subservient to your wife?

ADOLF: Yes, I do.] I like being a little worse than she is. For example, I've taught her to swim, and now I like to hear her boast that she's a stronger and bolder swimmer than I am. At first I pretend to be slow and timid to encourage her, and then one fine day I found I was in fact slower and more timid than she. It was if she'd really taken my courage from me.

GUSTAV: Have you taught her anything else?

ADOLF: Yes—between ourselves. I've taught her to spell. She couldn't before. But when she took over the household correspondence, I stopped writing, and—would you believe it?—I'm so out of practice that I now sometimes make mistakes. But do you think she remembers it was I who taught her to spell in the first place? Oh, no. I'm the idiot now.

GUSTAV: So you're the idiot already?

ADOLF: Only jokingly, of course.

GUSTAV: Of course! But this is cannibalism! [You know what cannibalism is? Savages eat their enemies to gain possession of their most enviable qualities.] The woman has eaten your soul, your courage, your learning——

ADOLF: And my faith in myself! It was I who encouraged her to write her first book——

GUSTAV [*pulls a face*]: Really?

ADOLF: I praised her, even when I thought it was rather cheap. It was I who introduced her into literary circles, where she was able to feed on the best minds. It was I who, through my personal intervention, protected her from criticism. It was I who fanned her belief in herself and kept it alive, fanned so hard that I had no energy left for my own work. I gave and gave and gave, till I had nothing left for myself. Do you know, when my success as a painter seemed to be overshadowing her and her reputation, I tried to sustain her belief in herself by belittling myself and my work. I talked so much about the unimportance of painting as an art, and found so many arguments to support my thesis, that in the end I found I believed it myself. So it was only a house of cards that you blew down.

GUSTAV: Forgive me for reminding you of this, but when we started this conversation you said she never took anything from you.

ADOLF: Not now. There isn't anything left to take.

GUSTAV: The snake is full. Now she vomits up her victim.

ADOLF: Perhaps she took more than I realise. [Things I wasn't aware of.]

GUSTAV: You can be sure she did. And she took without your noticing it. That's called stealing.

ADOLF: Perhaps she never educated me after all.

GUSTAV: No. You educated her. But she was clever enough to make you think that it was the other way round. How did she educate you, if I may ask?

ADOLF: Well, first of all—er——

GUSTAV: Yes?

ADOLF: Well, I——

GUSTAV: Never mind about yourself. What did she do?

ADOLF: I don't know.

GUSTAV: You see!

ADOLF: Anyway, she'd destroyed my faith, too, and I began to go further and further downhill until you came and gave me a new belief.

GUSTAV [*smiles*]: In sculpture?

ADOLF [*uncertainly*]: Yes.

GUSTAV: And you believe in it? That *passé*, abstract survival from man's infancy? You really believe that you can [work with pure form—the third dimension—that you can] satisfy the craving of our age for reality—that you can create illusion without the aid of colour? You really believe that?

ADOLF [*crushed*]: No.

GUSTAV: Neither do I.

ADOLF: Why did you say you did, then?

GUSTAV: I felt sorry for you.

ADOLF: Yes. I am to be pitied. For now I am bankrupt. I haven't even got her.

GUSTAV: What do you need her for?

ADOLF: What I needed God for, before I became an atheist. Something to worship——

GUSTAV: Bury your need to worship, and let some healthier plant grow on its grave. A little honest contempt, for example——

ADOLF: I can't live without something to worship——

[GUSTAV: Slave!

ADOLF: Without a woman to worship.]

GUSTAV: Oh, for Christ's sake, go back to your God, then, if you must have something to abase yourself before. [An atheist who worships women! A freethinker who can't think freely!] Don't you realise what this profound, mystical, sphinx-like quality in your wife really is? It's just stupidity. Look at this! She doesn't know when to use "ph" and when to use "f". Skirts, that's all. Dress her in trousers, draw a charcoal moustache under her nose, sit down and listen to her coldly and soberly, then you'll hear the difference. She's just a phonograph which plays back your words and other people's with most of the quality gone. Have you ever seen a naked woman? Yes, of course. A half-developed man, a child stunted in mid-growth, a youth with udders on his chest, a case of chronic anaemia who has regular haemhorrages thirteen times a year. What can become of that?

ADOLF: Assuming that everything you say is right, why do I still feel that she and I are one?

GUSTAV: A hallucination—the fascination of a skirt. Or—perhaps you have in fact become alike. [There has been a levelling. Her capillary power has sucked her up to your level.] [*Takes out his watch.*] We have been talking for six hours and your wife will be here soon. Shall we stop now so that you can get some rest?

ADOLF: No, don't leave me. I daren't be alone.

GUSTAV: It's only for a moment, then your wife'll be here.

ADOLF: Yes, she'll be here. It's strange—I long for her, but I'm afraid of her; [she caresses me, she's tender, but] her kisses stifle me, drain something from me, anaesthetise me.

I feel like the child in a circus whom the clown pinches backstage so that it'll look rosy-cheeked before the public.

GUSTAV: My friend, your condition alarms me. Without being a doctor, I can tell you that you are a dying man. One only has to look at your latest paintings to know that.

ADOLF: Really? How?

GUSTAV: Your colour is so watery and pale and thin that the canvas stares through it like a yellow corpse. I seem to see your sunken, putty-coloured cheeks——

ADOLF: Stop, stop!

GUSTAV: But it's not just my personal opinion. Haven't you read today's paper?

ADOLF [*starts up*]: No.

GUSTAV: Here it is, on the table.

ADOLF [*gropes towards the paper, but lacks the courage to take hold of it*]: Is there something about it here?

GUSTAV: Read it. Or would you like me to read it to you?

ADOLF: No.

GUSTAV: I'll go if you'd rather.

ADOLF: No, no, no! I don't know—I think I'm beginning to hate you—and yet I can't let you go. You haul me up out of the ice-cold water, but as soon as I'm out you hit me on the head and push me under again. As long as I kept my secrets to myself, I still had some entrails left inside me, but now I'm empty. There's a painting by one of the Italian masters which shows a torture scene. They are winding the entrails out of a saint on a winch. The martyr lies there and sees himself growing thinner and thinner while the roll on the winch grows thicker and thicker. It seems to me that you have been growing all the while you have been digging into me so that when you go you'll take all my entrails with you and leave only a shell behind.

CREDITORS

GUSTAV: What an imagination you've got! Still, your wife will be bringing home your heart soon.

ADOLF: No. Not now. You've burned her. You've laid everything in ashes. My art, my love, my hope, my faith.

GUSTAV: That had been done already.

ADOLF: At least there was something that could have been salvaged. Now it's too late. Murderer!

GUSTAV: We've only burned the rubbish. Now we can sow in the ashes.

ADOLF: I hate you. Curse you!

GUSTAV: That's a good sign. You've still some spirit left. Now I shall haul you up again. Adolf! Will you obey me?

ADOLF: Do what you want with me. I'll obey.

GUSTAV [*gets up*]: Look at me.

ADOLF [*looks at him*]: Now you're looking at me with those other eyes—that seem to attract me.

[GUSTAV: Now listen carefully.

ADOLF: Yes, but talk about yourself. Don't talk about me any more. I'm like an open wound, I can't bear to be touched.]

GUSTAV: [There's nothing to say about me. I'm a teacher of dead languages and a widower. That's all.] Take my hand.

ADOLF: How terribly powerful you are! It's like gripping an electrical machine.

GUSTAV: And I was once as weak as you. Get up!

ADOLF [*gets up, and falls around* GUSTAV's *neck*]: I am like a legless child, and my brain lies open.

GUSTAV: Walk across the floor.

ADOLF: I can't.

GUSTAV: Walk across the floor, or I'll hit you.

ADOLF [*straightens up*]: What did you say?

GUSTAV: I shall hit you, I said.

ADOLF [*takes a jump backwards, furious*]: You?

GUSTAV: There, you see! The blood went to your head, and your self-esteeem was aroused. Now I shall pass some electricity into you. Where is your wife?

ADOLF: Where is she?

GUSTAV: Yes.

ADOLF: She is—at—a meeting.

GUSTAV: Are you sure?

ADOLF: Quite sure.

GUSTAV: What kind of a meeting?

ADOLF: To discuss a children's home.

GUSTAV: Did you part friends?

ADOLF [*hesitates*]: Not friends.

GUSTAV: Enemies, then. What did you say to annoy her?

ADOLF: I'm frightened of you. How can you know this?

GUSTAV: It's simple. I have three known factors, and from them I work out the unknown. What did you say to her?

ADOLF: I said—I only said three words, but they were dreadful, and I regret them.

GUSTAV: Don't regret. What were they?

ADOLF: I said: "You old flirt!"

GUSTAV: And then?

ADOLF: That was all.

GUSTAV: No. You said something else, but you've forgotten it, perhaps because you dare not remember it. You've hidden it away in a secret drawer. Now you must open it.

ADOLF: I don't remember!

GUSTAV: But I know what it was. You said: "You ought to be ashamed of yourself. You're too old to get another lover."

ADOLF: Did I say that? I must have said it. But how do you know?

GUSTAV: I heard her telling the story on the steamer while I was on my way here.

ADOLF: To whom?

GUSTAV: To four young men she had with her. She has a weakness for clean young men already——

ADOLF: Oh, that doesn't mean anything.

GUSTAV: Like playing brother and sister when in fact you're playing mummy and daddy.

ADOLF: You've seen her, then?

GUSTAV: Yes, I have. But you've never seen her as she is when you're not there. That, my dear friend, is why a man can never know his wife. Have you a photograph of her?

ADOLF *takes a photograph out of his pocket-book, curious.*

GUSTAV: Were you there when this was taken?

ADOLF: No.

GUSTAV: Look at it. Is it like the picture you painted of her? No. The features are the same, but the expression is quite different. But you can't see that, because you project your own image of her in front of it. Look at this now, look at it as a painter, forget the original. What does it show? I can see nothing but an affected coquette, inviting me to flirt with her. Can't you see that cynical expression round her mouth, which she always hides from you? Can't you see that her eyes are looking for a man, someone else, not you? Can't you see that her neckline is too low, that she's prinked up her hair, that her sleeve has ridden up? Can't you see it all?

ADOLF: Yes, I can see it now.

GUSTAV: Beware, my friend.

ADOLF: Of what?

GUSTAV: Of her revenge. Remember you wounded her where it hurts most, when you told her she can no longer attract another lover. If you had told her that her writing was rubbish, she would simply have laughed at your bad taste, but now—believe me, if she has not avenged herself on you already, it won't be her fault.

ADOLF: I must know the truth.

GUSTAV: Find out.

ADOLF: Find out?

GUSTAV: I'll help you if you like. [*Steamer hoots in distance.*] There's the steamer. She'll be here soon.

ADOLF: I must go down to meet her.

GUSTAV: No. You must stay here. Be off-hand with her. If her conscience is clear, she'll give you a dressing-down, if she's guilty she'll cuddle up to you and kiss you.

[ADOLF: Are you absolutely sure about that?

GUSTAV: Not absolutely. The hare sometimes turns on its track and throws a false scent, but I'll ferret out the truth.] [*Points to the door behind the chair.*] I shall take up my post over there in my room, and keep a watch, while you act in here. Then, when the performance is over, we will change parts; I shall come in and charm the snake while you go into my room through the other door. Then we will meet and compare notes. But stick to your guns! If you start to falter, I shall bang twice on the floor with a chair.

ADOLF: All right, but don't go away. I must be sure you're in the next room.

GUSTAV: Don't worry, I shall be there. [But don't be afraid later, when you see me at work dissecting a human soul and laying out the bits and pieces here on the table. It sounds nasty if you're a beginner, but once you've seen it you won't regret the experience.] Remember one thing. Not a word about your having met me, or anyone, while she's been away. Not a word. [I'll ferret out her weaknesses myself.] Ssh, she's here already, up in her room. Singing to herself—that means she's furious. Shoulders back, now, and sit there; then she'll have to sit here, and I can watch you both.

[ADOLF: We've an hour left before dinner. There aren't any other guests, or we'd have heard the bell, so that means we'll be alone, I'm afraid.

GUSTAV: Are you feeling faint?

ADOLF: I don't feel anything. Yes, I feel afraid of what's coming. But I can't stop it. The stone's begun to roll downhill, but it wasn't the last raindrop that started it off, nor the first one, but the sum of them all put together.

GUSTAV: Let it roll. You'll have no peace till it's started. *Au revoir!*]

GUSTAV goes. ADOLF nods goodbye; stands looking at the photograph, tears it up, and throws the bits under the table. Then he sits down in his chair, fingers his cravat nervously, runs his hand through his hair, plays with his coat lapel, etc. TEKLA enters, walks straight towards him, and kisses him— friendly, open, gay and charming.

TEKLA: Good afternoon, Little Brother. How are you today?

ADOLF [*half conquered, tries to resist her, says jokingly*]: What have you been up to, kissing me like that?

TEKLA: All right, I'll tell you. I've been wickedly extravagant.

ADOLF: Have you been enjoying yourself?

TEKLA: Very much! Not at that ghastly meeting, though. That was what the French call *merde*. But, tell me, what has Little Brother been doing while Squirrel was away? [*Looks around the room as though she was looking for someone or trying to sniff out something.*]

ADOLF: Just sitting here, being bored.

TEKLA: No one to keep you company?

ADOLF: No, all alone.

TEKLA [*looks at him, then sits on the sofa*]: Who's been sitting here, then?

ADOLF: There? Nobody.

TEKLA: That's very strange. The sofa's still warm, and this cushion's rumpled. Have you had a woman here?

ADOLF: I? You don't mean it.

TEKLA: You're blushing! I think Little Brother's been telling fibs. Come over here. Tell Squirrel what you have on your conscience. [*Pulls him over to her. He sinks down with his head on her knees.*]

ADOLF [*smiles*]: You're a little devil. Do you know that?

TEKLA: No, I'm terribly ignorant about myself.

ADOLF: You never think about yourself.

TEKLA [*sniffs and glances around*]: I only think of myself—I'm a dreadful egotist. But why so philosophical?

ADOLF: Put your hand on my forehead.

TEKLA [*flippantly*]: Is he tied up in knots? Shall I make it better: [*Kisses his forehead.*] There! Is that better?

ADOLF: Now it's better.

Pause.

TEKLA: Well, what have you been amusing yourself with? Have you been painting something?

ADOLF: No, I've given up painting.

TEKLA: What? You've given up painting?

ADOLF: Yes. Don't scold me. I can't help it, but I just cannot paint any more.

TEKLA: What are you going to do now?

ADOLF: I'm going to be a sculptor.

TEKLA: More new ideas!

ADOLF: Yes, now don't make a scene. Look at that figure.

TEKLA [*takes the cloth off the wax figure*]: Well, look at this! Who's it meant to be?

ADOLF: Guess!

TEKLA [*softly*]: Is it little Squirrel? Shame on you!

ADOLF: Don't you think it's a good likeness?

TEKLA: How should I know, when it hasn't got any face?

ADOLF: Yes, but—there's so much else that's beautiful——

TEKLA [*slaps his cheek provokingly*]: Be quiet, now, or I'll kiss you.

ADOLF [*protecting himself*]: Take care! Someone might come.

TEKLA: What do I care? Can't I kiss my own husband? I've got my legal rights.

ADOLF: Yes but, you know, the people here don't believe we're really married, because we kiss so much. The fact that we quarrel now and then doesn't convince them because lovers do that too.

TEKLA: Why do we need to quarrel? Why can't you always be nice like you are now? Tell me. Don't you want to be nice? Don't you want us to be happy?

ADOLF: Of course I do, but——

TEKLA: What's wrong now? Who's given you the idea that you mustn't paint any more?

ADOLF: You always suspect there's someone else behind everything I think. You're jealous.

TEKLA: Yes, I am. I'm afraid someone might take you away from me.

ADOLF: *You're* afraid? You know I could never love any woman but you. Without you I couldn't live.

TEKLA: It's not women I'm afraid of. No, it's the friends who put ideas into your head.

ADOLF [*probing*]: You are afraid, then. What are you afraid of?

TEKLA [*gets up*]: There has been someone here! Who was it?

ADOLF: Can't you bear me looking at you?

TEKLA: Not like that. That's not the way you usually look at me.

ADOLF: How am I looking at you now?

TEKLA: Lowering your eyelid, and squinting——

ADOLF: Yes! I want to see what you look like behind that pretty face!

TEKLA: Well, stare away! I've got nothing to hide! But—you're talking differently, too—you're using expressions—[*probing*]—you're philosophising. [*Goes threateningly towards him.*] Who has been here?

ADOLF: Only my doctor.

TEKLA: Your doctor? What doctor?

ADOLF: The doctor from Strömstad.

TEKLA: What's his name?

ADOLF: Sjöberg.

TEKLA: What did he say?

ADOLF: He said—yes—he said among other things that I was in danger of becoming an epileptic——

TEKLA: Among other things? What other things?

ADOLF: Something very distressing.

TEKLA: What? Tell me.

ADOLF: He forbade us to live like married people for a while.

TEKLA: I knew it. They want to part us. I've noticed it for some time.

ADOLF: You couldn't have noticed it, because it isn't true.

TEKLA: Couldn't I?

ADOLF: How could you notice something which isn't there unless fear had so over-excited your imagination as to make you see things which don't exist? What are you afraid of? That I might see you through someone else's eyes for what you really are, instead of what I've always thought you were?

TEKLA: Kindly control your imagination, Adolf. That is what makes men beasts.

ADOLF: Where did you learn that? From the clean young men on the boat?

TEKLA [*without losing her composure*]: Yes; there are things to be learned from young people, too.

ADOLF: I believe you're already beginning to fall in love with youth.

TEKLA: I always have done; that is why I have loved you. Do you object?

ADOLF: No. But I'd prefer to feel I was the only one.

TEKLA [*banteringly*]: My heart is so big, Little Brother, that there is room in it for many others besides you.

ADOLF: But Little Brother does not want to have any other little brothers.

TEKLA: Come to Squirrel now and have your hair pulled for being jealous. No, that's not the word. I think you're envious! Come!

GUSTAV *strikes twice with his chair from the next room.*

ADOLF: No, I don't want to play. I want to talk seriously.

TEKLA [*banteringly*]: Dear God, he wants to talk seriously! You have become horribly serious, haven't you? [*Takes his head and kisses him.*] Laugh a little now. That's better.

ADOLF [*smiles unwilling*]: Damn you, I really believe you're a witch.

TEKLA: Indeed I am, so don't you start being quarrelsome, or I shall witch away your life.

ADOLF [*gets up*]: Tekla! Sit over there and give me your profile, so that I can put the face on your figure.

TEKLA: Like this? [*Turns her profile towards him.*]

ADOLF [*stares at her, pretends to start modelling*]: Don't think about me, now, think about someone else.

TEKLA: I shall think about my latest conquest.

ADOLF: The clean young man?

TEKLA: Yes, him. He had such a tiny little moustache, and cheeks like a juicy peach, so soft and pink I wanted to bite them.

ADOLF [*his expression darkens*]: Keep that expression round your mouth.

TEKLA: What expression?

ADOLF: That cynical, wanton expression—I've never noticed it before.

TEKLA [*grimaces*]: Like this?

ADOLF: Just like that. [*Gets up*]. Do you know how Bret Harte describes an adulterous wife?

TEKLA [*smiles*]: No, I have never read Bret—er——

ADOLF: As a pale creature who cannot blush.

TEKLA: Oh? But surely when she meets her lover she blushes, even though her husband and Mr. Bret may not be there to see her do it?

ADOLF: You know that?

TEKLA [*in the same tone of voice*]: Yes. Since her husband cannot bring the blood to her head, he never sees this charming spectacle.

ADOLF [*furious*]: Tekla!

TEKLA: Little silly!

ADOLF: Tekla!

TEKLA: Say "Squirrel" and I shall blush prettily for you. Would you like me to? Shall I?

ADOLF [*disarmed*]: I'm so angry with you, you little monster, I've a good mind to bite you.

TEKLA [*playfully*]: Come and bite me, then. Come. [*Stretches out her arms towards him.*]

ADOLF [*puts his arms round her neck and kisses her*]: Yes, I'll bite you to death.

TEKLA [*jokingly*]: Take care. Someone might come.

ADOLF: What do I care? I don't care about anything in the world as long as I have you.

TEKLA: And—when you no longer have me?

ADOLF: Then I shall die.

TEKLA: But you don't have to worry about that, because I'm so old that no one else wants me.

ADOLF: Tekla, you haven't forgotten what I said that morning. I take it back.

TEKLA: Can you explain to me why you are so jealous and at the same time so sure of yourself?

ADOLF: No, I can't explain anything. Perhaps the knowledge that someone else once owned you still rankles inside me. Sometimes I feel our love is a fiction, a defence pact, a passion elevated into an affair of honour, and I dread nothing so much as that he should know I was unhappy. Ah! I have never seen him, but the mere thought that somewhere a man is waiting for our marriage to break up, a man who curses me every day and will howl with joy when he hears I have failed, the mere thought of it drives me mad, drives me into your arms [—fascinates me, paralyses me].

TEKLA: Do you think I would ever allow him that pleasure? Do you think I want to prove him a true prophet?

ADOLF: No, I can't believe you would.

TEKLA: Keep calm, then.

ADOLF: I can't. Your incessant flirting drives me crazy. Why do you have to play this game?

TEKLA: It isn't a game. I want to be liked. That's all.

ADOLF: Yes, but only by men.

TEKLA: Of course. Don't you know that a woman is never liked by other women?

ADOLF: Have you heard from—him—lately?

TEKLA: Not for six months.

ADOLF: Do you never think about him?

TEKLA: No. [We've had no communication with each other since the child died.]

ADOLF: And you haven't seen him?

TEKLA: No. I have heard he lives somewhere here on the west coast. But what makes you worry your head about him?

ADOLF: I don't know. These last few days, when I've been alone, I've sometimes thought how he must have felt when he suddenly found himself alone.

TEKLA: I believe your conscience is beginning to prick you.

ADOLF: Yes.

TEKLA: You feel like a thief, don't you?

ADOLF: Almost.

TEKLA: Charming! One steals a woman as one steals a child or a chicken. So you regard me as his private property. Thank you.

ADOLF: No, I regard you as his wife. That's much more than a property. That can never be replaced.

TEKLA: Don't be silly. As soon as you hear that he has remarried, these stupid ideas will vanish. You have replaced him for me.

ADOLF: Have I? Did you ever love him?

TEKLA: Certainly I did.

ADOLF: But then——?

TEKLA: I grew tired of him.

ADOLF: What if you should tire of me, too?

TEKLA: I won't.

ADOLF: Suppose another man should turn up with just those qualities which you now look for in a man? Just suppose he did. You would leave me.

TEKLA: No.

ADOLF: If you were so attracted to him that you couldn't give him up? You'd give me up, it stands to reason.

TEKLA: No, not necessarily.

ADOLF: You couldn't love two men at the same time?

TEKLA: Yes. Why not?

ADOLF: I can't see that.

TEKLA: It's possible, even if you can't see it. All people weren't created alike.

ADOLF: Now I am beginning to understand.

TEKLA: Oh, really?

ADOLF: Oh, really.

Pause. ADOLF *is trying hard to remember something that eludes him.*

ADOLF: Tekla! Do you know I am beginning to find your outspokenness rather painful?

TEKLA: You always used to regard it as my supreme virtue. You taught it to me.

ADOLF: Yes, but now it seems to me you're using it as a mask to hide behind.

TEKLA: It's my new strategy, you see.

ADOLF: I'm beginning to dislike this place. Let's go home tonight.

TEKLA: What a silly idea! I've only just come, and I don't want to go back again.

ADOLF: No, but I want to.

TEKLA: What do I care what you want? Go.

ADOLF: I order you to follow me by the next boat.

TEKLA: You order me? What kind of talk is that?

ADOLF: Do you realise that you are my wife?

TEKLA: Do you realise that you are my husband?

ADOLF: Yes, and there's a difference between the two.

TEKLA: So that's the tone you're taking. You've never loved me.

ADOLF: Haven't I?

TEKLA: No. Loving means giving.

ADOLF: Loving means giving if one is a man. If one is a woman, it means taking. And I've always been the one who has given, given, given!

TEKLA: What have you given?

ADOLF: Everything!

TEKLA: A great deal that was. Well, suppose you have. I have accepted, haven't I? Are you now going to show me the bill for all the presents you have given me? And if I have accepted, that only goes to prove that I have loved you. A women only takes presents from her lover.

ADOLF: Lover, yes! You never said a truer word. I have been your lover, but never your husband.

TEKLA: How much more pleasant for you, not having to be my *chaperon*. But if you're not happy with your position, you'll have to go, for a husband is the last thing I want.

ADOLF: Yes, I've noticed that. These last months, when I saw you itching to sneak away like a thief, to find your own circle of friends where you could shine in my feathers, glitter with my jewels, I wanted to remind you of the debt you owed me. And then I was transformed into the unpleasant creditor, whom one doesn't want to have about the place; then you wanted to cancel the debt you owed me, and stopped drawing from my account and turned to other lenders. Then I became your husband, in spite of myself, and then you began to hate me. Well, now I shall be your husband whether you like it or not, since I may not be your lover.

TEKLA [*playfully*]: Don't talk such nonsense, you little idiot.

ADOLF: Look, it's dangerous to go round thinking everyone is an idiot except yourself.

TEKLA: Doesn't everyone think that?

ADOLF: And I'm beginning to suspect that he—your first husband—may not have been such an idiot after all.

TEKLA: Oh, God, I believe you're beginning to feel sorry for him.

ADOLF: Yes, almost.

TEKLA: Well, well. Perhaps you'd like to meet him, and pour out your heart to him? What a charming picture! But I too am beginning to feel a certain nostalgia for him. I'm getting tired of being a nanny. At least he was a man! Though he had the disadvantage of being my husband.

ADOLF: Oh, indeed? But you mustn't talk so loud, people can hear us.

TEKLA: What does that matter? They know we're married.

ADOLF: I see, you're beginning to go for strong men too, as well as clean young men.

TEKLA: I don't limit myself to one type. My heart is open to everyone, big and small, beautiful and ugly, young and old. I love the whole world.

ADOLF: Do you know what that means?

TEKLA: No, I don't know anything. I only *feel*.

ADOLF: It means age is beginning to tell.

TEKLA: Are you on to that again? You be careful.

ADOLF: You be careful, too.

TEKLA: Of what?

ADOLF [*holds up the paper-knife*]: This!

TEKLA [*teasingly*]: Little Brother mustn't play with such dangerous toys.

ADOLF: I'm not playing any longer.

TEKLA: Oh, I see, you're in earnest. Then I shall show you that you are wrong. But *you* will never see it, or know it, but everyone else will know it except you. But you'll suspect, you'll wonder, and you'll never have another peaceful minute. You'll feel you're looking ridiculous, you're being cuckolded, but you'll never have proof; because husbands never do have proof. You'll learn what it's like.

ADOLF: You hate me?

TEKLA: No, I don't hate you. I don't think I shall ever be able to hate you. But that's probably because you're a child.

ADOLF: Now, yes. But do you remember that time when the world was against us? You lay there screaming like a baby; then you sat on my knee, and I had to kiss you and lull you to sleep. In those days, *I* was your nurse. I had to see to it that you remembered to brush your hair before you went out, I had to take your boots to be mended, I had to see that there was food in the house. I had to sit by your side hour after hour, holding your hand, because you were afraid, afraid of the whole world, because you hadn't a single friend left, and the scandal had crushed you. I had to force courage into you until my mouth was dry and my head splitting. I had to make myself imagine that I was strong, make myself believe in the future, until I finally managed to bring you back to life as you lay there dead. Then you admired me; then *I* was the man, not the athlete you had left, I was the strong-willed magnetiser who massaged your slack muscles with my own nervous energy, charged your empty brain with new electricity. I put you back on your feet again, found you friends, built a little court for you for people who, for the sake of my friendship, were fooled into admiring you. I gave you control of me and my house. I painted you in my best pictures, [in rose and azure on a gold background,] and there wasn't an exhibition where you didn't hold pride of place. [Sometimes you were St. Cecilia, sometimes Mary Stuart, sometimes Joan of Arc.] I awoke people's interest in you, I compelled the public to look at you through my infatuated eyes, I forced your personality on them, pushed you down their throats, till you had gained their sympathy and could go ahead on your own. By then I was exhausted and I collapsed. The effort of lifting you into the limelight had overtaxed my strength, and I became ill. My illness embarrassed you, for now at last life was beginning to smile for you. I began to feel that you were driven by a secret longing to be rid of your creditor, the only witness of your degradation. Your love becomes like that of an elder sister, and I have to accept the role of Little Brother. Your tenderness remains, it even grows, but it is lined with a measure of pity, and that's largely made up of disdain, increasing to contempt as my sun sinks and yours rises. But somehow or other your inspiration seems to have dried up too, now that I can no longer replenish it, or rather now that you want to show that you no longer need to draw on me. And so we both sink. And now you must have someone to blame, someone new. Because you are weak and can never shoulder a debt yourself. So I became the scapegoat who had to be slaughtered. But when you cut my sinews, you didn't realise that you would hamstring yourself, because the years we have spent together have made us like twins. You were an offshoot of my stock, but you wanted to make yourself independent before you had taken fresh root, and you couldn't grow by yourself. The offshoot couldn't live without its stock; so they both died.

TEKLA: What you're really trying to say is that you have written my books?

ADOLF: No, you're saying that to make me out a liar. I haven't your talent for expressing myself bluntly, I've been talking for five minutes to give you all the nuances, all the undertones and overtones, but you're like a penny whistle, you can only play one note.

TEKLA: Yes, yes, yes, but the *resumé* of it all was that you have written my books.

ADOLF: No, there isn't any *resumé*. You cannot resolve a chord into one note. You cannot resolve a complex life to a single figure. I haven't said anything so insane as that I've written your books.

TEKLA: But you implied it?

ADOLF [*furious*]: I did not imply anything.

TEKLA: But the sum total of it all——

ADOLF [*demented*]: There is no sum total unless one adds, and I have not added, but when you divide there is a quotient, a long unending decimal quotient which won't go out. I have not added.

TEKLA: You may not be able to add, but I can.

ADOLF: I am sure you can, but I have not added.

TEKLA: But that's what you meant.

ADOLF [*impotently, closing his eyes*]: No, no, no—don't speak to me. I shall have a fit. Shut up. Leave me. You are clawing my brain apart with your rough pincers. You are tearing my thoughts to pieces. [*He becomes unconscious; stares vacantly and twiddles his thumbs.*]

TEKLA [*gently*]: How are you feeling? Are you ill? Adolf?

ADOLF *waves her away.*

TEKLA: Adolf!

ADOLF *shakes his head.*

TEKLA: Adolf!

ADOLF: Yes.

TEKLA: Admit that you were unfair to me just now.

ADOLF: Yes, yes, yes, yes, I admit.

TEKLA: And you ask my forgiveness.

ADOLF: Yes, yes, yes, yes, I ask your forgiveness. Just don't talk to me.

TEKLA: Kiss my hand.

ADOLF [*kisses her hand*]: I kiss your hand. Anything, only don't talk to me.

TEKLA: And now go out and get some fresh air before dinner.

ADOLF: Yes, I need it. And then we can pack and leave.

TEKLA: No.

ADOLF [*starts up*]: Why not? There must be some reason.

TEKLA: The reason is that I have promised to attend a *soirée* this evening.

ADOLF: Oh, so that's it.

TEKLA: Yes, that's it. And I have promised to take part.

ADOLF: Promised? You may have said that you were thinking of going, but that needn't stop you now from saying that you do not intend to go.

TEKLA: No, I'm not like you, I stand by my word.

ADOLF: Of course one should stand by one's word, but that doesn't mean one has to stand by every little thing one says. Or perhaps you have promised someone you'll go?

TEKLA: Yes.

ADOLF: Then you can ask to be freed from your promise, because your husband is ill.

TEKLA: I don't want to, and you're not so ill that you can't come with me.

ADOLF: Why do you always want to have me with you? Does it make you feel more safe?

TEKLA: I don't understand what you mean.

ADOLF: You always say that when you know I mean something you don't like.

TEKLA: Really? What is it that I don't like now?

ADOLF: No, no, no. Don't begin again. *Au revoir*. And be careful what you do.

> *He goes through the door upstage and exits right.* TEKLA *is left alone. A few moments later,* GUSTAV *enters. He goes straight towards the table to get a newspaper, pretending not to see* TEKLA.

TEKLA [*starts, but controls herself*]: Is it you?

GUSTAV: It is I. Forgive me——

TEKLA: How did you get here?

GUSTAV: I came by road, but—I shan't stay, since you——

TEKLA: No, please stay. It's been a long time.

GUSTAV: It's been a long time.

TEKLA: You've changed a good deal.

GUSTAV: And you are as charming as ever. Almost—younger. But forgive me, I shan't sour your happiness with my presence. If I'd known you were here, I'd never have——

TEKLA: I beg you—if you do not think it indelicate of me—stay!

GUSTAV: I have no objection, but I thought—ah, whatever I say it will hurt you.

TEKLA: Sit down for a minute. You won't hurt me, because you have, and always had, an unusual gift for tact and delicacy.

GUSTAV: You are too kind. But I am not sure that your husband would view my character in such a flattering light.

TEKLA: On the contrary, he has just been speaking most sympathetically of you.

GUSTAV: Ah? Well, time erases all things. It is like carving one's name on a living tree. Not even animosity can keep a permanent place in our natures.

TEKLA: Oh, but he's never felt any animosity towards you, because he's never seen you. I myself have always cherished a secret longing to see you and him friends for a moment; or at least to let you meet once in my presence, shake hands, and part.

GUSTAV: I too have cherished a secret longing, to see the person I love more dearly than my life safe in really good hands. I have, of course, heard many good opinions of him, I know and admire all his work, but none the less I should like, before I grow old, to press his hand, look him in the eyes, and beg him to take good care of the precious jewel which Providence has entrusted to his keeping. At the same time I should like to quench this involuntary hatred which lies, alas, within my heart, and find peace and humility of spirit to solace me for the remainder of my melancholy days.

TEKLA: You have spoken my own thoughts exactly; you have understood my feelings. Thank you.

GUSTAV: [I am of small account, and I was too insignificant to be able to overshadow you.] My dull life, my dreary work, my narrow circle of friends, were not for your aspiring soul. I admit it. But you, who have studied the human soul, understand what it costs me to have to say this.

[TEKLA: It is noble, it is great, to be able to admit one's shortcomings; and not everybody can do it. [*Sighs.*] But you were always honest, loyal and reliable—— I respect you—but——

GUSTAV: I wasn't—not then—but suffering purifies, grief ennobles, and—I have suffered——]

TEKLA: Poor Gustav. Can you forgive me? Can you?

GUSTAV: Forgive? Forgive what? It is I who must beg your forgiveness.

TEKLA [*turns away*]: Oh, dear. We are both crying. At our age.

GUSTAV [*turns gently*]: At our age? Yes. I am old. But you! You grow younger and younger.

He seats himself on the chair, left. TEKLA, *not noticing, sits on the sofa.*

TEKLA: Oh, no, do you really think so?

GUSTAV: And you dress so well.

TEKLA: Oh, you taught me to do that. Don't you remember that you discovered the colours that suited me best?

GUSTAV: No.

TEKLA: Yes, you did. Don't you remember? [*Laughs.*] I remember that you were even angry with me whenever I didn't wear a touch of poppy red.

GUSTAV: Angry? No! I was never angry with you.

TEKLA: Oh, yes. And when you were trying to teach me how to think. Remember that? I couldn't think at all in those days.

GUSTAV: Certainly you could. Everyone can think. And now you're really sharp, at least when you write.

TEKLA [*annoyed, says quickly*]: Well, as I was saying, it was lovely to see you again and in such a calm atmosphere.

GUSTAV: Well, I was never a trouble-maker, was I? Life with me was always peaceful.

TEKLA: Yes. Indeed it was.

GUSTAV: Oh? But I thought that was the way you wanted me. So you led me to believe when we were engaged.

TEKLA: In those days one didn't know what one wanted. And then one's mother had taught one that one ought not to contradict a gentleman.

GUSTAV: Well, now you've plenty of excitement. An artist's life is always eventful, and your husband does not seem to be a sluggard.

TEKLA: One can have too much of a good thing.

GUSTAV [*changing the subject*]: What! Do you still wear those ear-rings I gave you?

TEKLA [*embarrassed*]: Yes, why shouldn't I? We've never been enemies, and I thought I'd wear them as a sign, a reminder that we weren't bad friends. Anyway, one can't buy ear-rings like this any more. [*Takes one off.*]

GUSTAV: That's all very well, but what does your husband say about it?

TEKLA: What do I care what he says?

GUSTAV: You don't care? But isn't it rather an insult to him? I mean, doesn't it make him seem a bit ridiculous?

TEKLA [*briefly, as though to herself*]: He's that already.

GUSTAV [*notices that she is having difficulty in fixing her ear-ring into place*]: Will you allow me to help you?

TEKLA: Oh, yes, thank you.

GUSTAV [*fixes it in her ear*]: That little ear. What if your husband were to see us now?

TEKLA: Yes, then there'd be tears.

GUSTAV: Is he jealous?

TEKLA: Is he jealous? I should say he is.

Noise in room to right.

GUSTAV: Who lives in there?

TEKLA: I don't know. Well, tell me how things are with you, and what you're doing.

GUSTAV: Tell me how things are with you——

TEKLA *pensively and abstractedly removes the cloth from the wax figure.*

GUSTAV: What! Who's that? No! It's you!

TEKLA: Oh, no, I don't think so.

GUSTAV: But it's exactly like you.

TEKLA: Do you really think so?

GUSTAV: It reminds me of the old story: "But how did you know, Your Majesty?"

TEKLA [*shrieks with laughter*]: You're mad. Do you know any new stories?

GUSTAV: No; but you ought to know some.

TEKLA: No, I don't hear any these days.

GUSTAV: Is he shy?

TEKLA: As far as talking goes.

GUSTAV: Not otherwise?

TEKLA: He's so ill now.

GUSTAV: Poor girl. Well, serve Little Brother right for sticking his fingers into other people's stews.

TEKLA [*laughs*]: Oh, you're really mad.

GUSTAV: Do you remember, when we were newly married, we stayed in this room? Eh? It was furnished differently then. There used to be a chest of drawers over there, between the windows. And the bed stood there.

TEKLA: Be quiet!

GUSTAV: Look at me.

TEKLA: Yes, if you like.

They look at each other.

GUSTAV: Do you think one can forget what made so strong an impression?

TEKLA: No. One can't escape one's memories. Least of all the memories of youth.

GUSTAV: Do you remember when I first met you? You were a lovely child; a little slate on which your parents and governess had scrawled crows'-feet which I had to scratch out. Then I wrote new texts on you, texts of my own choosing, till you thought there was no room for more. That's the reason why I am glad I am not in your husband's shoes—ah, well, that's his business. But that's also why it is rather pleasant to meet you. Our minds think alike. Sitting here and talking to you is like decanting an old wine that I had bottled myself. I get my wine back again, but it has matured. And now that I am going to marry again, I have deliberately chosen a young girl whom I can educate according to my wish. For, my dear Tekla, a woman is a man's child, and if she isn't that, he will become her child, and then the world's upside down.

TEKLA: Are you going to get married again?

GUSTAV: Yes. I shall tempt Fortune once more, but this time I shall put a tight rein on her, so that she won't bolt.

TEKLA: Is she beautiful?

GUSTAV: Yes, to me she is. But perhaps I'm too old. It's strange, but now that fate has brought us together again, I'm beginning to doubt if I can play that game twice.

TEKLA: How do you mean?

GUSTAV: My roots are still in you. The old wounds bleed again. You are a dangerous woman, Tekla.

TEKLA: Really? And my husband says I shall never make another conquest.

GUSTAV: In other words, he has stopped loving you.

TEKLA: I don't know what he means by love.

GUSTAV: [You and he have played hide-and-seek for so long that you can no longer catch each other. It happens, you know. You've played the innocent so cleverly, you've quite sapped his courage.] Changing one's man has its dangers, you know. It has its dangers.

TEKLA: You are reproaching me?

GUSTAV: Not at all. What happens, happens with a kind of inevitability. If it had not happened, something else would have happened. But now it has happened, and it happened like that.

TEKLA: You understand so many things. I've never met anyone with whom it gives me so much pleasure to exchange ideas. You don't preach or moralise, you make so few demands upon people, one feels free when one's with you. Do you know, I'm jealous of your future wife?

GUSTAV: Do you know that I am jealous of your husband?

TEKLA [*gets up*]: And now we must part. For ever.

GUSTAV: Yes, now we must part. But not without a goodbye. Mm?

TEKLA [*uneasily*]: No.

GUSTAV [*follows her across the room*]: Yes. We shall say goodbye. We shall drown our memories in a drunkenness so deep that when we wake from it we shall have lost our memories. One can drink as deeply as that, you know. [*Puts his arm round her waist.*] His sick spirit drags you down, infects you with melancholy. I shall fill you with new life, I shall make your talent bloom again in its autumn like a September rose. I shall——

Two LADIES *in travelling clothes appear at the verandah door, look surprised, point, laugh, and go on their way.*

TEKLA [*tears herself loose*]: Who was that?

GUSTAV [*indifferently*]: Travellers.

TEKLA: Leave me. I'm afraid of you.

GUSTAV: Why?

TEKLA: You take my soul from me.

GUSTAV: And give you mine instead. Anyway, you have no soul, it's only an illusion.

TEKLA: You have a way of saying rude things that makes it impossible for one to be angry with you.

GUSTAV: That's because I have the first claim on you, and you know it. When? And where?

TEKLA: No. I feel sorry for him. I think he still loves me, and I don't want to hurt him.

GUSTAV: He doesn't love you. Do you want me to prove it?

TEKLA: Well, how can you prove it?

CREDITORS

GUSTAV [*picks up the fragments of the torn photograph from beneath the table*]: There. See for yourself.

TEKLA: Oh! How beastly of him!

GUSTAV: You see! Well. When? And where?

TEKLA: The little hypocrite.

GUSTAV: When?

TEKLA: He's catching the boat at eight o'clock tonight.

GUSTAV: Then——?

TEKLA: Nine o'clock. [*Noise from room to right.*] Who's making that noise in there?

GUSTAV [*goes to the keyhole*]: Let's see. No, there's a table lying on its side and a broken water carafe. Nothing else. Perhaps someone has locked a dog in there. Nine o'clock, then.

TEKLA: Right. He's only got himself to blame. The little hypocrite, preaching to me about truthfulness, and how he'd taught me to be truthful. But—wait a minute, wait a minute. He was very unfriendly when I got back this afternoon. He didn't come down to the jetty to meet me—and then—then he said something about the young men on the boat, which I pretended not to understand. But how could he have known about it? Wait—and then he went on about women, and said how you haunted him—and then he talked about becoming a sculptor, because that was the art of our time—just the way you used to talk in the old days.

GUSTAV: Really?

TEKLA: Really. Ah, now I understand. Now I begin to see what a vindictive bastard you are. You've been here, tearing him apart. It was you who sat on the sofa, it was you who put it into his head that he had epilepsy and that he ought to give up making love and prove himself a man by rebelling against his wife. It was you. How long have you been here?

GUSTAV: I have been here for eight days.

TEKLA: Then it was you I saw on the steamer?

GUSTAV: It was I.

TEKLA: And now you thought you would trap me.

GUSTAV: I have already done so.

TEKLA: Not yet.

GUSTAV: Oh, yes.

TEKLA: You sneaked up on my lamb like a wolf. You came with your vile plan to destroy my happiness, and you went ahead with it until I spotted what you were up to and stopped you.

GUSTAV: No, it didn't happen quite like that. In fact, it was like this. I wanted things to go badly for you, of course. But I was almost sure that this would happen without my interfering. Anyway, I've had no time for intriguing. But when I was out for a stroll and saw you on the steamer with your young gentlemen, I thought it was time I paid you a visit. I came here and at once your little lamb threw himself into the arms of the wolf. He took a liking to me as the result of a reflex action which I shall not be so impolite as to try to interpret. At first I felt sorry for him, because he was in the same predicament as I once found myself in. But then he began to rub up my old wounds—you know, the book, and the idiot—and then I felt a desire to take him to pieces and jumble them up so that he couldn't put them together again—and I succeeded, thanks to the work you had already put in on him. Then there was you. You were the mainspring in the watch, and you had to be wound up till you broke. And then——! [*Makes a noise like a spring breaking.*] When I came in just now, I wasn't quite sure what I was going to say. As a chess player I had various possible gambits ready, but which one I should use depended on how you would open the game. One thing led to another, luck played its part, and finally I mated you. Now I have you where I want you.

TEKLA: No, you haven't.

GUSTAV: Yes, I have. What you least wanted to happen has happened. The world—represented by two lady travellers, whose appearance was not contrived by me—for I am no Machiavelli—the world has seen how you became reconciled with your former husband and crept back remorsefully into his loyal embrace. Is that enough?

TEKLA: It should be enough for you to feel revenged. But, tell me, you who are so enlightened and so righteous, if we cannot act freely, since everything that happens is predetermined——

GUSTAV [*corrects her*]: Only up to a point.

TEKLA: It's the same thing.

GUSTAV: No, it's not.

TEKLA: How can you, who must regard me as innocent because my heredity and my environment drove me to act as I did, how can you think yourself entitled to take revenge on me?

GUSTAV: For the same reason. Because heredity and environment drove me to take my revenge. Fair play, don't you think? But do you know why you two drew the short straws in this contest? [TEKLA *gives him a contemptuous look.*] Why you were fooled by me? Because I am stronger than you, and cleverer. You and he were the idiots, not I. That shows you that a man isn't necessarily an idiot because he can't paint pictures and write novels. Remember that.

TEKLA: You are utterly without feeling?

GUSTAV: Utterly. But that, my dear, is why I am able to think—as you know from experience—and act, as you now also know from experience.

TEKLA: And all this just because I wounded your self-esteem.

GUSTAV: What do you mean, "just"? Don't go round wounding people's self-esteem. That is where people are most vulnerable.

TEKLA: You're a vindictive beast. I despise you.

GUSTAV: You're a wanton beast. I despise you.

TEKLA: Well, that's my nature, eh?

GUSTAV: "Well, that's my nature"! You should find out a little about other people's feelings before you abandon yourself to your own, or it will end in tears.

TEKLA: You can never forgive me for——

GUSTAV: I have forgiven you.

TEKLA: Have you?

GUSTAV: Certainly. Have I ever raised my hand against you in all these years? No. But now I no sooner come here than you collapse. Have I reproached you, moralised, preached at you? No. I exchanged a few jokes with your husband, and that was enough to disintegrate him. But why should I, who am the plaintiff, defend myself? Tekla! Have you nothing to reproach yourself with?

TEKLA: No, nothing at all. The Christians say that it is Providence which governs our actions, others call it fate. Whichever it is, we cannot be blamed.

GUSTAV: To a certain degree we cannot be blamed. But there is a margin of choice, and if we offend there, we are guilty and, sooner or later, the creditors will knock on the door. We are innocent, but responsible; innocent in the eyes of God—but he no longer exists—yet responsible to ourselves and our fellow-beings.

TEKLA: You have come to sue for payment, then.

GUSTAV: I have come to take back what you have stolen from me, not what I gave you freely. You stole my honour, and the only way I could get it back was by robbing you of yours.

TEKLA: Honour? Hm. And now you are satisfied.

GUSTAV: Now I am satisfied.

He rings for the PORTER.

TEKLA: And now you are going to meet your *fiancée*?

GUSTAV: I haven't got one, and I don't want one. And I am not going home, because I haven't got a home, nor do I want any.

The PORTER *enters.*

GUSTAV: Get my bill ready. I shall be leaving by the eight o'clock boat.

The PORTER *bows and exits.*

TEKLA: Can't we part friends?

GUSTAV: Friends? You use so many words which no longer have any meaning. Friends? What do you expect us to do, set up house together, all three of us? [You should bury our hatred by indemnifying me for my loss, but you can't. You have taken from me, and what you have taken you have consumed so that you cannot give it back to me.] Will it make you any happier if I were to say to you: "Forgive me for letting you claw my heart, forgive me for letting you rob me of my honour, forgive me for being a laughing-stock to my pupils every day for seven years, forgive me for [helping you to escape from your parents, for freeing you from the tyranny of your ignorance and superstitions, for] making you mistress of my house, [for giving you a position and friends,] for transforming you from a child into a woman?" Forgive me, as I have forgiven you. Now I cancel the debt you owe me. Go now, and settle your account with your other creditor.

TEKLA: Where is he? What have you done to him?

GUSTAV: Done to him? Do you still love him?

TEKLA: Yes.

GUSTAV: And just now? Was that true?

TEKLA: Yes.

GUSTAV: Do you know what you are?

TEKLA: You despise me?

GUSTAV: I pity you. [It is part of your character. I won't say it's a fault, but it is unfortunate because of the consequences it brings in its wake.] Poor Tekla! I almost begin to regret what I have done, although I am innocent, as you are. Still, it may be a useful experience for you to feel as you once made me feel. Do you know where your husband is?

TEKLA: Now I think I know. He's in there. And he has heard everything. And seen everything. And he who sees his own ghost dies.

> ADOLF *enters. He is deathly pale, and has a bloodstain on one of his cheeks. His eyes are quite still and staring, and there is white froth around his mouth.*

GUSTAV [*recoils*]: No, there he is. Settle your account with him, now, and see if he'll be as generous as I have been. Goodbye.

> *He goes left, but stops.*

TEKLA [*goes towards* ADOLF *with outstretched arms*]: Adolf!

> ADOLF *sinks down on the floor.*

TEKLA [*throws herself on to* ADOLF's *body and caresses him*]: Adolf! My beloved child! Are you alive? Speak, speak. Forgive your cruel Tekla. Forgive me, forgive me, forgive me! Little Brother, answer me, do you hear? No, oh God, he doesn't hear me. He's dead. Oh, God in Heaven, oh my God, help us, help us!

GUSTAV: It's the truth. She loves him too. Poor woman!

Introduction to
THE STRONGER

STRINDBERG wrote THE STRONGER in December 1888–January 1889, as part of the repertoire for his projected Experimental Theatre in Copenhagen. Following upon his row with Ludwig Hansen at Lyngby, his forcible expulsion from the castle, and the publicity given in the Danish newspapers to his affair with Hansen's seventeen-year-old sister, Martha Magdalene, his relations with his wife had, paradoxically, taken a turn for the better. She had stood by him, partly perhaps because she was anxious not to lose this opportunity of returning to the stage, and THE STRONGER is one of the very few examples of Strindberg's work which contains a sympathetic portrayal of his wife.

It was, like all his plays, based on fact. Since his marriage he had had various flirtations with other women, including, apart from Martha Magdalene, an actress named Helga Frankenfeldt, who had formerly been employed at the Royal Theatre in Stockholm, and Nathalia Larsen, the young Danish actress and authoress who was to share the leads at his experimental theatre with Siri. Siri seems not to have been particularly jealous of these rivals, possibly because they seemed the only means of diverting his own suspicions away from her; and, after each affair, he came back to her. "My friend and I are friends again—dear God, how tough love is!", he wrote on 27 September 1888 to his cousin, Johan Oscar Strindberg. At the time when he wrote this little playlet, it must have seemed to him that his wife was, after all, the strongest of all these women. The character of Mademoiselle Y appears to have been chiefly based on Helga Frankenfeldt, whom Strindberg had given up seeing in 1882 after she had insulted Siri at a party.

He offered Siri the role of Madame X, but she refused it. He then offered it to her rival, Nathalia Larsen, but she did not like it either. "You haven't understood the play," he wrote to her irritably on 7 January 1889. After unsuccessfully approaching two other actresses, including Johanne Krum who had played Laura in THE FATHER, he eventually succeeded in persuading Nathalia to accept the part; but in the end it was created by Siri. As described above (in the Introduction to MISS JULIE), MISS JULIE was banned by the censor on the day before the experimental theatre was to have opened, and THE STRONGER had to be hastily rehearsed with PARIAH to make up a triple bill the following week with CREDITORS. Nathalia was already fully occupied with rehearsing Tekla in the last-named play, and it was presumably thought that the strain of taking on another leading role would be too much for her. Mademoiselle Y was given to Fru Pio, who was acting Christine in MISS JULIE, and THE STRONGER received its first performance at the Dagmar Theatre in Copenhagen on 9 March 1889.

A few days before the première, Strindberg wrote Siri a few lines of advice concerning her part. As always, the precision and good sense of his remarks concerning practical theatrical details contrast amazingly with his hysteria on all other matters. "1. She is an actress, not just an ordinary respectable housewife. 2. She is the stronger, i.e. the softer. What is hard and stiff breaks, what is elastic gives and returns to its shape. 3. Poshly dressed—use the one you wore in MISS JULIE, or get something new. 4. If you get a new coat, beware of plain surfaces, and plain pleats, and buy a new hat! Something in fur, bonnet-shaped (not *à l'anglaise*) .5. Study it with meticulous care, but play it simply—but not too simply! Give it an undertone of 50% charlatanism, like Fru Hwasser* and Ibsen, and suggest depths that do not exist. 6. Change any phrases that don't come naturally, and work up to an exit that will bring applause, without making a meal of it. 7. Use your diaphragm when speaking, and don't squeak or rant...."

None of the three plays was adequately performed, and the

* Elise Hwasser had played Nora in A DOLL'S HOUSE at the Royal Theatre in Stockholm in 1880.

evening was less than a success. The critic of *Socialdemokraten*, however, thought that Siri acted "with charm and *noblesse*". Another observer noted that she "took repeated curtain-calls at the close of this *bagatelle*, which few people understood, but which they applauded because it was the end of the evening. Each time the curtain rose, it was she who stood upon the stage, and when there were calls for the author, who was not present, she addressed the audience, and promised to convey their greetings to him."

After the failure of the Experimental Theatre, THE STRONGER was forgotten until the turn of the century. As with so many of Strindberg's plays, it was Max Reinhardt who first realised and demonstrated its potential, with a production at his Kleines Theater in Berlin in 1902, in which Madame X was played by the distinguished actress Rosa Bertens. The play reached St. Petersburg in 1904 and Vienna in 1907, in which year it was played for the first time in Stockholm at Strindberg's own Intimate Theatre. It achieved the distinction of being the first Strindberg play to be performed in England, when the New Stage Club produced it at the Bloomsbury Hall on 29 November 1906 in a triple bill which also included Strindberg's playlet SIMOOM; and on 10 December 1909 it was revived at His Majesty's Theatre as curtain-raiser to a performance in Russian of Act 5 of Ostrovsky's IVAN THE TERRIBLE by Lydia Yavorskaia's company from St. Petersburg. Mlle Yavorskaia herself took the silent role of Mlle Y. in THE STRONGER, with Lady Tree as Mme X. Over the years, THE STRONGER has come to be recognised as a brilliantly effective curtain-raiser, and it has been frequently revived in Scandinavia, Germany and America, where Ruth Ford and Viveca Lindfors acted it at the Phoenix Theatre in 1956. It was last seen in London in 1961, at the Pembroke Theatre, Croydon, when Mme X. was played by Margaret Rutherford.

Dr. Gunnar Ollén has suggested that Strindberg may deliberately have made one of the characters silent in the hope that his wife might be able to play that role in productions outside Sweden, notably, perhaps, at the Théâtre Libre in Paris, the director of which, André Antoine, had just expressed a strong enthusiasm for Strindberg's work. If so, Strindberg was not the only major dramatist to have written an important non-speaking role for this reason. Frau Helene Weigel once told me that when her husband, Bertolt Brecht, wrote MOTHER COURAGE in Stockholm in 1938 he made the part of the Daughter dumb in order that his wife might be able to play it in Sweden, where he assumed it would receive its first production. As things turned out, MOTHER COURAGE was not performed in Sweden during Brecht's abbreviated stay there, and Helene Weigel never played the part, although later of course the Mother became her most famous role.

THE STRONGER

A Sketch
(1888-9)

CHARACTERS

MADAME X., a married actress
MADEMOISELLE Y., an unmarried actress
A WAITRESS

The corner of a café, of the kind frequented by ladies. Two small iron tables, a red plush sofa and some chairs. MADAME X. enters in winter clothes, with hat and cloak, and a delicate Japanese basket on her arm. MADEMOISELLE Y. is seated with a half-empty bottle of beer in front of her, reading an illustrated magazine, which she later changes for others.

MME X.: Why, Amelia darling! Fancy seeing you here! All alone on Christmas Eve, like a poor old bachelor!

MLLE Y. *looks up from her magazine, nods and goes on reading.*

MME X.: You know, it really hurts me to see you like this. Alone—alone in a café—and on Christmas Eve! I remember once when I was in Paris—there was a wedding breakfast in a restaurant—and the bride sat there reading a comic paper while the bridegroom was playing billiards with the witnesses! My word, I thought, if they start like this, how will they go on—and how will they end? He was playing billiards on his wedding day! And she was reading a comic paper, you're going to say. Well, but it isn't quite the same!

The WAITRESS *enters, places a cup of chocolate in front of* MME X. *and goes out.*

MME X.: You know what, Amelia? I really think you'd have done better to keep him. Don't you remember, I was the first person to say to you: "Forgive him!" Remember? You could have been married now, with a home. Do you remember last Christmas how happy you were with his parents in the country, and how you said that a happy home life was what really mattered, and that you'd like to get away from the theatre? Yes, Amelia, my dear—home's best—after the theatre—and children, you know—no, of course, you don't.

MLLE Y. *gives her a disdainful glance.*

MME X. [*takes a few sips from her cup, then opens her basket and shows her Christmas presents*]: Look what I've bought for my little darlings! [*Takes out a doll.*] See this! This is for Lisa. Look—she can roll her eyes and turn her head! Mm? And this little pistol is for Maja.

She loads it, and fires the cork, on its string, at MLLE Y., *who recoils in fear.*

MME X. Did it frighten you? You thought I wanted to shoot you? Mm? Darling, you can't have! If *you'd* wanted to shoot *me*, I could understand—for getting in your way—I know you can never forget that—though it really wasn't my fault. You still think I got them to terminate your contract. But I didn't. I didn't, though you think I did. Well, it's no use my talking, you won't believe me. [*Takes out a pair of embroidered slippers.*] And these are for my dear husband. I embroidered these tulips myself. I hate tulips, but he will have them on everything.

MLLE Y. *looks up from her magazine, with cynical curiosity.*

MME X. [*puts a hand into each slipper*]: Look what small feet he has! Mm? And you should see how daintily he walks! But of course you've never seen him in slippers. [MLLE Y. *laughs aloud.*] Look, I'll show you! [*Walks the slippers along the table.* MLLE Y. *laughs aloud again.*] And then, darling, when he gets angry, he stamps his foot like this. "What! Damn these maids, will they never learn how to make coffee? Oh, God! Now the cretins haven't trimmed the lamp!" Or there's a draught under the door and his feet are cold. "Ugh, it's freezing! Can't these confounded idiots keep the stove alight!"

She rubs the sole of one slipper against the upper part of the other. MLLE Y. *roars with laughter.*

MME X. And then he comes home and can't find his slippers, because Marie's hidden them under the chest of drawers.... Oh, but it's wicked to sit here and make fun of one's husband like this. He's a darling, actually—a real poppet! He's the kind of husband you ought to have had, Amelia! Why are you laughing? Mm? Mm? And then, you see, I know he's faithful to me. Oh, yes, I know. He told me himself—why are you giggling?—that when I was touring in Norway that horrid Frederique tried to seduce him! Can you imagine? The impertinence! [*Pause.*] I'd have scratched her eyes out if she'd shown her face while I was at home! [*Pause.*] It was lucky he told me about it himself. Imagine if I'd heard it from some gossip! [*Pause.*] But she wasn't the only one, you can be sure. I don't know why it is, but women always go crazy about my husband. They must think he has some pull at the theatre, because he works in the ministry. Perhaps you've been at him too! I was never quite sure about you—though I know now that he wasn't interested in you. I always felt you bore some grudge against him.

Pause. They look at each other uncertainly.

MME X. Come and have dinner with us this evening, Amelia, to show you aren't cross with us—aren't cross with me, anyway. I think it's so horrid being bad friends with anyone—especially you. Perhaps it's because I queered your pitch that time.... [*Gradually slower.*] Or—I don't know—why—really——!

Pause. MLLE Y. *gazes curiously at* MME X.

MME X. It's so strange about our friendship—when I first met you, I was afraid of you, so afraid I didn't dare let you out of my sight. Wherever I went, I took care to be near you—I didn't dare become your enemy, so I became your friend. But I always felt awkward when you came home to us, because I saw my husband couldn't stand you—and then I felt uncomfortable, as though my clothes didn't fit. I did everything to make him be nice to you, but without success. And then you went off and got engaged. Then you and he became great friends—as though you'd been afraid to show your true feelings while you were uncommitted—and then—what happened next? I didn't become jealous—funnily enough! And I remember, when our first baby was christened, and you stood as godmother, I made him kiss you—and he did, but you got so upset—that is, I didn't notice it at the time—I haven't thought of it since—haven't thought of it till—now! [*Rises suddenly.*] Why are you so silent? You haven't said a word all the time—you've just let me sit here talking! you've sat there staring at me, winding all these thoughts out of me like silk from a cocoon—thoughts—suspicions—? Let me see! Why did you break off your engagement? Why did you never come and visit us after that? Why won't you come and see us tonight?

MLLE Y. *seems about to speak.*

MME X.: No! You don't need to say anything—I see it all now! So *that* was why you—and why you—and why you——! Yes, of course! Now it all adds up! So that was it! Ugh, I don't want to sit at the same table as you!

Moves her things to the other table.

That was why I had to embroider tulips, which I hate, on his slippers—because you liked tulips! That was why—[*throws the slippers on the floor*]—we had to spend our holiday at Mälaren that summer, because you couldn't stand the sea—that was why my son had to be called Eskil, because that was your father's name—that was why I had to wear your colours, read your authors, eat your dishes, drink your drinks—your chocolate, for instance—that was why—oh, my God!—it's horrible, now I think of it—horrible! Everything, everything that belonged to you, entered into me. Even your passions! Your soul crept into mine like a worm into an apple, eating and eating, boring and boring, till there was nothing left but the skin and a little black mould. I wanted to run away from you, but I couldn't—you lay there like a snake with your black eyes, bewitching me—when I tried to use my wings they dragged me down. I lay in the water with my feet bound, and the more I tried to swim with my hands the deeper I sank, down, down, till I reached the bottom, where you lay like a giant crab ready to seize me in your claws! And I'm lying there now!

Ugh, how I hate you, hate you, hate you! But you—you just sit there, silent, calm, not caring—not caring whether it's night or day, summer or winter, whether other people are happy or miserable—unable to hate and unable to love—motionless like a stork over a rat-hole! You couldn't pounce on your victim, you couldn't hunt it, but you could wait for it! You sit here in your corner—do you know people call it the rat-trap because of you?—and read your papers to see if anyone's in trouble, or ill, or has got the sack from the theatre—you sit here reckoning your victims, calculating your opportunities like a pilot counting his shipwrecks, like a goddess receiving sacrifice!

Poor Amelia! Do you know, I feel sorry for you, because I know you're unhappy—unhappy like someone who's been hurt—and evil because you've been hurt. I can't be angry with you, though I'd like to be—because you're the one who's the baby, not me. Oh, that business with Bob doesn't bother me—why should it? And what does it matter whether you taught me to drink chocolate, or someone else did? It's all one in the end.

Takes a sip from her cup. Continues knowingly.

Anyway, chocolate's very healthy! And if you've taught me how to dress—*tant mieux*! It's just made my husband fonder of me—your loss has been my gain. And to judge by certain signs, I think you have lost him. I suppose you hoped I'd run away? But you're the one who's run away—and now you're sitting here regretting it ever happened. But I don't regret it! One mustn't be petty. And after all, why should I want to own something that no one else wants?

You know, when all's said and done, perhaps I really am the stronger of us two; now anyway. You never took anything from me, you only gave. And now I'm like the thief in the fairy tale—when you woke, I had gone off with your treasure!

Otherwise why did everything become worthless and sterile as soon as you touched it? You couldn't keep any man's love, for all your tulips and your passions—as I have done. Your authors never taught you how to live; but they taught me. You never had any little Eskil; you only had a father called Eskil.

And why are you always silent, silent, silent? I used to think it was because you were strong; but perhaps it was just that you had nothing to say. Because your head was empty! [*Gets up and picks up the slippers.*]

Now I'm going home—and taking the tulips with me—*your* tulips! You couldn't learn anything from other people, you could only give—and so you broke, like a dry reed. But I didn't!

Thank you, Amelia, for all the good lessons you've taught me. Thank you for teaching my husband to love! Now I am going home, to love him.

She goes.

Introduction to
PLAYING WITH FIRE

STRINDBERG'S EXPERIMENTAL THEATRE in Copenhagen folded very quickly, and he blamed its failure, quite unjustly, on his wife. "She did everything to destroy it and get herself an engagement at the Dagmar Theatre,"* he wrote to Edvard Brandes on 12 June 1889. "The Directress [i.e. Siri] never attended a rehearsal or a performance of PARIAH—in short, she never saw the play. I have never regarded it as my fault that, instead of *acting* Miss Julie, she flirted as a martyr, an oppressed woman, etc. That we didn't go on tour because our first effort in Malmö ended with an income (?loss) of 30 crowns and ruined our reputation because of the Directress's immodest behaviour at the hotel, plus the rumours which Herr Wied and Herr Schiwe's jealous fiancée spread about her, so that she ended by seeking refuge in alcoholism with Fröken David, and seems likely shortly to end in an alcoholics' home. That was the story of Strindberg's Experimental Theatre."

In fact, of course, the management had been incompetent, the actors inadequate and, since Strindberg himself hated attending rehearsals, there had been no proper supervision. The failure of the theatre, however, greatly discouraged Strindberg, and it was to be three years before he wrote another play.

This was a particularly wretched period of his life. He was virtually penniless, nagged by creditors, his marriage had become a mockery, and he felt that he had written himself out. It was only through loans from his brother and his publisher that he was able to survive.

In April 1889, shortly after the Copenhagen fiasco, he settled in Sweden for the first time for six years. He took no action about obtaining a divorce, though he spent less and less time with his family. Then, in 1891, a young Danish girl of

* i.e. in the regular company there.

uncertain parentage* named Marie David, whom they had first met a few years previously, returned from Paris and moved in to live with Siri and the children. Strindberg believed (possibly correctly, as things turned out) that she and Siri were having an affair, and he made his views public. Marie David promptly sued him for slander. Before the case came on, he and Siri at last decided to go through with their divorce, and on 24 March 1891 they were granted a year's judicial separation pending a decree absolute.

He began to conceive plans for another experimental theatre. This time it was to be in the dining-room of a restaurant in Djursholm, just north of Stockholm, where he was living alone. With this in view, he wrote during the spring of 1892 four one-act plays: THE FIRST WARNING, DEBIT AND CREDIT, IN THE FACE OF DEATH and A MOTHER'S LOVE. All were much below the level of his best work. In July 1892 Marie David's slander action came before the court, and was decided in her favour; he was condemned to pay a fine of 500 crowns. A few weeks later, on the island of Dalarö south of Stockholm, he wrote the bitter little comedy PLAYING WITH FIRE. It showed a return to his best form after his long silence and the sad string of failures.

PLAYING WITH FIRE was based on a visit which he had made the previous summer to the painter Robert Thegerström and his wife and parents on this same island of Dalarö. They had been friendly and helpful to him; but on midsummer day of 1892 Thegerström came to see Strindberg and dropped some unfortunate remark which caused Strindberg to break off their friendship. PLAYING WITH FIRE was Strindberg's spiteful revenge on the people who had befriended him; though it was also partially based on the visit which Strindberg had made to the Wrangels a decade earlier, when the Baron was in love with his cousin and was prepared to let his wife, Siri, have an affair with Strindberg.

* She believed herself to be the daughter of Georg Brandes, but the truth of this has never been fully established.

Introduction to PLAYING WITH FIRE

Bonnier at first refused to publish the play, on the ground that the characters were too easily identifiable and that he feared a libel action—a fear prompted, no doubt, by Strindberg's conviction in the Marie David case. Other publishers shared this view, and it was five years before PLAYING WITH FIRE was published in Sweden. In December 1893 it received its première, but was then ignored everywhere until well after the turn of the century when, like so many of Strindberg's plays, it at last came into its own.

In 1907 it was at last performed in Stockholm, under unpromising circumstances at a private soirée given in a restaurant by a young band of enthusiasts. These, however, included, in the role of the Friend, a young man of cosmopolitan parentage named Mauritz Stiller, who was later to become one of the early pioneer film directors. (He discovered a young girl named Greta Gustavsson, changed her name to Garbo and directed her in her first film, THE ATONEMENT OF GÖSTA BERLING.) The following spring, PLAYING WITH FIRE was staged at Strindberg's own Intimate Theatre in Stockholm; but it was harshly received and, as with so many of Strindberg's plays, it was left to the Germans to discover its merits and reveal them to the Swedes. In 1908, PLAYING WITH FIRE was staged in Munich, Mannheim and Berlin; in 1910 in Hamburg; and in 1911 in Karlsruhe and Baden-Baden, which must have provided an appropriate setting. The same year a production toured the Swedish provinces, and in 1912, the year of Strindberg's death, it was at last professionally performed in Stockholm, at the Little Theatre, with Mauritz Stiller back in his old part as the Friend. On this occasion the qualities of the play were at last recognised, and it has since been one of Strindberg's most popular plays in Sweden, having been produced on no less than seven occasions in Stockholm since 1945, as well as several times in provincial *stadsteatrar* and once on television. Ingmar Bergman directed it on sound radio in 1947, and again in 1961, this time with three of his most distinguished players in the leading parts: Max von Sydow as the Friend, Eva

Dahlbeck as the Daughter-in-Law and Ulf Palme as the Son. It was not performed in England until 1962, when it was presented by the Royal Shakespeare Company at the Aldwych Theatre in a double bill with Harold Pinter's THE COLLECTION.

PLAYING WITH FIRE is an easy play to misproduce; it requires a claustrophobic atmosphere of heat, boredom and sensuality of the kind from which English producers and actors tend to shy away, though perhaps less now than a few years ago. The set should be a sun-trap, with bright light beating in through glass and every window closed; it must not be airy. Of the six characters, all except the Mother are in heat for someone not their lawful partner. The Son and Daughter-in-Law have, as the Son suggests, been making love for much of the night, but there is no affection between them; they make love, as they do everything else, out of boredom. The scenes between the Daughter-in-Law and the Friend call for black comedy playing of a very high order. They are both smooth performers in the game of love, and they play cat and mouse with each other, each taking it in turns to be the cat. They use romantic and melodramatic clichés as part of their armoury, half-believing in them; they deceive themselves as easily as, perhaps more easily than, they deceive their victims. Such clichés are an essential weapon to any seducer, of either sex. If only one could have seen Noel Coward and Gertrude Lawrence in these two parts! (It is not the only Noel Coward part that Strindberg wrote; he would be a splendid Gustav in CREDITORS.)

Shortly after completing PLAYING WITH FIRE, Strindberg wrote the one-act play THE BOND, an account of a divorce suit closely based on his own. It was to be his last play for six years, until Part 1 of TO DAMASCUS in 1898. During the interval he came nearer to complete insanity than at any other time in his life—the period which he described memorably in his prose work INFERNO.

PLAYING WITH FIRE

A Comedy in One Act
(1892)

CHARACTERS

THE FATHER, 60, a *rentier*
THE MOTHER, 58
THE SON, 27, a painter
THE DAUGHTER-IN-LAW, 24
THE FRIEND, 26
THE COUSIN, a girl of 20

The action takes place in a seaside resort in Sweden on a summer morning towards the end of the last century.

This translation of PLAYING WITH FIRE was commissioned by the Royal Shakespeare Company, and was first performed on 18 June 1962 at the Aldwych Theatre, in a double bill with Harold Pinter's THE COLLECTION. The cast was:

THE FATHER	Michael Hordern
THE MOTHER	Gwen Nelson
THE SON	Colin Jeavons
THE DAUGHTER-IN-LAW	Sheila Allen
THE FRIEND	Kenneth Haigh
THE COUSIN	Patricia England

Décor by John Bury
Costumes by Motley
Produced by John Blatchley

Scene: a verandah with glass walls and roof, furnished as a living-room. Doors lead out to the garden, and to either side.

Scene 1

> *The* SON *is seated, painting. The* DAUGHTER-IN-LAW *enters, in a morning frock.*

SON: Is he up yet?

DAUGHTER-IN-LAW: Axel? How should I know?

SON: I thought you'd gone to look.

DAUGHTER-IN-LAW: Oh, for God's sake! If I didn't know you were incapable of being jealous, I'd begin to wonder.

SON: And if I didn't know that you were incapable of being unfaithful, I'd be getting a little restless myself.

DAUGHTER-IN-LAW: Why now, particularly?

SON: Didn't you hear? I said: "If——". You know I value no one's company as much as our friend Axel's, and since you so luckily share my sympathy for the poor fellow and his harrowed soul, everything's fine.

DAUGHTER-IN-LAW: Yes, he's a sad person, but sometimes he behaves very strangely. Why did he run away from us like that last summer, without saying goodbye? He didn't even take his clothes.

SON: Yes, that was very odd. I thought he was in love with Cousin Adèle.

DAUGHTER-IN-LAW: Oh, really?

SON: Yes, but I don't now. Mother thought he'd gone back to his wife and child.

DAUGHTER-IN-LAW: Why should he do that? Aren't they divorced?

SON: Not properly yet, but he's expecting it to come through any day now.

DAUGHTER-IN-LAW: So you thought he was in love with Adèle? You never told me. Yes, well, if they could get together I dare say it might work out quite well.

SON: Nonsense, she's as cold as a fish.

DAUGHTER-IN-LAW: Adèle? You don't know her.

SON: Oh, she's got an exquisite figure, but she hasn't an ounce of passion in her.

The DAUGHTER-IN-LAW *laughs.*

SON: Has she?

DAUGHTER-IN-LAW: If she once breaks through that shell of hers——

SON: Oh, really?

DAUGHTER-IN-LAW: You seem interested.

SON: In a sense.

DAUGHTER-IN-LAW: What sense?

SON: Well, you know she modelled for me once. As "The Swimmer"——

DAUGHTER-IN-LAW: Who hasn't? I do wish you'd have the decency not to show your sketches to everyone, though. Uh-huh, here comes your mother!

Scene 2

As before. The MOTHER *enters, badly dressed with a big Japanese hat and carrying a food-basket.*

SON: Oh God, mother, you do look a freak.

MOTHER: You're very polite!

DAUGHTER-IN-LAW: Knut'll never learn any manners. Well, what have you bought us for lunch?

MOTHER: Oh, I've found some lovely dabs——

SON: Oh no, not dabs! [*feels around in the basket*] Hullo, what are these? Ducklings?

DAUGHTER-IN-LAW: They're not very plump. Feel these breasts.

SON: I think all breasts are beautiful.

DAUGHTER-IN-LAW: Oh, you're disgusting.

MOTHER: Well, your friend turned up again last night.

SON: Our friend? Kerstin's friend, you mean. She's quite mad about him. When he arrived last night, I thought they were going to kiss each other.

MOTHER: You shouldn't make jokes like that, Knut. He who plays with fire——

SON: I know, but I'm too old to start learning. Anyway, do you think I look as though I need to be jealous?

MOTHER: It isn't a man's looks, is it, Kerstin?

DAUGHTER-IN-LAW: I don't understand what you mean.

MOTHER [*slaps her lightly on the cheek*]: Oh, Kerstin! Now you be careful!

SON: Kerstin hasn't got an evil thought in her head, and don't you start corrupting her, you old frump.

MOTHER: You two have such a nasty way of joking one never knows when you're being serious.

SON: I am always serious.

DAUGHTER-IN-LAW: I can believe that. You never laugh when you say these horrid things.

MOTHER: You're both very quarrelsome this morning. Didn't you sleep well last night?

SON: We didn't sleep at all.

MOTHER: You wicked boy! Well, my dears, I must be off, or your father will start cursing me.

SON: Father—yes, where is he?

MOTHER: Oh, I expect he's taking his constitutional with Adèle.

SON: Aren't you jealous, mother?

MOTHER: Oh, don't be so silly!

SON: Yes, but I am.

MOTHER: Of whom if I may ask?

SON: The old man, of course.

MOTHER: Poor Kerstin! You have married into a nice family!

DAUGHTER-IN-LAW: Yes, if I didn't know Knut so well, and hadn't already learned that artists are a different species, I'd hardly know what to think half the time.

SON: At least I'm an artist. Father and mother are just parasites——

MOTHER [*not angrily*]: You're a parasite if anyone was. You've never earned enough to feed yourself, and look how old you are! And your father wasn't a parasite when he built this house for you, you lazy good-for-nothing!

SON: Oh God, who'd be an only son! Buzz off now, or he'll start his cursing in here, and I don't want to have to listen to that. Hurry, I can see him coming.

MOTHER: I'll go out this way, then. [*Goes.*]

SON: There's a damned draught in this house. Blows right through you.

DAUGHTER-IN-LAW: Yes, your parents might leave us a little more in peace. And all this business of having to go and eat every meal with them instead of being able to keep house for ourselves——

SON: Just like putting out crumbs on the sill for the sparrows. Such fun to see how the little dears eat!

DAUGHTER-IN-LAW [*listens*]: Ssh! Try to put the old man in a good temper so that we don't have the usual morning scene.

SON: If only I could! But he isn't always in the mood to appreciate my jokes.

Scene 3

As before. The FATHER *enters, wearing a white waistcoat and black velvet jacket, and with a rose in his buttonhole. The* COUSIN *enters, and walks around for a while, then begins dusting.*

FATHER [*not removing his hat*]: It's cold this morning.

SON: So I see.

FATHER: How can you possibly see it?

SON: I can see your head's cold.

The FATHER *looks at him contemptuously.*

DAUGHTER-IN-LAW: Knut, how can you be so rude?

FATHER: A fool is a grief unto himself, and the father of a fool findeth no joy.

SON: Where do you get hold of all these proverbs?

DAUGHTER-IN-LAW [*to the* COUSIN]: The room has been dusted today, Adèle dear.

FATHER: A wise woman buildeth a house, but a fool destroyeth it.

SON: Hear that, Adèle?

COUSIN: I?

SON: Yes. Tell me, where does this proverb come from? "A beautiful woman who knoweth not discretion is like a sow with a gold ring in her snout."

DAUGHTER-IN-LAW: Knut, really!

FATHER: You had a visitor late last night?

SON: Did you think it was too late?

FATHER: I don't *think* anything. But it seems to me that a young man might choose a more suitable hour to pay his respects.

SON: You do think, then.

FATHER: Did you invite him?

SON: Why this inquisition? You'll be bringing out thumbscrews next.

FATHER: No, they're your speciality. As soon as I ask the smallest question you threaten to pack up and leave, although you know I built this house for you so that I might at least see you during the summer. When a man's as old as I am, he needs to live for others.

SON: Oh, you aren't old. Anyone'd think you were out courting today, with that rose in your buttonhole.

FATHER: There's a limit even to jokes. Don't you think so, Kerstin?

DAUGHTER-IN-LAW: Oh, Knut's impossible. If I didn't know that he means nothing by what he says——

FATHER: If he means nothing, he must be an idiot. [*Looks at an unfinished portrait of the* FRIEND.] Who's this meant to be?

SON: Can't you see? It's Kerstin's—it's *our* friend.

FATHER: That's a nasty expression he's wearing. He looks a wicked fellow, the way you've painted him.

DAUGHTER-IN-LAW: Yes, but he isn't.

FATHER: He who hath no religion is an evil man, and he who breaketh his marriage is an evil man.

DAUGHTER-IN-LAW: But he didn't break his marriage, he got the law to dissolve it.

FATHER: Knut used to spend his whole time abusing your friend. How come he's grown so fond of him?

SON: Because I didn't know him before and because I've got to know him now. Haven't you nagged enough for this morning?

FATHER: Have you heard this proverb——?

SON: I've heard all your proverbs and all your stories.

FATHER: "There is an hour for love, and there is an hour for hatred." Good morning! [*Goes.*]

Scene 4

As before, but without the FATHER.

DAUGHTER-IN-LAW [*to the* COUSIN, *who is about to water the flowers*]: The flowers have been watered, Adèle darling.

COUSIN: Don't call me darling. You know you hate me.

DAUGHTER-IN-LAW: I don't hate you, although you're the cause of every quarrel that takes place in this house.

SON: Oh Lord, are you two starting now?

DAUGHTER-IN-LAW: If only I could feel there was any kindness behind all the bother she takes about my house! But every service she performs is a reproach and a criticism.

COUSIN: You feel that because you neglect your house and your child. But I've only one object in all I do, and that's to be useful so that I don't have to feel I'm living on charity. But you! You! You!

SON [*goes closer to the* COUSIN *and looks at her*]: So you've got a temper, have you, Adèle? Then you must have passions too!

DAUGHTER-IN-LAW: What have her passions to do with you?

COUSIN: Yes, people who are poor mustn't have any feelings or opinions or will or passions! But marry someone rich and have a wedding in a church, and you can do what you like, your table's laid for you, your bed's made ready for you to creep into, you can live as you please—day *and* night!

DAUGHTER-IN-LAW: Have you no sense of shame?

COUSIN: But you take care! I've got eyes in my head. And ears too! [*Goes.*]

Scene 5

As before, but without the COUSIN.

SON: I honestly believe the Devil is loose today.

DAUGHTER-IN-LAW: You watch out for that girl, Knut. Has it ever occurred to you that your mother might die?

SON: Yes, well?

DAUGHTER-IN-LAW: And that your father might marry again?

SON: Adèle?

DAUGHTER-IN-LAW: Yes.

SON: Oh, nonsense. My God, we'd have to stop that! That'd mean she'd be my stepmother, and her children would share the inheritance.

DAUGHTER-IN-LAW: I have heard your father's already made a will in her favour.

SON: What do you suppose their relationship is, exactly?

DAUGHTER-IN-LAW: Everything. And nothing. One thing's certain, he's in love with the girl.

SON: In love! Well, possibly, but it hasn't gone beyond that.

DAUGHTER-IN-LAW: He's so infatuated with her that last year he started getting jealous of Axel.

SON: Well, couldn't we marry her off to him?

DAUGHTER-IN-LAW: Axel isn't so easy to hook.

SON: Oh, he's inflammable, like all widowers.

DAUGHTER-IN-LAW: Yes, but—poor man, he's much too good for a bitch like her.

SON: I don't know what it is this year, but the whole atmosphere in this place seems to me to have become absolutely suffocating. I feel as though a storm's about to brew up. Oh God, I do wish we could go abroad.

DAUGHTER-IN-LAW: You can't sell any of your paintings, and if we go your father will cut off our allowance. We must talk to Axel about it. He has a gift for solving other people's problems, though he can't manage his own.

SON: I don't know if it's wise to drag strangers into one's family squabbles——

DAUGHTER-IN-LAW: You call our only friend a stranger?

SON: Yes, but it isn't the same as being one of the family. Besides—I don't know—you know what Father says: "Always treat your friends as though they might become your enemies."

DAUGHTER-IN-LAW: For heaven's sake don't you start quoting proverbs. He's got another dreadful one: "Beware of the person you love."

SON: Yes, he's ghastly once he starts.

DAUGHTER-IN-LAW [*glances towards the door*]: Ah, at last! [*Goes to greet* AXEL.] Good morning, lazybones.

Scene 6

The FRIEND *enters in light-coloured summer clothes, with a blue tie and white tennis shoes.*

SON: Hullo, old man.

FRIEND: Good morning, my dear friends. You haven't been waiting for me?

DAUGHTER-IN-LAW: Indeed we have.

SON: My wife's been in absolute despair because you didn't manage to sleep last night.

FRIEND [*confused*]: What do you mean? I don't understand——
SON [*to* DAUGHTER-IN-LAW]: That made him blush!

The DAUGHTER-IN-LAW *looks curiously at the* FRIEND.

FRIEND: It's a glorious morning, and when one has slept beneath the roof of two happy people, one feels that life still has something to offer!

SON: You think we're very happy?

FRIEND: Yes. And your father is doubly so, for he has children and a grandchild through whom he can relive his memories. It is granted to a few mortals to enjoy so blissful an old age.

SON: "Envy no man."

FRIEND: Oh, but I don't envy you. On the contrary, I enjoy seeing how beautifully life can shape itself for some people. It gives me hope that it may possibly prove more friendly to me in the years to come. And especially when one remembers the painful experiences your father has undergone—bankrupt, exiled, rejected by his family——

SON: And now he has his own house and estate, and his son well married?

FRIEND: Exactly.

SON: Tell me, you were in love with my wife last year?

FRIEND: No, I wouldn't say that. I was a little infatuated with her—but that's all over now.

DAUGHTER-IN-LAW: You're very fickle.

FRIEND: In my infatuations, yes. Luckily for me.

SON: But why did you run away so suddenly last summer? Was it on account of—the other lady? Or was it Adèle, perhaps?

FRIEND [*embarrassed*]: Your questions are very intimate.

SON: It *was* Adèle! There, you see, Kerstin!

DAUGHTER-IN-LAW: I don't know why he needed to be frightened of her.

FRIEND: I'm not frightened of women, only of my feelings for women.

SON: You've a most extraordinary talent for evading the issue. It's impossible to pin you down.

FRIEND: Why should one want to pin me down rather than anyone else?

SON: Do you know what my father said about your portrait just now?

DAUGHTER-IN-LAW: Knut, really!

SON: He said you looked like a wicked man.

FRIEND: Then it must be a good likeness, for just now I am indeed a wicked man.

DAUGHTER-IN-LAW: Oh, you always go around boasting how wicked you are——

FRIEND: Perhaps because I'm trying to hide it?

DAUGHTER-IN-LAW: No, you're a good person, much better than you want to appear. But you oughtn't to frighten your friends away from you——

FRIEND: Do I frighten you?

DAUGHTER-IN-LAW: Yes, sometimes, when I don't understand you.

SON: You must marry again. That's all you need.

FRIEND: All! And whom should I marry?

SON: Adèle, for example.

FRIEND: Please let's not discuss that.

SON: Ah, I got you on the raw there! I see, so it was Adèle, then!

FRIEND: My dear friends, perhaps I ought to go and change into something more formal for lunch——

DAUGHTER-IN-LAW: No, don't change. You look charming as you are, and Adèle will fall madly in love with you.

SON: You hear? My wife thinks you're charming.

DAUGHTER-IN-LAW: Is it so dreadful to tell a man that his clothes suit him?

SON: It's a little unusual for a lady to flatter a gentleman. But then of course we're unusual people.

FRIEND: Will you come with me later to help me find a room?

DAUGHTER-IN-LAW: What! But aren't you going to stay with us?

FRIEND: No, that was never my intention.

SON: Oh, come!

DAUGHTER-IN-LAW: Why don't you want to stay with us? Tell us.

FRIEND: I don't know—I think you two ought to be left in peace—besides, we might get tired of one another.

DAUGHTER-IN-LAW: Are you tired of us already? No, but really, you can't possibly go and live in the village. People will start saying things——

FRIEND: Saying things? What kind of things?

DAUGHTER-IN-LAW: Oh, you know how people gossip——

SON: You're staying here, and there's an end of it. Let them talk! If you remain here you are obviously my wife's lover, and if you go and live in the village you have obviously quarrelled with her, or else I've thrown you out. For the sake of your honour I think it's preferable that you should be regarded as my wife's lover. Don't you agree?

FRIEND: You put the case very clearly, but I am mainly concerned with the question of your honour.

DAUGHTER-IN-LAW: I'm sure you have some secret reason you don't want to tell us.

FRIEND: To be perfectly frank—I dare not stay! Oh, yes! It's true! One melts so easily into other people's lives, one basks in their happiness, in the end one's feelings become inextricably entwined with theirs, and then it becomes so painful to part.

SON: But why should we part? Right, that's settled, you're staying here. Offer my wife your arm and let's go out for a walk.

The FRIEND, *somewhat embarrassed, offers the* DAUGHTER-IN-LAW *his arm.*

DAUGHTER-IN-LAW: I believe your arm's trembling! Knut, he's trembling!

SON: What a charming couple you make! My God, he really is trembling! If you feel cold, you'd better stay indoors.

FRIEND: If I may, I'll just sit here and read the papers.

DAUGHTER-IN-LAW: But do, please do! I'll send Adèle in to keep you company! Knut and I will just go out to do a little shopping. [*Beckons in the direction of the door.*] Come here, Adèle. I've got something for you.

Scene 7

As before, with ADÈLE.

FRIEND: Miss Adèle, will you keep me company while my host and hostess go shopping?

COUSIN: Keep you company? Are you afraid of the dark?

FRIEND: Yes, very.

The SON *and* DAUGHTER-IN-LAW *go.*

FRIEND [*makes sure they are alone*]: I don't want to miss this opportunity of having a private word with you, as a member of the family. May I?

COUSIN: By all means.

FRIEND: Well, you know how fond I am of these young people. Oh, you're smiling—I know what you're thinking. Yes, it's true that Mrs. Lenz does attract me as a woman, but I assure you I hold my feelings on so tight a rein that only for one brief moment did I fear they might run away with me.

COUSIN: It doesn't surprise me you're infatuated with Kerstin. She has a talent for making fools of men. What I can't understand is how you can find Knut's company so irresistible. He's utterly trivial, and has nothing like your talent or experience——

FRIEND: In other words, he is a child. But that's just what I find so relaxing, after a whole winter among intellectuals——

COUSIN: Playing with children can become tiring. But you never get tired of Knut. Why is that?

FRIEND: I haven't thought about it. You seem to have, though. What's your theory?

COUSIN: I think, without knowing it, you're in love with Kerstin.

FRIEND: No, I don't think so. I love them as a couple. I don't find the same pleasure in being with either of them alone as I do when the three of us are together. And to see any rift develop between them would set a gulf between them and me. But suppose you were right, suppose I was in love with Kerstin, what would that matter as long as I hide my feelings?

COUSIN: Feelings have a way of communicating themselves; and fire spreads.

FRIEND: Possibly, but I don't think there's any danger. After going through the misery of a divorce you can be sure I've no desire to see anything of that sort happen again, far less be the cause of it. Besides, Mrs. Lenz is in love with her husband——

COUSIN: In love? She's never been that. Their love's just dull husband-and-wife stuff. But Knut has a passionate nature, and one day he may get bored with strawberries and cream.

FRIEND: You know, you've obviously been engaged.

COUSIN: What do you mean?

FRIEND: You know this territory well. So I'll go further. Things seem to me to have changed considerably here since last year.

COUSIN: In what way?

FRIEND: There's a new atmosphere, a different way of talking and thinking. There's something that makes me uneasy.

COUSIN: You've noticed it? Yes, they're a strange family. The father's been doing nothing for ten years, living on his dividends; and the son's never done a stroke of work since he was born. They eat, sleep and wait for death, wasting time as amiably as they know how. No purpose in life, no ambition, no passions—but a great deal of sermonising. Have you noticed there's one word which recurs in this house every other hour? "What a *wicked* person!" It's used to cover every emergency.

FRIEND: You're remarkably eloquent. And penetrative.

COUSIN: Hatred is always penetrative.

FRIEND: Anyone who hates as you do must also be able to love.

COUSIN: Hm!

FRIEND: Miss Adèle, now that we have spoken ill of our friends, we must be friends ourselves, whatever we may feel.

COUSIN: Whatever we may feel!.

FRIEND: Give me your hand on that! But promise you don't hate—me.

COUSIN [*takes his hands, which he stretches towards her*]: How cold you hands are!

The DAUGHTER-IN-LAW is glimpsed for a moment in the doorway.

FRIEND: But yours are warm!

COUSIN: Ssh, there's Kerstin!

FRIEND: Then we must continue this conversation some other time——

Scene 8

The FRIEND. The COUSIN. The DAUGHTER-IN-LAW. A silence.

DAUGHTER-IN-LAW: What a silence! Do I intrude?

COUSIN: Not at all. Perhaps I'm the one who's intruding.

DAUGHTER-IN-LAW [*hands a letter to the FRIEND*]: Here's a letter for you. I see it's from a lady.

The FRIEND looks at the letter, and turns pale.

DAUGHTER-IN-LAW: How pale you've grown! If you're still cold you can borrow my shawl.

Takes off her shawl and puts it over his shoulders.

FRIEND: Thank you. That's warm, anyway.

COUSIN: Perhaps you'd like a cushion under your feet?

DAUGHTER-IN-LAW: It'd be better if you arranged to have a fire lit in his room. It gets so chilly down here.

COUSIN: It certainly does.

FRIEND: Oh, but you mustn't go to all this trouble for my sake! No, please!

COUSIN: Oh, it's no trouble. [*Goes.*]

Scene 9

The FRIEND. *The* DAUGHTER-IN-LAW.
Silence.

FRIEND: What a silence!

DAUGHTER-IN-LAW: Just like when I came in. What secrets did you two have?

FRIEND: Oh, I was just pouring out a few of my sorrows. It's a habit one has difficulty in outgrowing.

DAUGHTER-IN-LAW: Pour out a few for me, then. You're unhappy?

FRIEND: Chiefly because I can't work.

DAUGHTER-IN-LAW: And you can't work because——?

FRIEND: Because?

DAUGHTER-IN-LAW: Are you still in love with your wife?

FRIEND: No, not with her. But with her memory.

DAUGHTER-IN-LAW: Renew those memories, then.

FRIEND: Never!

DAUGHTER-IN-LAW: Was it her you ran away to last autumn?

FRIEND: No, it wasn't. It was to other women. Since you ask.

DAUGHTER-IN-LAW: Oh!

FRIEND: Well, when a gadfly stings you it's a relief to roll in the dirt. It toughens the skin.

DAUGHTER-IN-LAW: Shame on you!

FRIEND: Besides, there's consecrated dirt and—unconsecrated.

DAUGHTER-IN-LAW: What do you mean?

FRIEND: You're married, and we aren't children being prepared for confirmation; so—I mean that in marriage one rests in consecrated dirt, and outside marriage in unconsecrated dirt. But it's still dirt.

DAUGHTER-IN-LAW: Surely you don't compare——!

FRIEND: Yes, I do compare.

DAUGHTER-IN-LAW: What kind of a woman were you married to?

FRIEND: A modest young lady of excellent family.

DAUGHTER-IN-LAW: And you loved her?

FRIEND: Much too much.

DAUGHTER-IN-LAW: And then——?

FRIEND: We hated each other.

DAUGHTER-IN-LAW: But why? Why?

FRIEND: That is one of the many questions which life leaves unanswered.

DAUGHTER-IN-LAW: But there must be a reason.

FRIEND: I thought so too. But then I found that the reasons were the consequences of our hatred. Our quarrels didn't cause the split. It was just that when love ceased, the quarrels started. And that, you see, is why these so-called loveless marriages are the happy ones.

DAUGHTER-IN-LAW [*naïvely*]: Well, Knut and I have never had any serious quarrels.

FRIEND: That's a very revealing remark, Mrs. Lenz.

DAUGHTER-IN-LAW: Why, what have I said?

FRIEND: You have admitted that you have never loved your husband.

DAUGHTER-IN-LAW: Love? What is love?

FRIEND [*gets up*]: What a question, from a married woman! What is love? Well, it's one of the things which one does but can't define.

DAUGHTER-IN-LAW: Was your wife beautiful?

FRIEND: I thought so. She was like you, as a matter of fact.

DAUGHTER-IN-LAW: You think I'm beautiful, then?

FRIEND: Yes.

DAUGHTER-IN-LAW: My husband didn't think so until you said so. It's amazing how much he wants me when you're here. Your presence seems to inflame him.

FRIEND: I see. So that's why he's so glad to see me here. And—you?

DAUGHTER-IN-LAW: I?

FRIEND: Perhaps we should stop now, before we go too far.

DAUGHTER-IN-LAW [*angrily*]: What do you mean? What are you thinking?

FRIEND: Nothing bad, Mrs. Lenz. Nothing! Forgive me if I hurt you.

DAUGHTER-IN-LAW: You hurt me terribly. But I know how low your opinion of women is.

FRIEND: Not all women. You are to me——

DAUGHTER-IN-LAW: Yes?

FRIEND: My friend's wife, and therefore——

DAUGHTER-IN-LAW: And if I weren't?

FRIEND: Again I think we had better stop. Mrs. Lenz, you seem to me to be unused to having attentions paid to you by men——

DAUGHTER-IN-LAW: I am, and that's why I appreciate being liked. Just a little.

FRIEND: Just a little! You certainly ought to be happy if that is all you demand from life.

DAUGHTER-IN-LAW: What do you know of what I demand from life?

FRIEND: Are you ambitious? Do you ever feel the need to break out of your mould, to climb, to become something?

DAUGHTER-IN-LAW: No. Nothing like that, But this life's so monotonous—no work, no emotional excitements—nothing ever happens! Do you know, sometimes I feel so desperate that I long for something dreadful to happen—a pestilence, a fire—[*whispers*]—that my child should die! That I should die myself.

FRIEND: You know what that is? It's idleness, a surfeit of worldly contentment—perhaps something else, too——

DAUGHTER-IN-LAW: What?

FRIEND: Lust.

DAUGHTER-IN-LAW: What did you say?

FRIEND: I don't want to repeat the word, especially as I think you heard it. But as I don't mean anything ugly by it I can't really feel I have wounded you.

DAUGHTER-IN-LAW: Then you're unlike all other human beings. You hit your friends in the face, and they feel nothing.

FRIEND: There are said to be women who love being hit.

DAUGHTER-IN-LAW: Now I'm beginning to grow afraid of you.

FRIEND: Good.

DAUGHTER-IN-LAW: Who are you? What do you want? What is your purpose?

FRIEND: Don't start getting inquisitive about me, Mrs. Lenz.

DAUGHTER-IN-LAW: Now you're being impertinent again.

FRIEND: I'm just giving you a friendly piece of advice. Have you noticed we always quarrel when your husband is absent? That isn't a good omen.

DAUGHTER-IN-LAW: Of what?

FRIEND: Of lasting friendship. It suggests we need a safety valve.

DAUGHTER-IN-LAW: Sometimes I feel I could hate you.

FRIEND: That's a better omen. But have you **never** felt you could love me?

DAUGHTER-IN-LAW: Yes, sometimes.

FRIEND: When?

DAUGHTER-IN-LAW: I feel tempted to match your frankness. Well, it's when you talk to Adèle.

FRIEND: You are curiously like your husband. His passion always flares up when I am present. Miss Adèle and I seem to act as firelighters.

DAUGHTER-IN-LAW [*laughs*]: It sounds so funny when you put it that way, I can't bring myself to be angry.

FRIEND: You should never be angry. It's unbecoming to you, more than to most people. But to change the subject, where is your husband?

He gets up and looks out of the window. The DAUGHTER-IN-LAW *also looks out of the window.*

FRIEND: I didn't mean to draw your attention to what is happening down there in the park——

DAUGHTER-IN-LAW: Oh, it isn't the first time I've seen Knut kiss Adèle.

FRIEND: But it worries me that Miss Adèle cannot ignite your husband's feelings for you. There's so much in this house that worries me this year. I think something must be rotting underneath these floorboards.

DAUGHTER-IN-LAW: Oh? I haven't noticed anything. Anyway, it's only a game.

FRIEND: Yes, you play with matches, with hunting knives and dynamite. I think it's horrible.

Scene 10

As before. The FATHER *enters, with his hat on.*

FATHER: Is Knut here?

DAUGHTER-IN-LAW: No, he's gone out to do some shopping. Do you want him?

FATHER: Obviously, since I'm asking for him. Have you seen Adèle?

DAUGHTER-IN-LAW: No, not for some time.

FATHER [*notices the* FRIEND]: Oh, forgive me, I didn't see you. How are you?

FRIEND: Thank you, how are you, sir?

DAUGHTER-IN-LAW: Can I do anything?

FATHER: If you would. But perhaps I'm disturbing you. I'll come back later.

DAUGHTER-IN-LAW: How could you be disturbing us?

FATHER: Well, the fact is, I've got some mosquitoes in my bedroom, so I thought I'd ask if I might sleep in your spare room?

DAUGHTER-IN-LAW: What a pity. We've just promised that to Mr. Axel.

FATHER: Oh, I see, he's staying here. If I'd known that, of course I'd never have suggested——

FRIEND: I would never have accepted your son's offer if I had known that you——

FATHER: Oh, no, no, no—I don't want to be in the way. "Never come between the bark and the tree." [*Silence.*] Has Knut begun to paint yet?

DAUGHTER-IN-LAW: No, he doesn't feel in the mood.

FATHER: I've never known a time when he has. And less than ever nowadays.

DAUGHTER-IN-LAW: Is there anything else?

FATHER: No, it doesn't matter. Er—by the way, no need to mention anything to Knut about the room.

DAUGHTER-IN-LAW: I'll be delighted not to.

FATHER: I don't like causing trouble for nothing. It'd have been different if the room had been free, and I'd been able to have it, but since it's taken— Well, goodbye. [*Goes.*]

Scene 11

The FRIEND. *The* DAUGHTER-IN-LAW.

FRIEND: Mrs. Lenz, will you forgive me if I leave you for a short while?

DAUGHTER-IN-LAW: Where are you off to so suddenly?

FRIEND: That I can't tell you.

DAUGHTER-IN-LAW: You're going to look for a room! No, please, you mustn't do that!

FRIEND: Do you think I want to stay in your house after being told so plainly to go?

DAUGHTER-IN-LAW [*tries to take his hat*]: No, you mustn't go! We don't want you to go! Besides——!

Scene 12

As before. The SON.

SON: What's this? Are you two fighting? Or is this a declaration of love?

DAUGHTER-IN-LAW: Just a lovers' quarrel. Can you imagine, Knut, this restless man wants to go out again and look for a room just because Father said he wanted to have the spare room!

SON: Wanted to have the spare room? Oh yes, of course, he wants to see what you two are up to. And you're thinking of leaving just because of that? Go down on your knees to the lady and ask her pardon.

The FRIEND kneels.

SON: Kiss her foot. She has beautiful feet, you know.

FRIEND [*imprints a kiss on her foot, then gets up*]: Well, now I have asked your pardon for going out and looking for a room. *Au revoir*, then! [*Hastens out.*]

DAUGHTER-IN-LAW [*annoyed*]: Mr. Axel!

Scene 13

The SON. The DAUGHTER-IN-LAW.

DAUGHTER-IN-LAW: I really think it's indecent of the old man to stick his nose in like this and upset the whole household. Now we'll never have a moment's peace, day or night.

SON: A nice state of affairs! But you might have tried to hide your feelings just a little.

DAUGHTER-IN-LAW: What feelings? What do you mean? Knut—are you jealous?

SON: What on earth are you talking about? I was referring to your obviously hostile feelings towards my father.

DAUGHTER-IN-LAW [*changing the subject*]: Oh, let's stop talking about feelings. Here, put this tie on, and try to look like a human being. [*Takes a package from her pocket.*]

SON: Oh God, not another new tie! And blue again!

DAUGHTER-IN-LAW [*fastens a blue tie around KNUT's neck*]: Yes, and you must stop going around in these filthy clothes. And brush your moustache——

SON: Aren't you being a little obvious?

DAUGHTER-IN-LAW: What do you mean?

SON: Perhaps you'd like me to wear a white coat too. And tennis shoes.

DAUGHTER-IN-LAW: Yes, they'd suit you. You're beginning to get so fat and greasy.

SON: And I suppose you'd like me to get thin? And look a little harrowed? You wouldn't like me to get divorced too?

DAUGHTER-IN-LAW: Why, Knut! Now you *are* jealous!

SON: Yes, well, really you go too far. But it's strange! I am jealous, though I feel no envy or malice. I like this man so much I couldn't deny him anything. Anything!

DAUGHTER-IN-LAW: Anything? That's saying a lot.

SON: Well, it's the truth. It's mad, criminal, base, but if he asked me to let him sleep with you, I'd say yes.

DAUGHTER-IN-LAW: Now you're being horrible. I've had to put up with a lot from you, and——

SON: I can't help it. Do you know, sometimes I'm haunted by a vision, not only when I'm awake but when I'm asleep too. I see the two of you together—and it doesn't hurt me, I enjoy it, as though I were watching something very beautiful.

DAUGHTER-IN-LAW: This is revolting.

SON: It may be unusual, but you must admit it's damned interesting.

DAUGHTER-IN-LAW: Do you know, sometimes I think you want to be rid of me.

SON: You can't seriously think that!

DAUGHTER-IN-LAW: I do, sometimes. It seems to me you're nudging Axel forward the whole time so that he'll fall into my arms and you'll have a case against me and be able to get a divorce.

SON: Extraordinary! Tell me, Kerstin, have you and he never kissed each other?

DAUGHTER-IN-LAW: No, never. I swear it!

SON: Promise me that when the moment does come you'll tell me. Just say: "It's happened."

DAUGHTER-IN-LAW: Knut, for God's sake try to be sensible.

SON: But that's just what I am doing. You see, I don't want to be cuckolded. I don't want to give you up either, but I'd rather that than the other.

DAUGHTER-IN-LAW: Suppose you stop sermonising and let me start. What exactly is your relationship with Adèle?

SON: Only what you already know and approve.

DAUGHTER-IN-LAW: I've never approved of adultery.

SON: Ah, now you're changing your tone. What was innocent a moment ago is now a crime.

DAUGHTER-IN-LAW: My relationship with Axel was completely innocent a moment ago.

SON: It may be innocent today, but who knows what it may be tomorrow?

DAUGHTER-IN-LAW: Wait till tomorrow, then.

SON: No, I don't want to wait until it's too late.

DAUGHTER-IN-LAW: What do you want, then?

SON: I don't know. Yes—an end to all this. If there is one. We have woven the net ourselves, and now we sit caught in it. Oh, how I hate him when he isn't here! But as soon as I see him again, and he fixes his big eyes on me, I love him, like a brother, like a sister.... Now I understand why you have fallen under his influence. But I don't quite understand myself. It seems to me I've been going around here for so long among petticoats that I've become like a woman. Your love for him has infected me. You must love him tremendously, though you don't know it.

DAUGHTER-IN-LAW: It's true. And now you want to pretend it's my fault.

SON: Just as you are trying to pretend it's my fault.

DAUGHTER-IN-LAW: It is your fault!

SON: No, it's your fault. Now I *am* going mad!

DAUGHTER-IN-LAW: I can believe that.

SON: And you've no pity for me!

DAUGHTER-IN-LAW: Why should I pity you, when you plague the life out of me?

SON: You have never loved me.

DAUGHTER-IN-LAW: You have never loved me.

SON: Now we have started a quarrel that will last for the rest of our lives.

DAUGHTER-IN-LAW: Then let's stop while there's time. Go and have a swim and cool yourself down.

SON: You want to be alone.

Scene 14

The SON. *The* DAUGHTER-IN-LAW. *The* FRIEND.

FRIEND [*open and cheerful*]: Well, I'm in luck! As I was leaving, I happened to run into Miss Adèle, and she has a room——

DAUGHTER-IN-LAW: So she lets rooms too?

FRIEND: She knows of a room.

DAUGHTER-IN-LAW: She knows everything, that girl!

FRIEND [*to* SON, *offering him a cigarette*]: Cigarette?

SON [*crossly*]: No, thank you.

FRIEND: What a nice tie you've got!

SON: You think so?

FRIEND: You've been talking about me while I've been away. I can see it.

SON [*upset*]: Excuse me, I must go and have a swim. [*Hurries out.*]

Scene 15

The FRIEND. *The* DAUGHTER-IN-LAW.

FRIEND: What's wrong with him?

DAUGHTER-IN-LAW: Jealousy.

FRIEND: Oh! But he has no reason——

DAUGHTER-IN-LAW: He thinks he has. Where is this room of Adèle's that you were talking about?

FRIEND [*abstractedly*]: Adèle? Oh, yes—just opposite, in the pilot's cottage.

DAUGHTER-IN-LAW: That's convenient. You'll be able to see into her room. What a clever girl she is!

FRIEND: I'm sure such a thought never crossed Adèle's mind.

DAUGHTER-IN-LAW: Adèle? Have you become so intimate?

FRIEND: Mrs. Lenz, please don't raise ghosts which otherwise wouldn't see the light of day. Don't do it, or——

DAUGHTER-IN-LAW: Or you'll go again. But you mustn't go now. You haven't the right.

FRIEND [*lights a cigarette*]: Perhaps it is now my duty.

DAUGHTER-IN-LAW: If you are my friend, you will not leave me unprotected in this house, where my honour is threatened and where my incorrigible husband, with his parents' connivance, is free to indulge in whatever depravities he chooses! Would you believe it, he's sunk so low that he says if necessary he'll renounce me—to you!

FRIEND: That's a charming form of jealousy. And what did you reply?

DAUGHTER-IN-LAW: What could I reply?

FRIEND: The question was mine.

DAUGHTER-IN-LAW [*hysterically*]: You're playing with me like a cat! You can see how I'm caught in your net—I suffer and struggle to free myself, but I can't! Have pity on me, give me one kind look, don't sit there like a statue awaiting adoration and sacrifice! [*She falls on her knees.*] Oh, you're so strong, you can control your passions, you're so proud and high-minded, but that's because you have never loved, you've never loved as I have loved you!

FRIEND: Haven't I? Get up, Mrs. Lenz. Go over there and sit in that chair. The furthest one. That's right. Now I shall speak. [*Remains seated, with his cigarette in his hand.*] I have loved you, as you call it, from the first moment I saw you. Do you remember that sunset when we first met, last year? Your husband was painting down in the valley as I happened to pass. I was introduced to you, and we stood there talking till we grew tired and you sat down in the grass, and asked me to sit by your side. But the dew had fallen, and I was afraid of getting wet. Then you unbuttoned your coat and offered me one of its corners to sit on. To me it was as though you had opened your arms and asked me to rest my head in your lap. I was very unhappy, very tired and lonely, and it looked so warm and soft there inside your coat. I wanted to creep in under it and hide myself in your young and virginal bosom. But then I saw a faint smile in your innocent eyes. You were amused that a man like me could be embarrassed, and I became ashamed. We met again, often and often. Your husband seemed to enjoy my admiration of you, it was as though I had discovered his wife for him. I became your prisoner, and you played with me. Your husband didn't hesitate to tease me openly, even before strangers. His conceit and complacency hurt me at times, and there were moments when I felt tempted to shoulder him aside and try to take his place. Do you remember that afternoon when I invited you both to visit me on my birthday? You were to come later; and after we had waited an hour for you, you entered the room wearing a pansy-coloured skirt and a bodice embroidered with bright flowers. You had a shepherdess hat covered with yellow muslin, which flooded your whole body in sunshine and gold. And then, when you curtseyed and offered me your bouquet of roses, with the shy daring of a fourteen-year-old girl, I found you so overwhelmingly beautiful that I fell dumb, I could neither bid you welcome nor thank you for the flowers, but went outside and cried.

DAUGHTER-IN-LAW: At least you know how to hide your feelings.

FRIEND: And do you remember, later that night, after supper, how, hour after hour, we exchanged memories and our souls embraced; and then Knut, formally, and I suppose with your consent, invited me to come and spend the winter with you in town? And do you remember what I replied?

DAUGHTER-IN-LAW: You replied: "I dare not".

FRIEND: And the next morning, I was gone.

DAUGHTER-IN-LAW: And I cried the whole day. And Knut cried too!

FRIEND: Then what a flood of tears there'll be now!

DAUGHTER-IN-LAW: Now?

FRIEND: Sit still. Now that everything has been said, there is nothing left for us but to part.

DAUGHTER-IN-LAW: No! No! We mustn't part! Why can't things stay as they are? You're so calm, and I don't feel uneasy. What has Knut to do with our feelings, as long as we control them? We are just sitting here quite quietly talking about the past, like an old married couple remembering their youthful love.

FRIEND: Oh, you poor child! What kind of a marriage must yours have been if you can believe in friendship after a declaration of love? I am as calm as a sack of gunpowder above a match, I am as cold as a newly stoked furnace—ah! I have fought, I have tortured myself, but I cannot answer for myself.

DAUGHTER-IN-LAW: But I can answer for myself.

FRIEND: Yes, I can believe that. You can quench the flame the moment it flares up, but I—I live alone! God, what a hellish thought! Do you imagine that after this I could bear to live in this house on crumbs from the rich man's table, feeding on air, drinking the perfume of flowers, yet plagued every hour by a guilty conscience?

DAUGHTER-IN-LAW: Why should you have a guilty conscience? He doesn't hesitate to have a mistress whom he kisses.

FRIEND: Let's not try to shift the blame on to others—we mustn't do that. That way leads to the edge of the precipice, and then there'll be nothing left for us but to fall into the sea and drown. No, let us be original for once, let us show the world an example of how to behave honourably! The moment Knut enters this room, we will say to him: "It has happened, we love each other! Tell us what we must do!"

DAUGHTER-IN-LAW: Yes, that is great, that is noble! Yes, we'll do that. And then, let fate take its course! And we can do this with a clear conscience, for we have committed no crime.

FRIEND: But afterwards? He will of course ask me to leave.

DAUGHTER-IN-LAW: Or to stay.

FRIEND: On what condition? That everything shall remain as before? No, I couldn't bear that. Do you think that after this I could watch you caress each other, hear you shut your bedroom door at night——? No! I can't see how this will end. But he must know, otherwise I can never look him in the face again, never press his hand. We must tell him everything—and then, we'll see!

DAUGHTER-IN-LAW: Oh, if only this next hour were over! Tell me you love me, or I shan't have the courage to plunge the knife into him. Tell me you love me!

FRIEND [*remains seated, like the* DAUGHTER-IN-LAW]: I love you with my body and with my soul. I love your small feet which I see beneath the hem of your skirt. I love your small white teeth and your mouth ready for kisses, your ears, and your kind yet sensuous eyes. I love the whole of your light, airy body, which I long to throw over my shoulder and run away with into the forest. When I was young I once lifted a girl up in the street, cradled her on my arms and ran up four flights of stairs with her. I was young then, think what I could do now I am a grown man!

DAUGHTER-IN-LAW: Love my soul too!

FRIEND: I love your soul, because it is weaker than mine, fiery like mine, faithless as mine——

DAUGHTER-IN-LAW: Mayn't I get up and come to you now?

FRIEND: No! You mustn't!

DAUGHTER-IN-LAW: Knut is coming. I hear his footsteps, and I haven't the courage to speak until I have kissed you on the forehead.

FRIEND: Is he coming?

DAUGHTER-IN-LAW: Ssh!

Scene 16

The FRIEND. *The* DAUGHTER-IN-LAW. *The* FATHER *enters, his hat on his head, and goes straight across to the* FRIEND, *who starts and gets up.*

FATHER [*takes a newspaper from the table behind the* FRIEND]: Forgive me for disturbing you, I only wanted a newspaper. [*To the* DAUGHTER-IN-LAW.] Have you seen Adèle?

DAUGHTER-IN-LAW: That's the fifth time today you've asked for Adèle.

FATHER: Have you been counting? Aren't you going to have a bathe before lunch?

DAUGHTER-IN-LAW: No. Not today.

FATHER: You oughtn't to miss any opportunities of bathing, since your health's so delicate.

Silence. The FATHER *goes.*

Scene 17

The FRIEND. *The* DAUGHTER-IN-LAW.

FRIEND: No, I can't stay here any longer! I can't bear it!

DAUGHTER-IN-LAW [*goes close to him and looks at him, her eyes burning*]: Shall we run away?

FRIEND: No. But I shall run away.

DAUGHTER-IN-LAW: Then I will run away too! We shall die together!

FRIEND [*takes her in his arms and kisses her*]: Now we are lost! Oh, why did I do that? This is the end of honour and faith, the end of friendship, the end of peace! Fire of hell, that burns and parches all that was green and flowered! Ah!

They part and sit down again in their former chairs.

Scene 18

The FRIEND. *The* DAUGHTER-IN-LAW. *The* SON *enters.*

SON: Why are you sitting so far apart?

DAUGHTER-IN-LAW: Because——

SON: And looking so upset?

DAUGHTER-IN-LAW: Because—— [*A long pause.*] We love each other.

SON [*looks at them both for a moment, then says to the* FRIEND]: Is this true?

FRIEND: It is true.

SON [*sits down in a chair, somewhat overwhelmed*]: Why do you tell me this?

DAUGHTER-IN-LAW: Because we are honourable.

SON: Well, it's certainly original, but it's damned immodest.

DAUGHTER-IN-LAW: You said yourself that when the moment came——

SON: That's true. And the moment has come. I feel as though I'd known all this before, and yet it astonishes me so much, I can't comprehend it. Who is to blame? No one—and everyone! What shall we do now, and what's going to happen?

FRIEND: Have you any criticism to make of my conduct?

SON: None! You ran away when you perceived the danger. You rejected our invitation to you to come and live with us. You concealed your feelings so well that Kerstin thought you hated her. But why did you come back?

FRIEND: Because I thought my feelings were dead.

SON: That sounds plausible, and I believe you. All the same, we sit here confronted by a situation which is not our fault and which we could not have prevented. We tried to forestall the danger by pretending to be frank, and making fun of it, but it has closed in upon us and now it has struck. What are we to do? [*Silence.*] No one answers. But we mustn't sit here and watch the roof burn without doing something. [*Gets up.*] Let us think of the consequences.

FRIEND: The most proper solution would be for me to go?

SON: I think so.

DAUGHTER-IN-LAW [*wildly*]: No, you mustn't go! If you do, I'll follow you!

SON: Is this your idea of talking calmly?

DAUGHTER-IN-LAW: Love is not calm. [*Goes towards the* FRIEND.]

SON: At least spare me the spectacle of your lust. Consider my feelings a little, since I am comparatively innocent, and am always the one who suffers.

DAUGHTER-IN-LAW [*throws her arms around the* FRIEND's *neck*]: You mustn't go, do you hear?

SON [*takes his wife by the arm and separates her from the* FRIEND]: At least you can behave like decent human beings until I've left the room. [*To the* FRIEND.] Listen, my friend. We must come to some agreement quickly, for in a few minutes the gong will go for lunch. I see that you cannot conquer your love, whereas I, with a certain amount of effort, can conquer mine. For me to go on living with a woman who loves someone else could never be a satisfactory existence, since I should always regard myself as abetting a state of polygamy. Therefore—I shall abandon my claim to her, but not until I have your solemn promise that you will marry her.

FRIEND: I don't know why it is, but your noble offer humiliates me more than the knowledge of my guilt would have done if I had stolen her from you.

SON: I dare say, but it humiliates me less to give than to be robbed. I'll give you five minutes to settle the matter. Well, cheerio. [*Goes.*]

Scene 19

The FRIEND. *The* DAUGHTER-IN-LAW.

DAUGHTER-IN-LAW: Well?

FRIEND: Don't you see that my position is ridiculous?

DAUGHTER-IN-LAW: No. It isn't ridiculous to act honourably.

FRIEND: Not always, but in this instance the husband seems to me the least ridiculous of the three. One day you'll despise me.

DAUGHTER-IN-LAW: Is that all you have to say to me at a moment like this? Now, when nothing stands between us, and you could hold me in your arms with a clear conscience—*now* you hesitate?

FRIEND: Yes, I hesitate. Because this honesty of ours begins to seem like effrontery, this honourable behaviour smacks of callousness——

DAUGHTER-IN-LAW: Oh, it does, does it?

FRIEND: And I'm beginning to think that this smell of rottenness which I've noticed in this house emanates from you.

DAUGHTER-IN-LAW: Or from you! It was you who seduced me with your timid glances, with your pretence of coldness, with your brutalities that inflamed me like a whip! And now the seducer plays the man of honour! Oh!

FRIEND: Or one could put it like this. That it was you who——

DAUGHTER-IN-LAW: No, it was you, you, you! [*Throws herself on the sofa and screams.*] Help me! I'm dying! I'm dying!

The FRIEND *stands motionless.*

DAUGHTER-IN-LAW: Can't you help me? Have you no pity? Are you a wild beast? Don't you see I'm ill? Help me! Help me!

The FRIEND *remains as before.*

DAUGHTER-IN-LAW: Get me a doctor! At least do me the service every human being performs for a stranger! Call Adèle!

The FRIEND *goes.*

Scene 20

The DAUGHTER-IN-LAW. *The* SON *enters.*

SON: Well? What's the matter? [*To the* DAUGHTER-IN-LAW.] Couldn't you agree?

DAUGHTER-IN-LAW: Be quiet! For God's sake shut up!

SON: But why did he run out through the garden like that? He looked as though he was going to take the trees and bushes with him. I thought the seat of his trousers was on fire!

Scene 21

The DAUGHTER-IN-LAW. *The* SON. *The* MOTHER. *The* COUSIN. *Then the* FATHER.

MOTHER: Well, do you want to come and have lunch now?

SON: Thank you, yes. That's just what we need.

MOTHER: But where is Mr. Axel? Shall we wait for him or not?

SON: No, we won't wait for him. He's gone.

MOTHER: What a strange gentleman he is! And I've fried these lovely dabs——

The FATHER *enters.*

SON [*to* FATHER]: You can have that room now, if you want it.

FATHER: Thank you, I don't need it now.

SON: It's extraordinary the way you keep changing your mind.

FATHER: Well, I'm not the only one. But "he who knoweth his own mind is greater than he who conquereth cities."

SON: How about this? "Show not thy friend the door if thou wouldst see him more."

FATHER: That's very good! Where did you find that?

SON: I got it from Kerstin.

FATHER: From Kerstin? Really? Have you had your bathe, my child?

SON: No, she's just had a cold douche.

The gong is heard.

MOTHER: Ah, good, Now let's go and eat.

SON [*to* FATHER]: You take my wife in, and I'll escort Adèle.

FATHER: No, thanks. You keep Kerstin for yourself.

* Strindberg appears to have considered two alternative endings to PLAYING WITH FIRE, in addition to that printed above. The original manuscript of the play, long presumed lost, was discovered in the Bonnier archives in 1951. In this, after the Daughter-in-Law has collapsed and begged the Friend to call Adèle, the latter enters and tells the Friend that Kerstin is two months pregnant. The Friend leaves, the Son enters, and the play continues as above. This scene is deleted in the MS, but in blue chalk as opposed to the ink used by Strindberg in his corrections; the amendment was therefore probably made by the publisher, but this may have been at Strindberg's request.

In the German translation of the play, published in 1893, this scene does not appear. Instead, there is a much lighter one, in which the Friend remembers the letter lying unopened in his pocket, reads it, finds that his wife has after all refused him a divorce so that he and Kerstin cannot marry anyway, and takes his leave on this note. This (if it was written by Strindberg and not thought up by his German translator or publisher) makes a sad anticlimax, and when PLAYING WITH FIRE was first printed in Sweden, in 1897, Strindberg used neither of these endings but the one given above, in which the Friend simply walks out in the middle of Kerstin's hysterical fit. It seems to me that this should therefore be regarded as the definitive ending, in so far as any text can be regarded as definitive where Strindberg is concerned.

Introduction to
ERIK THE FOURTEENTH

STRINDBERG wrote ERIK THE FOURTEENTH during June and July of 1899, partly in Lund and partly in Furusund in the Stockholm archipelago.

Much had happened since that summer of 1892, when he had at last parted for good from Siri and written PLAYING WITH FIRE. His position then must have seemed even worse than after the failure of his experimental theatre in Copenhagen in 1889. He was homeless, separated from his children, treated with coolness by the Swedish publishers and theatres, worn out and poor. Several of his best plays, including THE FATHER and MISS JULIE, were still unperformed in Sweden. Disillusioned with the theatre, he turned his back on it and, like the Captain in THE FATHER, sought refuge in science, which had always interested him.

At the end of 1892 his friend Ola Hansson raised a fund to assist him, and he left Sweden for Germany. He settled in Berlin, where he led a wild bohemian life with a group of other writers and artists, including the Norwegian novelist Knut Hamsun and the Polish writer Stanislas Przybyszewski. Here, early in 1893, he met a young Austrian journalist named Frida Uhl, the daughter of a rich Viennese newspaper editor and art collector. They married that year, and she bore him a daughter. But their marriage lasted little more than a year, and late in 1894 Strindberg left her and made his way to Paris.

There, at last, success came to him, if only briefly. A few months earlier, in June 1894, CREDITORS had been produced by Lugné-Poe at the Théâtre de l'Œuvre, and had been well received. Now, in December 1894, THE FATHER was performed at the same theatre, and was excitedly acclaimed. For a few months Strindberg was interviewed and lionised. But this success brought him only three hundred francs, and by the spring all the talk had faded. His distaste for writing plays remained, and for two years he eked out a wretched existence in cheap hotels, immersed in his scientific experiments. With a dreadful single-mindedness he toiled to discover the origin of all matter, and to make gold.

For over a year he hovered on the brink of complete insanity. He was saved by, of all things for so confirmed an atheist, religion. Slowly and reluctantly he found himself groping towards a wavering faith. In December 1896 he returned from Paris to Sweden. It was, to him, a symbolic gesture; as though, by returning to the country of his birth, his time of exile might be ended. He settled in Lund, and there he found solace in the writings of the eighteenth-century theologian, Emmanuel Swedenborg. These deeply influenced the remaining years of his life. Swedenborg taught him to believe that life was not a chaos, but that he was being rightfully punished for his sins by a just God, and that everything was planned in detail by a wise and merciful Providence. Strindberg's belief that he was being persecuted became greatly reduced and, for the first time for years, he began to sleep well. In the summer of 1897, he wrote a terrifying account of the Purgatory through which he had passed; he called this book INFERNO. The following year, he wrote his first play for six years: the opening section of the trilogy TO DAMASCUS.

Each play in this trilogy forms a separate theatrical entity. They are dramas of wandering; Strindberg had often in the past identified himself with Ahasuerus, the Wandering Jew, and the Flying Dutchman. Now he likened himself to Saul, the persecutor whom God punished on the road to Damascus. Throughout these plays, one of the two principal protagonists remains invisible: God.

Such new content demanded a new form; and TO DAMASCUS is to the theatre what ULYSSES was to be to the novel and THE WASTE LAND to poetry. Strindberg had long felt that the division commonly made between the world of dreams and the world of reality was false. "It seems to me as though I walk in

Introduction to ERIK THE FOURTEENTH

my sleep", he had written back in 1887, "as though reality and imagination are one. . . . Everything that happens, however strange, seems inevitable." On 5 June 1898 he had written to the poet Gustav Fröding: "Don't use the word hallucination (or even delirium) as though it stood for something unreal. Hallucinations and delirium possess a certain kind of reality—or they are phantasmagoria consciously designed by the Invisible One to frighten us. They all have a symbolic meaning. For example, the projections of alcoholism are always the same: flies and rats. The direct progeny of filth."

In Paris, during his experiments in alchemy, he had associated with a circle of occultists, and had been especially attracted by their conception of the *doppelgänger* or dream ego. "Human beings", he wrote in 1897, "live a double life—our fancies, fantasies and dreams possess a kind of reality." In Paris, too, he had met Paul Gauguin and Edvard Munch, and had been influenced by the anti-naturalistic movement that was then taking place in painting; and he had read the symbolical one-act plays which Maurice Maeterlinck had written in the early 1890's. No one, however, had attempted to use symbolism on the scale of TO DAMASCUS. From start to finish of that mighty trilogy, reality and imagination are one.

He followed Parts I and II of TO DAMASCUS with another symbolical play, ADVENT, in the same year (1898). Then he returned to realistic writing and in 1899, with all his old feverish energy, he completed the tragi-comedy THERE ARE CRIMES AND CRIMES and three historical plays. The first of these was THE SAGA OF THE FOLKUNGS, set in fourteenth-century Sweden. He then composed GUSTAV VASA, a sequel to MASTER OLOF, his first theatrical success of twenty years before.

Gustav Vasa was the father of Erik the Fourteenth, an epileptic monarch who proposed unsuccessfully to Elizabeth I of England, married a commoner, and was ultimately deposed and murdered. Strindberg had long been interested in this character, and had attempted to write a play about him as early as 1870, but had burned the result. In 1872 he had written an article about a painting of Erik by Georg von Rosen in which he had criticised the traditional view of Göran Persson, the King's plebeian adviser, as a villain, and of Karin, Erik's queen, as an ethereal creature of legend. He wondered whether Göran might not have been maligned by historians; was he not perhaps a man born before his time who tried to champion the cause of the common people against the feudal lords? And was not Karin, the daughter of a common soldier, more likely to have been a down-to-earth peasant girl than a fairy-tale princess, with at least as much in common with Göran as with Erik?* The King, too, who had commonly been regarded as a mere lunatic, seemed to Strindberg a character worth reanalysing in the light of recent medical and psychological research. Perhaps he, like Strindberg, had been less mad than the world supposed him.

Strindberg began ERIK THE FOURTEENTH in Lund in mid-June, 1899, and sent it to his publisher on 1 August. On 17 October, GUSTAV VASA was performed at Svenska Teatern in Stockholm, and was a great success. As a result, ERIK THE FOURTEENTH was immediately put into rehearsal, and received its première at the same theatre on 30 November 1899. It was less favourably received on that occasion than its predecessor, but has since established itself in Scandinavia and Germany as one of Strindberg's most admired and most frequently performed plays. It also achieved a notable success in Moscow, where in 1921 it was the subject of a famous production at the Arts Theatre by Eugene Vachtangov (the play had been banned for its radical sentiments under the Tsarist régime, but was very much in tune with the atmosphere of post-revolutionary Russia). It remained in the Arts Theatre repertory for many years. In 1924 there was a distinguished production in Berlin at the Deutsches Theater, with Ernst Deutsch as the King; and in 1931, Michael Tchehov, who had acted the King in

* For more details about the historical background to the play, see page 291.

Vachtangov's production, visited Paris with his company and performed the play at the Théâtre de l'Atelier.

Since the Second World War there have been two particularly notable productions of ERIK THE FOURTEENTH in Sweden. In 1950, Alf Sjöberg directed it excitingly at the Royal Theatre in Stockholm, with Ulf Palme as the King and Lars Hanson as Göran Persson, and in 1956 Ingmar Bergman directed it equally excitingly, though quite differently, at Malmö, with Toivo Pawlo as the King, Bibi Andersson as Karin, Åke Fridell as Göran Persson, Max von Sydow as Duke Charles and Ingrid Thulin as Agda. In 1954 Alf Sjöberg based a film on Strindberg's play, entitled KARIN MÅNSDOTTER, with Jarl Kulle as the King, Ulf Palme as Göran Persson and Ulla Jacobsson as Karin. It was coolly received by the Swedish critics, though this translator found it a most powerful and moving experience. (But Sjöberg, like Orson Welles, has not received in his own country the credit due to him as a film director. Even his magnificent MISS JULIE was grudgingly accepted there.) In 1960, ERIK THE FOURTEENTH was produced in Paris by Jean Vilar for the T.N.P., with Daniel Gélin as the King, and it was a success in Warsaw in 1961 at the Teatr Polski, where it was directed by Zigmunt Hübner. It has not to date been performed in England in any medium.

ERIK THE FOURTEENTH

A Drama in Four Acts
(1899)

CHARACTERS

ERIK THE FOURTEENTH, King of Sweden
GÖRAN PERSSON, a commoner
SVANTE STURE, Lord High Steward of Sweden
NILS STURE \} his sons
ERIK STURE \}
NILS GYLLENSTJERNA, a nobleman.
KARIN MÅNSDOTTER, a commoner, mistress to the King
GUSTAV \} children of ERIK and KARIN
SIGRID \}
FRU PERSSON, mother to GÖRAN PERSSON
AGDA, a commoner, formerly a whore
MARIA, her three-year-old daughter
DUKE JOHAN, stepbrother to the King, (afterwards KING JOHAN III)
KATARINA STENBOCK, widow of the late KING GUSTAV VASA and stepmother to KING ERIK
PEDER WELAMSON, nephew to GÖRAN PERSSON
MAX, a Sergeant in the Royal Life Guards
DUKE CHARLES, stepbrother to the King (afterwards KING CHARLES IX)
A BRIDGEKEEPER
A COURTIER
PRIVATE MÅNS, father to KARIN MÅNSDOTTER
STEN LEJONHUFVUD, a nobleman
ABRAHAM STENBOCK, a nobleman, brother to the QUEEN MOTHER KATARINA STENBOCK
NIGEL, a goldsmith
SOLDIERS and CITIZENS

The action takes place in and around Stockholm and Uppsala between 1566 and 1568.

Act 1. A terrace of the Royal Palace in Stockholm

Act 2. A room in GÖRAN PERSSON's house

Act 3. Scene 1. A bridge over Lake Mälaren, eighty miles west of Stockholm

Scene 2. A room in Uppsala Castle.

Act 4. Scene 1. A room in PRIVATE MÅNS's house

Scene 2. A room in Gripsholm Castle

Scene 3. A room in the Royal Palace in Stockholm

HISTORICAL NOTE

Erik the Fourteenth was the eldest son of Gustav Vasa, the great liberator of his country and the founder of the Vasa dynasty. Before Gustav Vasa's expulsion of the Danes in 1523, the chief upholders of Swedish independence for the better part of a century had been the family of Sture, whose name was more or less synonymous with patriotism.

Gustav Vasa himself had close associations with the Stures. One of the greatest of them, Sten Sture the Younger, had been his uncle, and when the Danish King Christian II took Stockholm in 1520, Gustav Vasa had witnessed the execution of his own father and the disinterment and burning at the stake of Sten Sture's body. Erik the Fourteenth, however, had hated his father and was jealous of the Stures' power and reputation. When the play begins, the struggle between him and them is boiling up to its climax. They, for their part, in common with the rest of the nobility, resented his employment of commoners as his confidential secretaries (notably Göran Persson, the son of a priest) and his choice of a commoner, Karin Månsdotter, as his mistress.

M.M.

ACT ONE

A terrace in the Royal Palace in Stockholm. In the background is a balustrade of Tuscan columns; on it stand glazed vases containing flowers. Beneath in the distance can be seen the tops of trees and of beflagged masts; and in the extreme distance, the spires of churches and the gables of houses. On the terrace are benches, chairs and tables.

> KARIN MÅNSDOTTER *sits sewing at a table.* MAX, *a Sergeant in the Royal Life Guards, stands beside her, leaning on his pike.*

KARIN: Don't come so close! The King's at his window, spying on us.

MAX: Where?

KARIN: Up there on the right, but for God's sake don't look. How long is your watch?

MAX: Another half-hour.

KARIN: Oh, Max! You're my cousin—we've known each other since childhood——

MAX: Loved each other since childhood, you said once, Karin——

KARIN: Don't remind me of that. I have forfeited your love——

MAX: Why did you do it. You don't love him.

KARIN: Love? I don't know. In a way I do, the way one loves a child. I pitied him from the moment I saw him; he looked blind and bloodless, like a doll. I accepted our relationship as a duty, because he was calmer and more dignified when I was with him. I thought I could bring out what was best and most noble in him; and I felt I became better because he praised me. But now it's become dangerous; he worships me, he calls me his good angel—what'll happen when he wakes from this dream and finds I'm just an ordinary person? He'll hate me then, and call me a liar and a hypocrite——! Go away Max, quickly. He's moved——

MAX [*moves away*]: I met your father and mother yesterday.

KARIN: Did you? What did she say?

MAX: The same as before.

KARIN: She despises the King's whore. She's right. So do I. But what can I do? And—father?

MAX: He says next time he meets you on the bridge he'll shoulder you into the water.

KARIN: But my brothers and sisters——? Why don't they ever come to see me? Ah, well. I suppose even the poor and humble have a sense of pride——

MAX: You're only degrading yourself here. Leave it, and come away with me.

KARIN: And let you share my shame?

MAX: I would wipe out your shame. Through the sacred bond of marriage.

KARIN: And my children?

MAX: Would become mine.

KARIN: I almost believe you. But——

MAX: Ssh! I can see a pair of ears behind that hedge. Ears I'd like to see nailed to a gallows——

KARIN: It's Göran Persson. He's trying to worm his way back into the King's favour, after his disgrace——

MAX: You must stop that.

KARIN: If only I could! People think I can do anything now—but I've no power at all——

MAX: Come away with me.

KARIN: I can't. Erik says if I left him, he'd die.

MAX: Let him die.

KARIN: No! You mustn't want that! That's a sin! Oh, Max, please go now, or Göran will hear us.

MAX: Meet me this evening. Somewhere where we can talk undisturbed.

KARIN: No, I don't want to. I can't!

MAX: Karin, you know as well as I do the King's planning to get married. Have you thought what will happen to you then?

KARIN: When that time comes, I'll know it's my duty to go. But not before.

MAX: Then it'll be too late. Think of Elizabeth of England's father, Henry the Eighth. He didn't allow his wives to go on living, once he'd tired of them. They ended on the block. And now that murderer's daughter is to be your Queen. Your mere existence will be an affront to her, and she'll know how to remove it.

KARIN: How can you say such horrible things! Go away quickly, and don't look up. He's come out on to the balcony.

MAX: How can you see all this?

KARIN: In my sewing-basket. I keep a looking-glass there. Go—he's seen you, now he'll throw something——

A shower of large nails is thrown down at MAX.

MAX: He's throwing nails at me! Does he think I'm a troll?

KARIN: God forgive him, he believes in all evil powers, but no good ones. In the name of Jesus Christ, go!

MAX: All right. When you need me, Karin, send for me.

KARIN: Go! Go quickly, or he'll throw his hammer at you.

MAX: Then he *is* mad?

KARIN: Be quiet! And go, go, go!

> MAX *goes out.* GÖRAN PERSSON *enters from behind a bush, through which we have seen him peering.*

KARIN: What are you looking for?

GÖRAN: You, my dear. I bring good news.

KARIN: Can you bring anything good?

GÖRAN: Oh, once in a while—to others. But never to myself.

KARIN: Speak then, but don't let yourself be seen. The King's up there on the balcony. Don't turn round.

GÖRAN: My King is still displeased with me. But he does me wrong, for he'll never find a more loyal servant——

KARIN: So you say.

GÖRAN: It isn't often I can praise myself, I know. And when it does happen, I take no credit for it. Karin, listen! The King's attempt to woo the Queen of England has failed. This means new hope for you and your children. And for our country——

KARIN: Is this true?

GÖRAN: As true as I live. But the King has not yet heard the news. See that you're not the one who tells him. But make sure you're with him when the blow falls, for it will wound him as only a shattered hope can wound a man.

KARIN: Now I know you're speaking the truth, and that you are the King's friend, and mine.

GÖRAN: But he is not mine.

> *A steel hammer is thrown down at* GÖRAN, *but does not hit him.*

GÖRAN [*picks up the hammer, kisses it and puts it on a table*]: My life for my King!

KARIN: Go away, or he'll kill you!
GÖRAN: Let him!
KARIN: He's in an evil mood today. Take care——!

A flower vase is thrown down at GÖRAN, *but misses him.*

GÖRAN: He's throwing flowers at me! [*Breaks off a flower, smells it, and puts it in his buttonhole.* ERIK, *above, roars with laughter.*] He's laughing!
KARIN: I haven't heard him laugh for months! That's good!
GÖRAN [*shouts up*]: More, more!

A chair is thrown down and shatters into pieces. GÖRAN *gathers the bits and puts them in his pockets.*

KARIN [*laughs*]: Oh, this is crazy!
GÖRAN: Let me play the court jester, since Hercules can no longer make my lord laugh!
KARIN: Don't walk on the nails, Göran!
GÖRAN [*kicks off his shoes and walks on the nails*]: Yes, with my bare feet, if it will make my King happy.
ERIK [*from above*]: Göran.
GÖRAN: Göran is in disgrace.
ERIK [*from above*]: Göran! Wait! Stop!
KARIN [*to* GÖRAN]: Don't go.

An armful of shoes, cushions, and clothes is thrown down.

ERIK [*roars with laughter*]: Göran! Wait! I'm coming down!
GÖRAN: I'll come back when he needs me.
KARIN: Please God I may never regret this, but—Göran, stay! Erik is so unhappy——
GÖRAN: Erik isn't unhappy. He's just bored, and kings mustn't be bored, because then they become dangerous. I'll come and cheer him up. But there's something I have to do first. It's important——

KARIN: But be here when they break the news, or he'll vent his rage on us——

GÖRAN: Oh, I'll ride the whirlwind, like I used to before. He always came running after me when he'd done something crazy.

KARIN: Göran! One thing more. Did you hear what Sergeant Max and I were saying?

GÖRAN: Every word.

KARIN: I'm frightened of you. But we must be friends.

GÖRAN: That's certain, if nothing else.

KARIN: Please God I may never live to regret this!

GÖRAN: Karin, the bond that binds you and me was forged down there in the gutter. It's a bond of blood.

He goes. KING ERIK *enters right; at the same time, a* COURTIER *enters left.*

COURTIER: Your Majesty!

ERIK: Speak.

COURTIER: Nigel the goldsmith humbly begs leave to show Your Majesty the article you commanded him to make.

ERIK: Send him in. [*To* KARIN.] Now you're going to see something beautiful.

NIGEL *the goldsmith enters with a leather bag.*

Hullo, Nigel. You're a punctual fellow, and I like you. [*Points to a table.*] Put it there. [NIGEL *does so.*] Open it! [NIGEL *opens the bag and takes out a golden crown set with precious stones.*] Ah! [*Clasps his hands.*] Karin, look at this!

KARIN [*paces restlessly up and down*]: I see it, my lord. Very beautiful.

ERIK: Do you see? The lion of Sweden embracing the leopard of England!

KARIN: Erik, Erik!

ERIK: What's the matter?

KARIN: Who is to wear this crown?

ERIK: England's virgin queen—and mine! And when our hands meet across the sea, they will clasp Norway and Denmark too, and then Europe will be ours! That is the meaning of the six joined rings and the six jewels. [*He takes the crown and is about to put it on* KARIN's *head.*] Feel how heavy it is!

KARIN [*draws her head away*]: Much too heavy for me.

ERIK: Let me see how it looks. Come, now. Will you obey me?

KARIN: If it is obedience you demand, my lord, I am always your most dutiful servant.

ERIK [*puts the crown on her head*]: How well it suits you, Karin! Look at yourself in that mirror you keep in your sewing-basket, to spy on your king. By the way, wasn't Göran here? Where has the fool gone?

KARIN: He feared Your Majesty's disfavour.

ERIK: Idiot! Disfavour? Nonsense! Am I a man who harbours resentment? Didn't I send young Sture to take my offer to the Queen of England, although he'd proved himself a traitor in the Danish War, and had been punished for it?

KARIN: May I take the crown off now?

ERIK: Don't interrupt me when I'm talking. Oh, I know some people thought I did Sture an injustice, but I didn't let that stop me— All the same——

He begins to brood, seems abstracted and depressed, and stares vacantly. The QUEEN MOTHER, KATERINA, *walks past, apparently casually.*

ERIK [*rouses himself*]: What does my beloved stepmother want? Kindly take your exercise down there in the courtyard. Go away.

The QUEEN MOTHER looks at KARIN, who is embarrassed. ERIK snatches the crown from her.

Sweden, Norway, Denmark, England, Scotland, Ireland! Six jewels!

NIGEL *withdraws upstage.*

QUEEN MOTHER: Erik!

ERIK: King Erik, please.

QUEEN MOTHER: And—Queen Karin?

ERIK: Queen Elizabeth, if you've no objection. Or Mary of Scotland, or Renate of Lorraine, or, if the worst comes to the worst, Christina of Hesse!

QUEEN MOTHER: You're more pitiable than evil. Poor Erik! [*Goes.*]

ERIK: Don't pay any attention to that old hag's chatter, Karin. She thinks I'm to be pitied—she doesn't realise I have six crowns within my grasp. Oh yes, I have—Sture writes from England that my chances are decidedly bright— decidedly bright. He'll be here any day now. By the way, I had a dream the other night. Hm! Well, never mind that. Karin, you do love me, don't you, and you are happy at my success?

KARIN: I rejoice in your successes, but I grieve more than you do at your failures, and every mortal must be prepared for failures.

ERIK: Oh, I am! You've no idea what a clever game I'm playing just now. I've plenty of trumps in my hand. [*To* NIGEL.] You can go, Nigel. I'll talk to you later.

DUKE JOHAN *appears in the background.*

Come here, Redbeard. I've got something for you. I'm in a giving mood today.

KARIN [*to* ERIK]: Oh, don't bait him. He's so full of hatred already.

DUKE JOHAN *comes forward.*

ERIK: My beloved brother, upon mature consideration I have decided to accede to your request. Catherine of Poland shall be yours.

JOHAN: Your Majesty's gracious consent to a union which lies so close to my heart makes me most happy and grateful.

ERIK: Grateful too? Then don't forget, when you become the Emperor's kinsman, and your son inherits the Polish throne, that you have a Vasa to thank for your power! While I strengthen the North by my union with England, you with Poland will buttress our South and East; and then—well, you can imagine what'll result.

JOHAN: My noble brother's visions fly on eagles' wings, which I, a poor sparrow, lack the strength to follow.

ERIK: Good. Well, go in peace, and enjoy your good fortune, as I shall enjoy mine.

JOHAN: Forgive me, brother, but a decision of this magnitude customarily requires a seal and a signature.

ERIK: Oh, you're like a lawyer, you always want everything in writing. Here, you have my hand on it. And the mistress of my heart is sufficient witness.

JOHAN [*kisses* ERIK'S *hand, then* KARIN'S]: Thank you.

Goes quickly.

ERIK: He went quicker than he came. I always see a fox's brush trailing behind him. Don't you think he looks treacherous?

KARIN: I haven't noticed it.

ERIK: You always side with my enemies.

KARIN: You regard everyone as your enemy, Erik.

ERIK: Because they hate me! But I hate them too. Tell me, Karin, what were you talking about with that sergeant?

KARIN: That was my cousin, Max.

ERIK: It's unseemly for you to exchange confidences with a commoner.

KARIN: What right have I to be proud? I'm a commoner's daughter, and they call me a whore.

ERIK: The King's whore.

KARIN: Erik, Erik!

ERIK: Well, I'm only speaking the truth——

KARIN: What would you call our children, then?

ERIK: *My* children. That's different——

KARIN: How is it different?

ERIK: You want to pick a quarrel? Hm?

KARIN: No, no, no! Oh, if only I could tell you everything——

ERIK: Where's Göran? Every time you get quarrelsome, I long for Göran. Göran's the only person who understands the secret ways of my soul. He can say what *I* think, so that I hardly need to speak when he's around. He is my brother and my friend, and that's why you hate him.

KARIN: I don't hate him—least of all when he makes my lord happy——

ERIK: You don't hate him any longer? What's happened, then? He must have been saying things against me behind my back——

KARIN: Oh, my God—how unhappy you are! Erik, my poor Erik——!

ERIK: Poor? How dare you!

COURTIER [*enters*]: Herr Nils Sture presents his respects and craves audience of Your Majesty.

ERIK: At last!

KARIN [*gets up*]: May I go?

ERIK: No, stay. Do you envy your poor King?

KARIN: God pity you, you've nothing to envy.

ERIK: Your insolence goes too far! Beware of insolence, Karin. The gods hate nothing so much as insolence.

> SVANTE STURE *enters with his sons*, NILS STURE *and* ERIK STURE.

What's this, a pageant? Herr Nils! Are you making a triumphal entry into our Royal Palace?

SVANTE STURE: With respect, Your Majesty——

ERIK: Kindly allow our royal emissary to speak for himself. He's not making a will, he doesn't need witnesses.

SVANTE STURE: No; but a certain experience, too grievous to recall, has taught me, as the Head of the House of Sture, the wisdom of discussing matters of public import in public. Otherwise plain words and actions may be distorted and misrepresented——

ERIK [*stands by the table on which the crown rests*]: What's this, revenge? You wish to poison the most beautiful moment of my life by reminding me of the treason committed by your son, which I was gracious enough to pardon?

SVANTE STURE: He committed no treason.

ERIK: Great God in Heaven, the man refused to obey orders in time of war——

SVANTE STURE: He refused to commit atrocities——

ERIK: War's always atrocious, and anyone who hasn't the courage to deal with his enemies had better sit at home by the fire. I don't want to hear any more about that! Let Herr Nils deliver his message, and then get out, all of you!

NILS STURE: Most gracious Majesty, it grieves me deeply to deliver the reply that was entrusted to me——

ERIK: Where is the letter?

NILS STURE: I received no letter; only, alas, a verbal answer, which I must translate into a seemly form lest it should offend your ears and my tongue——

ERIK: Rejection?

NILS STURE [*after a pause*]: Yes.

ERIK: And you're pleased, by God!

NILS STURE: In Heaven's name, no!

ERIK: Yes, you devil, you're laughing at me!

SVANTE STURE: He did not laugh.

ERIK: Yes, he did, he was laughing to himself, up his sleeve—I saw him! And you too, you old fox. All three of you! I saw you! Karin, didn't *you* see them sniggering?

KARIN: No, by all that's holy——!

ERIK: You too! All hell is conspiring against me! Go, go, go, damn you! Get out, you devils! Get out!

> *He throws the crown over the balustrade, picks up from the floor the objects he had thrown down from above, and flings them after NILS and ERIK STURE, who have turned and begun to walk away.*

SVANTE STURE [*who has not moved*]: Alas for the country whose king is a madman!

ERIK: Are you calling me a madman, your King, you wretch, you dog!

KARIN: Erik, Erik!

ERIK: Hold your tongue!

SVANTE STURE [*goes*]: God have mercy on us all!

ERIK: I shan't have any mercy on you, be sure of that! [*To* KARIN.] Now you're happy, aren't you? Well, answer me! You don't need to, I know what you're thinking, I can read your thoughts and hear the words you're afraid to speak!

What else should you be but happy when I've been snubbed, when your rival has insulted me? Now you've got me to yourself, eh? Now you think I'm down, you think I'm beaten, so that you'll have to comfort me! You—comfort me!—when the mob is laughing at my failure and the lords are holding banquets to celebrate my defeat! And your father and mother, if I met them today I'd kill them—oh yes, this'll make them happy! And my step-mother! I can see her sitting there laughing and showing her black tooth—she's got a black tooth in her upper jaw, which they say my dear father gave her, God rest his soul! The whole of Sweden is happy today, except me! Me! [*Laughs wildly.*]

COURTIER [*enters*]: Herr Nils Gyllenstjerna.

ERIK: Gyllenstjerna! Thank God for him! That's my man—a *man*! Carry him here in a golden chair!

KARIN [*gets up*]: I'll go now.

ERIK: Yes, go to hell. [*Throws her sewing-basket after her.*] Go and start gossiping——!

NILS GYLLENSTJERNA *enters.*

Ah, Nils! Thank God for a sane man among all these imbeciles. Tell me, Nils, what's the truth about this English business? Is the woman upset?

GYLLENSTJERNA: No, Your Majesty. It's quite simple. Her heart, as the saying goes, belongs to the Earl of Leicester—hm——!

ERIK [*roars with laughter*]: You mean, he's her lover? She's a whore, then?

GYLLENSTJERNA: At any rate she is not a maiden, the Virgin Queen.

ERIK: His name's Leicester, you say. Couldn't he be killed?

GYLLENSTJERNA: I dare say, if one was prepared to pay.

ERIK: Will you kill him?

GYLLENSTJERNA: I?

ERIK: Ten thousand pounds? Well?

GYLLENSTJERNA: I? Is your Majesty serious?

ERIK: Serious? I'll give you the money in advance!

GYYLENSTJERNA: I mean, does Your Majesty seriously believe that I would act as a hired assassin?

ERIK: What's so offensive about that?

GYLLENSTJERNA: A Swedish nobleman——!

ERIK: And a Swedish King! Are you trying to teach me manners?

GYLLENSTJERNA: I came on other business, but since Your Majesty esteems me so little I must beg to be excused.

ERIK: Traitor! You too! It's all the same with you damned nobles who think you've a longer ancestry than the House of Vasa! Go to hell!

> NILS GYLLENSTJERNA *shakes his head and goes.*

Don't wag your head at me, you little bastard, or I'll wag it for you so that you won't know east from west! [NILS GYLLENSTJERNA *stops and looks at* ERIK.] Yes, stare at me! I won't fall to pieces!

> NILS GYLLENSTJERNA *shakes his head and goes.* ERIK, *left alone, paces up and down. He kicks aside the objects which are still lying on the ground; then he throws himself down on a couch covered with a tiger's skin, and begins to sob convulsively. After a while, his sobbing by imperceptible degrees turns to hysterical laughter; and this, equally imperceptibly, changes again to sobbing.*

GÖRAN PERSSON [*enters and goes forward to* ERIK. *He kneels*]: Your Majesty!

ERIK: Ah, Göran! I've been angry with you, but I'm not any longer. Sit down and talk to me.

GÖRAN: What does Your Majesty wish to know?

ERIK: Oh, stop this Majesty business. Call me Erik. Then we can talk. Have you heard the news?

GÖRAN: What news?

ERIK: I have rejected the Englishwoman.

GÖRAN: Oh, why?

ERIK: She was a whore. She had a lover—so that's finished. But what galls me is that these Stures think she's turned me down, and are going round spreading the story so as to make a fool of me.

GÖRAN: Good heavens!

ERIK: Göran, what's wrong with these Stures? Why do they always stand in our way? There's something about them, isn't there? What is it?

GÖRAN: Difficult to say. They've always been good people; a bit dull, but—— Of course, they're descended from Nattodag, who assassinated Engelbrecht——

ERIK: I'd forgotten that. Yes, they've blood on their heads. Perhaps that's why they've never become kings.

GÖRAN: But they've the blood of Saint Erik and the Folkungs in their veins; and of every noble house in Sweden. But why are you afraid of them? Fate, or whatever you want to call it, has ordained that Sweden shall be ruled by the House of Vasa.

ERIK: Why do I hate them?

GÖRAN: My royal friend, you use that word "hate" so often you'll end by imagining you're the enemy of the entire human race. Give it a rest. Words are creative, they're the spark that ends in the flame of reality, and if you repeat a word too often you end by bewitching yourself. Say "love" a little more often, and you'll start imagining that people love you.

ERIK: I've never heard you talk like this before. Göran! Are you speaking from experience?

GÖRAN: Yes, I am speaking from experience.

ERIK: Agda?

GÖRAN: No, it's—someone else.

ERIK: Is she beautiful?

GÖRAN: No. She's ugly really, but once, just for a moment, I glimpsed—what does Plato call it?—the prototype. You know that vision one sometimes gets of timeless beauty—well, I caught it for a moment behind the mask of her face, and ever since—well, I've loved her.

ERIK: How strange! When you used that word "love", which you always used to blush at, you suddenly became quite beautiful—transformed——

GÖRAN: Am I so hideously ugly?

ERIK: Absolutely appalling. Haven't you ever looked at yourself in a mirror?

GÖRAN: I avoid mirrors. But would you believe it, she thinks I'm beautiful! [*Laughs.*]

ERIK: Always?

GÖRAN: When I'm not being unkind to her.

ERIK [*laughs*]: I see. When you're being—nice.

GÖRAN [*embarrassed*]: If you like.

ERIK: You're a rascal, Göran. I don't understand you.

GÖRAN: So much the better, for my enemies.

ERIK: Are you planning to get married soon?

GÖRAN: Perhaps.

ERIK: Well, tell me whom I ought to marry.

GÖRAN: Princess Catherine of Poland, of course. Then we shall rule the Baltic and have the Emperor as our kinsman.

ERIK [*starts to his feet*]: Good God in Heaven! What a splendid idea! Yes, Göran, you're a remarkable man. I was saying just now to Karin, I don't need to think when you're around. I must send a messenger, at once! Hell and damnation! [*Claps his hands three times. A* COURTIER *enters.* ERIK *shouts at him wildly.*] Send someone after Duke Johan! Take him dead or alive! If he tries to escape, chop off his arms and legs! Run, run!

The COURTIER *goes.*

GÖRAN: What does all that mean?

ERIK: That scoundrel tricked me into promising him that he could marry Catherine of Poland. I gave him my hand on it.

GÖRAN: That's a pity.

ERIK: Isn't it just as though the devil himself had been shuffling the pack? Imagine him inheriting the Baltic—him, my stepmother's son, a kinsman of the Stures, a Jesuit, a Papist, becoming a cousin of the Emperor! Him!

GÖRAN: Erik, what have you done? Oh dear, if only you'd let me advise you. Think; Johan's heirs will be Kings of Poland, a country as big as France and whose territories extend into Russia. Johan's grandchildren could become Emperors of Austria! His wife already has a claim to the throne of Naples, through her Sforza ancestry. Oh dear, oh dear!

ERIK: We must crush the eagle before he leaves his egg.

GÖRAN: And we'll have the Catholics all over us—you know how Johan loves the Jesuits and everyone connected with the Pope. Erik, what have you done?

ERIK: I have committed the greatest folly of my life.

GÖRAN: Let it be the last.

ERIK: Haven't you noticed that there seems to be a curse on everything I try to do?

GÖRAN: You're just unlucky.

ERIK: What about you? You'll end on the gallows! But you know so much more than me, you shall be my counsellor. Do you know, before this mood came over me I was planning to——?

GÖRAN: Erik, if you make me your counsellor, I'm not just going to be a figurehead who'll take all the blame without ever having a say in anything. You must give me power and responsibility, so that I can act, and answer for my actions. Make me Protector.

ERIK: Right. You're Protector.

GÖRAN: While I await confirmation of my appointment by the Privy Council, may I——?

ERIK: There's no need for that. I rule this country.

GÖRAN: As Your Majesty pleases.

The COURTIER *enters.*

ERIK: Well?

COURTIER: Your Majesty, the Duke's ship has already sailed, with a favourable wind——

ERIK: Lost!

GÖRAN: Have him pursued! At once!

COURTIER: But the noble Lord Nils Gyllenstjerna bade me give you a message closely concerning this matter——

ERIK: Out with it! Quickly!

COURTIER: The situation appears to be that Duke Johan——

ERIK: Göran, Göran!

COURTIER: Duke Johan has already entered into a secret marriage with the Polish Princess.

ERIK *sits.*

GÖRAN: Now we're saved. Let me play the hand now.

ERIK: I don't understand.

GÖRAN: The Duke has contravened the Articles of Arboga by entering into an alliance with a foreign power. Send the fleet after him and seize him. Then we can put him on trial; impeach him. How's that?

ERIK: But what good will that do me?

GÖRAN: One enemy the less. And a dangerous one.

ERIK: Brother against brother. The Folkung Saga is not yet finished——

GÖRAN: No. Duke Johan has Folkung blood in his veins, and as long as he lives there will be no peace in this land. [*To the* COURTIER.] Order Admiral Horn to attend his Majesty immediately, that the pursuit may begin.

ERIK: Are you the King, or am I?

GÖRAN: For the moment, apparently, I am.

ERIK: You're too strong, Göran.

GÖRAN: No. You're too weak.

ACT TWO

A big room in GÖRAN PERSSON's house. In the corner on the right is a stove with cooking implements; beside it stands a table for eating. In the left-hand corner is GÖRAN's writing-table. GÖRAN is seated at it, writing. His mother, FRU PERSSON, is standing at the stove.

FRU PERSSON: Come and eat, Göran.

GÖRAN: Not now, mother.

FRU PERSSON: The food'll get ruined again.

GÖRAN: It won't get ruined; only cold. Be quiet now, there's a dear. [*Writes.*]

FRU PERSSON [*goes over to him*]: Göran, is it true you're working for the King again?

GÖRAN: Yes.

FRU PERSSON: Why didn't you tell me before?

GÖRAN: Some things I like to keep to myself.

FRU PERSSON: How much is he giving you?

GÖRAN: How much is he giving me? I haven't asked, and he's forgotten to mention it.

FRU PERSSON: What's the good of taking a job if you don't get paid for it?

GÖRAN: Yes, mother, I know that's how you look at it, but I feel differently.

FRU PERSSON: That's all very well for you, but I've got to find food to put on this table three times a day. Anyway, Göran, what d'you want to go back to the court for? Didn't you get humbled enough there in the old king's time?

GÖRAN: I was brought up on humiliation, mother. It doesn't hurt me any longer. I serve the King because I feel it's my calling—my duty, if you like. He's so weak; he's got a genius for making enemies of everyone——

FRU PERSSON: How can you help him? You're hardly able to stand on your own two feet.

GÖRAN: Oh, I shall manage.

FRU PERSSON: Oh, Göran, your good intentions always run ahead of you. Look what happened last time! Bringing Agda and her child here to live with us, because some fellow had left her in the lurch——

GÖRAN: Well, they're all right, aren't they? And better times are at hand for us all.

FRU PERSSON: You know what thanks you'll get for playing the gentleman——

GÖRAN: I don't want to hear any talk about playing the gentleman. I don't believe in that; and I don't want any thanks. A woman was in trouble, she asked for my help, and she got it. That's all.

FRU PERSSON: But now people are saying she's your whore.

GÖRAN: I've no doubt. But that only hurts her—worse luck!

FRU PERSSON: Are you so sure?

GÖRAN: What do you mean?

FRU PERSSON: Agda might start thinking you've intentions towards her, and then you'll get blamed for keeping her hanging about.

GÖRAN: Oh, mother, what haven't I been blamed for? Every crazy thing King Erik's ever done has been blamed on me— even this business with Karin. I tried to stop that, though I didn't manage to. But now I've realised she's the only person who can give the King any happiness and peace of mind, so she and I have become friends——

FRU PERSSON: You meddle too much, Göran. You'll end by burning your fingers.

GÖRAN: I don't think so.

FRU PERSSON: Put not thy trust in princes——

GÖRAN: I don't put my trust in anyone. Except myself. I wasn't born to wear a crown, but to rule; and since I can only rule through my King, I turn to him as a flower turns to the sun. When he sets, I shall die, and that'll be that.

FRU PERSSON: Do you like him?

GÖRAN: Yes and no. We're bound to each other by invisible ties. It's as though we'd been born in the same womb and under the same constellation. His hates are mine, his loves are mine; and that's the kind of thing that binds people together.

FRU PERSSON: Well, son, you go your own way. I can't follow you or stop you. Hush, here's Agda.

AGDA [*enters with her three-year-old daughter*, MARIA]: Good evening, Fru Persson. Good evening, Göran.

GÖRAN: Hullo, child. Come and kiss me, Maria.

MARIA [*goes over to the writing-table and fingers the papers*]: Good evening, uncle.

GÖRAN [*amiably*]: Stop messing about with those papers, you little monster. If you knew——!

MARIA: Why are you always writing, uncle?

GÖRAN: I wish I could tell you, Maria. Are you hungry? Let's sit down and start eating.

AGDA: Thank you, Göran. You break your bread for the hungry, while you——

GÖRAN: Oh, nonsense. Many's the time I've sat at other men's tables——

FRU PERSSON: He never eats anything himself.

GÖRAN: That's quite untrue. Once I cut loose, I'm a glutton. I can empty a bottle as well as the next man. Come on, eat.

They all sit down at the table. There is a loud knock on the door. GÖRAN gets up and draws a curtain across the part of the room in which the others are seated.

MARIA [*covers her face with her hands*]: Is that the bogey man? Oh, mummy, I'm frightened!

AGDA: Don't be silly, darling. There isn't any bogey man.

MARIA: Yes, there is! Anna said so, and I'm frightened of him.

SVANTE STURE [*enters and says haughtily to* GÖRAN]: Well, Mr. Secretary. Will you grant me the favour of a short conversation?

GÖRAN: A long one, if Your Excellency wishes——

SVANTE STURE: Your *Grace*, if you don't mind. But perhaps you don't know that I am now an Earl?

GÖRAN: I ought to. I made you one.

SVANTE STURE: Why, you impudent coxcomb——!

GÖRAN: Easy, now! Don't take that tone with me. It was at my suggestion that you were created the first Earl of Sweden.

SVANTE STURE: Good God! You mean I owe my title to an ex-jailbird——!

GÖRAN: Not so fast, Your Grace! When I was a young libertine I had to sleep off a bout of high spirits in the Tower. There's no shame in that. But you ought to spend the rest of your life there as a rebel and a traitor.

SVANTE STURE [*laughs*]: I'd like to see the man who'd put me there!

GÖRAN [*concealing the papers on his table*]: Only your services in the late King Gustav's reign have saved you from a punishment you richly deserved. In future, be careful!

SVANTE STURE: Of you—the brat of an unwed priest?

GÖRAN: My mother's sitting behind that curtain. Remember that.

SVANTE STURE: And the whore's bastard, too, I suppose?

GÖRAN: Shame on you, Herr Svante! A few hours ago I was praising you to the King; I said that the Stures have always been good men and patriots. I still want to believe that, but you do everything to degrade yourself with your overweening pride. Oh, yes, you're noblemen, but what's nobility? A horse with a man on it! You don't understand how to rule a country, and you don't want to learn anything except how to ride a horse and wield a sword. You despise the man who governs by the pen; but it's the pen that has planned this new age of ours, which has passed you by and which you don't understand. Human rights and human dignity, respect for the downtrodden and mercy for the guilty, these are new devices which have not been written into your coat of arms. I could have been an Earl too, but I didn't want to be one, because my destiny demands that I stay down here among the humble and lowly, where I was born——

SVANTE STURE: Are clerks and book-keepers to stand between the King and the lords of the realm?

GÖRAN: There is only going to be one lord in this realm, and no upstart princes are going to be allowed to stand between the King and his people. That's what the history of Sweden teaches us, from Ingjald, whom you call the Redeless because he burned little kings, through Birger Jarl and the Folkungs, right down to Christian the Tyrant, so called because he chopped off the heads of little kings. "The King and his People"—that's how our country's motto ought to read, and perhaps some day it will——

SVANTE STURE: When you dictate it?

GÖRAN: Who knows?

SVANTE STURE [*roars*]: Will you ask me to sit down, or must I stand?

MARIA [*behind the curtain*]: Why does the old man shout so loud, mummy?

AGDA: Hush, Maria dear!

GÖRAN: Stand or sit, as Your Excellency pleases. I have no rank, and am a little above all ranks——

SVANTE STURE: God damn your——

GÖRAN: Don't swear, Your Grace. There's a woman and a child sitting behind there——

SVANTE STURE: Are you teaching me manners?

GÖRAN: Why not? As President of the King's Council I begin by remonstrating; but for those who prove recalcitrant we have other methods at our disposal——

SVANTE STURE: The King's Council?

GÖRAN: Yes. I am the Supreme Judge of the Supreme Court——

SVANTE STURE: But I am a Privy Councillor——

GÖRAN: You are a Councillor who may be heard but need not be obeyed. I am the Protector of the Realm, who commands and does not obey—if we have to stand here boasting like horse-dealers——

SVANTE STURE: Protector? That's something new!

GÖRAN: Quite new. Here is my authority. With other papers of equal moment——

SVANTE STURE [*somewhat more respectful*]: But this is a revolution——

GÖRAN: Yes. The greatest there has been since the Reformation.

SVANTE STURE: And you think the lords and councillors of Sweden will submit to being deposed like this?

GÖRAN: I'm sure they will. King Erik has the army, the fleet and the people behind him.

SVANTE STURE: Could we have a window open? It smells so foul in here——

GÖRAN [*angrily*]: It's only the smell of cooking. As soon as you've gone we'll air the room. But you'd better go quickly. Quickly. You understand?

> SVANTE STURE *goes, but the feathers on his hat hit the beam above the door.*

Watch your head, Herr Svante!

SVANTE STURE [*comes back*]: I forgot my gloves.

GÖRAN [*picks up the gloves in the fire-tongs, and offers them at arm's length to* SVANTE STURE. SVANTE STURE *goes thoughtfully.* GÖRAN PERSSON *holds the door open for him, then spits after him*]: Curse you! And all your like! You have touched me and the ones I love, as the viper said.

MARIA: Was the old man angry with Uncle Göran, mummy?

GÖRAN [*gently*]: The old man has gone now, my dear. And he won't ever come back.

FRU PERSSON: Göran, Göran! Was that true what you were saying? Are you Protector, or whatever it's called?

GÖRAN: Certainly.

FRU PERSSON: Love thine enemies.

GÖRAN: That depends on them, and how they behave. In the next twenty-four hours they will decide their fate.

FRU PERSSON: *They* will?

GÖRAN: Yes. Earl Svante will go and tell his friends about this. But I have spies, and every threatening word these petty princes utter will be judged in Council. If they try to start a conspiracy, they're finished.

FRU PERSSON: Be noble, Göran——

GÖRAN: When the nobles start being noble, I will too.

SERGEANT MAX [*enters*]: You sent for me, Mr. Secretary?

GÖRAN: Sit down. Mother, leave us, will you? [*To* MAX *in a friendly but firm tone.*] Now listen, Max. I heard what you were saying to Karin——

MAX: I'm sure you did.

GÖRAN: Not so fast, lad. I don't for a moment doubt the sincerity of your feelings——

MAX: What have my feelings to do with you?

GÖRAN: Well, I don't want them to interfere with a life which is precious to us all, and to our country. Karin can become Queen if you leave her alone. And you don't need to bother about making an honest woman of her, because the King himself will take care of that.

MAX: He won't.

GÖRAN: Now listen to me, young man. What I'm saying to you now is as good as a royal command, and I command you never to see Karin again. If the King once suspects that Karin's affections are divided, it will be dangerous for him, and it'll mean the end of her. You say you love her. Good. Then show that you put her happiness above everything.

MAX: No! Not that way.

GÖRAN: Very well. Then you'll have to be removed to a safe distance. You see this letter. Take it—to Elvsborg Castle.

MAX: I refuse.

GÖRAN: Don't shout. You can easily be silenced.

MAX: David and Uriah?

GÖRAN [*lowers his voice*]: You are the seducer. You've trying to entice a woman who never belonged to you from the father of her children. Take my advice and go with this letter——

MAX: No.

GÖRAN: Then find yourself a confessor, for your hours are numbered.

MAX: Who will number them?

GÖRAN: I shall. Goodbye, Max.

MAX: By what authority do you dare judge me like this?

GÖRAN: By the authority of justice and the law, which condemns a man who tries to seduce another man's betrothed. Now you know. Well, that's all.

> KING ERIK *enters.* MAX, *frightened, creeps out, unseen by* ERIK.

GÖRAN [*pulls a bell-rope; a bell rings*]: Forgive me, Your Majesty——

ERIK [*gently*]: Of course. Are we alone?

GÖRAN: As good as. My mother's sitting in there; but let her listen. We have no secrets in this house.

ERIK [*through the curtain*]: Good evening, Fru Persson. Göran and I are good friends now, so you've nothing to fear.

FRU PERSSON: I know, Your Majesty. I'm not afraid.

ERIK: Good. Well, Göran, I've news for you.

GÖRAN: Good news?

ERIK: That depends on you, and what use you make of it——

GÖRAN: Well, one can sometimes use bad news to good effect.

ERIK: Then tell me what use you can make of this. As you know, Johan is already married to Catherine of Poland——

GÖRAN: That means Poland will support us against Russia.

ERIK: Couldn't it also mean that the Duke stands higher than the King?

GÖRAN: We'll see about that later!

ERIK: Now Johan has arrested my messenger and entrenched himself in Skansborg Castle with the whole of the Finnish Army——

ERIK THE FOURTEENTH

GÖRAN: That means that the Duke has taken up arms against his King, and thereby forfeited his liberty and his life.

ERIK: His liberty, anyway——

GÖRAN: *And* his life! That depends on the Estates. It's they who will judge him——

ERIK [*agitated*]: Not his life! There must be no bloodshed. Not now that I have children——

GÖRAN: Then he must be tried immediately, before the Estates adjourn.

ERIK: Very well. But no bloodshed. Otherwise—I couldn't sleep at night——

GÖRAN: Your great father, the founder of our realm, always held that one should pay no heed to family ties, friendship or personal obligations. The country before the individual!

ERIK: You're too strong for me, Göran.

GÖRAN: Nonsense. But as long as I have the strength, I shall defend your crown against your enemies.

ERIK: Have I enemies?

GÖRAN: Yes. The worst was here just now.

ERIK: Earl Sture?

GÖRAN: Yes. I'm afraid we overestimated that bunch. Earl Svante, having come here to insult me, started threatening the government and the new administration——

ERIK: Did he insult you? Why don't you let me give you a title, to put you on the same level as the nobles?

GÖRAN: No, I don't want that. I don't want to start competing with the nobility and end up by becoming a little king myself. As long as I am the representative of the common people, I am justified. Only my actions can ennoble or degrade me.

ERIK: Why do you always have to justify yourself, Göran?

GÖRAN: Oh——

ERIK: Don't forget that Johan is a cousin of the Stures; and clay and straw are not easily parted——

GÖRAN: I know. Well, they must be caught in the same net.

ERIK: It's strange, you know—I can never feel that I'm of the same blood as Johan or any of the nobles. My German mother, I suppose. Perhaps that's what has thwarted my plans for an ambitious marriage——

GÖRAN: You are married, Erik.

ERIK: I am and I'm not. Do you know—I sometimes feel it's good the way things are——

GÖRAN: Why not have the wedding soon?

ERIK: What would the nobles say to that?

GÖRAN: But how would they *feel*? Think of that!

ERIK [*rubs his hands*]: Yes, it'd make them smart, wouldn't it? [*Laughs.*] But you keep your nose out of this. By the way, how about your wedding?

GÖRAN: You keep your nose out of that!

ERIK [*laughs*]: It's funny, but I like you better since you became a slave of Cupid! I trust you more than I did before. Can't I see the Prototype just once?

GÖRAN: I must beg my royal friend not to jest about that which every man of honour must regard as sacred——

ERIK: You're a damned scoundrel, Göran!

GÖRAN: I was once, but I'm not any longer. But I have the feeling that—if she should betray me, then—then the old Göran would return——

ERIK: The old horned Göran who used to roam the brothels. [*Sings.*] "O come, my pretty maiden——!"

GÖRAN [*points to the curtain*]: Hush! Don't wake the ghosts of the past. I was foul then; I was vile, because no one loved me——

ERIK: You're a sentimentalist, Göran. Don't fool yourself into imagining that she loves you——

GÖRAN: What? What do you mean? Who said so? Who? Who?

ERIK: Come, come! I don't know anything. I only said that because that's the way things usually are——

GÖRAN: Erik, don't ever say that. Then the Devil re-enters my soul, where a little while ago I raised a tiny chapel to the Unknown God—[ERIK *laughs*.] It's strange how love stirs memories of one's childhood faith——

ERIK: Hm!

GÖRAN: Yes, you can smile! [*There is a knock on the door.*] Shall I open?

ERIK: Why not? There's only one person I'm afraid of meeting. [GÖRAN *looks at him questioningly*.] Karin's father. Private Måns——

GÖRAN [*takes a step back*]: Private Måns!

PRIVATE MÅNS [*enters stolidly, not immediately recognising* ERIK. *He hands a paper to* GÖRAN]: Will you be so good as to glance through this? [*He recognises* ERIK, *at first fearfully; then he slowly takes off his steel helmet.*] The King! I ought to kneel to you, but by God I can't, not even to save my head! [*Pause.*] Take my head, as you've taken my honour.

ERIK: Your honour can be restored to you, Måns——

MÅNS: By marrying her off to someone else? That's what I came about.

ERIK: How dare you speak like that of my betrothed, you insolent——!

MÅNS: Betrothed? You've shamed her, but now there's an honest man wants to mend what you've broken.

ERIK [*to* GÖRAN]: Must I stand here and be insulted by a simple peasant?

MÅNS: I wonder which of us is the simpler——?

ERIK [*to* GÖRAN]: Hold me, or I'll kill him!

MÅNS: I'm grandfather to your children, whether you like it or not. What does that make me to you?

ERIK: You are my Karin's father, and therefore I forgive you. What do you want?

MÅNS: What you can never give me back.

GÖRAN: Take your paper and go, Måns.

MÅNS: Then it'll have to happen without any papers. But happen it's going to!

ERIK: What's going to happen? Are you trying to trick Karin into leaving me and taking my children away from me?

MÅNS: If we can't agree, let the Estates judge.

ERIK: Do you come from the Devil?

MÅNS: No, from the Lord High Steward, Earl Svante Sture.

ERIK: Always the Stures! Private Måns, if you will be patient, you shall have justice.

MÅNS: I only want my daughter and my grandchildren. Mine, since you refuse to recognise them.

ERIK [*to* GÖRAN]: What does the law say?

GÖRAN: The law says that illegitimate children shall stay with the mother.

MÅNS: The law may say that. But there's another law that's written in the hearts of abandoned children. And that condemns a father who has no sense of honour to forfeit the love which he thinks belongs to him by right.

GÖRAN [*whispers to* ERIK]: Bribe him.

ERIK: Private Måns, I appoint you Sergeant——

MÅNS: No thanks, not me. The rich man thinks everything can be bought with money, but——

ERIK: But he is poorer than the humblest of his subjects.

MÅNS: That's about the strength of it. But as I didn't come here to beg, I must leave as poor as I came. [*Pause.*] Or even poorer. [*Goes.*]

ERIK: Must I stand still and listen to this——!

GÖRAN: That's a risk one has to take when one indulges in— irregularities.

ERIK: What shall I do, then?

GÖRAN: Marry her.

ERIK: But——

GÖRAN: There's no other way. How can you accuse Johan before the Estates if you yourself are the defendant in a lawsuit?

ERIK: Damnation! You're right as always. Let me go home and think this over. The Stures, the Stures, always the Stures! [*Looks around.*] You live like a pig, Göran. You must move, and get yourself fixed up decently— [*Jerks his thumb behind his back towards the curtain.*] What have you got hidden in there? [*Laughs.*]

GÖRAN: Be serious Erik, be serious! A difficult time is ahead; damned difficult——

ERIK: I know, but I'm too tired to think about that.

GÖRAN: I'll take care of everything, if you'll only let me handle matters and not try to interfere.

ERIK: You handle them, Göran. But don't let my hands feel the reins, for if they do I'll throw you off! Goodbye now. And for God's sake set yourself up decently. [*Towards the curtain.*] Goodbye, Fru Persson. [*To* GÖRAN.] Well, say goodbye to her for me. [*Goes.*]

> GÖRAN *pulls the bell-rope.* PEDER WELAMSON, *a tall, rough, one-eyed fellow, enters.*

GÖRAN: Do you know Sergeant Max, of the Life Guards?

PEDER: Yes, Protector.

GÖRAN: Take six strong men with you and meet him this evening at the green gate when he comes on his watch. Tie him up so that he can't make a noise and stuff him in a sack. But no blood, mind! Then throw him in the river and make sure he drowns.

PEDER WELAMSON: It shall be done, Protector.

GÖRAN: You've no scruples about doing this?

PEDER WELAMSON: None.

GÖRAN: That's how a faithful servant should be. And so am I to my King. Good luck.

　　PEDER WELAMSON *goes.*

GÖRAN [*towards the curtain*]: If you've a bit of cold left, mother, I'm ready to eat now.

FRU PERSSON: Well? Did you get any money?

GÖRAN: No, we had other things to talk about.

FRU PERSSON: I wasn't listening. But I heard a bit of what you were saying.

MARIA: Come and eat now, uncle!

GÖRAN: Yes, child. I'm coming.

ACT THREE

Scene 1

The shore of Lake Mälaren, about eighty miles west of Stockholm. Evening light. Across the centre of the stage runs a bridge; to the right of it, at the foot of a hill covered with oaks and hazels, stands the BRIDGEKEEPER's cottage. On the shore in the background is a fisherman's hut, with a boat and nets.

GÖRAN PERSSON *is talking to* NILS GYLLENSTJERNA.

GÖRAN: Herr Gyllenstjerna, you are, are you not, the King's friend, despite this unfortunate incident which occurred recently——?

GYLLENSTJERNA: I am a Gyllenstjerna, and a friend of the House of Vasa. But I will not act as an executioner.

GÖRAN: There's no question of that. Tell me, what is your opinion of Duke Johan's conduct, and of the sentence which has been passed on him?

GYLLENSTJERNA: Duke Johan has incited Finland and Poland to turn against his country, and the Estates have justly condemned him to death. King Erik's decision to reprieve him does honour to his goodness of heart.

GÖRAN: Quite. And what do you say to this decision of the Queen Mother and her kinsmen to give the criminal a triumphant welcome when he passes this way in a short while?

GYLLENSTJERNA: I say that by this action they will brand themselves as his accomplices, and will thereby merit the same punishment as the criminal himself.

GÖRAN: The Queen Mother is of course sacrosanct, but the Stures and the other nobles are not. At the first sign of their intention to acclaim the traitor I shall, therefore, have them arrested, here at the bridgehead, where the convoy is due to halt. I have already stationed soldiers in that fishing hut; but it would lend weight to my action if you, as a member of the nobility and a kinsman of the Stures, should give me your personal support.

GYLLENSTJERNA: I shall do my duty; provided there be nothing unlawful——

GÖRAN: Oh, everything will be quite lawful. And then the Estates will judge the Stures as they have judged Duke Johan.

GYLLENSTJERNA: In that case, I'm with you. But first I want to see whether the lords will dare to declare their sympathy with the traitor against our lawful King. My troop is stationed near by. If you fire a shot, I shall be here at once. Until then—— [*Goes.*]

GÖRAN: One word more, Herr Gyllenstjerna—— [*Goes after him.*]

The BRIDGEKEEPER *comes out of his hut, followed by* PEDER WELAMSON.

BRIDGEKEEPER: If I were you, I'd try to lay my hands on a hacksaw.

PEDER WELAMSON: A hacksaw?

BRIDGEKEEPER: Yes. It's like this; you saw through the supports of the bridge, and put a fellow on watch at the bridgehead. When their lordships come to waylay the Duke, the watchman says to them: "Don't go on the bridge!" He don't need to say it more than once, and not over-loud at that. Well, of course their lordships won't pay no notice to what he says, the bridge'll collapse, and nobody'll be to blame.

PEDER WELAMSON: Might do that, I suppose. Bit roundabout though, ain't it? And there's some folk as knows how to swim. T'other day, for instance, I drowned a Sergeant by the name of Max, over by the north bridge. We stuffed him in a sack like a kitten, with eight balls and chain at his feet; but you never saw the like! He swam like an otter, and we had to club him like an eel on twelfth night.

BRIDGEKEEPER: I see! So it was you that put an end to Max——

PEDER WELAMSON [*proudly*]: It was.

BRIDGEKEEPER: No harm done there. Them as disappears ain't seen again, and you don't have all this fuss and bother. All these trials and prosecutions, they're no good! There's always some flaw in the evidence; and there's so much blessed writing goes on, and if one fellow writes something down wrong the biggest villain in the world'll find himself acquitted. The Protector's a clever fellow, but he writes too much——

PEDER WELAMSON: Not always, he don't! But with the Duke you see, there's certain formalities as has to be observed——

BRIDGEKEEPER: Is the Duchess with him? The Polish wench?

PEDER WELAMSON: No, they say she's coming later——

BRIDGEKEEPER: Ah, well. [*Jerks his thumb over his shoulder.*] The castle's big and the walls are thick, and what happens inside don't get overheard.

GÖRAN [*enters*]: Peder Welamson!

PEDER WELAMSON: Your Excellency!

GÖRAN: Guard this bridgehead and don't let anyone cross from this side. The Duke and his escort will be coming from over there. [*Points to the other side of the bridge.*]

PEDER WELAMSON: I'll see to it.

GÖRAN [*to the* BRIDGEKEEPER]: Watchman! Keep your eyes open and note what happens, so that you'll be able to testify later.

BRIDGEKEEPER: Testify? Not much good in that—the other side always says you're lying——

GÖRAN: I'll take care of that. You do your duty. Quiet now, here come the outriders.

He withdraws upstage right. EARL VANTE STURE, NILS STURE *and* ERIK STURE *enter right, with several other lords and their retinues. All of them carry garlands and bouquets of flowers;* NILS STURE *has a large garland bearing the letters J and C in gold, with a ducal coronet above them.*

SVANTE STURE [*to* NILS STURE]: Now hang the garland across the centre of the bridge, so that our noble cousin's path to prison shall appear to lead through an arch of triumph. [*Looks at the garland.*] J for Johan and C for Catherine; but J also stands for Jagellonys, Catherine's great ancestor! Yes, I like that!

NILS STURE: And C could stand for Duke Charles.

ERIK STURE: Watch your tongue, brother!

SVANTE STURE: Quiet now, lads.

NILS STURE *goes towards the bridgehead carrying his garland.* PEDER WELAMSON *bars the way with his pike.*

PEDER WELAMSON: Keep back!

NILS STURE: Watch your manners, you one-eyed freak!

PEDER WELAMSON: Watch yours, puppy! If your father had taught you manners in your nursery you'd know better than to mock a man for his misfortune.

NILS STURE: That was no misfortune, that you lost one eyeball. Pity you didn't lose both!

PEDER WELAMSON: You foolish brat, may God strike you blind——!

SVANTE STURE: How dare a common soldier presume to——!

PEDER WELAMSON: The King's bodyguard presumes to obey his orders, and anyone who tries to pass here will find himself on his back.

SVANTE STURE: Someone else put those words into his mouth. The rabble acts as spokesman for the King! The servant takes precedence over the master, the pen over the sword, the bastard over the noble! Oh, Sweden, Sweden!

LEJONHUFVUD [*to* SVANTE STURE]: Do you know that this fellow is Göran Persson's nephew?

SVANTE STURE: I didn't, but he looks the part.

STENBOCK: That rogue Persson has one virtue, then.

LEJONHUFVUD: Surely not! What is it?

STENBOCK: That he possesses a sister. I wouldn't have believed it of him.

LEJONHUFVUD: Then he has another virtue. He doesn't appear to practise nepotism.

SVANTE STURE: If you go on like this you'll end by praising the scoundrel!

STENBOCK: Look out! Here comes the Duke!

Across the bridge from the left, riding in threes, come: firstly, three CAPTAINS *in full armour; then* DUKE JOHAN, *his hands manacled, between two* GUARDS; *finally, three* SOLDIERS *on horseback, followed by men on foot.* SVANTE STURE *and the other* LORDS *throw flowers and garlands.* NILS STURE *has hung his garland on the signpost.*

SVANTE STURE: Long live the Duke of Finland! Vivat!

ALL: Vivat! Vivat! Vivat!

DUKE JOHAN *raises his hands in acknowledgment. The procession goes out right while the* LORDS *stand and wave. A sharp whistle is heard, followed by a shot.* GÖRAN PERSSON *and* NILS GYLLENSTJERNA *enter upstage right, and* SOLDIERS *emerge from the fisherman's hut.*

GYLLENSTJERNA [*to* SVANTE *and the* LORDS]: I arrest you and your companions in the King's name!

SVANTE STURE: On what grounds?

GYLLENSTJERNA: Duke Johan has been deprived of his Dukedom by the Estates of the Realm. You and these other lords still acclaim him as Duke, thereby challenging the judgment of the law and declaring yourselves accomplices of the traitor. Soldiers, do your duty.

The SOLDIERS *seize the* LORDS.

SVANTE STURE: Is this the voice of a Swedish nobleman?

GYLLENSTJERNA: Yes, a descendant of Kristina Gyllenstjerna and a Sture, a name that has never yet been soiled by treachery. One of His Majesty's subjects has been brought to justice, and you stand waiting for him with flowers in your hands as though he were a bridegroom!

SVANTE STURE: The Duke is not one of the King's subjects——

GYLLENSTJERNA: Pardon me, Herr Svante, your memory has slipped. You yourself were present when the Articles of Arboga were drawn up, by which all the Dukes were declared subjects of the King. Go, gentlemen. Justice awaits you; the law before which we all must bow, whether we be lord or commoner.

SVANTE STURE: Very well. We Stures know how to take the evil with the good. And the morrow bringeth counsel.

NILS STURE [*to* GÖRAN]: And when the night comes, you will be gone. Let us go, my friends.

The LORDS *are escorted out right.*

GÖRAN: Thank you, Herr Gyllenstjerna. I can't command the fine phrases which are needed on such occasions as this. You have spoken well, and therefore, once more, I thank you. Now I must go to Uppsala and get to work!

GYLLENSTJERNA: Farewell then, Your Excellency; and judge them mercifully.

GÖRAN [*goes*]: I shan't do any judging. I shall leave that to the Estates. [*To* PEDER WELAMSON.] Peder Welamson! Gather up all these flowers and garlands.

PEDER WELAMSON: Right!

GÖRAN: And then we'll go inside and write down your testimony and the bridgekeeper's, point by point.

PEDER WELAMSON: Point by point! But—couldn't we do it without any writing——? You know, like——

GÖRAN: You forget you're my sister's son, and I'll forget I'm your mother's brother.

PEDER WELAMSON: Even as regards advancement?

GÖRAN: Especially as regards advancement! Look; these noblemen expect more of us common people than they do of themselves; so we must try to meet their expectations. You stay down in the valley; it's less windy there than up on the heights. Leave this to me. I'll see they end by praising the scoundrel!

Scene 2

A room in the Royal Castle at Uppsala. In the background a window provides a view across the courtyard of the windows of the Hall of State; they are illuminated, and are standing open. Through them, figures in the Hall can be indistinctly glimpsed, moving; but this only when the curtains are pulled aside. The crown is standing on a table.

ERIK [*dressed in his royal robe, opens a window*]: It's so damned hot——

GÖRAN [*standing by another window, is listening through it. He points through it*]: And it'll get hotter. Some of the Lords' places are empty; but the Clergy are packed in there like a crowd at an execution.

ERIK: They don't love me. Have you been in?

GÖRAN: I went in for a moment.

ERIK: How did it feel? Was the atmosphere hostile? I can usually sense at once whether people are my friends or my enemies.

GÖRAN: I always sense hostility when two or three people are gathered together, and so I'm always ready to strike. And I like to strike first——

ERIK [*points through the windows*]: Look! Isn't that Johan there? With the red beard——

GÖRAN: No, that's Magnus of Åbo. I know him.

ERIK [*clasps his forehead*]: Yes, but I saw Johan! I saw him! Give me my speech. It's been copied out clearly?

GÖRAN [*hands him a paper*]: Here it is—printed large, so a child could read it.

ERIK [*reads it*]: Good! But you have all the evidence too?

GÖRAN: All of it! From Nils Sture's seditious utterance to Earl Svante's acclamation of the traitor. They'll have to be damned cunning to get these fellows acquitted.

ERIK: And the witnesses?

GÖRAN: Downstairs in the servants' hall. Anyway, the written testimonies are sufficient.

ERIK: Can we begin soon, do you think?

GÖRAN [*glances through the window*]: The Speakers haven't taken their places yet, otherwise it seems pretty packed.

ERIK [*walks downstairs, puts the paper down on a chair, then takes the crown and sets it on his head*]: God, it's hot! This crown makes my very hair sweat!

KARIN MÅNSDOTTER [*enters*]: Forgive me, dearest, but the children have something they want to ask you. It's quite a simple request——

ERIK [*gently*]: What is it?

KARIN: They say they want to see the King.

ERIK: But they see me every day. Oh, I see. They mean the King in his crown; the Player King! Well, let them come in.

> GUSTAV *and* SIGRID, *hand in hand and carrying dolls, enter and kneel before* ERIK.

ERIK: Now then, you little sillies, don't lie on the floor! [*Bends down and picks them up, one in each arm.*] Look at the pretty toy!

> GUSTAV *and* SIGRID *finger the crown.*

ERIK [*kisses them and puts them down*]: You've never been as high as that before, have you?

GUSTAV [*fingers the ermines on* ERIK's *robe*]: Look, Sigrid! He's got rats on his cloak!

SIGRID [*hides her face*]: No, I don't want to look at wats!

> *She goes to the chair on which* ERIK *has put the paper and, unnoticed, wraps her doll in it.*

ERIK [*to* GUSTAV]: Well, Gösta, do you want to be King one day?

GUSTAV: Yes, if Mummy can become Queen.

ERIK: She is already more than Queen, my child!

GUSTAV: Am I more than a prince, then?

ERIK: Yes, do you know why? Because you're an angel, my son!

> COURTIER *enters and whispers to* GÖRAN PERSSON, *who goes across to the* KING.

GÖRAN: Everything is ready. Hurry!

ERIK [*to* KARIN *and the* CHILDREN]: God bless you and keep you all! All! [*Goes.*]

KARIN [*to* GÖRAN]: What's going to happen down there now?

GÖRAN: The King is to denounce the Lords before the Four Estates.

KARIN: You mean the Lords who are locked up in the dungeons below?

GÖRAN: Yes, them.

KARIN: Should people be imprisoned before they have been tried and condemned?

GÖRAN: Yes; if they're caught red-handed they're held in custody while they await trial. That's what's happened here.

KARIN: Oh, you do so many things I don't understand——

GÖRAN: Well, the law's a complicated business, and you can't take short cuts when a man's life is at stake. [*By the window.*] Listen! The King's speaking! Come here, you can see him!

KARIN: Draw the curtains, Göran. I don't want to look.

GÖRAN [*draws the curtains*]: As you wish, ma'am.

SIGRID: Mummy! Is that Göran Persson?

KARIN: Hush, Sigrid!

SIGRID: Is he the one they say is so horrid?

GÖRAN: Not to nice children. Only to people who do wicked things.

KARIN: I like you better when you frown than when you smile, Göran.

GÖRAN: Yes, I can believe that.

KARIN: I'd hate ever to have to thank you for anything.

GÖRAN: And yet you——

The COURTIER *enters and whispers to* GÖRAN, *who hurries out, alarmed.*

COURTIER [*to* KARIN]: Your Grace, the Queen Mother craves audience.

KARIN [*timidly*]: Audience? With me?

QUEEN MOTHER [*bursts in left, and throws herself on her knees*]: Mercy! Mercy for my brother and my kinsmen!

KARIN [*falls on her knees*]: Rise up, in the name of Heaven and of our Saviour! How can you think that I have the power to grant mercy—I, who only live on sufferance? Rise, Queen, great Gustav's noble widow! I am too humble even to receive your Majesty!

QUEEN MOTHER: Is it Karin Månsdotter who speaks, she who holds the fate of our country in her little hand? Rise up yourself, raise your hand and save my family, for the King is beside himself and raving!

KARIN: The King—raving? Why, I know nothing, I can do nothing! If I tried to say a word, he'd hit me! Only recently, he tried to kill me!

QUEEN MOTHER: Then it isn't true that he has made you Queen?

KARIN: I? Dear God, I am the least of the ladies of his court—if I can be counted so high——

QUEEN MOTHER: And he maltreats you? Why don't you go away, then?

KARIN: Where on earth could I go? My father hates the sight of me, and my brothers and sisters want nothing to do with me. The only friend I had left, my cousin Max, has disappeared, God knows where——

QUEEN MOTHER: Sergeant Max? Surely you know that he is——?

KARIN: What? Tell me!

QUEEN MOTHER: Max is dead. They have murdered him.

KARIN: Murder? Here? I'd feared that, but I didn't want to believe it. Oh, my God! Now it is I who beg you for protection, if you can feel pity for so poor a sinner!

QUEEN MOTHER [*thoughtfully*]: I see! Very well. Come with me to Hörningsholm. It is strongly fortified, and there are men gathered there ready to defend themselves against the raving madman who wields the sceptre.

KARIN: But my children?

QUEEN MOTHER: Bring your children with you.

KARIN: I've seen so much evil—I can scarcely believe in such kindness—

QUEEN MOTHER: Oh, don't talk of kindness. Believe what you like about my reasons for making this offer, but you can't stay here in this den of murderers. But be quick! Get your things packed at once! The King may be here in half an hour, and then you and your children will be lost!

KARIN: He has murdered my only friend, the noblest heart, who was ready to redress my wrongs. I forgive him, because he is so unhappy. But I can never see him again. [*She rings a bell. A* LADY IN WAITING *enters.*] Pack the children's clothes immediately, and bring them here. And bring their toys, so that the little ones won't cry on the journey, and want to come back home.

The LADY IN WAITING *goes out with* GUSTAV *and* SIGRID.

QUEEN MOTHER: What beautiful children you have! Does their father love them?

KARIN: He worships them. But he could kill them. Nowadays he only talks of killing——

QUEEN MOTHER [*thoughtfully*]: He'll miss them, then?

KARIN: One moment yes, the next, no. Poor Erik!

The LADY IN WAITING *enters with the* CHILDREN's *clothes and toys, and places them on chairs and tables.*

QUEEN MOTHER: Göran Persson has an evil influence on Erik, hasn't he?

KARIN: Rather the opposite! Göran is wise, and clever; and he tries to do what's right, as far as he can— But I'm frightened of him, all the same.

QUEEN MOTHER: Do you know what is happening in the Hall of State at this moment?

KARIN: They say it's something to do with the Lords, but I don't really understand.

QUEEN MOTHER: The King has sworn that they shall die——

KARIN: The Stures, too? The noble Stures, so beloved of the people——?

QUEEN MOTHER: Yes, the men who are sitting down there in the castle dungeons! My own brother, Abraham Stenbock, is lying there——

KARIN: Then I don't want to stay with him any longer. My children shall not be involved in any vendetta.

The buzz of voices, shouting and confusion are heard from the courtyard below.

QUEEN MOTHER [*at a window*]: Leave everything and let us fly, quickly! The King is coming! He's in a rage—I can see the foam on his mouth——

KARIN: Come with me! I know a way through the garden down to the river. [*Picks up some of the children's clothes.*] Help me to carry these. And now—God protect us!

She goes out with the QUEEN MOTHER. *From the courtyard there comes the clash of arms, and the sound of trumpets and of horses.* ERIK *enters, flings his crown upon a table and goes round looking for something, beside himself with rage.* GÖRAN PERSSON *enters.*

GÖRAN: Is the King here? What's happened? What in God's name has happened?

ERIK [*tears off his robe, rolls it up, throws it on the floor and kicks it*]: What has happened? Nothing has *happened*, it's all been planned, planned by Satan——!

GÖRAN: Speak intelligibly, and I'll put everything right.

ERIK: Very well. You know I'm no speaker, so I had everything written down. Well, I thought I had the paper in my pocket, so I open my attack on the traitors from memory, impromptu. Then I feel for the paper, but as I do so I see that red beard grin at me as only Johan can, and I can't find the paper! Then I went mad, rushed about, got the names and figures confused—it was as if someone had put their hand inside my head and jumbled everything up and dislocated the mechanism of my tongue! This someone, whom I don't hesitate to call Satan, made me confuse Svante Sture with Peder Welamson and vice versa. I said the Stures had decorated the bridge with wreaths instead of garlands, and all my old suspicions against the Stures which I've hitherto suppressed I blurted out, with a whole heap of accusations which I can't prove. First they laugh, then they catch me out in little mistakes about trivialities—and then, when six of their witnesses testified that Johan had been greeted with bunches of flowers and one wreath instead of with garlands, my evidence was dismissed as worthless! Imagine, Göran! If I'd had the Lords tried in the usual manner, according to the letter of the law, they'd have been convicted immediately because they'd been caught red-handed—but I had to be noble, God forgive me, because I had justice on my side! Noble! Damn nobility! And the Estates decided *for* the villains, they cheered the scoundrels, they commiserated with the swine, and now *we* stand there, we judges stand there in the dock, accused by the criminals! It seems that he who has Hell on his side is in the right!

GÖRAN: But the witnesses?

ERIK: The witnesses were challenged! Do you think a bridge-keeper or a common soldier are allowed to testify against lords? But they can testify *for* them! Sture's lackey they believed word for word, against me, the King! Stenbock's old nurse was quoted as though she was holy writ! Ivarsson's little son was adjudged competent to give evidence against all legal precedent, and was applauded!

GÖRAN: And the result?

ERIK: The Lords were acquitted.

GÖRAN: Let me think for a moment. Hm! Hm! Yes, we'll do it this way. The Estates shall be deemed unqualified to have judged the case, and it must come before the King's Council!

ERIK: Fool! We, that is you, stand accused in this matter, and can therefore no longer be accepted as an impartial judge.

GÖRAN: Damnation! Then I can see no way out but extra-legal procedure. Justice must be done, whatever the price.

ERIK: But not by unjust methods! We can't mock the law!

GÖRAN: No, by methods that are just, and that mock liars and false witnesses! The law condemns traitors to death. Therefore they must die.

ERIK: Tell me, why did red-beard grin when I couldn't find that paper? He knew where it was, of course; he must have conspired to steal it. That paper's got to be found, and whoever's hand it is found in I swear shall die! [*Looks around.*] What's this? Am I in the nursery? It looks just as though—— [*Rings.*] Göran! I'm frightened! [*Rings again.*] Why does no one come? It sounds so empty everywhere!

The COURTIER *enters.*

Where is Mademoiselle Karin? [*The* COURTIER *is silent.*] If you don't answer me at once, I'll kill you! Where is Mademoiselle Karin?

COURTIER: Her Grace has gone.

ERIK: Gone? With the children?

COURTIER: Yes, Your Majesty.

ERIK [*collapses on to a couch*]: Then *you* may kill *me*!

GÖRAN: Send after them! They can't have got far!

COURTIER: The Queen Mother has accompanied the fugitives to Hörningsholm——

ERIK: Hörningsholm! The Stures' castle! Always the Stures! Send ten thousand men to storm it! Burn it down! Starve them into submission——!

COURTIER: The Queen Mother was escorted by the Södermanland Regiment——

ERIK: Södermanland! Ha, that's Duke Charles! I daren't touch him; if I do, he'll release that devil Johan from Gripsholm! So it was the Queen Mother, that Sture bitch, who tricked my Karin into leaving me! And my pretty Karin went—a whore, Göran, they're all whores! But they took my children too, those Stures! That I shall never forgive! [*Draws a dagger and hacks at the table.*] Never! Never! [*Drives the dagger into the table.*]

GÖRAN: Was Nils Gyllenstjerna at the trial?

ERIK: Yes, when it started I saw him standing by the witnesses bench, but when the wind changed he disappeared. Everyone is abandoning me, except you, Göran!

GÖRAN [*to* COURTIER]: Tell Peder Welamson to come here. At once!

The COURTIER *goes.*

Listen, Erik. This is logical, isn't it? The common law condemns traitors to death. The Stures are traitors, therefore the Stures are condemned to death.

ERIK: Good!

GÖRAN: And——

NILS GYLLENSTJERNA [*enters*]: Pardon me, Your Majesty——

ERIK: Ah, here's the coward!

ERIK THE FOURTEENTH

GYLLENSTJERNA: That's easy to say, but what can a sane man do when he's faced by a pack of madmen?

ERIK: Tell me: do you regard the Stures as guilty?

GYLLENSTJERNA: I must believe my own eyes and ears, and a crime can be committed without the Estates of the Realm being there to see it. However, there is a rumour abroad—and this is why I have come—that Duke Johan has escaped.

ERIK [*starts to run around the room*]: Then all Hell is loose!

GÖRAN: Keep calm!

GYLLENSTJERNA: I also have a message for you, my lord Protector.

GÖRAN: Well, say it!

GYLLENSTJERNA: I would prefer to do so in private.

GÖRAN: We have no secrets here.

GYLLENSTJERNA [*presses an object into* GÖRAN'S *hand*]: A certain person has asked me to give you this and to say that she has exchanged it for another's——

GÖRAN: [*looks at the ring he has been given, then throws it behind his back out of the window. Then he takes a miniature from inside his shirt and crushes it beneath his foot.*]

ERIK [*who has been watching him, laughs*]: The Prototype! So she's proved a whore too! [*Laughs again.*]

GÖRAN: Now my blood begins to boil! To think that the best that life has to give can be the foulest—that Hell lies in Paradise, and angels are devils—that Satan is a white dove and the Holy Ghost a——!

ERIK: Stop!

GÖRAN: Have you turned superstitious! Go, Lord Gyllenstjerna, for here there is going to be such a sweeping and scouring as will scarce be matched till Doomsday! Go quickly, for we await a distinguished guest!

PEDER WELAMSON *enters.*

GYLLENSTJERNA: What you intend is unlawful. Yet—perhaps it is just—— [*He goes.*]

GÖRAN [*to* GYLLENSTJERNA]: Shut your mouth! [*To* PEDER WELAMSON.] Peder Welamson, there are rats in the cellar. Go down and kill them!

PEDER WELAMSON: Gladly! But——

ERIK: Do you hesitate?

PEDER WELAMSON: Oh, it isn't that. But there's something I want.

ERIK: What do you want? Do you want to become a baron, a count, a privy councillor? Speak! None of it's worth having; and it won't make you a whit better than those swine down in the cellars. I can't create Kings, but I can create Queen's! I can make a Queen out of a whore! If you want to be a Queen, I can make you one!

PEDER WELAMSON: I want to be a corporal.

ERIK: A corporal? What modesty! In truth, I have better friends than Johan! Very well, Corporal! Now serve your King!

PEDER WELAMSON: Could have been done cleanly in the first place, if there hadn't been all this writing. Ah, well—— [*Goes.*]

ERIK [*sits down in a chair*]: It's a beautiful Whitsun evening. [*Laughs.*] Green leaves and white lilies—I should have been sailing on the lake now, with Karin and the children. The children! Imagine, those wild beasts have stolen my babies—and everything they do is right and good. Why can some people do as they please, why? And now Johan has escaped!

GÖRAN [*has sat down at a desk and is writing*]: Why don't you send troops to catch him?

ERIK: Why don't you?

GÖRAN: I don't know. I can't fight against the Devil.

ERIK: Have you lost your courage?

GÖRAN: No, but I don't understand how this can have happened. It's against all logic, against probability, against justice! Is there a God who protects scoundrels, who helps traitors, who makes black white?

ERIK: So it seems.

GÖRAN: Listen! Someone's singing down there—a psalm——

ERIK [*listens*]: It's that old wild boar Svante——! The swine——!

GÖRAN: Yes, you can divide humanity into religious swine and irreligious swine; but they'll always stay swine.

ERIK: Have you any religion, Göran?

GÖRAN: I don't know. Just now a few bubbles seemed to be trying to fight their way up out of the swamp of childhood. But they burst and stank!

ERIK [*has reached out his hand and grasped a doll*]: Look at this! It's Sigrid's. She calls it Blind Bloodless—I know the names of their dolls, you see! Do you know, I've dreaded this moment more than any other moment of my life—the moment when the ones I love abandon me. But reality never equals expectation. I don't feel anything—I'm as calm as I never was before, in my whole life. I wish I could say that in a moment of happiness——! I wish to God it wasn't Whitsun Eve. That wakes so many happy memories. Of the children, especially. The best this wretched life has to give—— Last year we rowed on the lake. Sigrid and Gustav had new summer clothes, they were brightly coloured, and their mother had made them garlands of forget-me-nots which she put on their flaxen hair. It was high summer, and the children laughed and sang, and looked like angels. Then they went ashore in their bare feet to play ducks and drakes. Sigrid raised her little hand and the stone hit Gustav on the cheek. [*He sniffs.*] You should have seen how unhappy she was! How she stroked him and begged him to forgive her——! She kissed the soles of his feet to make him laugh!

Death and damnation! [*Leaps to his feet.*] Where are my children? Who has dared to touch the lion's young? The wild boar! Then the lion shall tear the wild boar's young! That's logic, isn't it? [*Draws his dagger.*] Damn them! Damn them!

GÖRAN: Leave that to the Corporal. If you get mixed up in this, all Hell will break loose.

ERIK: No, Göran. I shall myself be the instrument of divine justice, since the gods are asleep.

GÖRAN: Who cares about the gods?

ERIK: Exactly!

> *He goes out.* GÖRAN PERSSON *rings. The curtain descends for a moment. When it rises* GÖRAN *is still seated at his table writing.* ERIK *returns, greatly agitated.*

ERIK: It was a lie, of course, about Johan's escape. Everything is lies, the whole world, and heaven too; the Prince of the World is also called the Father of Lies, see the Gospel according to Saint Matthew, Chapter 8, Verses 11 and 12 in the Authorised ... However ... I wandered from room to room—imagine, those devils hadn't made the bed in our room—from chamber to chamber without meeting a soul. The whole castle's been abandoned like a sinking ship. Down in the kitchens it was horrible—the maids had stolen the spices and the food, bits of it were lying strewn around everywhere, and the footmen had knocked the heads off the wine bottles——! However——

GÖRAN: Did you go down into the cellars?

ERIK: Certainly not! But—how strange this room looks! There lies the crown and there the robe, the royal regalia of Sweden—but look at this little boot! Think of the little foot that has worn down this heel! It's Sigrid's—it's true, really, I am ashamed, but one can't escape one's fate and I've never managed to escape mine——! My father said I'd come to a bad end—how could he know that, if it hadn't been ordained—and who could have ordained it but He who willed that it should be so? But the worst was when the Corporal put out Nils's eye—the Corporal is one-eyed, as of course you know, and as he did it he said; "Here's a present from the One-Eyed Freak, an eye for an eye!" From which I assumed that Nils had at some time mocked the Corporal for his deformity. Which shows that life is a circle, and that Nils was, as the proverb says, hoist with his own petard.

GÖRAN: Are they dead, then?

ERIK: You mustn't ask so many questions, Göran. Then he stabbed Svante, the old wild boar, and Erik and the other ones—ssh! Now comes the worst part! When the Corporal was about to stab Svante, the old devil grew bold and declared that the Estates had acquitted him, and challenged me to prove my accusations. Imagine, the dog wants me to *prove* that he'd called me a madman to my face, *prove* that he'd thereby committed *lèse-majesté*, *prove* that he'd acclaimed a traitor——! That made me so mad that I ordered the Corporal to execute them—but then he cried: "Don't touch us! If you do, your children will die, for they have been taken as hostages!" Hostages! Can you realise what that word meant to me? I saw my little ones kneeling at Hörningsholm—before the block——! Then I wanted to cancel the order—but it was too late——

GÖRAN: What happened after that?

ERIK: It was a pitiable sight——! Every mortal attains a kind of sublimity at the moment of death; as though the mask fell off and the butterfly flew free. That was too much for me——

GÖRAN: Yes, but did *you* kill anyone?

ERIK: No. I just stabbed Nils in the arm, but that didn't kill him. Anyway, it was horrible, and I wish now it had never happened.

GÖRAN: Do you regret ordering criminals to be executed?

ERIK: But the hostages! Think of my children! And Nils' and Erik's mother—and my step-uncle, Abraham Stenbock—they killed him too! She'll never forgive that! Can you—settle this, Göran?

GÖRAN: No. I don't understand—I just don't understand anything. Don't you see? History takes its course and we can do nothing about it. I sit dumb and paralysed—I can't lift a finger—I can only wait, and ask: "What will happen now?"

ERIK: You can't help me any longer?

GÖRAN: No.

ERIK: I see. Then I shall go and look for the friend I should never have abandoned.

GÖRAN: You mean Karin?

ERIK: Yes.

GÖRAN: Well, go, then.

ERIK: What will happen now?

GÖRAN [*remains seated at his table, and drums with his fingers*]: If one only knew!

ACT FOUR

Scene 1

The kitchen in PRIVATE MÅNS's house. MÅNS is seated at the table. There is a knock on the door.

MÅNS: Come in!

   PEDER WELAMSON *enters*.

Hullo, Peder.

PEDER WELAMSON: Corporal, if you don't mind.

MÅNS: I see! I hope you earned your promotion honourably.

PEDER WELAMSON: I hope I did.

MÅNS: What have you been getting up to over there in Uppsala?

PEDER WELAMSON: We have been executing traitors.

MÅNS: In a just and lawful manner?

PEDER WELAMSON: The execution of traitors is always just.

MÅNS: You had full proof, then?

PEDER WELAMSON: Course I had proof. I was eyewitness. The King judged them guilty by royal decree, and I executed them.

MÅNS: Well, I've nothing against thinning these lords out a bit. But why did the King go mad afterwards?

PEDER WELAMSON: Mad? He just got a bit remorseful. That ain't mad.

MÅNS: They say he ran away into the forests. That true?

PEDER WELAMSON: He got desperate over the loss of his children, who'd been tricked away from him, so he went out into the night to look for them. Damned stupid! Well, he got lost in the forest and had to sleep on the ground in the rain. Couldn't find anything to eat, and got a fever which made him delirious. Anything else you want to know?

MÅNS: Is there any good in that man?

PEDER WELAMSON: Look here, Måns. I can understand you hating him, but the King's a human being. Think: the Estates condemned Duke Johan to death, but King Erik pardoned him, and now he's set him free. That's a noble action, though it ain't wise. He had those lords who'd plotted against him executed in a moment of impatience, but now he's asked their families to forgive him and given them large sums of money. That's noble too, ain't it?

MÅNS: Yes, but murder is murder.

PEDER WELAMSON: What do you mean, murder? He gave Nils a poke in the arm because he was cheeky, but that wasn't what killed him——

MÅNS: That makes no difference.

PEDER WELAMSON: What do you mean, makes no difference? Either he did murder them or he didn't murder them. You're a codfish, a conceited unreasonable old fox——

MÅNS: Don't shout. Someone's creeping around there outside the window, listening——

PEDER WELAMSON: Let 'em.

MÅNS: Has the King seen Karin?

PEDER WELAMSON: I don't know. I don't think so.

MÅNS: Why did she run away from him?

PEDER WELAMSON: The Queen Mother scared her.

MÅNS: What a bunch!

PEDER WELAMSON: Serve them right for getting mixed up with you.

MÅNS: Yes, they ought to have known better. You think I get any credit out of all this? Just the opposite. Other people can hide their shame, but mine's stuck up on a palace tower so the whole country can see it.

PEDER WELAMSON: There *is* someone moving around out there.

They turn towards the window. A pane is open, and through it KARIN MÅNSDOTTER'S *face can be seen, pale and distraught. It immediately disappears.*

MÅNS: Did you see what I saw?

PEDER WELAMSON: I saw. It was Karin. Look, Måns, you're prouder than the king himself, but it don't become you. Be a human being for once.

MÅNS: Give me that stick.

PEDER WELAMSON: I'd give it you all right, if you weren't so old.

MÅNS: Get out, before something happens to you!

PEDER WELAMSON [*goes towards the door*]: Me? [*Goes out, leaving the door open.*]

KARIN [*in the doorway*]: May I come in?

MÅNS: Are you hungry? That why you've come?

KARIN: No, it isn't that. Oh, father, I'm so unhappy——

MÅNS: The wages of sin is death.

KARIN: I know. But before I die, I want to see my brothers——

MÅNS: You won't do that.

KARIN: That would be the worst punishment you could give me. Oh, father, father——!

MÅNS [*takes the stick from the corner and sits down again*]: Don't come any closer, or I'll hit you.

KARIN: Forget I was once your daughter. Only think of me as a beggar who has been walking in the forest for so long that her feet can no longer carry her. May I sit down by the door like a tramp or a gipsy——?

MÅNS: Get up! And go—go till the earth burns your feet——!

KARIN [*goes towards the stove*]: You won't refuse me a drink of water from the pail——

MÅNS: Don't soil the vessel with your whore's lips. If you want food and drink, go out in the pigsty. That's where you belong——

KARIN [*goes nearer him*]: Beat me, but let me stay. Maybe I'm no worse than other women——

MÅNS *raises his stick.* KING ERIK *enters.*

ERIK: What are you doing, soldier?

MÅNS: I was about to thrash my child.

ERIK: Isn't it rather late to be thinking of that? If anyone has the right to do that, it is I. You have renounced your child.

MÅNS *is silent.*

If you had shown a little more courtesy, I would have asked you formally for your daughter's hand. As it is, I shall confine myself to inviting you to our wedding.

MÅNS *is silent.*

You think I have erred. I admit my errors, and now I am righting the wrong I have done you. But you, too, must forgive. Give Karin your hand!

MÅNS *remains as before; he looks scornful and unbelieving.*

You look as if you didn't regard me as sane. I suppose that's because you, who think yourself sane, are convinced you wouldn't act as I'm doing if you were in my shoes. But it shall be as I say; and you could have had a worse son-in-law than me.

MÅNS *remains silent.*

He refuses to answer me! Has any King ever been so humiliated? Don't you understand how highly I esteem your daughter when I tell you that I wish to make her our country's Queen—so that I come cap in hand to a coarse-mannered, stiff-necked ruffian like you! Was ever a father so cruel? I am going now, and I hope I may never live to regret this action. You will never understand it, because you do not understand what nobility means. Come, Karin! Come! [*Takes her by the hand, and goes towards the door; then turns*]. I forgive you, because I myself need forgiveness. A few moments ago, I regarded myself as the worst of mortals; but now I think myself a little better than you.

Scene 2

A turret room, furnished as a library. DUKE JOHAN is seated at a desk, bent over a folio volume. There is a knock at the door.

JOHAN: Come in! [DUKE CHARLES *enters*]. Well, have you slept on it.

CHARLES: Yes, I've slept on it.

JOHAN: Well? What conclusion have you come to?

CHARLES: That the elimination of ambitious lords is not a disaster for our country.

JOHAN: That seems to be the general opinion. But the country must not be ruled by a madman.

CHARLES: That's a delicate question. Is he a madman?

JOHAN: Of course he is!

CHARLES: I wonder. Pangs of conscience, remorse and repentance are not the characteristics of a madman.

JOHAN: But you haven't heard the latest. Do you realise that he, the King, has visited Private Måns in his house, offered a formal apology, asked for his daughter's hand, and made preparations for the wedding! He's already invited me. Your invitation's probably on its way.

CHARLES [*walks up and down thoughtfully*]: That's foolish, but it isn't mad.

JOHAN: No? Are you happy at the prospect of the Swedish crown being inherited by Private Måns's grandchildren?

CHARLES: I'd rather it didn't. But surely children born out of wedlock can't inherit the throne.

JOHAN: Can't they? Göran Persson, the cleverest scoundrel and the only intelligent politician in the country, can get the Estates to decree anything he wants. He persuaded them to condemn me to death, and I've no doubt he'll persuade them to adopt the bastards and make them legitimate.

CHARLES: Couldn't he be got rid of?

JOHAN: Try! No, I've a better idea. There'd be no Göran if there were no Erik; so——

CHARLES: Get rid of Erik? But he's our brother——

JOHAN: He says he isn't, because we didn't have the same mother.

CHARLES: Suppose, by working together, we did manage to effect a change in the administration——

JOHAN: Which we subsequently persuaded the Estates to ratify——

CHARLES: Johan, where did you learn such principles?

JOHAN: From my enemies.

CHARLES: A bad school. However, supposing we two should effect a change in the administration—what happens then?

JOHAN: We share the throne. The chair of Gustav Vasa is broad enough for two.

CHARLES: Will you give me your hand on this?

JOHAN [*stretches out his hand*]: Certainly.

CHARLES: Then we refuse his invitation to the wedding, and go instead to Stockholm?

JOHAN: Wouldn't it be better to let Erik think we're coming to the wedding?

CHARLES: That must depend on the circumstances. We don't know what move he'll make next. Let him show his hand first.

JOHAN: I almost believe you're shrewder than I am.

CHARLES: Let the game proceed, then. I trust you, Johan.

JOHAN: Trust me.

Scene 3

The hall of Uppsala Castle. ERIK and KARIN enter robed as King and Queen.

ERIK: Well now you are my wife, our country's mother and the first lady of our nobility. I bid you welcome to our royal palace. Our wedding was not as brilliant as I had hoped, since the Dukes absented themselves from the ceremony. But I'm sure they will be at the banquet——

KARIN: Erik, don't brood over this latest humiliation. Rather rejoice with me that our children now have parents who are man and wife——

ERIK: Everything in my life has been soiled and warped. Even this sacred day, when I lead my young bride to the Lord's altar, has to be a day of shame. And the children, God's blessing on our union, had to be hidden lest they should expose our shame before the world, which already knows of it!

KARIN: Don't be ungrateful, Erik! Remember those days and nights of terror, when you trembled for the fate of your children, because they were held hostage by our enemies——

ERIK: You are right; and our enemies were nobler than me, for they spared my children while I slew the Lords—! Yes, yes, those men are better than I am, and I am luckier than I deserve—much luckier!

KARIN: You ought really to be happy that you have survived these dangers as you have——

ERIK: I am happy—and it's just that that makes me uneasy. And it grieves me that I had to exclude Göran Persson from the ceremony, to please the Dukes——that was one of their conditions——

KARIN: Don't be miserable! Be thankful!

ERIK: I am thankful—though I don't really know why—I've only done what was right, and yet I have to beg forgiveness!

KARIN: Erik, Erik!

NILS GYLLENSTJERNA [*enters*]: Your Majesty, the people wish to see the royal bride and acclaim their country's Queen.

ERIK [*to* KARIN]: Do you want that?

KARIN: If it's the custom.

ERIK [*to* GYLLENSTJERNA]: Let them in.

NILS GYLLENSTJERNA *admits the* PEOPLE. MÅNS, FRU PERSSON, AGDA *and* MARIA *are among them.*

KARIN [*to* ERIK]: Say a friendly word to father. Just one!

ERIK: That man's prouder than I am—I don't need to make a bad business worse.

MÅNS [*to* KARIN]: Now that everything's been put to rights, I forgive you.

ERIK [*angrily*]: Forgive! Forgive what?

MÅNS: I thought once that Sergeant Max would be the one who'd raise up the fallen—the two of them were betrothed, in a manner of speaking—I mean, there wasn't anything *between* them, as the saying goes, that is—

KARIN: Father, father!

ERIK [*to* MÅNS]: Are you drunk, or has the Devil entered into you? Almighty God, what a wedding! There's Agda, from that damned brothel the Blue Dove. She used to be Jacob Israel's old concubine. A friend of the bride! And this bumpkin is my father-in-law! Death and damnation! But it's true, I must be thankful, and laugh and be happy. Oh, God, yes, I'm happy. [*To* GYLLENSTJERNA] Take this rabble out and feed them. I've probably half a dozen sisters-in-law among them who haven't deigned to speak to me before, and a brother-in-law or two who wants to borrow money! Get rid of them, Gyllenstjerna!

KARIN *goes out, weeping.*

[*Calls after her.*] Yes, that's the best thing you can do! [*The* PEOPLE *go out.*] If I could hear what those wretches are thinking, I'd have cause enough to hang the lot of them! Except Göran's mother, and she ought to have had the wit to stay at home. Her son had the sense to keep away—— [GÖRAN *enters.*] Well, here he is! I was just wishing you were here, Göran——

GÖRAN: I hope I haven't come too late——

ERIK: What have you been doing?

GÖRAN: I've been working on our friends at Uppsala; the Estates. I've news for you——

ERIK: Oh, God, what is it?

GÖRAN: After you left the castle, I found the indictment and the sworn testimonies. After a good deal of trouble I managed to summon the Estates again, and appeared before them in the role of prosecutor—— Well, to cut a long story short, the Estates have declared the Stures and the other Lords guilty!

ERIK: No! And I have begged their families for forgiveness, and have sent a proclamation all over the country declaring that all the men who were executed were innocent!

GÖRAN [*sinks down on a chair*]: Oh, God Almighty! Then we're finished. Oh, Erik, everything you touch goes wrong!

ERIK: Can't you find a way out of this for me, Göran?

GÖRAN: No. I can't clean up your messes any longer. Everything I build up you knock down. You were born unlucky.

ERIK: So that's why the Dukes didn't come to our wedding?

GÖRAN: Possibly. But someone warned them, too—

ERIK: Who? Who?

GÖRAN *is silent.*

You know! Speak!

GÖRAN: It pains me to have to say it, but——

ERIK: Karin? [GÖRAN *is silent.*] She! That whore, that false hypocrite! And I've gone and tied myself to her! Then she knew of the Estates' finding—but I didn't! That's the sort of thing I have to endure! [GÖRAN *is silent.*] And this is my reward for being noble! For pardoning Johan, for appeasing those scoundrels' families with good money! But why did I have to be wounded like this? By the only person on earth I loved and believed in! My hands and feet are chained— there's a rope round my neck! Who is this enemy I have to fight?

GÖRAN: Satan.

ERIK: I believe you're right! If only the Queen Mother would come—then the Dukes would come too—to the banquet! Imagine, that witch Elizabeth of England, when she learns I've married the daughter of a common soldier! That hurts me most of all! Oh God—! [*Laughs.*] The King of Sweden marries a vegetable seller, a Vasa celebrates his nuptials with a Månsdotter, who's been another common soldier's whore!

I suppose it was you who drowned him. Thank you for that. I got the blame, of course, and had to beg Karin to forgive me, for three days and three nights—I always have to beg for forgiveness when other people have committed villainies—! What a pity the Dukes didn't come. I'd have put gunpowder under their chairs and lit it myself!

NILS GYLLENSTJERNA *enters*.

All right, scream it out! [NILS GYLLENSTJERNA *is silent.*] More refusals! The Queen Mother begs to be excused!

GYLLENSTJERNA [*shows a heap of opened letters*]: Yes. And all the nobles beg to be excused.

ERIK: Ah! I, the King, honour rogues by inviting them to my wedding, and they don't come! Gyllenstjerna! Let the trumpets be sounded for the banquet to commence! Then call in the rabble and bid them sit down to the feast! All of them! My false jewel shall be given a setting worthy of her! Send out into the streets and the market places, bring beggars from the gutters and whores from the brothels—

GYLLENSTJERNA: Is Your Majesty serious?

ERIK: Do you mock me, dog? [*Goes over to the door in the background and throws it open. He gives a sign. A fanfare is blown and tables laid with food, etc., are carried in. Then he goes to the left-hand door and beckons in the* PEOPLE, *who seem half-drunk and timid.*] To the tables, scum! Come, let's have no false modesty! We won't wait for the bride; she'll be here in a moment. Sit down, you dogs! If you don't obey me, I'll kill you!

The RABBLE, *including* MÅNS, AGDA *and* MARIA, *but not* FRU PERSSON, *take their places at the tables*. GÖRAN PERSSON *remains seated in his chair, watching contemptuously*. NILS GYLLENSTJERNA *lays down his marshal's staff at* ERIK'*s feet and goes*.

ERIK: You've had your fill now, have you, lickspittle? You think yourself too good to serve this rabble? Look at the King's father-in-law—see how he sticks his fingers in this mouth—! [*Picks up the staff, breaks it and throws the pieces after* GYLLENSTJERNA.] Go to hell!

GYLLENSTJERNA: Now your last and only friend is leaving you. [*Goes out.*]

ERIK [*to* GÖRAN]: How beautiful that sounds. I'm still such a child, or such a fool, that I'm ready to believe the first rogue who utters a beautiful word! However—— [*Sits down beside* GÖRAN PERSSON.] Gyllenstjerna wasn't the best of men, nor the worst. They called him Lord Come-and-Go; full of righteousness and most unjust; brave as few men are, and cowardly as none; loyal as a dog and false as a cat——

GÖRAN: In a word, a man.

More PEOPLE *come in.*

ERIK [*to the* PEOPLE]: Welcome, good friends! The bride's father offers you hospitality! Eat, drink and be merry, for tomorrow you die! [*To* GÖRAN.] It's strange how I've always liked low people. Do you know, I really feel at home with these characters. But look at the lackeys, see how they turn up their noses——! [*Laughs.*]

GÖRAN: Do you really think common people are worse than aristocrats? I've never seen such coarseness as Svante Sture displayed when he visited me in any gutter or brothel.

ERIK: What sort of thing did he say?

GÖRAN: I'm ashamed for his sake to repeat the filth he uttered in the hearing of my mother and that child—— He didn't eat with his knife—that's about the best you could say of him.

ERIK [*to the* SERVANTS, *who are unwillingly handing round the food*]: Be polite to my guests, or I'll have your hides tanned for you! [*To* GÖRAN.] What are you brooding about?

GÖRAN: Your fate—and mine! I don't understand anything any longer. But I think our saga is moving towards its close. The air's so sultry, and I can hear so many things. In one ear I hear the tramp of horses, and in the other drumbeats. The kind they use at executions. Have you seen my mother lately?

ERIK: She was here just now to look at the bride.

GÖRAN: I can't think why, but I long for the old woman. I know she never talked about anything but money, but—I suppose she was right, really——

ERIK: Göran, you aren't hurt because I asked you to stay away from the wedding? I did it because of the Dukes——

GÖRAN: Do you think I don't understand? You think I bother about that? But there's one thing I'd like to ask you——

ERIK: What's that, Göran?

GÖRAN: You mustn't think I had any—anything to do with Agda. Jacob Israel's girl. It isn't true. I just took care of her because—well, you know those whims of—hm—chivalry we all have once in our lives——

ERIK: You're a good man really, Göran——

GÖRAN: Shut up! No, I'm sorry, but I can't stand people praising me; it's as if it wasn't true, or didn't concern me. [ERIK *clicks his tongue.*] You know what the Dukes' absence means?

ERIK: That they are swine.

GÖRAN: That we are condemned to death. That seems to me quite clear.

ERIK: Death? Yes, of course. You're right. Do you know what my greatest mistake was?

GÖRAN: No. I know nothing any longer. I understand nothing. That's why I'm finished. Once upon a time I used to dream I was a wise statesman; I thought I had a task in life—to defend the crown inherited by you from your great father, given by the people—not by the nobles—and worn by the grace of God. Well, it seems I was mistaken.

ERIK: Hasn't it ever struck you, Göran, that there are things which we don't understand, and aren't meant to understand?

GÖRAN: Yes. But haven't you often felt that, after all, you're a bit better than the rest of them?

ERIK: Yes. Have you?

GÖRAN: I have always believed that I have acted rightly——

ERIK: So have I. But I suppose the others did, too. Who has been wrong, then?

GÖRAN: Yes, answer that if you can. It's awful to think how little we know.

Pause.

ERIK: Göran, will you go and bring Karin back to me?

GÖRAN: Yes, if you forgive her.

ERIK: For what? Oh yes, of course—it was she who warned the Dukes. That was a nasty thing to do to me; but perhaps she was afraid of the children becoming involved in a vendetta. And me.

GÖRAN: She took away your gunpowder before you could use it, because she knew her Erik. Forgive her!

ERIK: I have already—in my heart. But look at these people! Now they've eaten all they can, and they're getting merry and would like to talk——! Göran, is life a comedy or a tragedy?

GÖRAN: Both. Equally. To me the whole thing's just a non-sense poem, though that doesn't say there isn't some hidden meaning to be found in it. You're sad, Erik?

ERIK: Yes; it's the old restlessness coming back. But who makes me restless? Who? Come with me, I want to see Karin and the children. Can you explain that—I know she isn't much better than me, but when I'm near her I feel calmer. I feel less of a compulsion to be evil.

GÖRAN: I can't explain anything.

ERIK: Sometimes it seems to me that I am her child; and sometimes that she is mine.

Pause.

GÖRAN [*listens*]: Hush! I can hear footsteps creeping up the stairs and along the corridors! They're tiptoeing through the doors and—opening windows——

ERIK: You hear it too?

NILS GYLLENSTJERNA *enters.*

ERIK: See who's here! Nils Göransson Come-and-Go, born Gyllenstjerna! [*Laughs.*]

GYLLENSTJERNA: Your Majesty! The garrison and the palace guards have been bribed! The Dukes must be much closer than we think?

ERIK: Why don't you go and welcome them, then?

GYLLENSTJERNA: I am not so base as that.

ERIK: What evidence have you for your suspicions?

GYLLENSTJERNA [*shows him a silver coin*]: This Judas money which has been distributed throughout the palace. It is already called the Blood Coinage, and has been struck from the silver Your Majesty gave as penance money for the Stures and the other lords.

ERIK: Can you make sense of this? The traitors are executed, I pay penance money, and with this money, they buy my head—and yours. Is not the world mad? Come with me to Karin.

GÖRAN: I'll come with you—as always—wherever you go.

ERIK [*to* GYLLENSTJERNA]: Go, Gyllenstjerna, and save your life! I thank you for the good service you have given me; the rest we'll forget. Let the people finish their fun. They are children whom no father dare provoke.

GYLLENSTJERNA [*on his knees to* ERIK]: God keep and protect good King Erik, our country's friend, the People's King!

ERIK: Do they call me that? Is some good said of me?

GYLLENSTJERNA: Yes. When the ear shows on the corn, and the farmers know that Saint Erik has blessed their harvest, they cross themselves and murmur: "God bless King Erik!"

ERIK: Hush! Madman and blasphemer, we believe in saints no longer——

GÖRAN: Nor in devils neither!

> GÖRAN *and* ERIK *go out right.* GYLLENSTJERNA *goes out left. Pause.*

MÅNS [*quite sober, but timidly, raising his beaker*]: Dear friends! This royal hospitality has been—we've all had a good time——!

MARIA [*loudly and clearly*]: Mummy, I want to do wee-wee!

AGDA: Hush, my angel.

MÅNS: Of course, I'm not the host—and I won't deny this is an unusual wedding rec—reception—some of us'd have liked to see the bride and bridegroom with us at the table——

MARIA: Mummy, I want to do wee-wee!

MÅNS: Wait a minute, child, and don't drink so much wine——

MARIA: Mummy, I want to do wee-wee!

MÅNS: Take the brat out, then, for God's sake!

AGDA [*gets up with* MARIA]: Come along, darling.

A MAN: Why can't the bloody child do it at home before she comes? Waiter! Let's have another look at that goose!

WOMAN: No, I asked first!

SECOND MAN: Hey, you! More salmon!

FOOTMAN: Do you know whose house you're in?

SECOND MAN: I'm in *our* house, you bloody sod, and it's our food, because we're the ones who've paid for it!

SECOND WOMAN: Loosen your belt, Måns lad.

MÅNS: Is someone insin- -insinuating that I've eaten too much?

SECOND WOMAN: No, I was talking to my son here.

THIRD MAN: Waiter! Call in the trumpeters! The trumpeters!

MÅNS: No, we don't want any trumpeters!

THIRD MAN: I wonder where the toffs are having their meal? Do they think they're too good to sit with us?

FIRST MAN: The King? He's mad, we all know that.

SECOND WOMAN: Course he's mad, otherwise we wouldn't be sitting here.

MÅNS: May I be allowed—? [*Buzz of voices.*] May I be *allowed* to say one *word*? *One* word? You wouldn't be sitting here if the King was less—sensible than he is. He's a bit strange—different, like—but he's shown himself better than most, 'cause he's willing to do what's right for a girl what's in trouble—and this dinner he's invited us poor people to—yes, well, we *are* poor—that shows he doesn't despise his bride's hum- -humble upbringing, as the saying is—— [*Trumpets are heard from various quarters outside.*] My good friends, these calls, as we soldiers call them, signify that this dinner, or banquet, is at an end. Let us therefore thank God for the good food he has given us——

FRU PERSSON [*enters*]: What's going on here?

MÅNS: Well, Mother Persson, there was a King as was going to hold a wedding and he sent out his servants to them as had been invited, but they didn't come, so then he said to his servants: "Go out into the highways and tell everyone you find to come to the wedding," and the servants went out and collected everyone they found, both good men and bad, so that the tables were all filled.

FRU PERSSON: Where's my son, Göran?

MÅNS: Inside with the King.

FRU PERSSON [*points*]: There?

MÅNS: There,

> FRU PERSSON *goes out right.*

My good friends! When the King returns, shout with me: "Long live King Erik the Fourteenth! Vivat!" Do you understand? Vivat! V-i-v-a-t!

ALL: Vivat!

PEDER WELAMSON [*enters hurriedly*]: Is the King here?

MÅNS: No. What's happened?

PEDER WELAMSON: The palace has been surprised! The Dukes are in the next room!

MÅNS [*gets up*]: Merciful Heaven! What'll become of us?

> *All the others get up from the table.*

PEDER WELAMSON: Of you? What'll become of me? The block, I reckon.

MÅNS: Nothing is so unsure as happiness, and when a man seems to have the world at his feet ill luck lurks behind his door. What shall we say? Where shall we fly?

PEDER WELAMSON [*takes a beaker and empties it*]: So long as it ain't the torture—but that Duke's a bastard——

FRU PERSSON [*runs in*]: Jesus Lord, the King is taken! And Göran—my son, my son!

MÅNS: And Karin—my daughter! My daughter!

FRU PERSSON: Yes, you can shout now! She won't come to you——

MÅNS: Why not?

FRU PERSSON: She's already joined her husband.

MÅNS: They're mad, the pair of them.

The doors in the background are thrown open. NILS GYLLENSTJERNA *enters.*

GYLLENSTJERNA: The King is coming!

All the PEOPLE *draw aside.*

MÅNS: But the King has been captured!

GYLLENSTJERNA: That one, yes. But not this one. Take care, good people, if you value your heads!

DUKE JOHAN *and* DUKE CHARLES *enter with their retinue.*

Long live King Johan the Third! Vivat!

ALL: Vivat! Long live Johan the Third!

JOHAN: Thank you. [*To* GYLLENSTJERNA.] Who are these?

GYLLENSTJERNA: They are King Erik's court.

JOHAN [*to* CHARLES]: I am a trifle near-sighted, but to my eyes this court looks somewhat strange. Are those bundles of rags I see over there?

CHARLES: Our brother did not love upstart princes. He loved humble people——

JOHAN: Yes, that was his weakness.

CHARLES [*lowers his voice*]: Or his strength. But yours is a tendency to forget promises——

JOHAN: What promises?

CHARLES: Was it not agreed that we should share the throne?

JOHAN: I don't remember that.

CHARLES: You damned scoundrel——!

JOHAN: Take care! There are many rooms at Gripsholm——

CHARLES: You should know them!

JOHAN [*to his retinue*]: Our civil strife is ended. Peace is restored, and we can face the future with new hope——

DUKE CHARLES *makes a sign to his retinue, and starts to walk away.*

Where are you going, brother?

CHARLES: My own way, which is no longer yours.

GYLLENSTJERNA: Oh, God! Must it begin again?

JOHAN: I think the world has gone mad.

CHARLES: Erik thought that too. Who knows——?

MARIA: Mummy, won't it be over soon?

CHARLES [*smiles*]: No, my child! Life is a war that never ends!

TRANSLATOR'S POSTSCRIPT

On being captured by Duke Johan's men, Erik capitulated, and the following year (1569) he was deposed in favour of Johan. For eight years he was kept a prisoner, at first in that same Gripsholm in which he had imprisoned Johan; thereafter he was regularly moved from prison to prison to preserve the secrecy of his whereabouts. For the first five years Karin voluntarily shared his captivity, and during this period she bore him two more sons, who both died in infancy. Then she was separated from him and exiled to Finland. Their son, Gustav, was taken from her and exiled to Poland. Erik died in prison in 1577, after nine years of captivity. Recently his embalmed body was dug up and, on being analysed, was found to be full of arsenic.

Karin lived to a ripe age in Finland, admired for her beauty and loved by all who came into contact with her. She never married again. Her son, Gustav, by now a melancholy recluse dabbling in alchemy, was allowed to see her again after a separation of twenty-one years; she recognised him only by some birth-marks. Soon afterwards, he was invited to Moscow by the Tsar of Russia, who received him with honour; but then it transpired that the Tsar wished to invade Sweden and set Gustav on the throne as a puppet monarch in place of his uncle. Gustav refused, and the Tsar imprisoned him for several years; he died in Russia shortly after his release. Sigrid, Erik's daughter, was allowed to marry a Swedish nobleman, and her son, Åke Tott, became one of Gustav Adolf's most famous generals.

Göran Persson was handed over to Duke Johan by Erik's own soldiers, and was publicly tortured and done to death with hideous cruelty. His maimed and decapitated body was hung on a gibbet in front of the window of the room where Erik was confined. Göran's mother was led on a horse to see her son's corpse, with her hands tied and a gag in her mouth to stop her screaming. As the horse turned to take her away, she fell to the ground and broke her neck. She was buried at the foot of the gallows on which her son's body hung.

Johan reigned for twenty-four years (1568-92), despite the enmity of his brother, Duke Charles. But when Johan died and his son, Sigismund, succeeded him, being then King of both Poland and Sweden, Duke Charles waged war on him and eventually wrested the crown from him, ascending the throne as Charles II. He reigned for thirteen years and was then succeeded by his son, the great Gustav II Adolf.

Introduction to
STORM

ERIK THE FOURTEENTH had been Strindberg's seventh full-length play within two years (1898-1899). This feverish activity continued for another two years, for in 1900 and 1901 he wrote no less than thirteen plays, all but one of them full-length: GUSTAV ADOLF, MIDSUMMER, CASPER'S SHROVE TUESDAY, EASTER, the two parts of THE DANCE OF DEATH, THE BRIDAL CROWN, SWANWHITE, CHARLES XII, the third part of TO DAMASCUS, ENGELBRECHT, QUEEN CHRISTINA and A DREAM PLAY.

In 1900, while looking for someone to play the Lady in TO DAMASCUS, which was about to receive its première, he saw a young Norwegian actress named Harriet Bosse act Puck in a performance of A MIDSUMMER NIGHT'S DREAM. Strindberg at once chose her for his play; the same year, he wrote EASTER especially for her; and the following May they married. The marriage was, however, a failure, and although she bore him a daughter they parted shortly afterwards.

During the four years since he had returned to the theatre, he had written much of his finest work. He was, however, the most uneven of all great writers, and in the two years after Harriet left him, 1902-1903, he produced little of value: a strange fragment called THE DUTCHMAN, GUSTAV III, and four inferior historical plays—THE NIGHTINGALE OF WITTENBERG (about Luther), and three sections of a "world-historical trilogy", dealing respectively with Moses, Socrates and Christ. This decline was not unpardonable, for no great dramatist has been so continually snubbed by his countrymen. Of his last twenty plays, only three had been produced, and one of these, EASTER, had been so inadequately staged that it had been a failure. His last eight plays had all been rejected by the Swedish theatres. A DREAM PLAY had to wait six years for its Swedish première, and THE DANCE OF DEATH nine years. Even MISS JULIE had not yet been performed in Sweden. For the next four years he turned his back on the theatre, writing non-dramatic works in both verse and prose. "The novel tempts me most", he wrote to Harriet on 15 April 1906. "I loathe the theatre. It is dishonest, superficial and calculating."

It seemed as though Strindberg as a dramatist belonged to the past. Fortunately, however, in 1906, there was a sudden revival of his reputation in Scandinavia. CREDITORS was successfully staged that January in Stockholm, and THERE ARE CRIMES AND CRIMES in March, while in April THE BRIDAL CROWN was produced in Helsingfors. In the autumn an imaginative production by August Falck of MISS JULIE toured the Swedish provinces, reaching Stockholm in December. The same month, GUSTAV VASA was revived in the capital; and the following April (1907) A DREAM PLAY was at last produced.

These successes revived Strindberg's old enthusiasm for starting an experimental theatre. He had been dreaming of this off and on for a quarter of a century; apart from the ill-fated Copenhagen project in 1889, he had considered doing something in Djursholm (1892), Berlin and London (both 1893), Paris (1894) and again in Stockholm since his return. But, apart from everything else, he had never had or been able to raise the money. In 1906, however, Max Reinhardt, who had long been a fervent admirer of Strindberg, had followed up his Kleines Theater in Berlin by founding his Kammarspiele; and, apart from the triumphant ventures by Antoine and Lugné-Poe in Paris during the nineties, Stanislavsky had made a success of the Moscow Arts and the Dublin Abbey was flourishing under W. B. Yeats and Lady Gregory.

Strindberg found a ready collaborator in the young actor-producer, August Falck, and in 1907 they leased a large ground-floor room near the Central Station in Stockholm and christened it the Intimate Theatre. It held, when they had adapted it, a hundred and sixty-one people, and it was for this theatre that he now began to write plays—not the full-length

Introduction to STORM

kind on which he had been concentrating since his INFERNO crisis, but plays lasting an hour to an hour and a half, such as he had written for the Copenhagen experimental theatre nineteen years earlier. The first of these "chamber plays", as he called them, was STORM.

He wrote it in January–February 1907, just after his fifty-eighth birthday, and the theme was his marriage with Harriet Bosse. Although they had now been parted for five years, he still felt closely bound to her, and kept contact with her by letter, telephone, and occasional meetings whenever she was in Stockholm. Lately, however, she had fallen in love with an actor named Gunnar Wingård, whom she was shortly to marry, and Strindberg was haunted, as he had been during the break-up of his marriage with Siri, by the thought of his daughter giving her love to a stepfather. STORM was a kind of warning to Harriet, just as CREDITORS had been a warning to Siri. In a letter which he wrote to Harriet the following year (April 1908) he described STORM as "a painful poem, with which to write you and our child out of my heart."

STORM is, even for Strindberg, a peculiarly personal play. The previous summer he had spent alone in their flat in Östermalm, the fashionable quarter of Stockholm. Then, as now, most of the inhabitants left town during the warm season, but in those days their places were not taken by tourists, and the city seemed deserted. He saw hardly anyone except his brother Axel, who used to come and play Beethoven to him on the piano. On the mantelpiece he kept a large photograph of Harriet, with candles on either side. On 17 July he noted that the previous evening the street lamps had been lit for the first time that summer (at one time he planned to entitle the play THE FIRST LAMP). A few weeks later, he wrote: "Today, 2 August, ideal weather at last. Thunder and rain. One can breathe."

After STORM, Strindberg wrote THE BURNT HOUSE and THE GHOST SONATA in quick succession, completing the three plays in the space of some ten weeks; and in May, he wrote THE

PELICAN. On 26 November 1907 the Intimate Theatre opened with a performance of the last-named play. But the Swedish critics and public remained as unsympathetic as ever. THE PELICAN was coldly received; THE BURNT HOUSE and THE GHOST SONATA were also greeted with disparaging reviews; and STORM, when presented there on 30 December 1907, fared no better. The fortunes of the theatre were only saved by the generosity of the new King's brother, Prince Eugen, who undertook to pay the rent, and by the success of a revival of MISS JULIE.

As with so many of Strindberg's plays, it took the Germans to reveal the merits of STORM to his countrymen. It was successfully staged in Dresden in 1912, and the following year was excitingly produced by Max Reinhardt at his Kammarspiele in Berlin, with Albert Bassermann in the lead. In 1915 Mauritz Stiller directed it brilliantly at the New Intimate Theatre in Stockholm, with the young Lars Hanson as the Gentleman. Reinhardt brought his production to Stockholm in 1920; and in 1933 Harriet Bosse, with what must have been mixed emotions, played the Wife in a production by Alf Sjöberg at Stockholm's Royal Theatre. STORM has since been revived several times in Scandinavia, and in 1960 it was directed for Swedish television by Ingmar Bergman. Jean Vilar played the Gentleman in a production at the Théâtre de Poche in Paris in 1943, but to date STORM has not been produced in England, except on sound radio in the Third Programme.

STORM

A Chamber Play

(1907)

CHARACTERS

THE GENTLEMAN, a retired civil servant
THE BROTHER, a Consul
STRONG, a café-owner
AGNES, his daughter
LOUISE, a cousin of the GENTLEMAN
GERDA, former wife of the GENTLEMAN
FISCHER, GERDA's new husband
A DRAYMAN
THE MILKMAID
THE ICE-MAN
THE POSTMAN
THE LAMPLIGHTER

Scene 1. Outside the House
Scene 2. Inside the House
Scene 3. Outside the House

Scene 1

The façade of a modern house.* The sub-section, below ground-level, is of granite; the upper part of brick, covered with yellow stucco. The surrounds of the windows, and other ornamentations, are in sandstone. In the middle of the granite sub-section is a low porch leading to the inner courtyard; it also contains the entrance to the café. On the right of the house is a garden, containing roses and other flowers. In the corner, a letter-box. Above the sub-section is the ground floor, with big windows standing open; four of these belong to a dining-room, elegantly furnished. Above the ground floor can be seen the first floor, the four central windows of which are covered by red blinds, illuminated from within. In front of the house is a pavement lined with trees. In the foreground, a green bench and a gas lamp.

> The CAFÉ-OWNER *comes out with a chair and sits on the pavement.*
> The GENTLEMAN *is seen at the table in the dining-room. Behind his back is a tall stove of green majolica; it has a shelf on which stands a large photograph flanked by vases of flowers and two candelabra. A young girl,* LOUISE, *dressed in light colours, is serving him the final course.*
> The BROTHER (*outside the house*) *enters left, and knocks with his stick on the window-pane.*

BROTHER: Have you nearly finished?

GENTLEMAN: I'm just coming.

BROTHER [*greets the* CAFÉ-OWNER]: Good evening, Mr. Strong. It's still very hot. . . . [*Sits on the bench.*]

* i.e. of around 1900.

CAFÉ-OWNER: Good evening, Consul. Yes, it's the worst time of the year. We've been making jam all day....

BROTHER: Really?... Been a good year for fruit?

CAFÉ-OWNER: Fair to middling. We had a cold spring, but this summer's been a scorcher. We've felt it here in town....

BROTHER: I came up from the country yesterday. When the evenings start to draw in, one longs for the city...

CAFÉ-OWNER: Me and the wife haven't got away all year. There ain't much doing in the shop, but we've got to stay and make ready for the winter. First there's the strawberries, then the cherries, and then the raspberries, and after them there's the gooseberries and melons, and all those autumn fruits....

BROTHER: Tell me, Mr. Strong. Are they going to sell this house?

CAFÉ-OWNER: Not that I know.

BROTHER: Do many people live here?

CAFÉ-OWNER: Ten families, I think. If you reckon the ones who live at the back. But none of them know each other. You don't hear no gossip in this house. They all seem to hide themselves away. Ten years I've lived here, and the first two years I never saw the people who lived next-door. Not a sound from them all day. But at night they got busy, with carriages rolling up and carting things away. It wasn't till the two years was up that I found it was an hospital, and what those carriages was fetching away was dead bodies.

BROTHER: How horrible!

CAFÉ-OWNER: People call this the silent house.

BROTHER: Yes, you don't often hear anyone speak here.

CAFÉ-OWNER: Some strange things have happened, though...

BROTHER: Tell me, Mr. Strong, who lives up there on the first floor, above my brother?

CAFÉ-OWNER: Up there behind those red blinds? Well, the man who had it died this summer, and it stood empty for a month. Last week some new people moved in, but I ain't seen them . . . don't know their names. They never seem to go out. Why do you ask?

BROTHER: Oh . . . I don't know. Those four red blinds look like the tabs of a theatre. I can imagine some dreadful tragedy being enacted behind them. . . . A palm-tree standing there like an iron whip, throwing its shadow on a curtain. . . . If only one could see the actors. . . .

CAFÉ-OWNER: I've seen plenty of people there. After dark.

BROTHER: Women or men?

CAFÉ-OWNER: Both . . . Well, I must get back to my stoves . . .

He goes in through the porch. In the drawing-room, the GENTLEMAN has risen and lights a cigar. He speaks from his window to the BROTHER.

GENTLEMAN: I shall be ready soon. Louise just has to sew a button on my glove.

BROTHER: Thinking of going into town?

GENTLEMAN: We might take a stroll. . . . Whom were you talking to?

BROTHER: Only the café-owner.

GENTLEMAN: Oh, him. Yes, he's a decent fellow. The only person I've spoken to this summer. . . .

BROTHER: Have you really stayed indoors every evening? Never been out?

GENTLEMAN: Never. These light evenings make me nervous. They're fine in the country, but here in town they seem unnatural; almost ghostly. I don't feel safe till they start lighting the lamps again. Then I can take my evening walk. That tires me, and I can sleep more easily. . . . [LOUISE *gives him the glove.*] Thank you, my child. You can leave the windows open. We get no mosquitoes here. I'm coming now.

After a few moments the GENTLEMAN *comes out through the garden and puts a letter in the postbox. He comes downstage and sits on the bench beside the* BROTHER.

BROTHER: But, tell me—*why* do you stay in town when you could be in the country?

GENTLEMAN: I don't know. I've lost the desire for movement. I'm chained to this house by memories. . . . Only in there can I find safety and peace. Yes, in there! It's interesting to see one's home from the outside. I imagine there's someone else pacing up and down in there . . . Just think—I've been doing that for ten years. . . .

BROTHER: Is it ten years?

GENTLEMAN: Yes, time goes quickly once it's past, but when it's with you it crawls. . . . The house was new then. I watched them putting the parquet flooring into the drawing-room, painting the walls and doors—and *she* chose the wallpaper—it's all still there. . . . Well, that's all past. The café-owner and I are the oldest inhabitants. He's had his troubles too. . . . He's the sort who never succeeds, always makes a mess of things. It's as though I'd lived his life, and borne his troubles as well as my own.

BROTHER: Does he drink?

GENTLEMAN: No. He isn't lazy, either; but he never gets anywhere. . . . But he and I know the story of this house. Couples have come in bridal carriages, and left in coffins. That letter-box at the corner has conveyed many a declaration of love. . . .

BROTHER: I hear you had a death this summer?

GENTLEMAN: Yes. Typhoid—a bank clerk. The apartment stood empty for a month. First the coffin came out; then the widow and children; and, finally, the furniture. . . .

BROTHER: Was that on the first floor?

GENTLEMAN: Up there, where the lights are on. There are new people there. I haven't seen them yet.

BROTHER: Not seen them?

GENTLEMAN: I never ask about the other tenants. If they choose to tell me anything, I listen, but I don't pass it on, or get involved. I want peace. The peace of age. . . .

BROTHER: Age, yes! It's good to be old. One hasn't so long to wait.

GENTLEMAN: Yes, it's good! I have settled my account with life, and have already begun to pack for the journey. Loneliness has its drawbacks, but at least no one has a claim on you. You are free. Free to come and go, to think and act, to eat and sleep, as you please.

A blind is raised on the first floor, but only a few inches, enough for us to glimpse a woman's dress. Then the blind is quickly lowered.

BROTHER: Someone's moving up there. Did you see?

GENTLEMAN: Yes. They're so furtive. It's worst at night. Sometimes they play music, badly. Sometimes they play cards and, long after midnight, carriages come and fetch. . . . But I never complain. People get their revenge; and what effect would it have? . . . It's best to know nothing.

A GENTLEMAN, bare-headed and wearing a dinner-jacket, comes out through the garden and puts a large bundle of letters in the letter-box. Then he goes.

BROTHER: He had a lot of letters!

GENTLEMAN: They looked like circulars.

BROTHER: Who was he?

GENTLEMAN: Must be from up there—the first floor——

BROTHER: Is that him? What do you make of him?

GENTLEMAN: I don't know. Musician—theatrical manager—operettas—dabbles in music-hall—gambler—Adonis—dilettante——

BROTHER: How white his skin was! That ought to mean black hair, but his was brown. Must have been dyed, or a wig. Evening dress at home—bit of a dandy. And did you see his hands as he put the letters in the box? As though they were mixing—taking and giving. . . .

A waltz is heard very faintly from the first floor.

BROTHER: A waltz? Perhaps they've a dancing-school. But they always play the same waltz. What's it called?

GENTLEMAN: Why, isn't that . . . *Pluie d'Or* . . . ? I know it by heart. . . .

BROTHER: You've played it yourself?

GENTLEMAN: Yes. That and *Alcazar*. . . .

LOUISE appears in the drawing-room, abstractedly replacing dried glasses on the sideboard.

BROTHER: Still satisfied with Louise?

GENTLEMAN: Very.

BROTHER: She's not getting married?

GENTLEMAN: Not that I know.

BROTHER: No *fiancé*?

GENTLEMAN: Why do you ask?

BROTHER: I wondered if perhaps you. . . ?

GENTLEMAN: I? No, thank you. I wasn't too old when I married last—we had a child at once—but now I am, and I want to grow old in peace. . . . Do you think I want to have someone running my house, someone to whom I must surrender my life, my honour and my possessions?

BROTHER: You kept your life and your possessions. . . .

GENTLEMAN: Not my honour?

BROTHER: Don't you know?

GENTLEMAN: What do you mean?

BROTHER: She destroyed your honour, when she left you....

GENTLEMAN: Have I been a corpse for five years without knowing it?

BROTHER: Didn't you know?

GENTLEMAN: No. You know what happened. It was my second marriage, and I was fifty. She was young, I had won her love, and she gave me her hand freely and without fear. I promised her that if ever she felt that I was too old for her, I would go my way and give her back her freedom. Nine months later our child was born. Neither of us wanted any more. Then our daughter began to grow away from me. I felt superfluous, so I walked out—or, more precisely, I took a boat, since we lived on an island, and that was the end of the story. I had kept my promise, and saved my honour. What more should I have done?

BROTHER: Yes, but she felt her honour had been impugned. She wanted to leave you. So she destroyed you, with silent accusations, which you never heard.

GENTLEMAN: Did she accuse herself too?

BROTHER: She had no reason.

GENTLEMAN: Well, she's all right, then.

BROTHER: Do you know what happened to her and the child afterwards?

GENTLEMAN: I don't want to know. Once I had gone through the horrors of parting, I regarded the affair as closed. This house had only beautiful memories for me, so I stayed here. But thank you for this valuable information——

BROTHER: What information?

GENTLEMAN: That she had nothing with which to accuse herself. If she had had, it would have been an accusation against me——

BROTHER: I think you're living under a delusion——

GENTLEMAN: Let me live under it, brother. A clean, or relatively clean conscience has always been for me a kind of diving suit—it enables me to plumb deep waters without drowning. [*Gets up.*] To think that I went through that, and survived! Well, now it's past. Shall we take a stroll down the avenue?

BROTHER: Yes, let's. Then we'll see them light the first lamp.

GENTLEMAN: Won't it be moonlight tonight? The august moon——?

BROTHER: A full moon, I think——

GENTLEMAN [*turns to the window and speaks through it*]: Louise, will you please give me my stick? My light summer cane. Just to hold.

LOUISE [*hands him a cane*]: This one, sir?

GENTLEMAN: Thank you, my child. Put out the lights in the drawing-room, if you've finished in there. . . . We'll be away some while. I can't say how long. . . .

The GENTLEMAN *and the* BROTHER *go out left.* LOUISE *at the window. The* CAFÉ-OWNER *comes out of the porch.*

CAFÉ-OWNER: Good evening, Miss Louise. Real close, isn't it? . . . Have the gentlemen gone?

LOUISE: Yes, they've gone for a walk down the avenue. . . . It's the first evening he's been out this summer.

CAFÉ-OWNER: We old people love the twilight. It hides our shortcomings—and other people's. Did you know my old woman's going blind? But she won't be operated on. There's nothing to look at, she says. Sometimes she wishes she was deaf, too.

LOUISE: Life can seem like that—sometimes.

CAFÉ-OWNER: You lead a nice quiet life in there. Comfortable, no worries. I never hear a voice raised or a door bang. Maybe it's a little too quiet for a young lady like you?

LOUISE: Good heavens, no! I love peace, and calm—one leaves things unsaid and ignores trivialities. . . .

CAFÉ-OWNER: You never have visitors?

LOUISE: Only the Consul. I never saw two brothers who loved each other as they do.

CAFÉ-OWNER: Which of them's the older?

LOUISE: I don't know. . . . There could be a year between them, they could even be twins. I don't know. They respect each other as though each was the elder.

AGNES *comes out of the house and tries to tiptoe past the* CAFÉ-OWNER.

CAFÉ-OWNER: Where are you going, my girl?

AGNES: Only for a little walk.

CAFÉ-OWNER: All right, but don't be long!

AGNES *goes*.

CAFÉ-OWNER: Do you think your master still grieves for his wife and child?

LOUIS: He doesn't grieve for them, or miss them. He doesn't want them back. But he lives with them in his memories. He only remembers what was beautiful . . .

CAFÉ-OWNER: But he sometimes worries about his daughter. . . .

LOUIS: Yes, well, that's natural. Her mother married again, and she has a stepfather. . . .

CAFÉ-OWNER: I have heard that when she left him she refused support, but then five years later sent along a lawyer with a bill for several thousand crowns. . . .

LOUISE [*deprecatingly*]: I don't know anything about that . . .

CAFÉ-OWNER: I reckon she's best the way he remembers her . . .

A DRAYMAN *enters with wine bottles in baskets*.

DRAYMAN: Excuse me, does a Mr. Fischer live here?

LOUISE: Mr. Fischer? Not that I know.

CAFÉ-OWNER: Perhaps that's him on the first floor? Try the bell up there, round the corner.

DRAYMAN [*goes out through the garden*]: First floor? Thank you.

LOUISE: Now we're in for another sleepless night, if he's taking those bottles up there!

CAFÉ-OWNER: What kind of people are they? Why do they never show themselves?

LOUISE: I suppose they use the back entrance. I've never seen them. But I hear them!

CAFÉ-OWNER: I've heard corks popping and doors banging—and other sounds. . . .

LOUISE: They never open the windows, even in this heat. Perhaps they're foreigners. Look, lightning! One, two, three. . . . It's only summer lightning. There's no thunder.

A VOICE [*from the basement*]: Strong dearie, come down and give me a hand with the syrup!

CAFÉ-OWNER: Coming, love! We're making jam, you see. Coming, coming!

He goes down to his shop. LOUISE *remains standing at the window.*

BROTHER [*enters slowly right*]: Isn't my brother back yet?

LOUISE: No, sir.

BROTHER: He went into a telephone kiosk and told me to go ahead. Well, I expect he'll be here soon. What's this? [*Bends down and picks up a postcard.*] What! "Boston Club after midnight. Fischer's". Who's Fischer? Do you know?

LOUISE: There was a man here with some wine looking for someone called Fischer. On the first floor—

BROTHER: First floor, Fischer's! Red blinds that glow like a cigar in the night. I think you've got bad company.

LOUISE: What is the Boston Club?

BROTHER: It could be quite innocent. I wonder, though. . . . But why this postcard? He must have dropped it just now. I'll put it in the box. . . . Fischer? I've heard that name before, in connection with something. I forget what. . . . Miss Louise, may I ask you a question? Does my brother never speak of . . . the past?

LOUISE: Never to me.

BROTHER: Miss Louise . . . may I ask . . . ?

LOUISE: Excuse me, here comes the evening milk. I must go and collect it . . .

She goes. The MILKMAID enters right and goes into the garden.

CAFÉ-OWNER [*comes out again, puffing, and takes off his white cap*]: In and out like a badger from its hole. . . . It's terrible down among those stoves. . . . And the evenings don't get any cooler. . . .

BROTHER: We'll have some rain, after that lightning. . . . It's noisy in town, but up here you're nice and quiet. Never a carriage, far less a tram. It's just like being in the country!

CAFÉ-OWNER: Yes, it's quiet all right. Too quiet for trade. I know my job, but I'm a bad salesman, always have been. I can't learn—or maybe it's something else—maybe I haven't the knack. If a customer thinks I'm trying to cheat him, do you know I blush! Then I get as angry as I can. But I don't seem able to get really angry nowadays. You lose it, the way you do everything.

BROTHER: Why don't you take a job somewhere?

CAFÉ-OWNER: No one'll have me.

BROTHER: Have you asked?

CAFÉ-OWNER: What'd be the use?

BROTHER: Oh——?

A long-drawn "O-oh!" is heard from the apartment above.

CAFÉ-OWNER: Mercy on us, what are they up to? Are they killing each other?

BROTHER: I don't like this new element that's entered the house. It's sinister—hangs over you, like a red thunder cloud. Who are they? Where do they come from? What do they want here?

CAFÉ-OWNER: It's dangerous to nose into other people's business. You only get involved . . .

BROTHER: Do you know anything about them?

CAFÉ-OWNER: No, I know nothing . . .

BROTHER: There's another cry . . . on the stairs . . .

CAFÉ-OWNER [*sidles out slowly*]: I don't want to get mixed up in this . . .

> GERDA, *the* GENTLEMAN'S *former wife, comes out into the garden, bare-headed and confused, with her hair down. The* BROTHER *goes towards her. They recognize each other. She shrinks away.*

BROTHER: So it's you? My former sister-in-law!

GERDA: It is I.

BROTHER: Why did you come here? Why didn't you leave my brother in peace?

GERDA [*distraught*]: They gave me the wrong name—I thought he'd moved—it isn't my fault——

BROTHER: Don't be afraid of me. You mustn't be afraid of me, Gerda. . . . Can I help you? What's happening up there?

GERDA: He hit me.

BROTHER: Is your little girl with you?

GERDA: Yes.

BROTHER: She has a stepfather, then?

GERDA: Yes.

BROTHER: Put up your hair, and calm yourself. I'll try to sort this out. But spare my brother....

GERDA: I suppose he hates me?

BROTHER: No. Don't you see how he looks after your flowers, here in your garden? He brought the soil here himself, in a basket, remember? Do you recognize your blue gentians and mignonette, your roses, Malmaison and Merveille de Lyon, which he grafted himself? Don't you see how he has kept your memory green, and your daughter's?

GERDA: Where is he now?

BROTHER: Taking a walk down the street. He'll be back in a minute with his evening paper. He'll come in the back entrance, and sit down in the drawing-room, to read. Keep still, and he won't notice you. But you must go back to your apartment——

GERDA: I can't do that. I can't go back to that man——

BROTHER: Who is he? What does he do?

GERDA: He—was a singer.

BROTHER: Was? What is he now? An adventurer?

GERDA: Yes.

BROTHER: Runs a gambling-house?

GERDA: Yes.

BROTHER: And your daughter? What's she? The decoy?

GERDA: Don't talk like that!

BROTHER: It's horrible!

GERDA: You take it too hard.

BROTHER: Should one take corruption lightly? Must what is pure and good be soiled? Why did you dishonour him, and why did you trick me into being your accomplice? I was fool enough to believe you, and argue your case to him.

GERDA: Have you forgotten? He was too old for me.

BROTHER: He wasn't then. You bore him a child. When he proposed to you, he asked you if you wanted to have a child by him. And he promised to give you back your freedom, when he had fulfilled his duty and begun to grow old.

GERDA: He left me. That was an insult.

BROTHER: Not to you. You were young, no one blamed you——

GERDA: He should have let me leave him.

BROTHER: Why? Did you want to dishonour him?

GERDA: It's the usual procedure.

BROTHER: How strangely your mind works! Anyway, you destroyed him, and fooled me into helping you. How can we restore his honour?

GERDA: We could only do that at my expense.

BROTHER: I can't follow your reasoning. Your mind only works in terms of hatred. But suppose we forget about his honour, and think about saving his daughter. How shall we do that?

GERDA: She is my child. The law has given her into my care, and my husband is her legal father....

BROTHER: How can you be so callous? You've become hard and cruel. Ssh! Here he is!

The GENTLEMAN enters left with a newspaper in his hand and goes pensively round to the back door, while the BROTHER and GERDA stand motionless, hidden by the corner of the garden. The BROTHER and GERDA come downstage. A few moments later the GENTLEMAN seats himself in the drawing-room and begins to read his paper.

GERDA: It's he!

BROTHER: Come here and look at your home! He's kept everything the way you left it. Don't be afraid, he can't see us here in the dark. The light blinds him, you see.

GERDA: He lied to me. . . .

BROTHER: How do you mean?

GERDA: He hasn't aged. He'd tired of me, that was all. Look at his collar, and cravat—the latest fashion. I'm sure he has a sweetheart.

BROTHER: You can see her portrait up there on the stove, between the candelabra.

GERDA: It's me—and our child! Does he still love me?

BROTHER: Your memory.

GERDA: How strange!

The GENTLEMAN stops reading and stares out through the window.

GERDA: He's looking at us!

BROTHER: Keep still.

GERDA: He's looking me straight in the eyes.

BROTHER: Keep still. He can't see you.

GERDA: He looks like a dead man. . . .

BROTHER: He has been killed.

GERDA: Why must you talk like that?

The BROTHER and GERDA are illuminated by a brilliant flash of lightning. The GENTLEMAN, in the drawing-room, rises in terror. GERDA slips quickly behind the corner of the garden.

GENTLEMAN: Karl Frederik! [*Comes to the window.*] Are you alone? I thought . . . Are you really alone?

BROTHER: As you see.

GENTLEMAN: It's so close. And these flowers give me a headache. . . . I'll just finish my paper. [*Goes back to his chair.*]

BROTHER [*at GERDA's side*]: Well, get back to your work. Do you want me to come up with you?

GERDA: Perhaps... But he'll be so angry....

BROTHER: But the child must be saved. And I am a lawyer.

GERDA: Very well. For the child's sake. Come with me.

They go.

GENTLEMAN [*from the room*]: Karl Frederik! Come and play chess. Karl Frederik!

Scene 2

Inside the drawing room. In the foreground, the stove. Left of it an open door leading to the pantry. To the right, a door leading to the hall. On the left, a sideboard with a telephone. On the right, a piano and a grandfather clock. Doors in both side walls.

LOUISE *enters.*

GENTLEMAN: Where has my brother gone?

LOUISE [*nervously*]: He was outside a moment ago. He can't be far off.

GENTLEMAN: They're making a dreadful noise up there. It feels as though they were tramping on my head. Now they're pulling out all the drawers as though they were getting ready to leave. Perhaps they're running away.... I wish you knew how to play chess.

LOUISE: I can play a little....

GENTLEMAN: Well, if you know the moves, I suppose we'll manage.... Sit down, my child. [*He arranges the pieces.*] What a noise they're making! The chandelier's shaking. And downstairs in the café they've lit all those stoves.... I think I'll move soon.

LOUISE: You ought to do that. I've often thought so.

GENTLEMAN: Why?

LOUISE: It isn't good to stay too long among memories.

GENTLEMAN: Why not? In time, all memories become beautiful.

LOUISE: But you may live another twenty years, and that's too long to sit among memories. They turn pale, and one fine day they may lose their colour.

GENTLEMAN: What a lot you know, child. Start now; move one of your pawns. But not the queen's, or you'll be mate in two moves.

LOUISE: I'll start with the knight, then....

GENTLEMAN: That's just as dangerous.

LOUISE: I think I will, anyway.

GENTLEMAN: Very well. Then I move my bishop's pawn...

The CAFÉ-OWNER *appears in the hall with a tray.*

LOUISE: There's Mr. Strong with the pastries. He moves so silently, like a little rat!

She gets up, goes into the hall, collects the tray and takes it into the pantry.

GENTLEMAN: Well, Mr. Strong, how is your wife?

CAFÉ-OWNER: Oh, thank you. It's her eyes, you know....

GENTLEMAN: Have you seen my brother?

CAFÉ-OWNER: I expect he's taking a walk.

GENTLEMAN: Is he alone?

CAFÉ-OWNER: Oh, yes, I think so.

GENTLEMAN: It's some time since you last saw this room.

CAFÉ-OWNER: Yes, must be ten years....

GENTLEMAN: When you came with the wedding cake.... Has it changed?

CAFÉ-OWNER: Not at all.... The palm trees have grown, of course. No, it hasn't changed....

GENTLEMAN: Nor will it, till you come with the funeral cake. After one has reached a certain age, nothing changes, everything stays the same. Things just slide forward like a toboggan on a hill. . . .

CAFÉ-OWNER: True enough.

GENTLEMAN: Life becomes calm. . . . No love, no friends, just the occasional visitor, otherwise one is alone. That way you can be yourself, no one lays claim to your feelings and sympathies. One loosens like an old tooth, and falls out, without any pain or sense of loss. Louise, for instance—a pretty young girl—the sight of whom enchants me like a painting one does not wish to own. Nothing disturbs our relationship. My brother and I meet like two old gentleman who never come too close or intrude on each other's confidence. By being neutral one keeps people at a distance, and human beings are more likeable at a distance. In short, I am content with old age, and its peace and quiet. [*Calls.*] Louise!

LOUISE [*in the doorway, amicably as always*]: I've fetched the laundry. I must count it. . . .

GENTLEMAN: Well, Mr. Strong, won't you sit down and talk? Perhaps you play chess?

CAFÉ-OWNER: I mustn't leave my saucepans. And at eleven o'clock I must light the oven. . . . Thanks all the same. . . .

GENTLEMAN: If you see my brother, ask him to come in and keep me company. . . .

CAFÉ-OWNER: I'll do that, sir. . . . I'll do that! [*Goes.*]

GENTLEMAN [*alone, moves the chessmen for a few seconds, then gets up and paces across the room*]: The peace of old age! Yes! [*Sits at the piano and strikes a few chords. Gets up and starts to pace again.*] Louise! Can't you leave that laundry?

LOUISE [*in the doorway*]: I mustn't do that. The woman's in a hurry. She has a husband and child waiting for her. . . .

GENTLEMAN: I see. [*Sits at the table and drums on it with his fingers. Tries to read the newspaper, but tires of it. Strikes matches and blows them out. Looks at the clock. There is a noise in the hall.*] Is that you, Karl Frederik?

POSTMAN [*enters*]: It's the postman. Excuse me coming in, but the door was open.

GENTLEMAN: Any letters for me?

POSTMAN: Only a postcard. [*Puts it down and goes.*]

GENTLEMAN [*reads the card*]: Herr Fischer again! The Boston Club! That's him upstairs. With the white hands and the dinner jacket. Addressed to me! What impertinence! I shall have to move. Fischer! [*Tears up the card. A noise in the hall.*] Is that you, Karl Frederik?

ICE-MAN: It's the ice-man.

GENTLEMAN: Thank God for some ice, in this heat. Mind those bottles. And lean it at an angle, so that I can hear it drip as it melts. It's my water-clock, measuring time, slow time. . . . Tell me, where do you get that ice from? . . . Has he gone? They all go, home, to listen to the sound of their own voices, and find company. . . . [*Pause.*] Is that you, Karl Frederik?

Upstairs a piano plays Chopin's Fantasie Impromptu, *opus 66; but only the first part.*

GENTLEMAN [*listens, awakes, looks up at the ceiling*]: Who's that playing? My impromptu! [*Puts his hand over his eyes and listens. The* BROTHER *enters from the hall.*]

GENTLEMAN: Is that you, Karl Frederik?

The music stops.

BROTHER: Yes.

GENTLEMAN: Where have you been all this time?

BROTHER: I had some business to attend to. Have you been alone?

GENTLEMAN: Of course. Come and play chess.

BROTHER: I'd rather chat. And it's good for you to hear your own voice.

GENTLEMAN: True. But we always speak of the past. . . .

BROTHER: It helps one to forget the present. . . .

GENTLEMAN: There is no present. What is happening now is vacuum, nothingness. Forward or back. Preferably forward, for there hope lies.

BROTHER [*at the table*]: Hope of what?

GENTLEMAN: Of change.

BROTHER: Good! You mean you've had enough of the peace of old age?

GENTLEMAN: Perhaps.

BROTHER: Certainly! If you could choose now between loneliness and the past. . . .

GENTLEMAN: No ghosts, though.

BROTHER: But your memories——?

GENTLEMAN: They are not ghosts. They are poems, based on reality. But if the dead walked, *they* would be ghosts.

BROTHER: But tell me, in your memory, which do you love more, the woman or the child?

GENTLEMAN: Both. I cannot separate them. That is why I never asked to keep the child.

BROTHER: But was that right? Didn't it occur to you that there might be a stepfather?

GENTLEMAN: I didn't think so far ahead. But since then, I have—reflected on—that fact.

BROTHER: A stepfather who might maltreat, perhaps even degrade, your daughter?

GENTLEMAN: Ssh!

BROTHER: What is it?

GENTLEMAN: I thought I heard footsteps—those light, tripping footsteps in the corridor when she came to look for me. It was the child I loved most. She was never frightened of me —she feared nothing, knew nothing of life's disillusions, had no secrets.... I remember her first encounter with human depravity. She saw a pretty child in the park, and ran towards her with open arms to kiss her. The pretty child responded to this kindness by biting her in the cheek and then sticking out her tongue. You should have seen my little Anne Charlotte then. She stood petrified, not by the pain, but by the horror of seeing this abyss which men call the human heart open before her. I saw it once, when from behind the loveliest eyes there suddenly appeared a strange expression like that of a savage beast; it so terrified me that I looked to see if there was another person standing behind her and using her face as a mask. But why do we sit here talking about this? Is it the heat, or the thunder, or what?

BROTHER: Loneliness makes for brooding, and you need company. This summer in town seems to have affected you.

GENTLEMAN: It's only these last weeks. That illness and death up there so upset me that I almost felt it had happened to me. The café-owner's sorrows and troubles seemed to become mine, so that now I pace to and fro, worrying about his finances, his wife's eyes, his future.... And now, each night, I've been dreaming of my own little Anne-Charlotte. I see her in danger, lost, unrecognised, nameless; and before I sleep, when my hearing becomes intolerably sharp, I hear her small footsteps And once, I heard her voice....

BROTHER: Where is she, then?

GENTLEMAN: Ah....

BROTHER: Suppose you met her in the street....

GENTLEMAN: I think I'd go mad, or faint.... Once I spent a long time abroad when my little sister was growing up.... After some years I came back, and met on the quayside a young girl who took me in her arms. I saw with horror two eyes that bored into mine, with a strange expression of the most awful horror at not being recognised. "It's me!" she repeated several times before I realised it was my own sister! That's how I imagine it would be to meet my daughter again. At that age, five years alter a person beyond recognition. Imagine, not to know one's own child! To meet her as a stranger! I couldn't bear that. No, I'd rather keep her as she was, four years old, up there on my altar. I don't want to find myself the father to someone else.... [*Pause.*] Is that Louise there in the linen-room? It smells clean, and brings back memories... yes, the housekeeper in the linen-room, the good fairy who protects and renews; the woman with the iron who smooths out the roughnesses and removes the wrinkles... the wrinkles... [*Pause.*] Now—I'll—go—in and write a letter. Wait here. I'll be back in a few minutes.

He goes out left. The BROTHER *coughs.*

GERDA [*appears in the hall*]: Are you...? [*The grandfather clock strikes.*] Oh, God! That sound!... I've carried it in my ears for ten years. That clock, which was always wrong but measured out the hours for five long years, day and night. [*Looks around.*] My piano... my palms... the dining-table—he's kept it well—polished like a shield! My sideboard! The Knight on his horse—and Eve, Eve with her basket of apples. ... In the right-hand drawer, at the back, there used to be a thermometer.... [*Pause.*] I wonder if it's still there.... [*Goes to the sideboard and pulls out the right-hand drawer.*] Yes, here it is.

BROTHER: Has it some special significance?

GERDA: In the end it became a symbol. Of impermanence. When we came to live here, we left the thermometer lying about—we were going to have it outside the window.... I promised to fix it there... forgot... he promised to do it, and forgot. Then we nagged each other about it, and in the end, to be rid of it, I hid it in this drawer.... I came to hate it, and so did he. You know what it signified? No one believed our marriage would last, because from the first we dropped our masks and flaunted our differences. Those first months we lived on the wing ... ready to flee at any moment. We were the thermometer—and here it lies, still—up and down, always changing, like the weather. [*She puts it down and goes over to the chessboard*]. My chessboard! He bought it to while away the long days of waiting, before the child came. Whom does he play with now?

BROTHER: With me.

GERDA: Where is he?

BROTHER: Gone to his room to write a letter.

GERDA: Where?

BROTHER [*points left*]: There.

GERDA [*winces*]: And he has been pacing to and fro in here for five years?

BROTHER: For ten years. Five of them alone.

GERDA: But he loves loneliness?

BROTHER: I think he's had enough.

GERDA: Will he throw me out?

BROTHER: Try and see. You risk nothing. He is always polite.

GERDA: I didn't make that tablecloth. ...

BROTHER: Of course, you risk one thing. He may ask after the child.

GERDA: But he must help me to find her!

BROTHER: Where do you think Fischer's gone? And why has he run away?

GERDA: To escape his creditors. And to make me come after him—he's taken the girl as a hostage.

BROTHER: The ballet. Her father mustn't know that. He hates the stage.

GERDA [*sits at the chessboard and arranges the pieces abstractedly*]: The stage. I've been on that.

BROTHER: You?

GERDA: As an accompanist.

BROTHER: Poor Gerda!

GERDA: Why? I loved the life. When I sat here as a prisoner, it wasn't the warder's fault, but the prison's, that I was unhappy.

BROTHER: But now you've had enough?

GERDA: Now I love peace and loneliness . . . above all, my child.

BROTHER: Ssh! He's coming!

GERDA [*rises to run away, but falls back in her chair*]: Oh——!

BROTHER: I'll leave you now. Don't think what you're going to say. Let it come by itself, like a move at chess.

GERDA: What I'm most frightened of is the first look he'll give me. I'll be able to read in that whether I've become more beautiful . . . or whether I have grown old and ugly. . . .

BROTHER [*goes out right*]: If he finds you aged, he won't be afraid to come close to you. If he finds you as young as before, he will have no hope. He's shyer than you think. Here he is!

> The GENTLEMAN *walks slowly past the left-hand door, leading to the pantry, which is standing open. He has a letter in his hand. He disappears, but immediately reappears in the hall, and goes out of the front door.*

BROTHER [*in the right-hand doorway*]: He's gone to the letter box.

GERDA: I can't go through with it. How can I ask *him* to help me divorce this man? I daren't. I must go.

BROTHER: Stay! You know how kind-hearted he is. He will help you, for the child's sake.

GERDA: No, no!

BROTHER: He is the only one who can help you.

> *The* GENTLEMAN *walks briskly in from the hall, nods at* GERDA, *whom he short-sightedly mistakes for* LOUISE, *goes to the telephone on the sideboard, and turns the handle. As he does so, he speaks casually to* GERDA.

GENTLEMAN: Finished already? Put back the pieces, Louise, and we'll begin again. From the beginning. . . .

> GERDA, *petrified, does not understand.*

GENTLEMAN [*with his back to* GERDA, *speaks into the telephone*]: Hullo! Hullo, is that you, Mother! Thank you, I'm fine. I'm playing chess with Louise, but she's a little tired. She's had a bit of trouble—no, it's over now, and everything's all right. No, nothing important. Isn't this heat dreadful! A thundercloud's just gone over, straight over our heads, but it didn't rain. False alarm. What's that? The Fischers! Yes, but they're leaving soon. Why? I don't know why. Mm? Mm? Yes, it leaves at a quarter past six—no, the outer route, through the islands—it gets in at, wait, let me see, 8.25. Did you have a nice time? [*Chuckles*]. Yes, he's crazy once he starts. What did Maria say about that? What kind of summer have I had? Oh, you know—Louise and I have kept each other company—she's so easy to get along with. Yes, she's a sweet girl, sweet. No, thank you, I do not! [GERDA, *beginning to understand, rises, horrified.*] My eyes? Yes, I'm getting shortsighted, but I feel like old Strong's wife—what is there to look at? Wish I was deaf too! Deaf and blind! Those people upstairs make such a din at night. . . . It's some gambling club. . . . Damn it, they've cut us off. Probably listening . . .

> *He turns the handle again.* LOUISE *appears in the doorway to the hall, unseen by the* GENTLEMAN. GERDA *looks at her with a mixture of admiration and hatred.* LOUISE *goes out through the door, right.*

GENTLEMAN [*at the telephone*]: Are you there? Fancy, they cut us off, trying to listen! Tomorrow, then, 6.15. Thank you—the same to you. Yes, I will! Goodbye, Mother!

He rings off. LOUISE has gone. GERDA is standing in the middle of the room. The GENTLEMAN turns round, sees GERDA, and slowly recognises her. He clutches at his heart.

GENTLEMAN: Dear God! Is it you! Wasn't Louise here just now? [GERDA *does not speak. He says dully.*] How—how did you come here?

GERDA: Forgive me—I was passing, and felt a longing to see my old home.... The windows were open....

Pause.

GENTLEMAN: Do you think it has changed?

GERDA: It's the same—but different—somehow different...

GENTLEMAN [*unwillingly*]: Are you—happy?

GERDA: Ye-es. I've got what I wanted.

GENTLEMAN: And the child?

GERDA: Oh, she's growing. Happy. Enjoying life.

GENTLEMAN: Then I won't question you further. [*Pause.*] Do you want anything? Can I help you in any way?

GERDA: Thank you, but... I don't need anything. I see you're happy too. [*Pause.*] Do you want to see Anne-Charlotte?

Pause.

GENTLEMAN: I don't think so, since you tell me she's happy. It's so difficult to go back—it's like lessons you know but the teacher thinks you don't. I'm so removed from all this—I've been in another country—and I can't re-establish contact with the past—I don't wish to seem impolite, but please don't sit down—you're another man's wife—and you're not the same person as the one I divorced.

GERDA: Am I so—changed?

GENTLEMAN: A stranger. Voice, look, movements....

GERDA: Have I aged?

GENTLEMAN: I don't know. They say that after three years no particle of a human body remains—in five years, everything has been renewed—so you who stand there are a different person from the one who sat and suffered here. I hardly dare use your name, you're such a complete stranger to me! And I suppose it would be the same with my daughter.

GERDA: Don't talk like that. I'd rather you were angry with me.

GENTLEMAN: Why should I be angry?

GERDA: For all the pain I caused you.

GENTLEMAN: Did you? I don't feel it.

GERDA: Didn't you read my deposition?

GENTLEMAN: No. I left that to my lawyer. [*Sits.*]

GERDA: Or the judgment?

GENTLEMAN: I didn't read that either. Since I don't intend to re-marry, I have no use for such papers.

Pause. GERDA *sits.*

GENTLEMAN: What did it say? That I was too old? [GERDA *is silent.*] Well, it was true, so don't let that embarrass you. I wrote just the same in my deposition, and begged the court to grant you your freedom.

GERDA: You wrote that. . . ?

GENTLEMAN: I wrote, not that I *was*, but that I was becoming too old for you.

GERDA [*nettled*]: For me?

GENTLEMAN: Yes. I couldn't say I'd been too old when we married, or the birth of our child might have been misinterpreted. She was our child, wasn't she?

GERDA: You know she was. But . . .

GENTLEMAN: Should I be ashamed of my age? Yes, if I started dancing the Boston, and playing cards at night—then I'd soon find myself in a wheel-chair or on the operating table. Then there'd be cause for shame.

GERDA: You don't look old. . . .

GENTLEMAN: Did you think divorce would kill me? [GERDA *is silent.*] There are people who say that you killed me. Do you think I look dead? [GERDA *is silent, embarrassed.*] I hear your friends drew pictures of me in their little papers, but I never saw them, and they've been waste paper now for five years. You needn't have a bad conscience for my sake.

GERDA: Why did you marry me?

GENTLEMAN: You know why a man marries. And you know I didn't have to beg for your love. Don't you remember how we laughed at all the wise counsellors who warned you? But why you encouraged me I've never been able to understand. . . . When, after our wedding, you didn't look at me but behaved as though you were at someone else's wedding, I thought perhaps you'd made a bet that you'd murder me. My subordinates all hated me—naturally, I was their boss—but they quickly became your friends. As soon as I acquired an enemy, he became your friend. Which made me think: "Thou shalt not hate thine enemies, but thou shalt not love *my* enemies!" However, when I saw how things were, I decided to pack it in. But first I wanted to have a living witness to the fact that you'd been lying about me, so I waited until our child was born.

GERDA: How could you be so deceitful?

GENTLEMAN: I kept my mouth shut; but I never lied to you. You turned my friends into detectives—you even turned my own brother against me. But, worst of all, by your idle chatter you made people doubt your child's legitimacy!

GERDA: I told them that was untrue.

GENTLEMAN: A rumour that has been started can't be scotched.

And the worst thing was that this lying rumour reached the child's ears, so that she regards her mother as a——

GERDA: Oh, no!

GENTLEMAN: Yes, she does! You built a tower on a foundation of lies, and now it is collapsing upon you!

GERDA: It isn't true!

GENTLEMAN: Oh, yes, it is. A little while ago I met Anne-Charlotte....

GERDA: You met her?

GENTLEMAN: On the stairs. She called me uncle. You know what an uncle is? An old friend of the household, and of the mother. And I hear that at school, too, she refers to me as her uncle. It's horrible for the child!

GERDA: You met her!

GENTLEMAN: Yes. I didn't feel required to tell anyone. Haven't I the right to silence? In any case, I found the encounter so disturbing that I wiped it from my memory as though it had never happened.

GERDA: How can I repair the wrong I have done you?

GENTLEMAN: You? You cannot repair it. I can only do that myself. [*They give each other a long, intense look.*] That is to say, I have already repaired it....

GERDA: Can't I make amends somehow? Couldn't you forget...?

GENTLEMAN: What do you mean?

GERDA: Mend what has been broken.

GENTLEMAN: You mean re-tie the knot, start again, make you my mistress? No, thank you. I don't want you.

GERDA: How can you say that to me!

GENTLEMAN: Now you know how it feels.

Pause.

GERDA: That's a pretty tablecloth....

GENTLEMAN: Yes, it is pretty.

GERDA: Where did you get it?

Pause. LOUISE *appears in the doorway to the pantry with a bill in her hand.*

GENTLEMAN [*turns*]: Is that a bill?

GERDA *gets up and pulls her gloves on violently.*

GENTLEMAN [*takes out money for the bill*]: Eighteen crowns, seventy-two öre. Here is the exact sum.

LOUISE: May I have a word with you?

The GENTLEMAN *gets up and goes to the door, where* LOUISE *whispers to him.*

GENTLEMAN: Oh, my God!...

LOUISE *goes.*

GENTLEMAN: Poor Gerda!

GERDA: What do you mean? You think I'm jealous of your maid?

GENTLEMAN: No; I didn't mean that.

GERDA: Yes, you did. And you meant you were too old for me, but not for her. I understand the insult.... She's pretty, I don't deny, as servants go....

GENTLEMAN: Poor Gerda!

GERDA: Why do you say that?

GENTLEMAN: Because I feel sorry for you. Jealous of my servant! That's punishment enough....

GERDA: I—jealous?

GENTLEMAN: Then why are you so angry about my dear little cousin?

GERDA: Cousin?

GENTLEMAN: Oh, no, child. I gave that up long ago.... I am content with my loneliness.... [*The telephone rings. The* GENTLEMAN *answers it.*] Herr Fischer? No, he doesn't live here. Yes, speaking. He's run away? With whom has he run away? Agnes Strong! Dear God! How old is she? Eighteen! A child!

GERDA: I knew he'd leave me. But with a woman——! I suppose you're happy now.

GENTLEMAN: No; I'm not happy. Though it comforts me to see that there is justice in the world. Life hurries on, and now you sit where I once sat.

GERDA: She is eighteen. I am twenty-nine. I am too old, too old for him!

GENTLEMAN: Everything is relative, even age. But to other matters. Where is your child?

GERDA: My child! I'd forgotten her! My child! Oh, God—help me! He's taken the child with him—he loved Anne Charlotte like his own daughter.... Take me to the police! Come with me!

GENTLEMAN: I? Now you are asking too much.

GERDA: Help me!

GENTLEMAN [*goes to the door right*]: Karl Frederik, will you call a cab and go with Gerda to the police station? Would you mind?

BROTHER [*enters*]: Of course. In God's name, we are human beings!

GENTLEMAN: Quickly! But say nothing to Mr. Strong. There is still time to put things right. Poor man! And poor Gerda! Hurry!

GERDA [*looks out through the window*]: It's beginning to rain. Lend me an umbrella.... Eighteen.... Only eighteen! Hurry! [*Goes out with the* BROTHER.]

GENTLEMAN [*alone*]: The peace of old age! And my child in the hands of an adventurer! Louise! [LOUISE *enters*.] Come and play chess with me.

LOUISE: Has the Consul. . . ?

GENTLEMAN: He's had to go out. . . . Is it still raining?

LOUISE: No; it's stopping now.

GENTLEMAN: Then I'll take a walk and get cool. [*Pause.*] You're a good, sensible girl. You knew the café-owner's daughter?

LOUISE: Only very slightly.

GENTLEMAN: Was she beautiful?

LOUISE: Ye-es.

GENTLEMAN: Did you know the people upstairs?

LOUISE: I've never seen them.

GENTLEMAN: You're being evasive.

LOUISE: I've learned to keep my ears shut in this house.

GENTLEMAN: Deafness can go too far, and become dangerous. Make some tea, and I'll go out in the cool. And one thing, my child. You see what is happening. But don't ask me any questions.

LOUISE: I? No, sir. I'm not inquisitive.

GENTLEMAN: Thank you.

Scene 3

Outside the house, as in Scene One. There is a light on in the CAFÉ-OWNER's basement. The lights are also burning on the first floor, where the windows stand open and the blinds are raised. The CAFÉ-OWNER is standing outside his door.

GENTLEMAN [*on the green bench*]: That shower was nice.

CAFÉ-OWNER: A real blessing. It'll help the raspberries. . . .

GENTLEMAN: Would you keep me a few litres! We're tired of making our own jam. It only stands and ferments, and goes mouldy....

CAFÉ-OWNER: Yes, I know. Jam's like naughty children; you've got to watch it. Some say it helps if you add chemicals. But I don't understand these new-fangled innovations....

GENTLEMAN: Chemicals. I suppose they act as an antiseptic. Yes; that might help....

CAFÉ-OWNER: Yes; but it alters the taste. It's an innovation....

GENTLEMAN: Mr. Strong, do you have a telephone?

CAFÉ-OWNER: No; I've no telephone....

GENTLEMAN: Haven't you?

CAFÉ-OWNER: Why do you ask?

GENTLEMAN: Oh, I was just thinking.... It can be useful sometimes.... Customers.... Important messages....

CAFÉ-OWNER: Maybe. But sometimes it's good to avoid ... messages.

GENTLEMAN: True. True. Yes. My heart always gives a little jump when I hear the bell. One never knows what it may be.... And I want peace ... peace!

CAFÉ-OWNER: Me too.

GENTLEMAN [*looks at his watch*]: They'll be lighting the lamps soon.

CAFÉ-OWNER: He must have forgotten us. He's already lit them in the avenue....

GENTLEMAN: Then he'll be here soon. It'll be good to see our lamp burning again ...

The telephone rings in the drawing-room. LOUISE *comes in. The* GENTLEMAN *rises, puts his hand to his heart, and tries to listen, but no words are audible.* LOUISE *comes out through the garden.*

GENTLEMAN [*uneasily*]: What news?

LOUISE: Nothing.

GENTLEMAN: Was that my brother?

LOUISE: No, it was . . . her.

GENTLEMAN: What did she want?

LOUISE: To speak with you.

GENTLEMAN: I won't! Must I console my executioner? I have done it before, but now I'm tired of it. Look up there! They've fled from the light—empty rooms are more horrible with the lights on than in the dark. . . . One sees the ghosts. [*Half to himself*]. And—Agnes——! [*Indicates the* CAFÉ-OWNER.] Do you think he knows?

LOUISE: It's hard to say. He doesn't talk about his troubles. No one does in this silent house.

GENTLEMAN: Ought we to tell him?

LOUISE. No, for God's sake. . . .

GENTLEMAN: But it can't be the first time she's caused him trouble?

LOUISE: He never talks about her. . . .

GENTLEMAN: It's horrible! Please God this'll soon end! [*The telephone rings in the drawing-room.*] Now it's ringing again. Don't answer it. I don't want to know anything. My child! In that company! An adventurer and a whore! My God! Poor Gerda!

LOUISE: It's best to know. I'll go and answer it. You must do something.

GENTLEMAN: I can't. I can receive impressions; I cannot act.

LOUISE: If you turn your back on a danger, it will destroy you. If you don't try to avert it, it will strike you down.

GENTLEMAN: If one doesn't allow oneself to get involved, one cannot be hurt.

LOUISE: Why?

GENTLEMAN: Everything solves itself if you don't interfere. How could I influence a situation like this, where so many passions are involved? I can't stifle their heat or alter their direction.

LOUISE: But the child?

GENTLEMAN: I have relinquished my rights ... and in any case—to be honest, I don't feel it's my business—since *she* came in here and destroyed my memories. She destroyed all my hidden treasures, and now I have nothing left.

LOUISE: Now you are free!

GENTLEMAN: I feel so empty. Like a deserted house. And up there—it's like ... after a fire.

LOUISE: Who's that?

AGNES enters, upset and frightened. She composes herself, and goes towards the back door, where the CAFÉ-OWNER is sitting.

LOUISE [*to* GENTLEMAN]: It's Agnes! What can this mean?

GENTLEMAN: Agnes! Then everything will be all right!

CAFÉ-OWNER [*quite calmly*]: Good evening, my child. Where have you been?

AGNES: Out for a walk.

CAFÉ-OWNER: Your mother's been asking about you.

AGNES: Has she? Well, here I am.

CAFÉ-OWNER: Run downstairs and help her light the small oven, will you?

AGNES: Is she angry with me?

CAFÉ-OWNER: She couldn't be angry with you!

AGNES: She is sometimes, but she never says anything.

CAFÉ-OWNER: Well, that's best, child. No use listening to harsh words.

AGNES goes into the house.

GENTLEMAN [*to* LOUISE]: Does he know, or not?

LOUISE: Let us hope he never knows. . . .

GENTLEMAN: But what has happened? Have they quarrelled? [*To the* CAFÉ-OWNER.] Mr. Strong!

CAFÉ-OWNER: Did you call me?

GENTLEMAN: I was just thinking. Did you see anyone leave the house a few minutes ago?

CAFÉ-OWNER: I saw the ice-man. And the postman, I think.

GENTLEMAN: I see. [*To* LOUISE.] Perhaps there's been a mistake. Someone must have got things wrong—I don't understand this. . . . Perhaps they're playing a trick on him. What did she say on the telephone?

LOUISE: She wanted to speak to you.

GENTLEMAN: How did she sound? Was she upset?

LOUISE: Yes.

GENTLEMAN: I find it somewhat impudent of her to turn to me in such a situation. . . .

LOUISE: But the child!

GENTLEMAN: Imagine. I met my daughter on the stairs, and when I asked her if she recognised me, she called me uncle, and then informed me that her father lived upstairs. . . . Of course, he is her stepfather and has legal custody. . . . They've been slandering me to her, destroying my good name——

LOUISE: There's a cab stopping at the corner!

The CAFÉ-OWNER *goes indoors.*

GENTLEMAN: Oh, God, please don't let them come back. I don't want them round my neck again. Imagine—hearing my child singing the praises of her father—*him*—and then it'll all begin again—"Why did you marry me?"—"You know quite well. Why did you accept me?"—"You know quite well . . ."—and so on, and on, until the end of time.

LOUISE: It's the Consul!

GENTLEMAN: How does he look?

LOUISE: He's walking slowly.

GENTLEMAN: He's preparing what he's going to say. Does he look pleased?

LOUISE: Not exactly. Thoughtful. . . .

GENTLEMAN: I see. . . . It was always the same. As soon as he came near that woman, he betrayed me. . . . She could charm anyone, except me. To me she was coarse, simple, ugly, stupid—and to others she was sensitive, lovable, beautiful, intelligent. All the hatred that I aroused through my self-sufficiency gathered itself round her in a cloud of sympathy for my persecutor. Through her they tried to control and influence me, wound me, ultimately kill me.

LOUISE: I'll go in and wait by the telephone. This storm will pass now surely——

GENTLEMAN: People can't stand self-sufficiency; they want others to obey them; all my subordinates, right down to the night-watchman, wanted me to obey them; when I wouldn't they called me a tyrant. The servants at home wanted me to obey them, and eat warmed-up food, and when I wouldn't they incited my wife against me. And, finally, my wife wanted me to obey our child. And when I left, they united together against the tyrant—me! Hurry in now, Louise, and we'll spring the mine out here.

The BROTHER *enters left.*

GENTLEMAN: What happened? Never mind the details——

BROTHER: Can we sit down? I'm feeling a little tired. . . .

GENTLEMAN: The seat's wet . . .

BROTHER: You've been sitting on it, so it can't hurt me.

GENTLEMAN: As you please. Where is my child?

BROTHER: May I begin at the beginning?

GENTLEMAN: Begin.

BROTHER [*slowly*]: I went with Gerda to the station. At the ticket office, I saw him and Agnes....

GENTLEMAN: Agnes was with him, then?

BROTHER: Yes; and your child. Gerda stayed outside, and I went in. As I did so, he gave Agnes the tickets. But when she saw that they were third-class, she threw them in his face and went out to get a cab.

GENTLEMAN: Ugh!

BROTHER: As I was expostulating with the fellow, Gerda ran in, seized the child and disappeared into the crowd....

GENTLEMAN: What did he say?

BROTHER: Oh—you know. "I can explain everything," etcetera.

GENTLEMAN: Let me hear. I suppose he wasn't as bad as we'd imagined? He had his good points?

BROTHER: Well——

GENTLEMAN: I thought as much. But I trust you won't ask me to sit here and listen to you singing the praises of my enemy?

BROTHER: Not his praises—but there were extenuating circumstances——

GENTLEMAN: Did you ever listen to me when I tried to give you the true picture? Oh yes, you listened—and answered with the silence of disbelief. You always sided with injustice, you only believed lies, because—you were in love with Gerda. But you had another motive too....

BROTHER: No more, please, brother. You only see things from your viewpoint.

GENTLEMAN: Do you expect me to see them from my enemy's? Must I raise my hand against myself?

BROTHER: I am not your enemy.

GENTLEMAN: Yes. When you befriend those who have done me wrong. Where is my child?

BROTHER: I don't know.

GENTLEMAN: How did it end?

BROTHER: He left, alone.

GENTLEMAN: And the others?

BROTHER: Disappeared.

GENTLEMAN: Then they may come back here. [*Pause.*] You're sure they didn't go with him?

BROTHER: No, he travelled alone.

GENTLEMAN: Well, I'm rid of him, anyway. But there's still the mother, and the child.

BROTHER: Why are the lights on up there?

GENTLEMAN: They forgot to put them out.

BROTHER: I'll go up. . . .

GENTLEMAN: No; don't go! Oh, God—don't let them come back! Please don't let it begin again!

BROTHER: But it's going to be all right. . . .

GENTLEMAN: The worst is still to come. . . . Do you think they'll come back?

BROTHER: She won't. She'd have to apologise to you in front of Louise.

GENTLEMAN: I'd forgotten that. Yes; she did me the honour of being jealous! I begin to think there is justice in the world!

BROTHER: And then she found that Agnes was younger——

GENTLEMAN: Poor Gerda! But in cases like this one mustn't speak to people of justice, and Nemesis. . . . It isn't true that people love justice. One must spare their feelings—and Nemesis—that's only for other people. . . . It's ringing again. It sounds like a rattlesnake!

LOUISE *answers the telephone. Pause.*

GENTLEMAN [*to* LOUISE]: Did the snake bite?

LOUISE [*at the window*]: May I have a word with you, please?

GENTLEMAN [*goes to the window*]: Well?

LOUISE: Your—your wife has gone with her mother to Dalarna. She intends to live there. With the child.

GENTLEMAN [*to* BROTHER]: Mother and child in the country ... a good home. It's solved itself ... [*Sighs with relief.*]

LOUISE: And she asked me to go upstairs and put out the lights.

GENTLEMAN: Do so, Louise, at once. And pull down the blinds.

LOUISE *goes. The* CAFÉ-OWNER *comes out.*

CAFÉ-OWNER [*looks up*]: I think the storm's passed over.

GENTLEMAN: The sky certainly seems clearer. We'll be able to see the moon.

BROTHER: Thank God for that rain!

CAFÉ-OWNER: Yes; it's been a real blessing.

GENTLEMAN: Look! Here comes the lamplighter. At last!

The LAMPLIGHTER *enters and lights the lamp.*

GENTLEMAN: The first lamp! Now it is autumn. Our season, my friends! It is beginning to grow dark; but wisdom comes, and lights her lantern to guide our footsteps.

LOUISE *appears upstairs. Immediately it becomes dark up there.*

GENTLEMAN [*to* LOUISE]: Close the windows and pull down the blinds. Let our memories be put to bed, and sleep in peace. The peace of old age! This autumn I shall leave this silent house.

Introduction to
THE GHOST SONATA

STRINDBERG wrote THE GHOST SONATA in February-March 1908, immediately after STORM and THE BURNT HOUSE. It was the third of the "chamber plays" composed for his Intimate Theatre, which he was to open that November; he completed the three of them in less than ten weeks.

He was living alone in the apartment in Stockholm which he had previously shared with Harriet Bosse and their daughter, Anne-Marie. He had recently had a recurrence of psoriasis, the humiliating and painful skin disease which had discomfited him in Paris during his scientific experiments, and the slightest contact with anything, even a pen, made his hands bleed. According to his sister Anna, the first symptoms of the stomach cancer which was to kill him five years later had also manifested themselves.* He thus wrote THE GHOST SONATA in a state of almost permanent physical pain. This made him more than usually impossible to live with, and six servants left him within forty days, including, two days before he finished the play, his cook. It is not surprising that THE GHOST SONATA, and THE PELICAN which followed it, are so much crueller and more bitter than STORM, which he wrote in loneliness, but in apparent resignation.

THE GHOST SONATA marks a return to that mood of cynicism and disillusionment with the world of the living which we find so often in his earlier work. In 1905 he had written: "Life is so horribly ugly, we human beings so utterly evil, that if a writer were to portray *everything* he saw and heard no one could bear to read it. There are things which I remember having seen and heard in good, respectable and well-liked people, but which I have blotted out from my mind because I could not bring

* In the original draft of the play, the Daughter's illness is identified as being cancer of the womb.

myself to speak of them and do not wish to remember them. Breeding and education are only masks to hide our bestiality, and virtue is a sham. The best we can hope for is to conceal our wretchedness. Life is so cynical that only a swine can be happy in it; and any man who sees beauty in life's ugliness *is* a swine! Life is a punishment. A hell. For some a purgatory, for none a paradise. We are compelled to commit evil and to torment our fellow mortals."

On 27 March 1907 he wrote to his German translator, Emil Schering: "I am sending you today a second Chamber Play (opus 3), called A [sic] GHOST SONATA (subtitled KAMA-LOKA, though that needn't be printed). It is *schauderhaft* like life, when the veil falls from our eyes and we see *Das Ding an Sich*. It has shape and content, the wisdom that comes with age, as our knowledge increases and we learn to understand. This is how 'The Weaver' weaves men's destinies; secrets like these are to be found in *every* home. People are too proud to admit it; most of them boast of their imagined luck, and hide their misery. The Colonel acts out his private comedy to the end; illusion (Maya) has become reality to him—the Mummy awakens first, one cannot wake the others.... I have suffered as though in Kama-Loka* (Scheol) during the writing of it and my hands have bled (literally). What has saved my soul from darkness during this work has been my religion (= Anschluss with Jensits). The hope of a better life to come; the firm conviction that we live in a world of madness and delusion (illusion) from which we must fight our way free. For me things have become brighter, and I have written with the feeling that this is my 'Last Sonata!'"

A week later, he wrote again to Schering: "Now I am assuredly entering into something new. I long for the light, have always done so, but have not found it. Is it the end that is approaching? I don't know, but I feel that it is so. Life is, as it

---

* Kama-Loka—"a kind of ghost or dream world through which mortals, or some mortals, have to wander before they enter the peace of death's kingdom" (Olle Holmberg).

were, squeezing me out, or driving me out, and I have long since rested all my hopes on 'the other side', with which I am in contact (through Swedenborg). A feeling has also come over me that I have completed my work, that I have nothing more to say. My whole life often seems to me to have been planned like a play, so that I might both suffer and depict suffering."

While he was writing THE GHOST SONATA, preparations were under way for the first production of A DREAM PLAY that April, and this may partly explain why he returned to a certain degree to the technique of the earlier play and of TO DAMASCUS. In his preface to A DREAM PLAY, Strindberg had written: "In this dream play, the author has, as in his former dream play, TO DAMASCUS, attempted to imitate the inconsequent yet transparently logical shape of a dream. Everything can happen, everything is possible and probable. Time and place do not exist; on an insignificant basis of reality the imagination spins, weaving new patterns; a mixture of memories, experiences, free fancies, incongruities and improvisations. The characters split, double, multiply, evaporate, condense, disperse, assemble. But one consciousness rules over them all, that of the dreamer; for him there are no secrets, no illogicalities, no scruples, no laws. He neither acquits nor condemns, but merely relates; and, just as a dream is more often painful than happy, so an undertone of melancholy and of pity for all mortal beings accompanies this flickering tale."

The characters in THE GHOST SONATA are based on people whom Strindberg saw in his respectable suburb of Östermalm. On his walks he sometimes came across a rich old man in a wheel-chair who ostentatiously dispensed charity to beggars. Through the window of a house he observed a youngish man playing cards with three old people who looked like mummies. The Daughter and the Student may have been modelled on his own daughter, Greta, and her fiancé, Henry Philp, to whom she had become engaged the previous December; he was very fond of both these young people, who seemed untouched by evil in an evil world.* The Mummy and the Colonel appear to have been based, like the two protagonists in THE DANCE OF DEATH, on his sister Anna and her husband, Hugo Philp (the parents of Henry Philp); they had been kind to Strindberg and, as was his habit, he had turned violently against them. In 1900 Hugo Philp had put a "von" before his name, which may have given Strindberg the idea of making the Colonel falsely claim to be a nobleman. The soya or colorite bottle carried by the Cook held some particular significance for Strindberg, for he specifically commanded Schering not to omit it from his translation. "N.B.! Don't forget the soya bottle, the colorite which I have had to put up with for thirteen days; I have been eating coloured water", he wrote to him on 7 April 1907. Presumably his cook had given up the struggle. The Japanese screen stood in the Philps' home; and the idea of a death screen was given him by a niece, who was a hospital nurse and told him of the procedure in a ward when a patient dies. Böcklin's *Island of the Dead*, mentioned in the final stage direction, was one of Strindberg's favourite paintings, and when the Intimate Theatre opened that winter reproductions of it and of the same painter's *Island of the Living* hung on either side of the proscenium arch.

THE GHOST SONATA was first acted at the Intimate Theatre on 21 January 1908, and was, like the other three chamber plays which preceded it, STORM, THE BURNT HOUSE and THE PELICAN, violently condemned by the critics. Again, it was Max Reinhardt who first revealed the play's possibilities when he staged it in 1916 at his Kammarspiele in Berlin, a production the fame of which spread to many countries even in that dark time. The same year he took his production to Gothenburg and Stockholm, where it created a considerable sensation. Paul Wegener played Hummel and Gertrud Eysoldt the Mummy. In 1917 the play was produced in Munich, in 1920 in Copenhagen (with Reinhardt as guest producer), in 1921 in Oslo and

* Greta Strindberg was killed in a railway accident in the same year that her father died (1912) at the age of thirty-one.

Introduction to THE GHOST SONATA

in 1922 in Vienna. In 1924, at the instigation of Eugene O'Neill, the Provincetown Players presented THE GHOST SONATA in New York; in 1925 it was successfully staged in Rome at Bragaglia's experimental theatre; and in 1926 it at last reached England, when J. B. Fagan presented it at the Oxford Playhouse. The following year Fagan brought his production to the Globe Theatre in London for two matinées; some critics, including James Agate, were impressed, but the general public reaction was one of bewilderment.*

The past quarter of a century has seen several notable revivals of THE GHOST SONATA in Sweden. In 1941 a young student named Ingmar Bergman aroused attention with an imaginative production at Medborgarhuset in Stockholm, and the following year Olof Molander, a pioneer among Strindberg interpreters, staged it powerfully at the Royal Theatre, with Lars Hanson as Hummel and Märta Ekström as the Mummy. Molander has since reproduced the play on several occasions, most recently in 1962, when his production visited the Festival des Théâtres des Nations in Paris and created something of a *furore*. Hummel was brilliantly played by Anders Henrikson. Ingmar Bergman directed the play again in 1954, at Malmö, with the thirty-stone actor, Bengt-Åke Bengtsson, as another remarkable Hummel.

THE GHOST SONATA has not been professionally staged in England since 1927 (although there have been several performances by amateurs, especially at the universities), but on 16 March 1962 it was televised by the B.B.C. in a production by Stuart Burge, which, as several critics remarked, was probably watched by more people than had seen the play during the previous fifty-five years of its existence. Robert Helpmann played Hummel, and Beatrix Lehmann the Mummy, and it is a measure of the development of theatrical taste in the last thirty years that the public reaction from this huge audience was predominantly favourable. A telerecording of this production was subsequently seen in the United States and in Australia.

* For the cast of this production, see p. 479.

Strindberg wrote seven plays after THE GHOST SONATA, but of these only THE PELICAN and his last play, THE GREAT HIGHWAY (and perhaps the fragment, TOTEN-INSEL) can be counted among his best. His Intimate Theatre finally failed and closed in 1910, and he devoted the last three years of his life to writing pamphlets on politics, sociology and philology. He died of stomach cancer on 14 May 1912, aged sixty-three.

THE GHOST SONATA

A Chamber Play
(1907)

This translation of THE GHOST SONATA was commissioned by the British Broadcasting Corporation and was first performed on B.B.C. Television on 16 March 1962. The cast was:

THE OLD MAN	Robert Helpmann
THE STUDENT	Jeremy Brett
THE MILKMAID	Linda Gardner
THE CARETAKER'S WIFE	Miki Iveria
THE DEAD MAN	George McGrath
THE DARK LADY	Yvonne Coulette
THE COLONEL	William Mervyn
THE MUMMY	Beatrix Lehmann
THE DAUGHTER	Ann Bell
THE NOBLEMAN	Arthur Lawrence
JOHANSSON	Thomas Heathcote
BENGTSSON	John Kidd
THE FIANCÉE	Jane Eccles
THE COOK	Anna Wing
A MAIDSERVANT	Mary McMillen

Designed by Clifford Hatts
Produced by Stuart Burge

CHARACTERS

THE OLD MAN

THE STUDENT

THE MILKMAID, a vision

THE CARETAKER'S WIFE

THE DEAD MAN, a Consul

THE DARK LADY, daughter to the Caretaker's Wife by the Dead Man

THE COLONEL

THE MUMMY, wife to the Colonel

THE "COLONEL'S DAUGHTER", in reality the Old Man's daughter

THE NOBLEMAN, known as BARON SKANSKORG, engaged to the Caretaker's Daughter

JOHANSSON, servant to the Old Man

BENGTSSON, footman to the Colonel

THE FIANCÉE, a white-haired old lady, formerly engaged to the Old Man

THE COOK

A MAIDSERVANT

BEGGARS

The ground floor and first floor of a fashionable house. Only a corner of it is visible. The ground floor ends in a circular drawing-room, the first floor in a balcony with a flagstaff.

As the blinds are raised in the drawing-room they reveal through the open windows a white marble statue of a young woman, surrounded by palms which are bathed in bright sunlight. In the window to the left stand vases of hyacinths, blue, white and pink.

Over the railing of the balcony, at the corner of the first floor, hangs a blue silk eiderdown, with two white pillows. The windows to the left are draped with white sheets. It is a clear Sunday morning.

Downstage, in front of the house, is a green bench. Downstage right, a public fountain. To the left is a pillar, with posters pasted round it.

Upstage left is the front entrance to the house. Through it we can see the staircase, which is of white marble, with banisters of mahogany and brass. On the pavement outside, laurels in tubs stand on either side of the door.

The corner of the house which contains the round drawing-room also looks on to a side street which leads upstage.

To the left of the entrance, on the ground floor, is a window with a mirror outside it set at an angle.

As the curtain rises, the bells of several churches can be heard pealing in the distance.

The doors of the house are open. A WOMAN *dressed in dark clothes is standing motionless on the staircase. The* CARETAKER'S WIFE *is cleaning the front step; then she polishes the brass on the front door, and waters the laurels.*

In a wheel chair by the pillar, the OLD MAN *sits reading the paper. He has white hair, a white beard, and spectacles.*

The MILKMAID *enters from the left, carrying bottles in a wire basket. She is in summer clothes, with brown shoes, black stockings and a white cap. She takes off the cap and hangs it on the fountain, wipes the sweat from her forehead, drinks from the cup, washes her hands and arranges her hair, using the water as a mirror.*

A steamship's bell rings, and the bass notes of an organ in a nearby church intermittently pierce the silence.

After a few moments of this silence, when the MILKMAID *has finished her toilet, the* STUDENT *enters from the left, sleepless and unshaven. He goes straight to the fountain.*

Pause.

STUDENT: May I have the cup?

THE MILKMAID *hugs the cup to her.*

You've finished with it, haven't you?

THE MILKMAID *looks at him frightened.*

OLD MAN [*to himself*]: Who's he talking to? I can't see anyone. Is he mad? [*He continues to watch them in great amazement.*]

STUDENT: What are you staring at? Am I so repulsive? Oh, I see. I haven't slept all night, so of course you think I've been dissipating. [*She still stares at him with the same expression.*]

Drinking punch, hm? Does my breath smell of punch? [*Her expression remains unchanged.*] I haven't shaved—oh, I know. Give me a drink of water, girl—I've earned it. [*Pause.*] Oh, very well. I suppose I'll have to tell you. I've been bandaging wounds all night, and tending the injured; I was there when the house collapsed yesterday evening. Now you know.

The Milkmaid *rinses the cup and gives him a drink.*

Thank you.

The Milkmaid *does not move.*

[*Slowly.*] Will you do me a service? [*Pause.*] It's like this. My eyes are swollen, as you can see, but I daren't touch them with my hands because I've been fingering open wounds and dead bodies. Will you take this handkerchief, moisten it in the clean water and bathe my eyes? Will you do that? Will you be my Good Samaritan? [*She hesitates, but does as he asks.*] Thank you, dear friend. [*Takes out his purse. She makes a gesture of refusal.*] Oh—forgive me for being so thoughtless—I'm not really awake——

Old Man [*to the* Student]: Pardon my addressing you, but did I hear you say you witnessed that accident last night? I've just been reading about it in the paper——

Student: Oh, have they got hold of it already?

Old Man: Yes, the whole story's here. And your photograph; but they regret they were unable to discover the name of the brilliant young student who——

Student [*looks at the paper*]: Really? That's me! Well, well.

Old Man: Whom were you talking to just now?

Student: Didn't you see her?

Pause.

Old Man: Would it be impertinent of me to ask—to be allowed the honour of knowing—your name?

STUDENT: What'd be the point? I don't want any publicity; once you become famous people start saying foul things about you. Depreciation's become a fine art nowadays. Anyway, I'm not looking for any reward——

OLD MAN: You are rich?

STUDENT: Quite the contrary. I'm ab-absolutely penniless.

OLD MAN: Wait a moment! I seem to know that voice. When I was young I had a friend who couldn't say absinthe, he always said ab-absinthe. He's the only person I've ever come across with that particular stammer. And now you! I wonder if you could possibly be any relation to a wholesale merchant of the name of Arkenholz?

STUDENT: He was my father.

OLD MAN: The ways of fate are strange. I saw you once, when you were a little child—under very painful circumstances——

STUDENT: Yes. I'm said to have been born into this world in the home of a bankrupt.

OLD MAN: Precisely.

STUDENT: Perhaps I may ask your name?

OLD MAN: My name is Hummel.

STUDENT: Are *you*——? Yes—now I remember——

OLD MAN: You've often heard my name mentioned by your family?

STUDENT: Yes.

OLD MAN: Mentioned, I dare say, with a certain—distaste?

THE STUDENT *is silent.*

Oh, yes—I can imagine! I've no doubt they told you it was I who ruined your father? People who ruin themselves by idiotic speculation always swear they've been ruined by the one man they failed to fool. [*Pause.*] The truth of the matter is that your father swindled me out of seventeen thousand crowns—a sum which at the time represented my entire savings.

STUDENT: It's strange how a story can exist in two such different versions.

OLD MAN: You think I'm not telling you the truth.

STUDENT: What else am I to think? My father never lied?

OLD MAN: True, true. One's own father never lies. But I am a father, too; so——

STUDENT: What are you trying to tell me?

OLD MAN: I saved your father from complete destitution, and he rewarded me with hatred—the dreadful hatred of a man tied to another by the knot of gratitude. He taught his family to spit on my name.

STUDENT: Perhaps you made him ungrateful by poisoning your charity with unnecessary humiliations?

OLD MAN: All charity is humiliating, my dear sir.

STUDENT: What do you want from me?

OLD MAN: Oh, not money. If you would just perform one or two trivial services for me, I shall think myself well repaid. I am, as you see, a cripple. Some say it is my own fault, others blame my parents. I prefer to believe that life itself is to blame; she's a cunning snarer; sidestep one pit and you walk straight into the next. Be that as it may, I cannot run up stairs or pull bell-ropes, and therefore I say to you: "Please help me."

STUDENT: What can I do?

OLD MAN: First of all, push my chair so that I can read these posters. I want to see what they're playing tonight at the theatre——

STUDENT [*pushes the wheel chair*]: Haven't you a servant?

OLD MAN: Yes, but he's gone on an errand. He'll be back soon. So you're a medical student, are you?

STUDENT: No, I'm studying languages. I haven't really decided yet what I'm going to be——

OLD MAN: Ah-ha! Are you any good at arithmetic?

STUDENT: I know a little.

OLD MAN: Good! Would you like a job?

STUDENT: Yes. Why not?

OLD MAN: Excellent! [*Reads one of the posters.*] They're giving a matinée this afternoon of *The Valkyrie*. The Colonel'll be there with his daughter. He always sits at the end of the sixth row. I'll put you beside them. Go into that telephone kiosk, will you, and book a ticket for seat number 82 in the sixth row?

STUDENT: You want me to go to the opera this afternoon?

OLD MAN: Yes. Just do as I tell you and you'll be well rewarded. I want you to be happy, to find wealth and honour. By tomorrow your gallant deeds of rescue will be in every mouth, and your name will have a considerable market value——

STUDENT [*goes towards the telephone kiosk*]: This is a strange adventure.

OLD MAN: Are you a gambler?

STUDENT: Yes. That's my tragedy.

OLD MAN: It shall be your fortune. Go along and do your telephoning.

> *He reads his newspaper. The* WOMAN *dressed in dark clothes has come out on to the pavement and is talking to the* CARETAKER'S WIFE. *The* OLD MAN *listens, but the audience cannot hear what they say. The* STUDENT *returns.*

OLD MAN: Have you done it?

STUDENT: Yes.

OLD MAN: You see that house?

STUDENT: Yes. I've noticed it before. I was walking past it yesterday, as the sun was shining in its windows. I thought of all the beauty and luxury there must be inside, and said to my companion: "If only one had an apartment there, four floors up, with a beautiful young wife, two pretty children and a private income of 20,000 crowns a year."

OLD MAN: You said that, did you, did you indeed? Well, now; I love this house, too——

STUDENT: You speculate in houses?

OLD MAN: Mm—yes. But not the way you mean——

STUDENT: You know the people who live there?

OLD MAN: Every one of them. When you live to be as old as I am, you know everyone, who their fathers were and their forefathers, and you find you're related to all of them in some way or other. I'm eighty; but no-one knows me; not really —I'm interested in people's destinies——

The blind in the round drawing-room is raised. The COLONEL *is seen within, dressed in mufti. After looking at the thermometer, he turns back into the room and stops in front of the marble statue.*

OLD MAN: Look, there's the Colonel. You'll be sitting next to him this afternoon——

STUDENT: Is that—the Colonel? I don't understand what any of this means—it's like a fairy tale——

OLD MAN: My whole life is a book of fairy tales, my dear sir; and although each tale is different, a single thread links them, there is a *leitmotif* that recurs continually——

STUDENT: Whom does the marble statue represent?

OLD MAN: His wife, of course.

STUDENT: Was she so beautiful?

OLD MAN: Mm—yes. Yes.

STUDENT: Tell me.

OLD MAN: Ah, my dear boy, we must not judge our fellow mortals. If I were to tell you that he struck her, that she left him, that she came back to him, and re-married him, and that she now sits in there in the shape of a mummy, worshipping her own statue, you would think I was mad.

STUDENT: I don't understand.

OLD MAN: I didn't suppose you would. Then we have the hyacinth window. That's where his daughter lives. She's out riding, but she'll be home soon——

STUDENT: Who is the dark lady talking to the caretaker's wife?

OLD MAN: Well, that's a bit complicated. It's to do with the dead man upstairs—up there, where you can see the white sheets——

STUDENT: Who was he?

OLD MAN: A human being, like us; but vain—vain. If you were a Sunday child, in a few minutes you would see him come out through the door to look at the consulate flag flying at half-mast. He was a consul, and loved crowns and lions, plumed hats and coloured ribbons——

STUDENT: Sunday child, you said. They say I was born on a Sunday——

OLD MAN: You don't say! Were you really? I might have guessed it from the colour of your eyes. Then you can see what others cannot see. Have you noticed that?

STUDENT: I don't know what other people can see, but sometimes—well, I'd rather not talk about it.

OLD MAN: I knew it. Come on, you can tell me. I understand about these things——

STUDENT: Well—yesterday, for example. I felt myself drawn to that quite ordinary little street in which, in a few minutes, a house was to collapse. I walked down it and stopped in front of this building—I'd never seen it before. Then I noticed a crack in the wall and heard the floorboards snapping. I ran forward and snatched hold of a child who was walking close by the wall. The next moment, the house collapsed. I was safe. But in my arms, where I thought I was holding the child, there was nothing.

OLD MAN: Extraordinary. I guessed as much. But tell me something. Why were you gesticulating like that at the fountain just now? And why were you talking to yourself?

STUDENT: Didn't you see the milkmaid?

OLD MAN [*recoils*]: Milkmaid?

STUDENT: Yes, the one who gave me the cup?

OLD MAN: Ah-ha? So that's how it is? Well, I can't see, but I can——

A white-haired woman sits down by the window beside the angled mirror.

OLD MAN: Look at that old woman in the window. You see her? Good. She was my fiancée once—sixty years ago. I was twenty. Don't be afraid, she doesn't recognise me. We see each other every day, but I don't feel anything, though we once vowed to be eternally true to each other. Eternally.

STUDENT: How little your generation understood of life. We don't talk to our girls like that nowadays.

OLD MAN: Forgive us, my boy, we knew no better. But can you see that this old woman was once young and beautiful?

STUDENT: No. Yes, she has an attractive glance. Though—I can't see her eyes——

The CARETAKER'S WIFE *comes out with a basket and scatters pine twigs.**

OLD MAN: Ah, yes. The caretaker's wife. The dark lady over there is her daughter, by the dead man. That's how her husband got the job as caretaker. But the dark lady has a lover; a nobleman, with great expectations. He's getting divorced from his wife—she's giving him a fine house so as to be rid of him. This noble lover is son-in-law to the dead man—you can see his bedclothes being aired up there on the balcony. Complicated, isn't it?

* A custom in Sweden when someone has died.

STUDENT: Confoundedly complicated.

OLD MAN: Yes; it's a complicated house, inside and out. Yet it looks quite ordinary, doesn't it?

STUDENT: But who was the dead man, then?

OLD MAN: You asked me just now, and I told you. If you could see round the corner to the back entrance, you'd see a crowd of paupers whom he used to help. When he felt inclined——

STUDENT: He was a kind man, then?

OLD MAN: Sometimes.

STUDENT: Not always?

OLD MAN: No. People are like that. Now, my dear sir, move my chair a little so that it gets the sun. I'm so horribly cold; when one can't move, the blood stiffens. I'm going to die soon, I know that, but there are one or two things I've got to do before I go. Take my hand, feel how cold I am.

STUDENT [*recoils*]: It's horrible!

OLD MAN: Don't leave me. I'm tired, I'm lonely, but I haven't always been like this, you know. I've an interminably long life behind me—oh, interminably long. I've made people unhappy, and people have made me unhappy—I suppose the one cancels out the other—but before I die I want to see you happy. Our destinies are wedded—through your father—and in other ways, too.

STUDENT: Let go of my hand, you're draining my strength, you're freezing me. What do you want?

OLD MAN: Be patient. You will see and understand. Here comes the young lady.

STUDENT: The Colonel's daughter?

OLD MAN: Yes! His daughter! Look at her! Did you ever see such a masterpiece?

STUDENT: She's like the marble statue in there.

OLD MAN: That's her mother.

STUDENT: Yes—you're right! I never saw such a woman—of woman born. Happy the man who leads her to the altar and to his home!

OLD MAN: Ah—you see it, then? Not everyone appreciates her beauty. Good, good; it is written so.

The DAUGHTER enters from the left in a fashionable English riding habit, with breeches, and walks slowly, without looking at anyone, to the door. She pauses, and says a few words to the CARETAKER'S WIFE; then she enters the house. The STUDENT puts his hand to his eyes.

OLD MAN: Are you crying?

STUDENT: When one stands face to face with the unattainable, what else can one do but despair?

OLD MAN: I can open doors, and human hearts, if only I can find a hand to perform my will. Serve me, and you will win her.

STUDENT: Is this a pact? Must I sell my soul?

OLD MAN: Sell nothing! Listen. All my life I have taken; now I have a longing to give. To give! But no one will take anything from me. I am rich, very rich, but I have no heirs—only a rascal, who plagues the life out of me. Be a son to me, be my heir while I am still alive, enjoy life so that I can watch you enjoy it—if only from a distance.

STUDENT: What must I do?

OLD MAN: First, go and listen to *The Valkyrie*.

STUDENT: I've agreed to that. What else?

OLD MAN: Tonight you shall sit in there, in the round drawing-room.

STUDENT: How shall I get in there?

OLD MAN: Through *The Valkyrie*!

STUDENT: Why have you chosen me as your medium? Did you know me before?

OLD MAN: Yes, of course. I've had my eye on you for a long time. But look up there, now—on the balcony! The maid's hoisting the flag to half mast for the consul. Now she's turning the bedclothes. You see the blue eiderdown? That was made for two to sleep under. Now it serves for one.

The DAUGHTER, who has changed her clothes, enters and waters the hyacinths in the window.

That's my little girl—look at her, look! She's talking to the flowers—isn't she like a blue hyacinth herself? She's giving them drink—just plain water, but they turn it into colour and perfume. Here comes the Colonel with his newspaper. He's showing her the paragraph about the accident. Now he's pointing at your photograph! She's interested; she's reading of your bravery. It's clouding over, what if it should rain? I'll be in a fine pickle stuck here if Johansson doesn't get back soon.

It clouds over and becomes dark. The OLD LADY at the mirror shuts her window.

Now my fiancée's shutting her window... seventy-nine... that mirror's the only one she uses, because she can't see herself in it, only the outside world. and that from two angles—but the world can see her, she hasn't thought of that. She's a beautiful old lady, though....

The DEAD MAN, in his winding-sheet, emerges from the door.

STUDENT: God Almighty, what do I see now?

OLD MAN: What do you see?

STUDENT: Can't you see? There—in the doorway! The dead man?

OLD MAN: I see nothing. But I was expecting this. Tell me.

STUDENT: He's going out into the street. [*Pause.*] Now he's turning his head and looking at the flag.

OLD MAN: What did I tell you? Next he'll count the wreaths: and read the names on the cards. Woe to those whose names he cannot find!

STUDENT: Now he's going round the corner——

OLD MAN: He's going to count the beggars at the back door. It always looks good to have the poor at one's funeral. "Accompanied to his grave by the blessings of the people." Yes, he won't have my blessing, though. Between ourselves, he was a dreadful scoundrel——

STUDENT: But charitable——

OLD MAN: A charitable scoundrel, whose only dream in life was to have a beautiful funeral. When he felt that the end was near, he fleeced the estate of 50,000 crowns. Now his daughter's living with another woman's husband, worrying whether she'll get her inheritance. He can hear everything we say, the rogue, and serve him right! Ah, here's Johansson.

JOHANSSON *enters from the left.*

OLD MAN: Well, what news? [JOHANSSON *speaks inaudibly.*] Not at home? Fool! Anything on the telegraph? Nothing. Go on. Six o'clock this evening? That's good. Special edition? With his full name? Arkenholz . . . student . . . born . . . parents . . . Excellent! Oh, I think it's starting to rain. What did he say? I see, I see. . . . Didn't want to. . . ? Well he must. . . . Here comes the noble lover. Push me round the corner, Johansson, I want to hear what the beggars are saying. Arkenholz, wait for me here; you understand? Hurry, hurry!

JOHANSSON *pushes the wheel-chair round the corner. The* STUDENT *remains where he is, watching the* DAUGHTER, *who is now raking the earth in the flowerpots.*

NOBLEMAN [*in mourning, addresses the* DARK LADY, *who has*

come out on to the pavement.] Well, what can we do about it? We'll just have to wait.

LADY: I cannot wait.

NOBLEMAN: Is that so? Better leave town, then.

DARK LADY: I don't want to do that.

NOBLEMAN: Come over here, or they'll hear what we're saying.

They go over by the pillar and continue their conversation inaudibly.

JOHANSSON [*enters from the right and addresses the* STUDENT.] The master says please not to forget the other matter.

STUDENT: Does your master own this house?

JOHANSSON: Yes.

STUDENT: Tell me—who is he?

JOHANSSON: Ah! He's a lot of things—and he *has* been everything.

STUDENT: Is he sane?

JOHANSSON: Depends what you mean by that. All his life he says he's been looking for a Sunday child. Might not be true, of course.

STUDENT: What does he want? Is he a miser?

JOHANSSON: He wants power. All day he drives round in his chariot like the great god Thor. He looks at houses, knocks them down, opens up streets, builds over public squares— and he breaks into houses, too, creeps in through windows, mucks around with people's destinies, kills his enemies, and never forgives. But would you believe it, sir, this little cripple used to be a Don Juan once. Always lost his women in the end, though.

STUDENT: Oh, why was that?

JOHANSSON: Well, he's crafty, you see. Got them to leave him once he'd tired of them. Now he's become a horse-thief—

only he don't steal horses, he steals human beings. All sorts of ways. Me, now for example. He literally stole me from out of the hands of justice. I'd committed a—hm—little blunder, and he was the only one who knew about it. Well, instead of putting me inside he made me his slave. Which I do just for my food, which ain't the best——

STUDENT: What does he want to do in this house?

JOHANSSON: Ah, that I wouldn't like to say. It's all very complicated.

STUDENT: I think I'm getting out of this.

JOHANSSON: Look, the young lady's dropped her bracelet through the window.

The DAUGHTER has dropped her bracelet through the open window. The STUDENT goes slowly forward, picks it up and hands it to her. She thanks him stiffly. The STUDENT goes back to JOHANSSON.

JOHANSSON: Mm, so you're thinking of going? That's not so easy, once he's got his net over your head. He's afraid of nothing between earth and heaven—oh, yes, one thing. Or rather, one person——

STUDENT: Wait a moment. I think I know.

JOHANSSON: How can you?

STUDENT: I can guess. Is it—a little milkmaid?

JOHANSSON: He always turns his face away when he meets a milkcart. And he talks in his sleep—says he was once in Hamburg——

STUDENT: Can one believe that man?

JOHANSSON: You can believe him all right. Whatever he says.

STUDENT: What's he doing round the corner now?

JOHANSSON: Listening to the beggars. Drops a word—picks each brick out, grain by grain, till the house collapses.

Figuratively speaking, of course. I'm an educated man, you know. Used to be a bookseller—once. You going now?

STUDENT: I don't want to seem ungrateful. This man saved my father once, and now he's only asking a small service of me in return——

JOHANSSON: What's that?

STUDENT: He wants me to go and see *The Valkyrie*.

JOHANSSON: Can't understand that. But he's always thinking up new ideas. Look, now he's talking to the policeman. He always keeps in with the police—uses them, implicates them in his affairs, ties their hands with false hopes and promises, and all the time pumps them for information. You'll see—before the night's over he'll have nosed his way into that round room.

STUDENT: What does he want there? What is there between him and the Colonel?

JOHANSSON: Ah—I could make a guess, but I ain't sure. You'll see for yourself when you get there.

STUDENT: I shall never be admitted there.

JOHANSSON: That depends on you. Go to *The Valkyrie*——

STUDENT: You mean, then I might——?

JOHANSSON: If that's what he's told you to do. Look at him now, riding in his war chariot! Look at the beggars drawing him in triumph! They won't get a penny for their pains—just a nod to remind them they'll get a blow-out at his funeral.

OLD MAN [*enters, standing in his wheel-chair, drawn by a beggar and followed by others*]: Hail to the noble youth who, at the peril of his own life, saved many lives in yesterday's disaster. Hail, Arkenholz!

> The BEGGARS *take off their caps, but do not cheer. The* DAUGHTER *waves her handkerchief at her window. The* COLONEL *stares out through his window. The* OLD WOMAN

stands up at her window. The MAID *on the balcony hoists the flag to the top of the mast.*

OLD MAN: Clap your hands, fellow citizens! It is Sunday, but the ass at the well and the ear in the field absolve us by their toil. Although I am not a Sunday child, yet I possess the gift of prophecy, and also the gift of healing. I once summoned a drowning girl back to life. It was in Hamburg—one Sunday morning—as it might be now——

The MILKMAID *enters, seen only by the* STUDENT *and the* OLD MAN. *She stretches up her arms like a drowning person, and stares fixedly at the* OLD MAN.

OLD MAN [*sits down and cringes in terror*]: Johansson, take me away! Quickly! Arkenholz, do not forget *The Valkyrie*!

STUDENT: What does all this mean?

JOHANSSON: We shall see. We shall see.

Inside the round drawing-room. Upstage, a cylindrical, white-tiled stove, with mirrors in it. A pendulum clock; candelabra. On the right is an entrance hall, with a perspective of a green room containing mahogany furniture. On the left stands the statue, shadowed by palms. There is a curtain that can be drawn to conceal it. Upstage left is the door to the hyacinth room, where the DAUGHTER sits, reading. The COLONEL'S back is visible as he sits writing in the green room.

BENGTSSON, *the* COLONEL'S *footman, enters from the hall dressed in livery, with* JOHANSSON, *who is wearing tails and a white cravat.*

BENGTSSON: Right, then. You do the serving, and I'll take their clothes. Ever done this kind of thing before?

JOHANSSON: I spend all day pushing his chariot, as you know, but I sometimes serve at parties of an evening. It's always been my dream to enter this house. Queer bunch, aren't they?

BENGTSSON: Uh-huh. Bit out of the ordinary.

JOHANSSON: Musical evening, or what?

BENGTSSON: No—just the usual spook supper. That's what we call it. They sit round drinking tea, none of them utters a word—unless maybe the Colonel talks on his own. They nibble little cakes, all together. Sounds like rats in an attic.

JOHANSSON: Why do you call it the spook supper?

BENGTSSON: Well, they look like spooks. They've been doing this for twenty years, always the same bunch saying the same things, or keeping their traps shut for fear of making fools of themselves.

JOHANSSON: Hasn't he a wife here, too?

BENGTSSON: Yes, but she's mad. Sits in a cupboard, because her eyes can't stand the light. In here. [*Points to a door concealed in the wall.*]

JOHANSSON: In there?

BENGTSSON: Yes. I told you they're a bit out of the ordinary.

JOHANSSON: What does she look like?

BENGTSSON: Like a mummy. Care to see her? [*Opens the concealed door.*] Look, there she is.

JOHANSSON: Jesus Chr——!

MUMMY [*in the voice of a small child*]: Why are you opening the door? Haven't I said it's to be kept shut!

BENGTSSON [*talking baby-talk*]: Now, now, now, now. Little girlie must be good, and she'll get a sweetie. Pretty Poll!

MUMMY [*speaks like a parrot*]: Pretty Poll! Is Jacob there? Funny man.

BENGTSSON: She thinks she's a parrot. Could be she is. [*To* MUMMY.] Now then, Polly, whistle for us.

The MUMMY *whistles.*

JOHANSSON: I've seen a good deal in my time, but never the likes of this.

BENGTSSON: Well, you know, when a house gets old it starts to decay, and when people sit for years in the same room torturing each other, they go off their nut. Madam here, now—quiet, Polly!—this mummy's been sitting here for forty years. Same husband, same furniture, same relatives, same friends. [*Shuts the door on the* MUMMY *again.*] As to what's gone on in this house—well, I shouldn't like to commit myself. See this statue? That's her when she was young.

JOHANSSON: My God! *This*—the mummy?

BENGTSSON: Yes. Enough to make you cry, isn't it? And that's not all. Somehow or other—imagination, maybe—she's become just like a parrot in all sorts of little ways. Can't stand cripples, for example. Or invalids. Can't even bear the sight of her own daughter, because she's ill——

JOHANSSON: The young lady? Is she ill?

BENGTSSON: Didn't you know?

JOHANSSON: No. What about the Colonel? What sort of a man's he?

BENGTSSON: You'll see.

JOHANSSON [*looks at the statue*]: It's horrible. How old is—Madam—now?

BENGTSSON: No-one knows. They say that when she was thirty-five she looked nineteen, and got the Colonel to believe she was. In this very house. Know what that black Japanese screen's for, over by the chaise longue? That's called the death screen. They put it out when someone's going to die—like in a hospital——

JOHANSSON: What a horrible house! And that young student was pining his heart out to get in here, as though it was Paradise——

BENGTSSON: What student? Oh, him. The one who's coming this evening. The Colonel and his daughter met him at the opera. They both fell for him. Hm! Now it's my turn to ask you a question. Who's—er—behind him? That old boy in the wheel chair?

JOHANSSON: Yes. Yes. He coming too?

BENGTSSON: He hasn't been invited.

JOHANSSON: He'll come uninvited. If need be.

The OLD MAN appears in the entrance lobby, wearing a long, black frock-coat and top hat. He edges silently forward on his crutches and listens.

BENGTSSON: Real old robber, I've heard.

JOHANSSON: One of the worst.

BENGTSSON: Looks like Old Nick himself.

JOHANSSON: He's a magician, too. He can pass through closed doors——

OLD MAN [*on them, seizes* JOHANSSON *by the ear*]: Villain! Beware! [*To* BENGTSSON]. Tell the Colonel I have arrived.

BENGTSSON: But he's expecting guests——

OLD MAN: I know. But he's been half-expecting me; if not exactly looking forward to it.

BENGTSSON: Oh, I see. What name shall I say? Mr. Hummel?

OLD MAN: Yes.

BENGTSSON goes through the lobby to the green room, the door of which is then closed.

OLD MAN [*to* JOHANSSON]: Clear out. [JOHANSSON *hesitates*.] Clear out!

JOHANSSON goes out into the hall. The OLD MAN looks round the room; stops amazed in front of the statue.

OLD MAN: Amelia! It's she! Yes! It's she! [*Wanders round the room, fingering things; arranges his wig in front of the mirror; goes back to the statue.*]

MUMMY [*from the cupboard*]: Pretty Poll!

OLD MAN [*starts*]: What was that? Is there a parrot in the room? But I don't see one.

MUMMY: Is Jacob there?

OLD MAN: It's a ghost!

MUMMY: Jacob!

OLD MAN: I'm frightened! So this is the kind of thing they've been concealing! [*Looks at a painting, his back towards the cupboard.*] That's him! Him!

MUMMY [*comes up behind the* OLD MAN *and tweaks his wig*]: Funny Man! Is it Funny Man?

OLD MAN [*jumps into the air*]: God Almighty! Who is it?

MUMMY [*in an ordinary human voice*]: Is it Jacob?

OLD MAN: My name *is* Jacob——

MUMMY [*with emotion*]: And my name is Amelia.

OLD MAN: No, no, no! Oh, Lord Jesus——

MUMMY: This is how I look now. Yes. And I used to look like that. One lives and learns. I stay in the cupboard mostly, to avoid seeing people—and being seen. What are you looking for in here, Jacob?

OLD MAN: My child. Our child.

MUMMY: She's sitting over there.

OLD MAN: Where?

MUMMY: There. In the hyacinth room.

OLD MAN [*looks at the* DAUGHTER]: Yes—it's she! [*Pause.*] What does her father say? I mean—the Colonel—your husband——

MUMMY: I lost my temper with him once, and told him everything——

OLD MAN: Yes?

MUMMY: He didn't believe me. He just replied: "That's what all wives say when they want to murder their husbands." It was a beastly thing to do. His life's a lie too, though. Even his pedigree. Sometimes I look at the List of Nobility and think to myself: "She's got a false birth certificate, like a little kitchen slut. People get sent to prison for that."

OLD MAN: Lots of people lie about their birth. You did once —to me——

MUMMY: My mother made me. I wasn't to blame. But the crime which you and I committed—you were to blame for that.

OLD MAN: No it was your husband's fault; he stole my sweetheart from me. I was born like that—I can't forgive until I've punished. To me, that's a command, a duty— I still feel so.

MUMMY: What are you looking for in this house? What do you want? How did you get in? Is it my daughter—? If you touch her, you shall die.

OLD MAN: I only wish her well.

MUMMY: But you must spare her father. I mean, my husband——

OLD MAN: No!

MUMMY: Then you shall die. In this room, behind that screen——

OLD MAN: That may be. But once I have fastened my teeth into someone, I cannot let go.

MUMMY: You want her to marry the student. Why? He's nothing. No money——

OLD MAN: I shall make him rich.

MUMMY: Were you invited for this evening?

OLD MAN: No. But I shall invite myself to this ghost supper.

MUMMY: Do you know who's coming?

OLD MAN: Not for sure.

MUMMY: The baron—the one who lives upstairs—the son-in-law of the man who was buried this afternoon——

OLD MAN: Oh, the one who's getting divorced so that he can marry the caretaker's daughter! He was once your lover.

MUMMY: And the woman to whom you were once betrothed—and whom my husband seduced——

OLD MAN: A pretty bunch!

MUMMY: Oh, God! If we could die! If we could only die!

OLD MAN: Why do you all keep on meeting?

MUMMY: Our crimes bind us; our secrets, and our guilt. We have tried to break away many times. But we always come back.

OLD MAN: I think I hear the Colonel.

MUMMY: I'll go in to Adèle, then. [*Pause.*] Jacob, mind what you do. Spare him. [*Pause.* She goes.]

The COLONEL *enters, cold and reserved.*

COLONEL: Please be seated.

The OLD MAN *sits, slowly. Pause. The* COLONEL *looks at him.*

You wrote this letter?

OLD MAN: Yes.

COLONEL: Your name is Hummel?

OLD MAN: Yes [*Pause.*]

COLONEL: I know you have purchased all my notes of hand, and that I am therefore in your power. What do you want?

OLD MAN: Payment. In some form.

COLONEL: What form?

OLD MAN: Something quite simple. Let's not talk about money. I merely ask that you tolerate me in your house, as your guest.

COLONEL: If so trifling a service can be of use to you——

OLD MAN: Thank you.

COLONEL: What else?

OLD MAN: Dismiss Bengtsson.

COLONEL: But why should I do that? My trusted servant, who has been with me all his life—who wears his country's medal for loyal and faithful service? Why should I dismiss him?

OLD MAN: He possesses these virtues only in your imagination. He is not the man he appears to be.

COLONEL: Who is?

OLD MAN [*recoils*]: True. But Bengtsson must go.

COLONEL: Are you going to decide what happens in my own home?

OLD MAN: Yes. I own everything you see here. Furniture, curtains, china, linen. Other things, too.

COLONEL: What other things?

OLD MAN: Everything. Everything you see. It is all mine.

COLONEL: Very well. All that is yours. But my patent of nobility and my good name—they at least are still mine.

OLD MAN: No. Not even those. [*Pause.*] You're not a nobleman.

COLONEL: How dare you?

OLD MAN [*takes out a paper*]: If you read this letter from the College of Heralds you will see that the family whose name you bear has been extinct for a hundred years.

COLONEL [*reads*]: I—have heard rumours to this effect, it is true— But I inherited the title from my father—— [*Reads.*] No. It is true. You are right. I am not a nobleman. Even that is taken from me. I can no longer wear this ring. Take it. It belongs to you.

OLD MAN [*puts on the ring*]: Good. Now let's continue. You're not a Colonel either.

COLONEL: Not a Colonel?

OLD MAN: No. Because of your name you were commissioned colonel in the American Volunteers, but since the Cuban War and the reorganization of the American Army all such commissions have been cancelled.

COLONEL: Is that true?

OLD MAN [*puts his hand towards his pocket*]: Would you like to read about it?

COLONEL: No—there's no need. Who are you, that you claim the right to sit there and strip me like this?

OLD MAN: You'll find out. Talking of stripping—I suppose you do know who you really are?

COLONEL: You have the effrontery——!

OLD MAN: Take off your wig and look at yourself in the glass; take out your teeth, shave off your moustaches; get Bengtsson to unlace your corset. Perhaps then a certain footman may recognise himself; who used to sponge food from a certain cook in a certain kitchen——

The COLONEL *reaches towards the bell on the table.*

OLD MAN [*stops him*]: Don't touch that bell. Don't call for Bengtsson. If you do, I shall have him arrested. Your guests are arriving. Keep calm, now; we'll go on playing our old parts for a little longer.

COLONEL: Who are you? I seem to recognise the expression in your eyes—and voice——

OLD MAN: Ask no more. Be silent, and obey.

STUDENT [*enters and bows to the* COLONEL]: Sir!

COLONEL: Welcome, young man. Your noble conduct in this great disaster has made your name a household word, and I count it an honour to be permitted to receive you in my home——

STUDENT: Colonel—my humble origins—your famous name —your noble heritage——

COLONEL: Hm—may I present—Mr. Arkenholz, Mr. Hummel. Will you be so good as to go in and introduce yourself to the ladies? I have a little business to finish with Mr. Hummel.

The STUDENT is shown into the hyacinth room, where he remains visible, engaged in shy conversation with the DAUGHTER.

COLONEL: A superb young man—musician—singer—poet— If only he were of noble stock—my peer genealogically— I wouldn't set my face against having him as a—hm, yes——

OLD MAN: As a what?

COLONEL: My daughter——

OLD MAN: *Your* daughter? Talking of her, why does she always sit in there?

COLONEL: She feels a compulsion to sit in the hyacinth room when she isn't out of doors. It's a quirk she has—— Ah, here comes Mademoiselle Beata von Holsteinkrona—a charming old lady—tremendously wealthy—a great benefactress——

OLD MAN [*to himself*]: My true love!

The FIANCÉE curtsies and sits. The NOBLEMAN, a secretive figure dressed in mourning, enters and sits.

COLONEL: Baron Skanskorg——

OLD MAN [*aside, without getting up*]: I think he's the fellow who stole those jewels. [*To the* COLONEL.] Let out the mummy, and the party'll be complete.

COLONEL [*at the doorway to the hyacinth room*]: Polly!

MUMMY [*enters*]: Funny man!

COLONEL: Shall we have the young people in, too?

OLD MAN: No. Not the young. Let them be spared.

They all sit in a dumb circle.

COLONEL: Shall we take tea?

OLD MAN: Why? None of us likes tea. Why pretend we do?

Pause.

COLONEL: Shall we talk, then?

OLD MAN [*slowly and with pauses*]: About the weather, which we know? Ask after each other's health? We know that, too. I prefer silence. Then one can hear thoughts, and see the past. Silence hides nothing. Words conceal. I read the other day that differences of language arose through the need of primitive peoples to keep their tribal secrets private. Languages are cyphers; it's only a question of finding the key; but secrets can be exposed without the key, especially when it's a question of proving one's parentage. Legal proof is another matter, of course; a couple of false witnesses can furnish that—provided their testimonies agree. But in cases such as the one I have in mind, there are no witnesses, for nature has endowed man with a sense of shame which seeks to hide that which should be hid. Nevertheless, the time sometimes comes when that which is most secret must be revealed, when the mask is stripped from the deceiver's face, when the identity of the criminal is exposed. [*Pause. They all look at each other in silence.*] What a silence! [*Long silence.*] Here, for example, in this respectable house, this exquisite home, where beauty, culture and wealth are united—— [*Long silence.*] We who sit here, we know what we are—hm?— I don't need to underline that. And you all know me, though you pretend you don't. In that room sits my daughter—yes, *mine*! You know that, too. She has lost the desire to live—she doesn't know why—this air foul with crime and treachery and falsehood has withered her. I have tried to find her a friend through whom she may discover light and warmth—the light and the warmth that a noble action engenders. [*Long silence*]. That was why I came to this house; to burn out the weeds, expose the crimes, balance the ledger, so that these young people may start life afresh in this home which I have given them. [*Long silence.*] Now I give you leave to depart in peace, each of you in your turn. Anyone who stays I shall have arrested. [*Long silence.*] Listen to the clock ticking, the clock of death on the wall. Do you hear what she's saying? "'Tis time—'tis time". In a little while, she will strike, and your time will be up; then you may depart, but not till then. But before she strikes, she whispers this threat. Listen! She's warning you! "The clock—can—strike". I too, can strike! [*He strikes the table with his crutch.*] You hear?

MUMMY [*goes over to the clock and stops the pendulum. Then she says clearly and earnestly.*] But I can halt time. I can wipe out the past, undo what has been done. Not with bribes, not with threats; but through suffering and contrition. [*Goes over to the* OLD MAN.] We are weak and pitiable creatures; we know that. We have erred, and sinned, like all mortals. We are not what we seem, for our true selves live within us, condemning our failings. But that you, Jacob Hummel, sit here wearing your false name and judge us, proves you worse than us, wretched as we are. You are not what you seem any more than we are. You are a robber of souls, for you robbed me of mine with your false promises; you murdered the consul they buried today, you strangled him with your notes of hand; and now you have stolen the student's soul for a feigned debt of his father, who never owed you a penny.

The OLD MAN *has tried to rise and interrupt her, but has fallen back in his chair, and shrunk small. During what follows, he shrinks smaller and smaller.*

MUMMY: But there is a black spot in your life. I don't know the full truth about it; but I can guess. And I fancy Bengtsson knows. [*Rings the bell on the table.*]

OLD MAN: No! Not Bengtsson! Not him!

MUMMY: Ah! Then he does know. [*Rings again.*]

The little MILKMAID *appears in the door leading from the hall, unseen by anyone except the* OLD MAN, *who cringes in terror. The* MILKMAID *disappears as* BENGTSSON *enters.*

MUMMY: Bentgsson, do you know this man?

BENGTSSON: Yes; I know him, and he knows me. Life has its ups and downs; he has served in my house, as I now serve in this one. He hung around my cook for two years. So that he could get away by three o'clock, we had to have dinner ready by two; and then we had to make do with the warmed-up remains of what he'd left. He drank the juice from the meat, too, so that we had to eke out what was left with water. He sat there like a vampire sucking all the goodness out of our home, and left us skeletons; then, when we called the cook a thief, he had us put in prison. Later, I met this man in Hamburg, under another name. He'd become a usurer—another kind of bloodsucker; besides which, he was accused of having lured a young girl out on the ice to drown her, because she'd been witness to a crime he was afraid might get discovered——

MUMMY [*puts her hand over the* OLD MAN's *face.*] You see yourself. Now give me your notes of hand. And the deeds of the house.

JOHANSSON *appears in the door leading to the hall, and watches the scene with interest, realising it means his release from slavery. The* OLD MAN *takes out a bundle of papers and throws them on the table.*

MUMMY [*strokes the* OLD MAN's *back*]: Pretty parrot. Jacob? Jacob?

THE GHOST SONATA

OLD MAN [*in a parrot's voice*]: Jacob's here! Cacadora! Dora!

MUMMY: Can the clock strike?

OLD MAN [*clucks*]: The clock can strike. [*Imitates a cuckoo clock.*] Cuc-koo, cuc-koo, cuc-koo.

MUMMY [*opens the cupboard door*]: Now the clock has struck. Get up and go into the cupboard where I have sat for twenty years, mourning our folly. In it there hangs a rope. Let it remind you of the rope with which you strangled the Consul upstairs, and thought to strangle your benefactor. Go!

The OLD MAN *goes into the cupboard. The* MUMMY *shuts the door.*

Bengtsson! Put out the screen. The death screen.

BENGTSSON *puts the screen in front of the door.*

It is accomplished. May God have mercy on his soul.

ALL: Amen.

Long silence.

In the hyacinth room, the DAUGHTER *becomes visible. She plays on a harp as the student sings.*

SONG [*preceded by a prelude*]:
I saw the sun.
I seemed to see the Hidden One.
Man reaps as he sows.
The doer of good shall receive blessing.
Answer not with evil what was done in anger.
Repay with goodness him thou hast robbed.
He who hath done no wrong hath nought to fear.
Innocence is goodness.

A room somewhat bizarrely decorated in Oriental style. Hyacinths of all colours, everywhere. On the top of the tiled stove sits a large statue of Buddha, with a flat root on his knees. Out of it rises the stalk of an Ascalon flower, with its globe of white, star-shaped petals.

Upstage right a door leads out to the round drawing room, where the COLONEL and the MUMMY sit silent, doing nothing. Part of the death screen is also visible. On the left, a door leads out to the kitchen and pantry.

The STUDENT *and the* DAUGHTER *are at the table, she seated at her harp, he standing.*

DAUGHTER: Sing for my flowers.

STUDENT: Is the hyacinth your flower?

DAUGHTER: It is my only flower. You love the hyacinth, too?

STUDENT: Above all other flowers. I love its slim figure, which rises erect and virginal from its roots, rests on water, and sinks its pure, white tendrils in the colourless stream. I love its colours; the white of snow and innocence, the honey-gold of sweetness, the rose-pink of youth, the scarlet of maturity; but above all the blue—the blue of deep eyes, of dew, of steadfastness. I love them all, more than gold or pearls. I have loved hyacinths ever since I was a child. I have worshipped them, because they embody everything I lack. And yet——

DAUGHTER: Yes.

STUDENT: My love is unrequited, for these beautiful flowers hate me.

DAUGHTER: Why do you say that?

STUDENT: Their perfume, strong and clean with the first zephyrs of spring, which have passed over melting snow, confuses my senses, deafens me, blinds me, drives me from my room, shoots me with poisoned arrows which sadden my heart and set my head aflame. Don't you know the legend of this flower?

DAUGHTER: Tell me.

STUDENT: First, I will tell you its meaning. The root, resting on the water or buried in the soil, is the earth. The stalk shoots up, straight as the axis of the world, and on the top of it rest the star-flowers with their six-headed petals.

DAUGHTER: Stars over the earth! How beautiful! Where did you find that vision, how did you see it?

STUDENT: Where? In your eyes. It is an image of the world. Buddha sits with the earth on his knees, brooding over it, watching it grow outwards and upwards, transforming itself into a heaven. This unhappy earth shall become a heaven! It is that that Buddha awaits.

DAUGHTER: Yes—now I see it! Is not the snow-flower starred with six points like the hyacinth lily?

STUDENT: Yes. Snow-flowers are falling stars——

DAUGHTER: And the snowdrop is a snow-star, risen from the snow.

STUDENT: But Sirius, the largest and most beautiful of the stars of the firmament in its gold and red, is the narcissus with its gold and red cup and its six white petals——

DAUGHTER: Have you seen the Ascalon flower?

STUDENT: Yes—yes, I have. It carries its blooms in a sphere like the sphere of heaven, strewn with white flowers.

DAUGHTER: Yes! Ah, God—how wonderful! Who first imagined this vision?

STUDENT: You.

DAUGHTER: You.

STUDENT: You and I together. We have given birth to a vision. We are wed.

DAUGHTER: Not yet.

STUDENT: What remains?

DAUGHTER: The waiting, the trials, the patience.

STUDENT: Good! Try me. [*Pause.*] Tell me—why do your parents sit so silently in there, never saying a word?

DAUGHTER: They have nothing to say to each other, for neither will believe what the other says. My father once said: "What is the point of our talking? We cannot deceive each other."

STUDENT: How horrible.

DAUGHTER: Here comes the cook. Look at her! How big and fat she is!

STUDENT: What does she want?

DAUGHTER: She wants to ask me about dinner. I look after the house while my mother is ill——

STUDENT: Must we bother about what happens in the kitchen?

DAUGHTER: We have to eat. Look at the cook—I can't look at her——

STUDENT: Who is this ogress?

DAUGHTER: One of the Hummels—that breed of vampires. She is devouring us——

STUDENT: Why don't you dismiss her?

DAUGHTER: She won't go. We have no control over her. She is our punishment for our sins. Can't you see? We are wasting away. We are being consumed.

STUDENT: Doesn't she give you any food?

DAUGHTER: Oh, yes. She cooks us many dishes, but there is no nourishment in them. She boils the meat till it is nothing but sinews and water, while she herself drinks the juice from it. When she roasts she cooks the meat till the goodness is gone; she drinks the gravy and the blood. Everything she touches loses its moisture, as though her eyes sucked it dry. She drinks the coffee and leaves us the dregs, she drinks the wine from the bottles and fills them with water——

STUDENT: Drive her out of the house!

DAUGHTER: We can't.

STUDENT: Why not?

DAUGHTER: We don't know. She won't go. No one has any control over her. She has drained the strength from us.

STUDENT: Can I send her away?

DAUGHTER: No. It is ordained. She must stay with us. She asks what we will have for dinner. I reply. She objects. And in the end, she does as she pleases.

STUDENT: Let her decide the meals, then.

DAUGHTER: She will not.

STUDENT: This is a strange house. It is bewitched.

DAUGHTER: Yes. Ah! She turned away when she saw you!

COOK [*in the doorway*]: No, that wasn't why. [*Grins, showing her teeth.*]

STUDENT: Get out!

COOK: When I feel like it. [*Pause.*] Now I feel like it. [*Goes.*]

DAUGHTER: Never mind. You must learn patience. She is one of the trials we have to endure in this house. We have a maid, too. We have to dust everywhere after her.

STUDENT: My head reels. *Cor in aethere.* Sing to me!

DAUGHTER: Wait!

STUDENT: Sing to me!

DAUGHTER: Be patient. This room is called the room of trial. It is beautiful to look at, but consists only of imperfections——

STUDENT: Incredible. But we must turn a blind eye to them. It is beautiful, but a little cold. Why don't you have a fire lit?

DAUGHTER: Because it smokes.

STUDENT: Can't you have the chimney cleaned?

DAUGHTER: That doesn't help. You see that desk?

STUDENT: It's very beautiful.

DAUGHTER: But it won't stand straight. Each day I put a cork disc under its leg, but the maid takes it away when she dusts, and I have to cut a new one. Every morning the pen is clogged with ink, and the inkwell too. I have to wash them after she's gone, every day of my life. [*Pause.*] What's the worst thing you know?

STUDENT: Counting laundry. Ugh!

DAUGHTER: That's what I have to do. Ugh!

STUDENT: What else?

DAUGHTER: To be woken in the middle of the night, and have to get up to fasten the window-catch, because the maid's forgotten to.

STUDENT: What else?

DAUGHTER: To climb up a ladder and mend the cord of the damper on the stove, when she's wrenched it loose.

STUDENT: What else?

DAUGHTER: To clean up after her, and dust behind her, and light the fire after her—she only puts in the wood. To open the damper, dry the glasses, re-lay the table, uncork the bottles, open the windows to air the rooms, re-make my bed, clean the water carafe when it grows green with slime, buy matches and soap, which we're always out of, dry the lamps and trim the wicks so that they won't smoke—I have to fill them myself so that they won't go out when we have guests——

STUDENT: Sing to me!

DAUGHTER: Wait! First the toil, the toil of holding the dirt of life at bay.

STUDENT: But you're rich. Why don't you keep two maids?

DAUGHTER: It wouldn't help, even if we had three. Life is hard

—sometimes I grow tired. Imagine if there were a nursery as well!

STUDENT: The greatest joy of all——

DAUGHTER: The most expensive. Is life worth so much trouble?

STUDENT: It depends what one wants in return. I would shrink from nothing to win your hand.

DAUGHTER: Don't talk like that. You can never win me.

STUDENT: Why not?

DAUGHTER: You mustn't ask.

Pause.

STUDENT: You dropped your bracelet out of the window.

DAUGHTER: Because my hand has grown so thin——

Pause. The COOK *appears, with a Japanese bottle in her hand.*

DAUGHTER: It's she who is devouring me. Devouring us all.

STUDENT: What's she got in her hand?

DAUGHTER: The colorite bottle with the scorpion lettering. It contains soya, to make water into stock. We use it instead of gravy, and to cook cabbage in, and to make turtle soup——

STUDENT: Get out!

COOK: You drain the goodness out of us, and we drain it from you. We take the blood and give you back the water—with the colorite. This is colorite. I'm going now, but I'm staying in this house as long as I want. [*Goes.*]

STUDENT: Why does Bengtsson wear a medal?

DAUGHTER: For faithful service.

STUDENT: Has he no faults?

DAUGHTER: Yes, very great ones. But you don't get medals for them.

They both laugh.

STUDENT: You have many secrets in this house.

DAUGHTER: Like everyone else. Let us keep ours.

Pause.

STUDENT: Do you love honesty?

DAUGHTER: Yes. Quite.

STUDENT: Sometimes I'm seized with a passionate desire to say everything I think; but I know that if people were really honest the world would come to an end. [*Pause.*] The other day I was at a funeral. In the church. It was very impressive, very beautiful.

DAUGHTER: Was it Hummel's?

STUDENT: Yes. My benefactor. At the head of the coffin stood an old friend of the dead man, holding the funeral mace. The priest impressed me deeply by his dignified bearing and his moving sermon. I wept. We all wept. Afterwards we went to a hotel. There I learned that the man with the mace had been in love with the dead man's son. [*The* DAUGHTER *looks at him, not understanding.*] And that the dead man had borrowed money from his son's admirer. [*Pause.*] And the next day the priest was arrested for stealing from the church funds. Pretty, isn't it?

DAUGHTER: Horrible.

Pause.

STUDENT: Do you know what I'm thinking? About you?

DAUGHTER: Don't tell me. If you do, I shall die.

STUDENT: I must, or I shall die.

DAUGHTER: In madhouses, people say everything they think.

STUDENT: I know. My father died in a madhouse.

DAUGHTER: Was he sick?

STUDENT: No. He was perfectly well; just mad. He only showed it once; I'll tell you how. He was surrounded, as we all are, by a circle of—associates; he called them friends, the word was shorter and more convenient. They were a gang of scoundrels, of course; most people are. But he had to have someone to talk to, he couldn't bear to be alone. One doesn't ordinarily tell people what one thinks of them, and neither did he. He knew they were false and treacherous; but he was a wise man, and had been well brought up, so he was always polite to everyone. But one day he gave a great party. It was in the evening; he was tired after his day's work, and tired with the strain of listening to his guests and exchanging spiteful gossip with them.

The DAUGHTER *shudders.*

Well, he rapped on the table for silence, and stood up with his glass to make a speech. Then the safety-catch flew off, and as he talked he stripped the company naked, flinging their hypocrisy in their faces. Then he sat down exhausted on the middle of the table, and told them all to go to hell.

DAUGHTER: Oh!

STUDENT: I was there, and I shall never forget what happened next. My mother hit him, he hit her, the guests rushed for the door—and Father was taken to the madhouse, where he died. [*Pause.*] Water which has remained stationary and silent for too long becomes rotten. It's the same with this house. Something has rotted here, too. And when I saw you walk through the door for the first time, I thought it was Paradise. I stood there one Sunday morning, and gazed in through the windows. I saw a Colonel who was not a Colonel, I found a noble benefactor who turned out to be a crook, and had to hang himself, I saw a mummy that was not a mummy, and a maid. . . . Where is virginity to be found? Or beauty? Only in flowers and trees . . . and in my head when I am dressed in my Sunday clothes. Where are faith and honour to be found? In fairy tales and games that children play. Where can I find anything that will fulfil its promise? Only in my imagination. Your flowers have poisoned me, and I have poisoned you in return. I asked you to be my wife and share my home, we wrote poems, we sang and played. And then the cook came in. *Sursum corda*! Try once more to strike fire and purple from your golden harp! Try, I beg you! I command you—on my knees. Then I shall do it myself. [*Takes the harp, but no sound comes from the strings.*] It is deaf and dumb. Why should the most beautiful flowers be the most poisonous? It is a curse that hangs over all creation, all life. Why would you not be my bride? Because the source of life is poisoned in you. Now I can feel that vampire in the kitchen beginning to suck my blood— perhaps she's a Lamia who lives on the blood of children— it's always in the kitchen that children's hearts are nipped, if it hasn't already happened in the bedroom. There are poisons which blind and poisons which open the eyes. I must have been born with the second kind in my veins, because I can't see beauty in ugliness or call evil good—I can't! Jesus Christ descended into hell when he wandered through this madhouse, this brothel, this morgue which we call earth. The madmen killed him when he tried to set them free, and released a robber instead; the robber always gets the sympathy. Alas for us all, alas! O Saviour of the World, save us! We are dying.

The DAUGHTER *has crumpled in her chair. She rings.* BENGTSSON *enters.*

DAUGHTER: Bring the screen. Quickly! I am dying.

BENGTSSON *comes back with the screen, which he opens and places in front of the* DAUGHTER.

STUDENT: The deliverer cometh. Welcome, Thou pale and gentle One. And you, beautiful, unhappy, innocent creature, who must suffer for the guilt of others, sleep! Sleep dreamlessly, and when you wake again may you be greeted by a sun that will not burn, in a home without dust, by friends ignorant of dishonour, by a love that knows no imperfections. O wise and gentle Buddha, who sitteth waiting for a heaven to rise up out of the earth, grant us patience in our time of trial, and grant us purity of will, that thy hopes may be fulfilled.

The harp's strings begin to whisper. The room becomes filled with a white light.

SONG:
I saw the sun.
I seemed to see the Hidden One.
Man reaps as he sows.
The doer of good shall receive blessing.
Answer not with evil what was done in anger.
Repay with goodness him thou hast robbed.
He who hath done no wrong hath nought to fear.
Innocence is goodness.

A moaning is heard from behind the screen.

STUDENT: Unhappy child, born into this world of delusion, guilt, suffering and death, this world that is for ever changing, for ever erring, for ever in pain! The Lord of Heaven be merciful to you on your journey.

The room disappears. Böcklin's painting of the Island of the Dead *appears in the background. Soft music, calm and gently melancholy, is heard from the island outside.*

THE PLAYS OF STRINDBERG
(1849-1912)
with their dates of composition

PRE-INFERNO
1869. A Birthday Gift (lost)
 The Freethinker
1870. Hermione
 In Rome
1871. The Outlaw
1872-1877. Master Olof
1876-1877. Anno 48
1880. The Secret of the Guild
1882. Lucky Peter's Journey
 Sir Bengt's Wife
1886-1887. The Robbers (The Comrades)
1887. The Father
1888. Miss Julie
 Creditors
1888-1889. The Stronger
1889. Pariah
 The People of Hemsö
 Simoom
1892. The Keys of Heaven
 The First Warning
 Debit and Credit
 In the Face of Death
 A Mother's Love
 Playing with Fire
 The Bond

POST-INFERNO
1898. To Damascus, Part I
 To Damascus, Part II
 Advent
1899. There are Crimes and Crimes
 The Saga of the Folkungs
 Gustav Vasa
 Erik the Fourteenth
1900. Gustav Adolf
 Midsummer
 Casper's Shrove Tuesday
 Easter
 The Dance of Death, Part I
 The Dance of Death, Part II
1901. The Bridal Crown
 Swanwhite
 Charles XII
 To Damascus, Part III
 Engelbrecht
 Queen Christina
 A Dream Play
1902. Gustav III
 The Dutchman (fragment)
 The Nightingale of Wittenberg
1903. Exodus (Moses)
 Hellas (Socrates)
 The Lamb and the Beast (Christ)
1907. Storm
 The Burnt House
 The Ghost Sonata
 Toten-Insel (fragment)
 The Pelican
1908. The Last Knight
 Abu Casem's Slippers
 The Protector
 The Earl of Bjälbo
1909. The Black Glove
 The Great Highway

AUGUST STRINDBERG was born in 1849, the third of twelve children, and grew up in an atmosphere of poverty, neglect, and religious fanaticism. For a while he was a lay preacher, then had a varied career as a tutor, painter, editor, journalist, telegrapher and librarian, losing each of his jobs in turn. He was married—and divorced—three times. Despite his personal problems and deep despair, he continued to write, and on his death in 1912 he left behind a huge body of work and was acknowledged even then as the greatest modern writer in Sweden.

MICHAEL MEYER was educated at Wellington College and Christ Church, Oxford. He has lectured on English Literature and Language in Sweden, and since 1950 has been a free-lance writer and translator. He is the author of a novel, *The End of the Corridor,* and of several stage, television and radio plays. His translations of Ibsen and Strindberg have been used extensively for stage productions. Mr. Meyer was awarded the Swedish Academy Gold Medal in 1964 for this volume of translations.

The Best of the World's Best Books
COMPLETE LIST OF TITLES IN
THE MODERN LIBRARY

A series of handsome, cloth-bound books, formerly available only in expensive editions.

76	ADAMS, HENRY: *The Education of Henry Adams*
310	AESCHYLUS: *The Complete Greek Tragedies*, VOL. I
311	AESCHYLUS: *The Complete Greek Tragedies*, VOL. II
101	AIKEN, CONRAD (editor): *A Comprehensive Anthology of American Poetry*
127	AIKEN, CONRAD (editor): *20th-Century American Poetry*
145	ALEICHEM, SHOLOM: *Selected Stories*
104	ANDERSON, SHERWOOD: *Winesburg, Ohio*
259	AQUINAS, ST. THOMAS: *Introduction to St. Thomas Aquinas*
248	ARISTOTLE: *Introduction to Aristotle*
228	ARISTOTLE: *Politics*
246	ARISTOTLE: *Rhetoric and Poetics*
160	AUDEN, W. H.: *Selected Poetry*
263	AUGUSTINE, ST.: *Confessions*
264	AUSTEN, JANE: *Pride and Prejudice* and *Sense and Sensibility*
256	BACON, FRANCIS: *Selected Writings*
299	BALZAC: *Cousin Bette*
193	BALZAC: *Droll Stories*
245	BALZAC: *Père Goriot* and *Eugénie Grandet*
116	BEERBOHM, MAX: *Zuleika Dobson*
22	BELLAMY, EDWARD: *Looking Backward*
362	BELLOW, SAUL: *The Adventures of Augie March*
184	BENNETT, ARNOLD: *The Old Wives' Tale*
231	BERGSON, HENRI: *Creative Evolution*
285	BLAKE, WILLIAM: *Selected Poetry and Prose*
71	BOCCACCIO: *The Decameron*
282	BOSWELL, JAMES: *The Life of Samuel Johnson*
64	BRONTË, CHARLOTTE: *Jane Eyre*
106	BRONTË, EMILY: *Wuthering Heights*
198	BROWNING, ROBERT: *Selected Poetry*
15	BUCK, PEARL: *The Good Earth*
32	BURCKHARDT, JACOB: *The Civilization of the Renaissance in* [Italy
241	BURK, JOHN N.: *The Life and Works of Beethoven*
289	BURKE, EDMUND: *Selected Writings*
136	BUTLER, SAMUEL: *Erewhon and Erewhon Revisited*
13	BUTLER, SAMUEL: *The Way of All Flesh*
195	BYRON, LORD: *Selected Poetry*
24	BYRON, LORD: *Don Juan*
295	CAESAR, JULIUS: *The Gallic War and Other Writings*
51	CALDWELL, ERSKINE: *God's Little Acre*

249	CALDWELL, ERSKINE: *Tobacco Road*
352	CAMUS, ALBERT: *The Fall & Exile and the Kingdom*
109	CAMUS, ALBERT: *The Plague*
349	CAMUS, ALBERT: *Notebooks 1935–1942*
353	CAPOTE, TRUMAN: *Selected Writings*
339	CAMUS, ALBERT: *Resistance, Rebellion and Death*
79	CARROLL, LEWIS: *Alice in Wonderland*, etc.
165	CASANOVA, JACQUES: *Memoirs of Casanova*
150	CELLINI, BENVENUTO: *Autobiography of Cellini*
174	CERVANTES: *Don Quixote*
161	CHAUCER: *The Canterbury Tales*
171	CHEKHOV, ANTON: *Best Plays*
50	CHEKHOV, ANTON: *Short Stories*
272	CICERO: *Basic Works*
279	COLERIDGE: *Selected Poetry and Prose*
251	COLETTE: *Six Novels*
235	COMMAGER, HENRY STEELE & NEVINS, ALLAN: *A Short History of the United States*
306	CONFUCIUS: *The Wisdom of Confucius*
186	CONRAD, JOSEPH: *Lord Jim*
275	CONRAD, JOSEPH: *Nostromo*
34	CONRAD, JOSEPH: *Victory*
105	COOPER, JAMES FENIMORE: *The Pathfinder*
194	CORNEILLE & RACINE: *Six Plays by Corneille and Racine*
130	CRANE, STEPHEN: *The Red Badge of Courage*
370	CUMMING, ROBERT D. (editor): *The Philosophy of Jean-Paul Sartre*
214	CUMMINGS, E. E.: *The Enormous Room*
236	DANA, RICHARD HENRY: *Two Years Before the Mast*
208	DANTE: *The Divine Comedy*
122	DEFOE, DANIEL: *Moll Flanders*
92	DEFOE, DANIEL: *Robinson Crusoe* and *A Journal of the Plague Year*
43	DESCARTES, RENÉ: *Philosophical Writings*
173	DEWEY, JOHN: *Human Nature and Conduct*
348	DEWEY, JOHN: *John Dewey on Education*
110	DICKENS, CHARLES: *David Copperfield*
204	DICKENS, CHARLES: *Pickwick Papers*
308	DICKENS, CHARLES: *Our Mutual Friend*
189	DICKENS, CHARLES: *A Tale of Two Cities*
25	DICKINSON, EMILY: *Selected Poems*
23	DINESEN, ISAK: *Out of Africa*
54	DINESEN, ISAK: *Seven Gothic Tales*
12	DONNE, JOHN: *Complete Poetry and Selected Prose*
205	DOS PASSOS, JOHN: *Three Soldiers*
293	DOSTOYEVSKY, FYODOR: *Best Short Stories*
151	DOSTOYEVSKY, FYODOR: *The Brothers Karamazov*
199	DOSTOYEVSKY, FYODOR: *Crime and Punishment*
55	DOSTOYEVSKY, FYODOR: *The Possessed*
5	DOUGLAS, NORMAN: *South Wind*
206	DOYLE, SIR ARTHUR CONAN: *The Adventure and Memoirs of Sherlock Holmes*
8	DREISER, THEODORE: *Sister Carrie*
69	DUMAS, ALEXANDRE: *Camille*

143	DUMAS, ALEXANDRE: *The Three Musketeers*
227	DU MAURIER, DAPHNE: *Rebecca*
338	ELLISON, RALPH: *Invisible Man*
192	EMERSON, RALPH WALDO: *The Journals*
91	EMERSON, RALPH WALDO: *Essays and Other Writings*
331	ERASMUS, DESIDERIUS: *The Praise of Folly*
314	EURIPIDES: *The Complete Greek Tragedies*, VOL. V
315	EURIPIDES: *The Complete Greek Tragedies*, VOL. VI
316	EURIPIDES: *The Complete Greek Tragedies*, VOL. VII
271	FAULKNER, WILLIAM: *Absalom, Absalom!*
368	FAULKNER, WILLIAM: *A Fable*
175	FAULKNER, WILLIAM: *Go Down, Moses*
351	FAULKNER, WILLIAM: *Intruder in the Dust*
88	FAULKNER, WILLIAM: *Light in August*
61	FAULKNER, WILLIAM: *Sanctuary*
187	FAULKNER, WILLIAM: *The Sound and the Fury*
324	FAULKNER, WILLIAM: *Selected Short Stories*
117	FIELDING, HENRY: *Joseph Andrews*
185	FIELDING, HENRY: *Tom Jones*
28	FLAUBERT, GUSTAVE: *Madame Bovary*
102	FORESTER, C. S.: *The African Queen*
210	FRANCE, ANATOLE: *Penguin Island*
298	FRANK, ANNE: *Diary of a Young Girl*
39	FRANKLIN, BENJAMIN: *Autobiography*, etc.
96	FREUD, SIGMUND: *The Interpretation of Dreams*
358	GENET, JEAN: *Our Lady of the Flowers*
36	GEORGE, HENRY: *Progress and Poverty*
327	GIDE, ANDRÉ: *The Counterfeiters*
177	GOETHE: *Faust*
40	GOGOL, NICHOLAI: *Dead Souls*
291	GOLDSMITH, OLIVER: *The Vicar of Wakefield and Other [Writings*
20	GRAVES, ROBERT: *I, Claudius*
286	GUNTHER, JOHN: *Death Be Not Proud*
265	HACKETT, FRANCIS: *The Personal History of Henry the Eighth*
163	HAGGARD, H. RIDER: *She* and *King Solomon's Mines*
320	HAMILTON, EDITH: *The Greek Way*
135	HARDY, THOMAS: *Jude the Obscure*
17	HARDY, THOMAS: *The Mayor of Casterbridge*
121	HARDY, THOMAS: *The Return of the Native*
72	HARDY, THOMAS: *Tess of the D'Urbervilles*
233	HART & KAUFMAN: *Six Plays*
329	HART, MOSS: *Act One*
250	HARTE, BRET: *Best Stories*
93	HAWTHORNE, NATHANIEL: *The Scarlet Letter*
239	HEGEL: *The Philosophy of Hegel*
375	HELLER, JOSEPH: *Catch-22*
223	HELLMAN, LILLIAN: *Six Plays*
26	HENRY, O.: *Best Short Stories*
255	HERODOTUS: *The Persian Wars*
328	HERSEY, JOHN: *Hiroshima*
334	HESSE, HERMAN: *Steppenwolf*
166	HOMER: *The Iliad*

167	HOMER: *The Odyssey*
141	HORACE: *Complete Works*
302	HOWARD, JOHN TASKER: *World's Great Operas*
366	HOWE, IRVING (editor): *Selected Short Stories of Isaac Bashevis Singer*
277	HOWELLS, WILLIAM DEAN: *The Rise of Silas Lapham*
89	HUDSON, W. H.: *Green Mansions*
35	HUGO, VICTOR: *The Hunchback of Notre Dame*
340	HUME, DAVID: *Philosophy*
209	HUXLEY, ALDOUS: *Antic Hay*
48	HUXLEY, ALDOUS: *Brave New World*
180	HUXLEY, ALDOUS: *Point Counter Point*
305	IBSEN, HENRIK: *Six Plays*
307	IBSEN, HENRIK: *The Wild Duck and Other Plays*
240	IRVING, WASHINGTON: *Selected Writings*
16	JAMES, HENRY: *The Bostonians*
107	JAMES, HENRY: *The Portrait of a Lady*
169	JAMES, HENRY: *The Turn of the Screw*
269	JAMES, HENRY: *Washington Square*
244	JAMES, HENRY: *The Wings of the Dove*
114	JAMES, WILLIAM: *The Philosophy of William James*
70	JAMES, WILLIAM: *The Varieties of Religious Experience*
234	JEFFERSON, THOMAS: *The Life and Selected Writings*
355	JOHNSON, SAMUEL: *Johnson's Dictionary: A Modern Selection*
363	JOHNSON, SAMUEL: *A Johnson Reader*
124	JOYCE, JAMES: *Dubliners*
300	JUNG, C. G.: *Basic Writings*
318	KAFKA, FRANZ: *The Trial*
283	KAFKA, FRANZ: *Selected Stories*
297	KANT: *Critique of Pure Reason*
266	KANT: *The Philosophy of Kant*
233	KAUFMAN & HART: *Six Plays*
273	KEATS: *Complete Poetry and Selected Prose*
303	KIERKEGAARD, SØREN: *A Kierkegaard Anthology*
99	KIPLING, RUDYARD: *Kim*
74	KOESTLER, ARTHUR: *Darkness at Noon*
262	LAOTSE: *The Wisdom of Laotse*
148	LAWRENCE, D. H.: *Lady Chatterley's Lover*
128	LAWRENCE, D. H.: *The Rainbow*
333	LAWRENCE, D. H.: *Sons and Lovers*
68	LAWRENCE, D. H.: *Women in Love*
252	LEWIS, SINCLAIR: *Dodsworth*
221	LEWIS, SINCLAIR: *Cass Timberlane*
325	LIVY: *A History of Rome*
56	LONGFELLOW, HENRY W.: *Poems*
77	LOUŸS, PIERRE: *Aphrodite*
95	LUDWIG, EMIL: *Napoleon*
65	MACHIAVELLI: *The Prince and The Discourses*
321	MAILER, NORMAN: *The Naked and the Dead*
317	MALAMUD, BERNARD: *Two Novels*

33	MALRAUX, ANDRÉ: *Man's Fate*
309	MALTHUS, THOMAS ROBERT: *On Population*
360	MANN, THOMAS: *Confessions of Felix Krull*
365	MANN, THOMAS: *Doctor Faustus*
182	MARQUAND, JOHN P.: *The Late George Apley*
202	MARX, KARL: *Capital and Other Writings*
14	MAUGHAM, W. SOMERSET: *Best Short Stories*
270	MAUGHAM, W. SOMERSET: *Cakes and Ale*
27	MAUGHAM, W. SOMERSET: *The Moon and Sixpence*
176	MAUGHAM, W. SOMERSET: *Of Human Bondage*
98	MAUPASSANT, GUY DE: *Best Short Stories*
46	MAUROIS, ANDRÉ: *Disraeli*
119	MELVILLE, HERMAN: *Moby Dick*
253	MEREDITH, GEORGE: *The Egoist*
134	MEREDITH, GEORGE: *The Ordeal of Richard Feverel*
138	MEREJKOWSKI, DMITRI: *The Romance of Leonardo da Vinci*
296	MICHENER, JAMES A.: *Selected Writings*
322	MILL, JOHN STUART: *Selections*
132	MILTON, JOHN: *Complete Poetry and Selected Prose*
78	MOLIÈRE: *Eight Plays*
218	MONTAIGNE: *Selected Essays*
343	NASH, OGDEN: *Verses From 1929 On*
235	NEVINS, ALLAN & COMMAGER, HENRY STEELE: *A Short History of the United States*
113	NEWMAN, CARDINAL JOHN H.: *Apologia Pro Vita Sua*
9	NIETZSCHE, FRIEDRICH: *Thus Spake Zarathustra*
81	NOSTRADAMUS: *Oracles*
67	ODETS, CLIFFORD: *Six Plays*
42	O'HARA, JOHN: *Appointment in Samarra*
211	O'HARA, JOHN: *Selected Short Stories*
323	O'HARA, JOHN: *Butterfield 8*
342	O'NEILL, EUGENE: *Ah, Wilderness! and Two Other Plays*
146	O'NEILL, EUGENE: *The Emperor Jones, Anna Christie and The Hairy Ape*
111	O'NEILL, EUGENE: *The Long Voyage Home: Seven Plays of [the Sea*
232	PALGRAVE, FRANCIS (editor): *The Golden Treasury*
123	PARKER, DOROTHY: *Collected Short Stories*
237	PARKER, DOROTHY: *Collected Poetry*
267	PARKMAN, FRANCIS: *The Oregon Trail*
164	PASCAL, BLAISE: *Penseés and The Provincial Letters*
86	PATER, WALTER: *The Renaissance*
103	PEPYS, SAMUEL: *Passages from the Diary*
247	PERELMAN, S. J.: *The Best of S. J. Perelman*
153	PLATO: *The Republic*
181	PLATO: *The Works of Plato*
82	POE, EDGAR ALLAN: *Selected Poetry and Prose*
196	POLO, MARCO: *The Travels of Marco Polo*
257	POPE, ALEXANDER: *Selected Works*
284	PORTER, KATHERINE ANNE: *Flowering Judas*
45	PORTER, KATHERINE ANNE: *Pale Horse, Pale Rider*
371	POWERS, J. F.: *Morte d'Urban*
120	PROUST, MARCEL: *The Captive*

220	PROUST, MARCEL: *Cities of the Plain*
213	PROUST, MARCEL: *The Guermantes Way*
278	PROUST, MARCEL: *The Past Recaptured*
59	PROUST, MARCEL: *Swann's Way*
260	PROUST, MARCEL: *The Sweet Cheat Gone*
172	PROUST, MARCEL: *Within a Budding Grove*
372	PYNCHON, THOMAS: *V.*

194	RACINE & CORNEILLE: *Six Plays by Corneille and Racine*
62	READE, CHARLES: *The Cloister and the Hearth*
215	REED, JOHN: *Ten Days That Shook the World*
140	RENAN, ERNEST: *The Life of Jesus*
336	RENAULT, MARY: *The Last of the Wine*
10	RICHARDSON, SAMUEL: *Clarissa*
200	RODGERS & HAMMERSTEIN: *Six Plays*
154	ROSTAND, EDMOND: *Cyrano de Bergerac*
374	ROTH, PHILIP: *Goodbye, Columbus*
243	ROUSSEAU, JEAN JACQUES: *The Confessions*
53	RUNYON, DAMON: *Famous Stories*
137	RUSSELL, BERTRAND: *Selected Papers of Betrand Russell*

280	SAKI: *Short Stories*
301	SALINGER, J. D.: *Nine Stories*
90	SALINGER, J. D.: *The Catcher in the Rye*
292	SANTAYANA, GEORGE: *The Sense of Beauty*
335	SARTRE, JEAN-PAUL: *The Age of Reason*
370	SARTRE, JEAN-PAUL: *The Philosophy of Jean-Paul Sartre*
52	SCHOPENHAUER: *The Philosophy of Schopenhauer*
281	SCHULBERG, BUDD: *What Makes Sammy Run?*
2,3	SHAKESPEARE, WILLIAM: *Tragedies*—complete, 2 vols.
4,5	SHAKESPEARE, WILLIAM: *Comedies*—complete, 2 vols.
6	SHAKESPEARE, WILLIAM: *Histories* ⎫ complete, 2 vols.
7	SHAKESPEARE, WILLIAM: *Histories, Poems* ⎭
19	SHAW, BERNARD: *Four Plays* [and the Lion
294	SHAW, BERNARD: *Saint Joan, Major Barbara,* and *Androcles*
112	SHAW, IRWIN: *The Young Lions*
319	SHAW, IRWIN: *Selected Short Stories*
274	SHELLEY: *Selected Poetry and Prose*
366	SINGER, ISAAC BASHEVIS: *Selected Short Stories*
159	SMOLLETT, TOBIAS: *Humphry Clinker*
312	SOPHOCLES I: *Complete Greek Tragedies,* VOL. III
313	SOPHOCLES II: *Complete Greek Tragedies,* VOL. IV
373	SPARK, MURIEL: *Memento Mori* and *The Ballad of Peckham Rye*
60	SPINOZA: *The Philosophy of Spinoza*
332	STEIN, GERTRUDE: *Selected Writings*
115	STEINBECK, JOHN: *In Dubious Battle*
29	STEINBECK, JOHN: *Of Mice and Men*
216	STEINBECK, JOHN: *Tortilla Flat*
157	STENDHAL: *The Red and the Black*
147	STERNE, LAURENCE: *Tristram Shandy*
254	STEWART, GEORGE R.: *Storm*
31	STOKER, BRAM: *Dracula*
11	STONE, IRVING: *Lust for Life*
261	STOWE, HARRIET BEECHER: *Uncle Tom's Cabin*

212	STRACHEY, LYTTON: *Eminent Victorians*
369	STRINDBERG: *The Plays of Strindberg*, VOL. I, Translated by Michael Meyer
351	STYRON, WILLIAM: *Lie Down in Darkness*
188	SUETONIUS: *Lives of the Twelve Caesars*
100	SWIFT, JONATHAN: *Gulliver's Travels and Other Writings*
49	SYMONDS, JOHN A.: *The Life of Michelangelo*
222	TACITUS: *Complete Works*
230	TENNYSON: *Selected Poetry*
80	THACKERAY, WILLIAM: *Henry Esmond*
131	THACKERAY, WILLIAM: *Vanity Fair*
38	THOMPSON, FRANCIS: *Complete Poems*
155	THOREAU, HENRY DAVID: *Walden and Other Writings*
58	THUCYDIDES: *Complete Writings*
85	THURBER, JAMES: *The Thurber Carnival*
37	TOLSTOY, LEO: *Anna Karenina*—tr. revised
347	TOLSTOY, LEO: *Selected Essays*
354	TOLSTOY, LEO: *Short Novels*
367	TOLSTOY, LEO: *Short Novels*, VOL. II
346	TOLSTOY, LEO: *Short Stories*
361	TOLSTOY, LEO: *Short Stories*, VOL. II
41	TROLLOPE, ANTHONY: *Barchester Towers* and *The Warden*
21	TURGENEV, IVAN: *Fathers and Sons*
162	TWAIN, MARK: *A Connecticut Yankee in King Arthur's Court*
357	UPDIKE, JOHN: *The Poorhouse Fair* and *Rabbit, Run*
190	VASARI, GIORGIO: *Lives of the Most Eminent Painters, Sculptors and Architects*
63	VEBLEN, THORSTEIN: *The Theory of the Leisure Class*
156	VINCI, LEONARDO DA: *The Notebooks*
75	VIRGIL: *The Aeneid, Eclogues* and *Georgics*
47	VOLTAIRE: *Candide and Other Writings*
178	WALPOLE, HUGH: *Fortitude*
170	WARREN, ROBERT PENN: *All The King's Men*
219	WEBB, MARY: *Precious Bane*
225	WEIDMAN, JEROME: *I Can Get It for You Wholesale*
197	WELLS, H. G.: *Tono Bungay*
290	WELTY, EUDORA: *Selected Stories*
299	WHARTON, EDITH: *The Age of Innocence*
97	WHITMAN, WALT: *Leaves of Grass*
125	WILDE, OSCAR: *Dorian Gray* and *De Profundis*
83	WILDE, OSCAR: *The Plays of Oscar Wilde*
84	WILDE, OSCAR: *Poems* and *Fairy Tales*
126	WODEHOUSE, P. J.: *Selected Stories*
268	WORDSWORTH: *Selected Poetry*
44	YEATS, W. B. (editor): *Irish Fairy and Folk Tales*
179	YOUNG, G. F.: *The Medici*
207	ZIMMERN, ALFRED: *The Greek Commonwealth*
142	ZOLA, ÉMILE: *Nana*

MISCELLANEOUS

- 288 *An Anthology of Irish Literature*
- 330 *Anthology of Medieval Lyrics*
- 326 *The Apocrypha*
- 201 *The Arabian Nights' Entertainments*
- 87   *Best American Humorous Short Stories*
- 18   *Best Russian Short Stories*
- 129 *Best Spanish Stories*
       Complete Greek Tragedies
- 310 VOL. I (Aeschylus I); 311 VOL. II (Aeschylus II); 312 VOL. III (Sophocles I); 313 VOL. IV (Sophocles II); 314 VOL. V (Euripides I); 315 VOL. VI (Euripides II)
- 359 *Complete Poems and Selected Letters of Michelangelo*
- 101 *A Comprehensive Anthology of American Poetry*
- 226 *The Consolation of Philosophy*
- 94   *Eight Famous Elizabethan Plays*
- 345 *Eight Spanish Plays of the Golden Age*
- 224 *Eighteenth-Century Plays*
- 73   *Famous Ghost Stories*
- 139 *The Federalist*
- 30   *Five Great Modern Irish Plays*
- 144 *Fourteen Great Detective Stories*
- 108 *Great German Short Novels and Stories*
- 168 *Great Modern Short Stories*
- 238 *Great Tales of the American West*
- 203 *The Greek Poets*
- 356 *Hellenistic Philosophy*
- 364 *The Hindu Tradition*
- 217 *The Latin Poets*
- 149 *The Making of Man: An Outline of Anthropology*
- 183 *Making of Society*
- 344 *Medieval Philosophy*
- 133 *Medieval Romances*
- 1   *The Modern Library Dictionary*
- 258 *New Voices in the American Theatre*
- 152 *Outline of Abnormal Psychology*
- 66   *Outline of Psychoanalysis*
- 287 *Restoration Plays*
- 337 *Roman Comedies*
- 158 *Seven Famous Greek Plays*
- 57   *The Short Bible*
- 276 *Six Modern American Plays*
- 38   *Six American Plays for Today*
- 118 *Stories of Modern Italy*
- 127 *Twentieth-Century American Poetry*—revised
- 341 *Twenty German Poets*

MODERN LIBRARY GIANTS

A series of sturdily bound and handsomely printed, full-sized library editions of books formerly available only in expensive sets. These volumes contain from 600 to 1,400 pages each.

THE MODERN LIBRARY GIANTS REPRESENT A SELECTION OF THE WORLD'S GREATEST BOOKS

- G76 ANDERSEN & GRIMM: *Tales*
- G74 AUGUSTINE, ST.: *The City of God*
- G58 AUSTEN, JANE: *Complete Novels*
- G70 BLAKE, WILLIAM & DONNE, JOHN: *Complete Poetry*
- G2 BOSWELL, JAMES: *Life of Samuel Johnson*
- G95 BROCKWAY, WALLACE & WEINSTOCK, HERBERT: *The World of Opera*
- G17 BROWNING, ROBERT: *Poems and Plays*
- G14 BULFINCH: *Mythology* (ILLUSTRATED)
- G35 BURY, J. B.: *A History of Greece*
- G13 CARLYLE, THOMAS: *The French Revolution*
- G28 CARROLL, LEWIS: *Complete Works*
- G15 CERVANTES: *Don Quixote*
- G33 COLLINS, WILKIE: *The Moonstone* and *The Woman in White*
- G94 COOPER, JAMES FENIMORE: *The Leatherstocking Saga*
- G27 DARWIN, CHARLES: *Origin of Species* and *The Descent of Man*
- G43 DEWEY, JOHN: *Intelligence in the Modern World*
- G70 DONNE, JOHN & BLAKE, WILLIAM: *Complete Poetry*
- G36 DOSTOYEVSKY, FYODOR: *The Brothers Karamazov*
- G60 DOSTOYEVSKY, FYODOR: *The Idiot*
- G51 ELIOT, GEORGE: *Best-Known Novels*
- G41 FARRELL, JAMES T.: *Studs Lonigan*
- G82 FAULKNER, WILLIAM: *The Faulkner Reader*
- G39 FREUD, SIGMUND: *The Basic Writings*
- G6, G7, G8 GIBBON, EDWARD: *The Decline and Fall of the Roman Empire* (COMPLETE IN THREE VOLUMES)
- G25 GILBERT & SULLIVAN: *Complete Plays*
- G76 GRIMM & ANDERSEN: *Tales*
- G37 HAWTHORNE, NATHANIEL: *Compl. Novels & Selected Tales*
- G78 HOLMES, OLIVER WENDELL: *The Mind and Faith of Justice Holmes*
- G19 HOMER: *Complete Works*
- G3 HUGO, VICTOR: *Les Miserables*
- G18 IBSEN, HENRIK: *Eleven Plays*
- G11 JAMES, HENRY: *Short Stories*
- G52 JOYCE, JAMES: *Ulysses*
- G4 KEATS & SHELLEY: *Complete Poems*
- G24 LAMB, CHARLES: *The Complete Works and Letters*
- G20 LINCOLN, ABRAHAM: *The Life and Writings of Abraham Lincoln*
- G84 MANN, THOMAS: *Stories of Three Decades*
- G26 MARX, KARL: *Capital*
- G57 MELVILLE, HERMAN: *Selected Writings*
- G38 MURASAKA, LADY: *The Tale of Genji*
- G30 MYERS, GUSTAVUS: *History of the Great American Fortunes*
- G34 NIETZSCHE, FRIEDRICH: *The Philosophy of Nietzsche*
- G88 O'HARA, JOHN: *49 Stories*
- G55 O'NEILL, EUGENE: *Nine Plays*
- G68 PAINE, TOM: *Selected Work*

G86	PASTERNAK, BORIS: *Doctor Zhivago*
G5	PLUTARCH: *Lives* (The Dryden Translation)
G40	POE, EDGAR ALLAN: *Complete Tales and Poems*
G29	PRESCOTT, WILLIAM H.: *The Conquest of Mexico* and *The Conquest of Peru*
G62	PUSHKIN: *Poems, Prose and Plays*
G65	RABELAIS: *Complete Works*
G12	SCOTT, SIR WALTER: *The Most Popular Novels* (Quentin Durward, Ivanhoe & Kenilworth)
G4	SHELLEY & KEATS: *Complete Poems*
G32	SMITH, ADAM: *The Wealth of Nations*
G61	SPAETH, SIGMUND: *A Guide to Great Orchestral Music*
G92	SPENGLER, OSWALD: *The Decline of the West* (one volume)
G91	SPENSER, EDMUND: *Selected Poetry*
G75	STEVENSON, ROBERT LOUIS: *Selected Writings*
G53	SUE, EUGENE: *The Wandering Jew*
G42	TENNYSON: *The Poems and Plays*
G23	TOLSTOY, LEO: *Anna Karenina*—tr. revised
G1	TOLSTOY, LEO: *War and Peace*
G49	TWAIN, MARK: *Tom Sawyer* and *Huckleberry Finn*
G50	WHITMAN, WALT: *Leaves of Grass*
G83	WILSON, EDMUND: *The Shock of Recognition*

MISCELLANEOUS

G77	*An Anthology of Famous American Stories*
G54	*An Anthology of Famous British Stories*
G67	*Anthology of Famous English and American Poetry*
G81	*An Encyclopedia of Modern American Humor*
G47	*The English Philosophers from Bacon to Mill*
G16	*The European Philosophers from Descartes to Nietzsche*
G31	*Famous Science-Fiction Stories*
G85	*Great Ages and Ideas of the Jewish People*
G89	*Great Classical Myths*
G72	*Great Tales of Terror and the Supernatural*
G9	*Great Voices of the Reformation*
G87	*Medieval Epics*
G48	*The Metropolitan Opera Guide*
G46	*A New Anthology of Modern Poetry*
G69	*One Hundred and One Years' Entertainment*
G93	*Parodies: An Anthology from Chaucer to Beerbohm and After*
G90	*Philosophies of Art and Beauty: Readings in Aesthetics from Plato to Heidegger*
G21	*Sixteen Famous American Plays*
G63	*Sixteen Famous British Plays*
G71	*Sixteen Famous European Plays*
G45	*Stoic and Epicurean Philosophers*
G22	*Thirty Famous One-Act Plays*
G66	*Three Famous Murder Novels, Before the Fact,* FRANCIS ILES, *Trent's Last Case,* E. C. BENTLEY, *The House of the Arrow,* A. E. W. MASON
G10	*Twelve Famous Plays of the Restoration and Eighteenth Century* (1660–1820): Dryden, Congreve, Wycherley, Gay, etc.
G56	*The Wisdom of Catholicism*
G59	*The Wisdom of China and India*
G79	*The Wisdom of Israel*